D0987424

THE
ORIGINS
OF
CHRISTIANITY

A CRITICAL INTRODUCTION

edited by
R.Joseph
Hoffmann

Prometheus Books
Buffalo, New York

Published 1985 by Prometheus Books
700 East Amherst Street, Buffalo, New York 14215

Library of Congress Catalog Card Number: 85-62744
ISBN 0-87975-308-0

Printed in the United States of America

Contents

Epilogue

Introduction

Traditionally, introductions to the New Testament have been one-volume surveys of the canonical Christian writings. Based on a German theological model, such introductions are commonly the work of a single author and represent a particular confessional or religious stance toward the Gospels and letters—conservative or liberal, Methodist, Roman Catholic, or whatever. The disadvantages of such an approach are clear enough, or ought to be. Students coming to the study of the New Testament for the first time are likely to be unaware that the introductory text prescribed for a course is loaded with the theological or doctrinal freight of its author. Told, for example, that the Gospel of Mark was written before the year 70 C.E. (Common Era; old style, A.D.) or that the First Letter to Timothy was written by the apostle Paul, those unfamiliar with the problems of text, dating, and authorship or unacquainted with the Greek language will be inclined to accept such statements as hard fact.

If one can trust the textbook conclusions of other disciplines, the reasoning goes, why not trust the Bible. Indeed, to pursue the critical investigation of a book whose authenticity is thought to be guaranteed by the highest authority of all will seem unnecessary to some and sacrilegious to others. It may even seem odd, given such assumptions, that the New Testament needs "introducing" at all.

The problem of how to write an introduction to the New Testament is patent to the nature of the study of Christian origins. Specifically, it is the problem of extracting historical information from literature that was not written for the purpose of supplying such information. The Gospels and the letters of Paul and those ascribed to other apostles, the books of Acts and Revelation, are the primary documentation for the growth of a movement. Indeed, one can almost say, they are the only documentation, since the movement spread nearly unnoticed by non-Christian writers for the first two hundred years of its existence, and the humble Galilean preacher, proclaimed Christ (Messiah) by adherents of the new sect, was scarcely mentioned in the histories of Suetonius, Josephus, and Tacitus.

What has survived as the primary artifact of earliest Christianity is the body of literature we know as the New Testament, a collection of semitheological narratives, letters to churches, forged epistles contrived to put down various sorts of heresies, romantic legends about the travels of the apostles and early missionaries, traditions (strung together without much regard for consistency) about what Jesus said, who he was, how he died, and apocalyptic predictions of the new age. Altogether—since it was never meant to be taken as a coherent unity by its writers and compilers, working as they did in splendid isolation from one another—the New Testament is a treasure chest of literary types, theological perspectives and church traditions. Its diversity far outweighs the artificial unity imposed upon it by the list-making bishops of the third and fourth centuries. Its theological survival has had less to do with doctrinal coherence than with the intriguing jumble of ideas theologians have always found at hand upon lifting its cover. Here, we have Jesus saying he is the son of God (Mark 14:62); there (Mark 10:18), denying it; here, decreeing a man may divorce his wife for cause (Matt. 19:9); there, that divorce is, without exception, forbidden (Mark 10:9). It has been remarked without undue exaggeration that the seeds of the Reformation were planted in the canon. To an almost unrealized extent, the charter documents of the Christian faith, with their opposing theologies, are the cause of the fracturing of Christianity, a fact that may make enlightened folk skeptical of any return to "Bible teaching" as the cure for denominational strife, or doubtful that the term *fundamentalism* has any meaning at all.

In order to approach the New Testament intelligently, one must first acknowledge the character of the literature under consideration. In the first place, this involves looking at the intention of the authors of the various books. What sort of literature did they think they were writing? For what reason were the Gospels created—in order to supply biographical details or for some loftier purpose? As a matter of fact, the Gospels make no secret of their authors' intentions: "Jesus did many other things," writes the editor of the fourth Gospel, tantalizing his readers, "but these are written [in this book] so that you may believe and believing you may have life in his name" (John 20:30-31).

For "John" (as tradition names the writer), the story is meant to serve a single purpose; the material has been deliberately selected and arranged in order to win converts for the Christian church. "Luke" follows a similar tack, suggesting to Theophilus, the recipient of the book, that he is undertaking to compile from the many accounts available to him "an orderly narrative" to set the record straight (Luke 1:1-2).

These hints in our written Gospels point to an earlier time, when the Gospel was not a coherent narrative beginning with the birth and ending with the resurrection of Jesus, but an oral message preached by wandering missionaries from Jerusalem to Greece and beyond: "I would have you know," writes Paul to the Galatians, "that the gospel which was preached by me is not man's gospel, for I did not receive it from a man, nor was I taught it" (Gal. 1:11-12).

Such references also point up the fact that at the most basic level, the

Gospels and the letters preserved for us in the New Testament are the missionary propaganda of early Christianity. Their purpose is not to supply information but to do a combination of things: 1. to convince those outside the emerging cult of Christ that Jesus of Nazareth was the promised son of man and son of God (Mark 1:1-2); 2. to offer advice of a practical or ethical nature to the members of the cult (e.g., Matt. 5-7); 3. to demonstrate (especially to the rabbis) that Jesus' death did not occur in contradiction of prophecy but in accordance with it (Matt. 17:22); 4. to assuage fear and doubt about the delay of the end of time (eschaton) prophesied by Jesus (e.g., Matt. 12:38-42; II Pet. 3:8-9); 5. to provide testimony to the effect that the divinity of Jesus was attested by various signs and wonders (John 20:30-31); 6. to defend an emerging doctrinal system from the attacks of heretics—or from those considered to be in some way (subject to fluctuations of opinion) wrongheaded about the message of Jesus and the nature of his relationsip to God (Titus 3:10-11). 7. Perhaps of first-rank importance is the reason Paul cites for the preaching of the Gospel: to serve as an antidote to the stringency of Jewish law and as the charter of a new, relatively libertarian religion based on faith in the "promise" of God as revealed in Jesus Christ (Rom. 3:27 ff.). The desire to provide an objective historical picture of Jesus does not figure in this list of intentions, but this, given the nature of the literature, is as it might be: books written by Christians for Christians and for those interested in learning something about the beliefs of the new religion. Put bluntly, the New Testament is a collection of books that tell the church's story as the church, in its first-century diversity, wanted it told.

The New Testament is therefore our best source for discovering how the cult of Christ developed and how its original belief in the imminent return of Jesus and his judgment of the world as the son of man (bar nasha; Gk., huios anthropou) was transformed into an elaborate theological structure comparable in scope and equipped to outlast the other Hellenistic mystery religions. While an historical individual, Joshua (Gk., Iesous) of Nazareth, is assumed to be the subject of this collection of writings, it is the real object of the Gospels and letters that must determine how we use the New Testament sources and even how much confidence we can place in their historical assertions.

To say this will seem puzzling or perhaps sacrilegious. But it is really no different with other sorts of literature of far less apparent propagandist coloring. Josephus' Jewish Wars, for example, written within a few decades of the Gospels, remains our best source for the history of the altercation that led in 70 C.E. to the burning of the Temple by Roman legions under Titus. But Josephus writes with the purpose of absolving the Jewish people of responsibility for the uprisings, pinning the blame instead on reckless insurgents who led the people astray. His hidden agenda is to defend the Jews from the slander that they were, by Roman standards, an ungovernable people; the telling of the story is the vehicle for achieving this aim.

For a counterbalance to Josephus' version of affairs, one has only to refer to Tacitus (Hist., V), who offers his readers a rather different set of reasons for the destruction of Jerusalem. "Their customs," he opines, "owe their strength to their very badness. . . . They regard the rest of mankind with hatred and as enemies; they sit apart at meals; they sleep apart, and as a nation they are singularly prone to lust—though they refrain from intercourse with foreign women. Among themselves nothing is unlawful. Circumcision was adopted by them as a mark of their difference from other men." It is thus Tacitus' opinion that the arrogance and isolationist tendencies of the Jews (leading in the long run to wars of national liberation) are responsible for the misfortune that has befallen them.

In such cases—and they could be multiplied without difficulty—the "truth" of what happened, in the sense of a photographic reproduction of events and their causes, cannot be ascertained by choosing the interpretation of one historian over another's story. Indeed, even photographic reproduction requires the use of a lens, a focus; it is limited by the conjunction of what the camera "sees" and what the recorder, given the parameters of his own vision, wishes it to see.

And so historical knowledge goes: the testimony of any reporter is only as good as his point of observation, only as reliable as he wishes to make it. Self-interest or chauvinism may be great or small, but even the most disinterested historical narrative is only relatively objective. One can point to modern German history as a case in point. In popular historical writing, American, British, and French commentators find it as unnecessary to distinguish between the "Germans" and the "Nazis" as Tacitus did to distinguish the Zealots from the Jews. On the other hand, contemporary German history books insist on the point that National Socialism, and not some national flaw in the German character, was responsible for Hitler, the war, and the destruction that led to the partitioning of Berlin and the creation of two Germanies. The question to ask in such cases is not who is *right* but who is telling the story, to whom, and for what purpose.

"Rightness," at least in the sense of fidelity to the events as they happened, is never easily achieved, and in the case of ancient history, where events cannot be known except by interpretations of events, photographic accuracy is impossible. Thus, in the study of ancient history, a reporter's angle of vision is often the only access we have to the events of the past. By analogy, we know that historians then as now were obliged to select, edit, and refine material, some of which they derived from their predecessors, who in turn had their own angle of vision and loyalties. One can see, therefore, that the "accuracy" of any historical narrative—even when the desire to report details faithfully is part of the reporter's intention—is limited by the writer's focus and interest; by the amount of material available to him—or the amount he wishes to consult; by his inherent sense of proportion and his cultural values; even by the anticipated reaction of the projected readership.

All of these considerations apply to our reading of the Gospels. As we saw, the author of the Gospel of John did not hesitate to announce that he omitted much more material than he included in his book and is clear that what he selected was chosen with the purpose of advancing the message of the new cult. The term *gospel* (Gk., *euangelion*, announcement, news) as Mark uses it means not history but hype—an advertisement for the cult told in the form of a story about Jesus Christ, whom he decided to call the son of God. In approaching the Gospels, we must realize that we are dealing with literature of a distinct kind with distinctive limitations.

The approach in this book will be an attempt to avoid the twin dangers of parochialism and theory. Designed as an anthology, the collection offers the student a balanced overview of New Testament times, the intellectual and religious environment of the first century, the origins of the Gospel tradition, and of the putative historical elements contained in the Gospels, together with their legendary embellishments. From first to last, the essays presented here are designed to enhance the reader's appreciation of the New Testament. Doubtless this design will not appeal to everyone. After all, it can be argued, we read the New Testament not to learn history but to learn about Jesus. In part this is so, but because of the nature of the sources and the aim of the writers, the New Testament presents its protagonist, to use Paul's great image, through a glass darkly.

The glass of vision itself—the primary object of this investigation—belongs to the early Christians, people whose world-view we do not share, whose opinions on art, science, and literature we would find naive, whose sense of justice would appall even the tougher among us, and whose religious affections, including even their understanding of the Christian cult to which they were attracted, would strike many as foolish.

Having said what may seem excessively harsh, I must immediately caution that we have no need to blame the early Christians for being people of their time or to dismiss the Gospels as so many superstitious scribblings. Any *historical* appreciation of the Gospels requires us to acknowledge that the religious ideas of humankind are interesting in their own right. Only a misguided Comtean view of history as progresss permits us to think that our distance from the early Christians marks our superiority to them and their beliefs. The early history of Christianity is a seminal chapter in the intellectual and social history of Western civilization; to know what Christians believed is to know something about ourselves— what we believe and why, and for good or ill, whether it is still worth believing.

Fideists throughout the ages have discouraged such inquiry as leading to the dissolution of moral values or the end of Judeo-Christian society. But such discouragement is hopelessly uninformed, given the fact that there is nothing in Judeo-Christian society (whatever that may mean) that cannot but be better understood by a glance backward to antecedent cultures and civilizations. At the opposite extreme, liberal theologians serve up a steady diet of the Gospel according to trend, fad, and survey, making Jesus our "contemporary" with such alarming facility that the true historical background—the Roman Judea that might have produced an apocalyptic preacher like Jesus of Nazareth—fades into insignificance.

The German Bible critics of the last century, obsessed with the Hegelian notion that truth works itself out in history, regarded New Testament scholarship as the discovery of "what really happened." In the early decades of this century, especially in the period between the two world wars, a general intellectual pessimism set in, at least with respect to knowing "what really happened" in the case of Jesus of Nazareth. One couldn't know; one might never know. The Christ of the church had so efficiently displaced the Jesus of history that no conclusion heretofore reached about the date of the Gospels, their order of composition, or their relationship to the letters of Paul, seemed secure. As Wilhelm Wrede pointed out, even the earliest Gospel (if it was earliest), Mark, was thoroughly influenced by Hellenistic ideas and heavy with the aroma of the mystery religions.

The discovery, beneath the layers of ancient theology, of an obscure Galilean rabbi who had been raised to life and godhood by the ingenuous hopes of his followers, a clutch of apocalyptic enthusiasts who shared their leader's misguided vision, brought the nonparochial study of the Gospels nearly to a standstill. What is worse, the discovery invited a theological reaction so severe that the generation of New Testament scholars trained after World War II, especially those in Germany, found themselves mired in a discipline now devoted to saving (at any cost) rather than investigating the Gospels. If the road to the historical Jesus led only to the front door of the church, they reasoned, then a different route must be tried.

And so it was that New Testament scholars following the lead of the acknowledged master, Rudolph Bultmann of Marburg, retreated from what they called the "historicism" of the past and shifted the focus away from questions about the historical Jesus to questions about the "meaning" of the Gospel—or more precisely, Christian proclamation (kerygma)—in its contemporary setting. If the historical Jesus could not be known, at least the Christ of the church's preaching would survive.

After a hiatus of some fifty years, scholars are again beginning to ask what really happened. But they are freer than were their German predecessors in terms of the sorts of questions they ask and the conclusions they are prepared to accept. Initially, and inevitably, the recognition that the Gospels do not provide any direct access to the teaching of Jesus was a depressing one; more devastating was the idea that the Protestant "principle"—that the churches of the Reformation stood nearer to the intention of Jesus than did medieval Catholicism—could not be established, since increasingly it looked as if Jesus had not intended to start a church at all. These recognitions, insofar as they no longer surprise us, need no longer be put aside as "impolite" or inappropriate. If, as the great historian Adolph von Harnack imagined, the future of theology depends on the work of the historians of religion, then no answer we attempt will be without its consequences for the church.

The essays included here represent the best answers of the past century and are likely to be the ones that determine the course of New Testament study for the next generation.

Part One

The Religious and Cultural Background

Introduction

The essays in this section deal with various aspects of Hellenistic civilization—from the period beginning roughly with the death of Alexander the Great in 323 B.C.E. (before the Common Era; old style, B.C.) through the accession of Octavian (Caesar Augustus) in 27 B.C.E. Politically, the Hellenistic era was a time of consolidation and ferment. Great empires, like that of the Persians, were transformed into satellites of the Macedonian empire; new empires, such as those of the Ptolemies in Egypt and the Seleucids in Syria, were born and infused with the spirit of Greek civilization. The religious life of people throughout the ancient Near East was affected by the triumph of Hellenism as well. In general, there was a gradual movement away from the old tribal deities—the Baals, the celestial pantheons of gods, and the even more primitive fertility and vegetation cults—to a philosophical interpretation of the activity of the gods and their nature.

Aristotelian and Platonic speculation about the nature and causes of the universe merged with this theology to produce a teleological perspective corresponding, in some measure at least, to the new political realities that attended the creation of the Hellenistic kingdoms: God's (or the gods') plan for the universe was more and more assumed to be the establishment of order and peace. The death of Alexander brought an end to the process of "Hellenization"—that is, the benevolent imposition of Greek ideas, language, and religion on foreign territories—but the idealism that had fired the process lived on among Alexander's warring lieutenants throughout the Mediterranean, North Africa, and Syria-Palestine.

It is a popular misconception that the New Testament writings belong to Jewish Palestine. They do not. Written in Greek, the *lingua franca* of Alexander's empire, the Gospels were designed to appeal to the common people—people who, like Paul, considered themselves citizens of the world Rome had created on the ancient foundation of the Hellenistic kings. To read the Gospel is to enter this world, a world populated by gods, magicians, and healers, cults devoted to assorted divinities and divine men (not least, the emperor himself), divisions of time and space into sacred and profane spheres, rules governing every aspect of human behavior from eating to sexual intercourse to casual conversation with strangers.

The Gospels are a species of Hellenistic literature—or, put differently, they are a literary artifact of their time and culture. To know something of Alexander's legacy and of the customs prevalent in the *oikoumene* (the name given to the trans-cultural dominion he and his successors controlled) is thus an essential element in the study of Christian origins and the formation of Christian literature.

Eduard Lohse

The Political History of Judaism

EDUARD LOHSE was born in Hamburg, Germany, in 1924. He studied at the University of Mainz, where he received his doctorate in theology in 1949. From 1953 to 1956 he served as a lecturer at Mainz, becoming professor at the University of Kiel in 1956 and at Göttingen in 1964. Since 1971 he has been Protestant bishop of Hanover. Lohse's publications include *Mark's Witnesses to Jesus Christ* (1955), *Israel und die Christenheit* (1960), and *Die Geschichte des Leidens und Sterbens Jesu Christi* (1964), and *The New Testament Environment* (1971).

Judaism in the time of the New Testament is the legacy of its changeful history in the preceding centuries. Like their neighbors, the Jews lived at times under the dominion of the great powers which successively ruled the Near East, and although from time to time they, like other smaller tribes, were allowed a relatively unhindered life of their own, at other times they suffered interference with and dictation of their style of life. Each of these succeeding powers continued to influence the history of the land and its inhabitants, so that in the New Testament period their effects are clearly recognizable. Hence the situation in which Judaism found itself in the time of Jesus can be adequately described only against the background of the historical past by which it was molded.

PALESTINE UNDER THE RULE OF THE PERSIANS

The history of Judaism begins with the time of the *Babylonian exile*. After the destruction of Samaria by the Assyrians in 722 B.C., the ten tribes of Israel, which had settled in the northern part of the country, disappeared. In 587 B.C. Judea was finally conquered by Babylon, Jerusalem was destroyed, and the upper stratum of the population was deported to Babylon. These Judeans were able to preserve their unity as a people and their belief in the God of Israel. Though they were forbidden to continue the temple cultus, they held fast to the law of their God and obeyed the commandments of the sabbath and of circumcision—signs by which Israel constantly made itself aware of its separation and distinction from all other peoples. This produced the intellectual and spiritual precondition that made possible, after the end of the Babylonian rule, a new beginning in the land of their fathers.

The turning point came with the victory of the Persian king *Cyrus*, who with powerful blows put an end to the neo-Babylonian empire. In 539 B.C. he marched triumphantly into Babylon and thereupon became ruler not only over Mesopotamia but also over Syria and Palestine. The Persians followed a policy toward the foreign nations that came under their dominion different from that pursued earlier by the Assyrians and Babylonians. The latter, after the conquest of the countries, had transplanted entire populations, or at least deported the upper stratum; they had everywhere enforced their cult as the state religion. The Persians, on the other hand, neither forced large-scale resettlements nor required that one single state religion be acknowledged. Instead, they made allowances for various local conditions, permitted any peculiar customs of the people to be continued, let the people conduct their daily lives as previously, and sought thereby to win their allegiance. For official business the Persian government employed not its own language, but the Aramaic language, which was widely used in Syria and Palestine. This policy also afforded Judaism the opportunity to develop its own life with the express support of the government. Shortly after the conquest of Babylon, King Cyrus issued a decree ordering that the House of God in Jerusalem be rebuilt and the furnishings which Nebuchadnezzar had taken from the temple be restored (Ezra 6:3-5). Presumably, however, few of the Jews living in exile at first took advantage of the permission to return to their homeland. And the remnant of the Jewish population in Palestine lived in such modest circumstances that reconstruction of the temple began only slowly and with difficulty.

In the fifth century there arose among the Jews who had remained in Mesopotamia a strong impetus for the consolidation of the Jewish community in Jerusalem. Upon commission of the great king, first Nehemiah, then Ezra came to Palestine to set things in order. Nehemiah undertook to surround Jerusalem with fortified walls and exacted from the Jews a sworn promise not to enter into any marriages with members of alien neighboring tribes. Ezra taught the city's inhabitants the Law and, on order from the king, put it into effect. It can be assumed, with a high degree of probability, that this Law embraced the five books of Moses, i.e., the Pentateuch, in which the ancient traditions of Israel had been collected and arranged. By virtue of the fact that the Jews were under obligation to obey the law and a royal decree had confirmed its authority, Israel's Law now served as the Persian law of the land in Jerusalem and Judea. Hence the cultus of the Jewish community stood under the protection of the Persian government, and the community could develop its life without hindrance according to the prescriptions of the Law.

These circumstances evoked both envy and jealousy on the part of the neighboring peoples, and in particular among the inhabitants of *Samaria*. In the north of Palestine, after the conquest by the Assyrians, foreign settlers had become residents of the land, and these had mixed with the population that remained (II Kings 17). Their descendants, it is true, worshiped Yahweh as the God of the land, who gave fertilty and growth to the soil, but they were not recognized by the Jews as true Israelites. Hence the Jerusalem community, which had been urged by Nehemiah and Ezra not to enter into any alliances with other peoples, separated itself from them and would have no dealings with them. This harsh separation and the king's heavy favoring of Jerusalem created bitterness among the people in the region of Samaria, which led to increased alienation between north and south and finally to the political separation of the provinces of Samaria and Judea. Insofar as the Samaritan people worshiped Yahweh as the God of Israel, they had continued to go to Jerusalem, the capital of the neighboring but unfriendly province, in order to offer sacrifices and to worship in the temple there. Now political dissension gave rise to the desire on the part of the Samaritans to erect a sanctuary of their own so that they might become wholly independent of Jerusalem.

Thus, at first, the Samaritans still belonged to the cultic community of Jerusalem; for only this way is it possible to explain the fact that the Samaritans have in common with the Jews the five books of Moses as Holy Scripture, but not the remaining parts of the Old Testament Canon: the prophetic writings and the books of poetry. The separation between Jews and Samaritans must have come after the completion of the Pentateuch and before the canonical boundaries of the other parts of the Old Testament had been fixed. Although the Jewish historian Josephus relates that it was only under Alexander the Great that the Samaritans first received permission to erect a temple on Mount Gerizim (*Jewish Antiquities* XIII. 74–79), their sanctuary had probably already been built by this time. Since before its collapse the Persian Empire suffered serious upheavals, it must have been in this time at the earliest that it became possible to secure the agreement of the great king to the building of the holy places of the Samaritans. The Samaritans proudly point out that in the Law of Moses Jerusalem is not explicitly named, but their holy mountain, Gerizim, is (Deut. 11:29; 27:12–13).

From the time the Samaritans possessed their own sanctuary, such bitter enmity prevailed in their relationship with the Jews, that the eventual result was conflict tantamount to outright warfare, and in the year 128 B.C. the Jews under

John Hyrcanus destroyed the temple on Mount Gerizim. Although the Samaritans could not rebuild it, still they clung unwaveringly to Gerizim as their holy place. Even today the small Samaritan community annually celebrates in this place the Passover feast according to the age-old usage that it has preserved.

In Jesus' time, Jews and Samaritans had no dealings with each other (John 4:9). To the Jews, the Samaritans were of an alien tribe (Luke 17:18). "Samaritan" was used as a term of abuse and, specifically, was applied to persons considered demented (John 8:48). If Jewish pilgrims on their way to feasts in Jerusalem wished to take a route through Samaritan territory, they could expect hindrances and hostile treatment on the way (Luke 9:51-56). It is true that the Samaritans referred to the patriarchs as their ancestors (John 4:12), but the Jews did not allow this claim. Jesus cited, not the act of a Jew, but that of a Samaritan, as an example of love for one's neighbor unselfishly demonstrated (Luke 10:30-37). And it is told that a Samaritan, not a Jew, after being cured of leprosy, gave praise to God (Luke 17:11-19). After some initial hesitation (Matt. 10:5-6), the primitive community overcame the alienation that existed between Jews and Samaritans and carried the gospel to Samaria (Acts 8:4-25). The old dispute over whether one should worship on Mount Gerizim or in Jerusalem (John 4:20) was now of no importance, "for God is spirit, and those who worship him must worship him in spirit and in truth" (John 4:24).

PALESTINE UNDER ALEXANDER THE GREAT AND THE RULE OF THE EGYPTIANS

In the battle of Issus (333 B.C.), *Alexander the Great* conquered the Persian king Darius III and, by means of this victory, opened the way via Syria and Palestine to Egypt. Only slight resistance could be offered to the rapid advance of the Macedonian forces. The strong island fortress of Tyre was able to maintain itself until a seven-month-long siege brought about its capitulation. Gaza held out for two months; then this city also fell. After overcoming these obstacles, Alexander was able to march along the Mediterranean coast directly to Egypt. The victorious king did not remain for the conquest and occupation of the inland districts, but left this task to his generals. Judea submitted to the commander Parmenio without offering any resistance. Samaria, the seat of the Persian governor, was conquered by Perdiccas and his soldiers. The Jews were deeply impressed by the strength of the Greek army and acknowledged the superior power of the new lords without delay. Since the Jews submitted peaceably, the rights that they possessed under Persian rule were preserved for them. The Jerusalem community was permitted to continue practicing its cult without hindrance.

The lack of outward change occasioned with respect to the legal situation of the Jewish community by the change in rulers contrasted sharply with the later profound effect caused by the entrance of the *Greeks* into the country. Although in earlier times Greek traders, merchants, and travelers had come to Palestine, now the trade and the manner of life of the Greeks reached into all parts of the country. The peoples of the Near East opened themselves to the Greek influence—manners, culture, and intellectual materials—so that the descendants of the ancient Phoenicians and Philistines exchanged their language for Greek, and, thereby, became so completely absorbed into the world of Hellenism that they lost their distinctive culture. Greek settlements and cities were founded, but Greeks also settled in already existing cities. The conquered fortress of Tyre was resettled with Greeks; the city of Samaria, which had offered resistance, received Macedonians as inhabitants. Many cities adopted not only a Greek name but also Greek civil law. From this time on, therefore, the Jews in Palestine lived in close proximity to the Greeks, who enforced their language as the language of trade. Anyone who was not able to speak Greek was regarded as a barbarian. Many Jews learned the language of the aliens (which was spoken in all the countries which Alexander the Great had reached in his triumphal march) so that in New Testament times many people in Palestine could understand and speak Greek. If one had dealings with the representatives of the Roman occupation forces, one could make oneself understood with Greek. When Paul was arrested in Jerusalem and wanted to defend himself before the masses of the people—thus the book of Acts reports—people were surprised that he spoke Hebrew, or Aramaic, and not Greek (Acts 22:2). Apparently people would have been able to understand one language as well as the other without difficulty.

Along with the language there came into the country the Hellenistic civilization as well, for the Greek settlers brought along their own patterns of life and clung to them. Greek buildings appeared, theaters and baths were erected in the cities, and sports were pursued in the gymnasia. *Greek customs* were adopted; in festive meals, people ate while reclining at the table (see Mark 14:18 par. 22 par.). They came to enjoy the medical skill that the Greeks had developed to a high degree (Mark 5:26 par.). As the Greeks sought to develop a train of thought in conversation and through the interplay of question and answer to find the solution to a problem, so now the Jews also learned to debate and, in didactic conversation, to inquire about and to attempt to clarify the truth of the divine will. These examples show how the Jews also learned to adapt themselves to the new conditions and to find their way about in them. The attraction which people in many Jewish circles felt for the superior civilization and culture of the Greeks increased to the extent that in the second century B.C. there were Jews in Jerusalem who in all seriousness believed that they were kinsmen of the Spartans, who were famed for their just laws. I Maccabees tells of a letter which Areus, the king of Sparta, is supposed to have written to the high priest Onias; this letter states that an ancient writing has been discovered which identifies Spartans and Jews as brothers and both as descendants of the tribe of Abraham (1 Macc. 12:21). This development might finally have led to complete Hellenization of Jerusalem and Judea, as had happened with the land of the Phoenicians and Philistines. But the Law that was received from the fathers and recorded in the

Hebrew language obligated the community to keep the old faith, to order its worship according to the law of Moses, and to remain aware that God had set Israel, his people, apart from all the other nations.

The sudden death of Alexander the Great at the age of thirty-three, in 323 B.C., plunged his hastily constructed empire into political confusion. Alexander's military commanders fell into a dispute about their respective jurisdictions, and the unity of the empire collapsed. The governor Ptolemy, who resided in Egypt, sent forces to occupy Palestine and at first brought it under his control. But Antigonus, who governed Syria, contested Ptolemy's claim to Palestine and usurped his rule (315 B.C.). However, when Antigonus later succeeded in re-conquering the old Persian Empire almost in its entirety, the other former governors under Alexander became envious of his success and joined forces against him. As a result, Ptolemy succeeded in regaining control of Palestine and acquired the southern part of Syria, as well. Therewith circumstances were decided which were to prevail for the next one hundred years. Palestine, which so often in its history had been the source of discord between the great powers in Egypt and Mesopotamia, stood under the overlordship of Egypt, now a Hellenistic state, so that the Hellenistic influence in Palestine continued unchanged.

The Ptolemies apparently followed the example of the Persians and Alexander the Great in refraining from meddling in the internal affairs of the cultic community in Jerusalem. The leadership of Judaism lay in the hands of its high priest, who was able to order and guide its interests with the consent of the Hellenistic rulers of Egypt. Standing with him in the Sanhedrin were priests and elders, the heads of the influential families of Jerusalem. It cannot be determined with certainty when this supreme Jewish authority came into existence. Its origin could in fact date from the Persian period, but there is unequivocal evidence for its existence only beginning with the Hellenistic period. In the first century B.C., the priests and elders were joined by a third group. The Sanhedrin is frequently mentioned in the New Testament, primarily in the passion narratives, in this context (Mark 10:33 par.; 11:27 par.; 14:43 par.; et passim). When occasionally only two groups are named—the chief priests and scribes (Mark 1:18 par.; 14:1 par.; et passim), or the chief priests and elders (Matt. 21:45; 26:3, 47; et passim)—or when only the chief priests are cited as representatives of the Sanhedrin (Mark 14:55 par. et passim), what is meant is always the supreme Jewish authority which came together under the leadership of the high priest, to regulate all secular and spiritual matters which affected the Jewish population.

PALESTINE UNDER THE RULE OF SYRIA
AND THE MACCABEAN STRUGGLE FOR FREEDOM

After a first fruitless attempt, about the end of the third or the beginning of the second century B.C., the Syrian king Antiochus III (223–187 B.C.) succeeded in wresting Palestine from Egypt. The Ptolemies were obliged to withdraw and leave the country to the Syrians. Since the Jews had recognized in time that the scales were tipping in the Syrians' favor and during the hostilities had fought on their side, after the victory they were treated accordingly by the Syrians. Efforts were made to repair the damage which Jerusalem had suffered during the war, and to their existing rights further privileges were added. Up to a certain amount, the expenses required for the temple cult were to be defrayed by funds from the state's treasury, and the members of the council of elders and the scribes were granted freedom from taxation.

Yet the friendly relations were not to continue for long. Syria was ruled by the dynasty of the Seleucids, which had been founded by Seleucus after the death of Alexander the Great. The Seleucids strove, by promoting Hellenistic culture, to bind the diverse peoples of their kingdom closer together. Large groups of the Jews were receptive to this policy, and even among the priesthood in Jerusalem there were many who adjusted to the process of Hellenization. The high priest, as head of the Jewish people, was responsible for enforcing the laws and decrees of the Syrian king. Since he was also responsible for seeing that the taxes owed were paid on time, the Syrians could also turn to him when they wished to collect more money. When *Antiochus IV* assumed the reign in Syria in the year 175 B.C., the high priest in Jerusalem was *Onias*, a devout observer of the law. Nevertherless he had opponents within the priesthood, above all in the person of his brother Joshua and generally among the adherents to the Hellenizing movement. Joshua rendered his name into Greek as Jason, offered the Syrians a considerable sum of money which was to be brought in through the raising of taxes, and succeeded in having Onias relieved of his office and himself installed as high priest. The change in the office of high priest was accomplished without any resistance on the part of the defeated party. Onias was murdered some years later in Antioch; his son of the same name fled to Egypt and, with the support of the Ptolemies, around 160 B.C. established a temple in Leontopolis, where a sacrificial cult modeled after that of the temple in Jerusalem was adopted and continued until A.D. 73. Nevertheless the significance of this sanctuary remained slight, since even the Egyptian Jews continued to adhere to the temple in Jerusalem. In Jerusalem, it is true, Jason enforced the performance of the temple cult in accordance with the prescriptions of the Law, but he vigorously advanced the process of Hellenizaton. A gymnasium was built, where the young men played sports unclothed; and even priests took part in this activity. Jewish participants under these circumstances became ashamed of their circumcision, which the Greeks ridiculed; hence many of them underwent an operation to undo their circumcision (1 Macc. 1:15)—a practice which still occurred frequently among Jews even in Paul's time (see 1 Cor. 7:18). When Jason had been in office three years, a certain *Menelaus* offered the Syrian king an even larger sum of money for the position of high priest than Jason had once paid, and thereupon was given Jason's place. The office of high priest had become a political entity which could be bought and sold.

The Romans, who after their victorious struggle against Hannibal had also made their military and political influence felt in the Orient, intervened in favor of the Ptolemies, who were ruling in Egypt, and against the party of Antiochus of Syria. Antiochus had made war against Egypt, but was forced to interrupt his undertaking when the Romans commanded him to stop. After the abortive Egyptian campaign, the rumor spread in Jerusalem that Antiochus had lost his life. Jason, who had been expelled from his office, sought to use this opportunity to drive out Menelaus by armed force and once again succeeded in taking upon himself both the office of the high priest and the rule over Jerusalem. When Antiochus learned of these events, enraged, he intervened and restored Menelaus to the office of high priest. Yet the latter could preserve his position only with the support of the Syrians and therefore offered no resistance to them when in 169 B.C. Antiochus replenished his own treasury, which had been emptied in the war, by plundering the Jerusalem temple: the precious furnishings of the temple, the altar of incense, the seven-branched lampstand, and the table of the shew-bread were removed to Antioch (1 Macc. 1:20–24).

This first offense against the holy place was soon followed by a second, still harsher attack. The Hellenization of Jerusalem and Judea, which in fact had encountered some resistance but for the most part had made significant progress, was to be completed with force; and thereby the Jewish community's indigenous way of life was to be abolished. The walls of Jerusalem were torn down, and a fortress was built on the hill of the ancient city of David (the Acra). The Jews were forbidden, on pain of death, to keep the sabbath and to circumcise their children. The king's inspectors traveled throughout the country in order to supervise the fulfillment of these decrees. In Jerusalem a pagan altar was erected on the site of the altar of burnt offering, and sacrifices were offered there to the supreme God, the Olympian Zeus (167 B.C.). Even swine were offered as sacrificial animals. Greeks were able to interpret this change as an expression of the view that in all cults ultimately the one God was worshiped, and that it was a matter of arbitrary choice whether his name was Yahweh, Baal of heaven, or Zeus; but for the Jews, the profanation of the holy place signified the abomination of desolation (see Dan. 11:31; 12:11). People saw in this event a sign of the last times and even later always spoke of the abomination of desolation as a phenomenon which was to occur shortly before the end of this age (Mark 13:14 par.). These events brought an extremely dangerous crisis for Judaism, whose end appeared to be imminent. But the believing community did not passively let itself be detached from the faith of the fathers. The book of Daniel was composed as a writ of consolation for the oppressed community; persecution and suffering were understood as signs of the last times, soon to be brought to an end by an act of God. Pious Jews preferred to accept suffering and death rather than to renounce their obedience to the Law (2 Macc. 7).

In contrast to the city residents who opened themselves to the influences of the Hellenistic culture and civilization, the people of the countryside held stubbornly to the faith of their fathers. Within their circles resistance to Syrian policy increased and, as a result of an incident which occurred in the little village of Modein, not far from Lydda, escalated to outright rebellion against the alien rule. When the king's inspectors came to this place to compel the Jews to offer pagan sacrifices, the old priest *Mattathias*—the head of a family which was called, after its ancestor, the Hasmoneans—killed a Jew who was ready to offer a sacrifice on the altar, and also slew the royal official who had demanded that the sacrifices be made. This act created a great sensation. Mattathias and his sons had to flee and to withdraw into the hills of the wilderness of Judea (1 Macc. 1:15–28), where a host of Jews ready for battle soon gathered around them. From this base, they at first carried out small forays here and there to destroy pagan temples which had been erected throughout the countryside or to punish apostate Jews. When the old priest Mattathias died soon thereafter, his son *Judas* took over the leadership of the warriors. He acquired the surname "the Maccabean," which probably means "the hammer-like one" (from the Aramaic *makkaba,* meaning "the hammer"). He was regarded by his friends as an able warrior, and was feared by his adversaries. Judas was soon not content with small-scale guerrilla activities and attacks, and ventured to undertake large-scale attacks on the Syrians. Hence the Syrians were compelled to show resistance. The king, Antiochus, who was fighting the Parthians in the East, sent his commander Lysias to Palestine. Judas continued to be successful against him, defeated the Syrians in several battles, marched in triumph to Jerusalem, occupied the desecrated holy place, and reestablished the worship of the God of Israel prescribed by the Law. On the twenty-fifth of Kislev (i.e., in December) of the year 164 B.C., the altar was consecrated anew; and with an eight-day feast, worship in accordance with the Law was begun again. Ever since, Judaism has annually commemorated this event in the Feast of Dedication (Hebrew *Hanukkah*) (see John 10:22), during which lamps are lighted as a sign that shadows and darkness must inevitably give way to the light.

Notwithstanding these victories, the Syrians still occupied the fortress in Jerusalem. After a few smaller military undertakings, Judas began to besiege the fortress, and thereby provoked a counteraction from the Syrians. In place of King Antiochus, who had died during a campaign against the Parthians, the general Lysias was ruling as guardian of the king's minor son and regent of the kingdom. He sent a well-equipped army, which defeated the Jews and encircled Jerusalem. In this cramped situation Judas and his army were aided by an outbreak of disputes over the Syrian throne. Another general sought to depose Lysias. In order to be free to deal with his opposition, Lysias made an agreement with the Jews: he allowed them free exercise of their religion in return for their acknowledgment of Syrian sovereignty. From then on this compromise remained in force. Despite continual confusion in Syria over the occupancy of the throne, no Syrian ruler ever called this treaty into question.

Large segments of the Jewish populace were satisfied with this outcome of the Maccabean struggle for freedom, especially since after some time the deserted office of the high priest could again be filled. Menelaus, who had thoroughly misused the office, had been removed by the Maccabean reform.

Under the reign of the Syrian king Demetrius, who in 162 B.C. had seized power, Hellenistic sympathizers in Jerusalem presented petitions and registered complaints that they were being suppressed by Judas. The king listened to them and installed as high priest a man named Alkimus, who indeed was a friend of Hellenization, but was also of the Aaronic family. Since the cult was again being performed in accordance with the prescriptions of the Law and a believing Jew could live unmolested, the devout ones (Hebrew *chasidim*) who had resisted the Syrian policy of tyranny saw their goal achieved. They were prepared to recognize the high priest who had been installed by the Syrians as the lawful holder of the office. But Judas and his friends distrusted the Syrians. What concerned them was not the reestablishment of proper worship; instead, they wished to take further steps—to achieve political independence—by which alone they felt effective protection against the Syrian-Hellenistic influence could be achieved.

Therefore Judas challenged the high priest Alkimus, who then called on the Syrians for help. There ensued a series of various military engagements, in the course of which Judas was killed in 160 B.C. His followers were bloodily persecuted by the Syrians wherever they could be seized. The bands of fighters withdrew into the wilderness, and in Judas' place, his brother *Jonathan* became their leader. Although the rebel force **was** only a small one and the situation was extremely difficult, Jonathan succeeded in making an impact on his enemies. Owing to his skill in exploiting the continuing disputes over the throne in Syria, he was able to weaken the contesting parties by fighting first on one side, then on the other. He managed to secure concessions from every side and in this way enlarged the area that lay under his influence: the southern part of Samaria, whose inhabitants held to the temple in Jerusalem, became subject to his jurisdiction. Since the demise of Alkimus, who had died at the end of the year 160 B.C., the office of the high priest had remained unfilled. Now Jonathan succeeded in securing the agreement of the Syrians to allow him to assume this office (153 B.C.). Thus, a man who had constantly stained himself in war, who indeed came from a rural, priestly family but was not of Zadokite origin, became high priest of Israel. The devout persons who once had shared in the Maccabean revolt were deeply concerned over this development.

When Jonathan was murdered in 143 B.C. through the treachery of the Syrians, *Simon*, the third of the brothers, assumed the leadership of the struggle. He succeeded also in gaining for himself the same position which Jonathan had attained. He became not only military commander and leader of Judaism, but its high priest as well. While Jonathan was able to expand the territory governed by him, Simon besieged and expelled the Syrian garrison in the fortress of Jerusalem. Since Jerusalem was not completely free of foreign rule, Simon was able also to gain independence abroad. He succeeded in persuading the Syrians to concede freedom of taxation to the Jews (142 B.C.), and minted his own Jewish coins. The office of high priest, field commander, and leader of the Jews was conferred upon him in 140 B.C. as hereditary, and thus the dynasty of the Hasmoneans, which was acknowledged even by the Romans, was founded. The Jewish community had achieved far-reaching independence, and under Simon's rule experienced peaceful relationships once again. People breathed a sigh of relief: Simon's rule was praised as a time of peace and happiness:

> People could cultivate their land in peace, and the land gave its yield and the trees in the field, their fruit. The elders sat about the streets and conferred with each other about the common good, and the young men clothed themselves with the decoration of battle dress. He [Simon] provided the cities with food and equipped them with fortifications, so that his glorious name was sounded as far as the ends of the earth. He created peace in the land, and Israel rejoiced greatly. Everyone sat under his own vine and under his fig tree, and no one was afraid. No one any longer made war in the land, and in that time the kings were humbled. He aided all the wretched ones among his people; he was full of zeal for the Law and rooted out every apostate and evildoer. He made the sanctuary splendid and increased the furnishings of the sanctuary. (1 Macc. 14:8-15)

In these words from 1 Maccabees the age of Simon is rapturously extolled, and the peaceful conditions are interpreted as a fulfillment of the divine promise: each one would sit under his vine and under his fig tree, and no one would make him afraid (Mic. 4:4). The wise rule of Simon, his compassion for the needy, and his zeal for the Law and the temple are described as having features like those attributed to the messiah in the eschatological expectation. Yet this portrayal was by no means convincing to all the Jews. Many priests and other devout people sharply disapproved of the rule of the Hasmoneans, who came neither from a high-priestly family nor from the family of David yet had combined the office of high priest with the capacity of ruler over Israel. Previously, and seemingly inevitably, under Jonathan such a merger had led to disputes between members of the devout groups on the one hand, and the high priest and his followers on the other; and these disputes led to the withdrawal of a group of strict law-observing Jews into the desert, to lead their lives on the shores of the Dead Sea in rigid obedience to the Law. They would never have agreed with the praise voiced in 1 Maccabees concerning the government of Simon.

Simon's rule came to a sudden end when in 134 B.C. he fell victim to a murderous attack plotted by a son-in-law of Ptolemy. Yet the murderer did not succeed in gaining Simon's place for himself. Instead, the rule fell to Simon's son, John Hyrcanus, in accordance with the designation of the people under Simon's rule.

THE HASMONEAN KINGDOM

After one last attempt by the Syrians to gain influence in the affairs of Palestine was defeated (128 B.C.), *John Hyrcanus* acquired a free hand to govern the entire country. He undertook military campaigns in the vicinity of Judea; however, he did not carry out these campaigns in the vicinity of Judea; however, he did not carry out these campaigns with a people's army which fought for Israel's faith, but with a band of mercenaries whom he had purposely gathered and who willingly did whatever he commanded. Though Jonathan and Simon had already succeeded in expanding the Jewish sphere of power, Hyrcanus was concerned with extending his rule still further. In 128 B.C., the temple on Mount Gerizim was destroyed and thereby the Samaritans were deprived of their holy place. He made another thrust into Idumea, the territory of the ancient Edom, whereby the local populace was converted to Judaism by force and their land was brought under Jewish rule. A campaign against Samaria ended equally successfully: in 107 B.C. that Hellenized city was conquered and destroyed.

Although Hyrcanus' policy in his military undertakings turned out well, he received little acclaim from the masses and outright rejection in the circles of the pious. The latter were concerned with shaping their lives according to the law of God, and therefore they disapproved of the Hasmoneans' drive for power as worldly action on the part of the rulers. The society of the Pharisees was an offshoot of the groups of law-observing Jews who had supported the Maccabean revolt. Although they had originally stood close to the Hasmoneans, a serious breach now occurred, so that Hyrcanus sought support not among the Pharisees, but among those who conceived of politics from a realistic viewpoint and did not wish to isolate themselves even from Hellenism. At first Hyrcanus had proceeded in accordance with the Pharisaic understanding of the Law, but he gradually turned away from this and drew closer to the Sadducees, who were sympathetic to his efforts. The tradition reports that a sudden break came between Hyrcanus and the Pharisees. According to this account, when Hyrcanus once asked a gathering of Pharisees to tell him plainly if they believed that he was departing from the right way at any point, no one at first uttered any criticism, and all were full of praise. But then a Pharisee named Eleazar arose and demanded of Hyrcanus that he lay aside the position of high priest, because in the time of Antiochus Epiphanes, Hyrcanus' mother had been in prison. It was possible for a woman to have been violated while in prison; therefore, the son of such a mother might not be fit for the office in which the highest degree of priestly purity is required. Hyrcanus was so angered by this assertion that he regarded it as an expression of the opinion held by all the Pharisees, and thus broke with them. The narrative stresses the fact that the Hasmonean rulers did not, in the view of the pious, satisfy the prescription of the Law concerning the purity of the high priest. To Hyrcanus the post of field commander and ruler over the Jews was more important than the cultic task of the high priest, although the coins which he minted bore either the inscription "The high priest John and the commonwealth of the Jews," or "The high priest John, the head of the commonwealth of the Jews."

After the death of Hyrcanus the son *Aristobulus* seized the rule for himself. Hyrcanus had in fact decreed that after him his wife should govern; but Aristobulus threw his mother and three of his brothers into prison. He shared the rule only with his brother Antigonus, until others planted suspicions about the latter in his mind and caused him to order Antigonus' assassination. Aristobulus conducted himself in the manner of the kings of petty Oriental states and was the first Jewish ruler to secure for himself the title of king. He continued the military campaigns, won successes in Galilee, and compelled the people of the conquered territories to practice circumcision. Yet the forced conversion to Judaism did not further religious aims, but served to subjugate persons to the power of the king. Abroad he represented himself as a friend of the Greeks, and in this respect, also followed the example of other Oriental rulers.

After a short reign Aristobulus died in 103 B.C. His wife, Salome Alexandra, freed the brothers of the deceased king from prison, handed over the rule to the eldest of these, and became his wife. The new ruler grecized his name from Jonathan to Jannaeus, and called himself *Alexander Jannaeus*. He too waged many wars and, like his predecessor, continued for the most part to be successful. After he had conquered the region on the coast of the Mediterranean Sea and had undertaken some thrusts into the country east of the Jordan, he was able, but only with difficulty, to assert himself in the dispute with the rising kingdom of the Nabataeans. By means of his campaigns he united an area the scope of which corresponded approximately to that of Israel and Judah in the time of King Solomon; but his kingdom was not solidly established. Since the inhabitants of the conquered portions were either expelled or forced to become Jews, there was constant unrest, and the king was obliged to hasten from one corner of his country to the other to suppress or prevent rebellion. Because the rule of the Hasmoneans could not sustain itself through a broad sense of support among its own people, it remained insecurely established. The devout stood in open opposition to the policy of the ruler, who as the man of war he was, nevertheless, simultaneously had to fill the post of high priest. He did not shrink from enforcing his will with cruelty and ruthlessness or from suppressing the Pharisees and their adherents with violence. The tension rose so high that it led to armed conflict. It is told in the tradition that Jannaeus captured eight hundred rebels, brought them to Jerusalem, and had them crucified. In company with his women he arranged a banquet in front of the crosses and had the wives and children of the crucified men slain before their eyes. Since the cruel punishment of crucifixion had never before been employed in Israel, the frightful vengeance with which Alexander Jannaeus punished his opponents by "hanging men up alive" (4QpNah. I. 6–7) evoked horror and fear among the people. Jannaeus indeed destroyed the open resistance by means of the terror, but the inward rejection of the populace continued.

On his deathbed Alexander Jannaeus advised his wife, *Salome Alexandra,* to be reconciled again with the Pharisees. After the king's death she took over the government and directed it for nine years with prudence and wisdom (76–67 B.C.). Although she was indeed queen, she could not, as a woman, perform a priestly office; so her son *Hyrcanus II,* a weak and not very energetic man, was installed as high priest. Salome brought about an agreement with the Pharisees, granting them an influence upon the political destiny of the land. Scribes of the Pharisees' company became members of the Sanhedrin, to which only chief priests and elders had previously belonged, and here were able to make their opinions felt and often to put them into effect. Anyone who had fled from Jannaeus' tyrannical rule could return home. The company of the Sadducees, whose opinion had been determinative in the supreme council of the Jews, saw themselves put at a disadvantage. Alliances with them and with all who were dissatisfied with the queen's government were formed by her younger son Aristobulus II, who was vigorously striving to gain power. In view of these tensions, Salome used the reins of power with caution and avoided initiating any military undertakings. She sought instead to safeguard peace abroad, in order to achieve internal pacification of the country as well. Hence, in the Pharisaic tradition, her reign is glorified as a blessed and peaceful time. It is said that in the years of Simon ben Schatach, who was the most outstanding scribe in the time of Queen Salome Alexandra, the rain fell so abundantly that the grains of wheat grew as large as kidneys, the grains of barley as large as olive seeds, and the lentils as large as gold *denarii*.

When Salome Alexandra died in 67 B.C., her son Hyrcanus II legally should have succeeded her in the office of king, but his brother *Aristobulus II* contested the position with him. Armed conflict began, in which the soldiers of Aristobulus proved to be superior to those of Hyrcanus. Hyrcanus was abandoned by his people, who went over to the stronger side. Therefore, he was obliged to accept an agreement whereby the dignity of high priest and king passed over to Aristobulus. Yet even with this the conflict did not end. For now *Antipater*, whose father had been royal governor in Idumea under Alexander Jannaeus, took his position on the side of the supplanted Hyrcanus. He lured the Nabataean king, Aretas, to their side by promising him the return of the cities which Jannaeus had taken from him. Aretas and Antipater marched with their troops to Jerusalem and began to besiege the city. But before matters could come to a decisive stage, the superior power of Rome appeared on the scene. From that time onward, this power was to determine the fate of the Near East and thus of Palestine as well. When *Pompey* approached with his legions, the weak kingdom of the Seleucids collapsed and was incorporated into the Roman realm as the province of Syria. Both of the parties fighting over the power in Judea appealed to Pompey, in order to win him to their side. But the people let him know that he might abolish the kingship altogether and restore the ancient rule of the priests. The kingdom of the Hasmoneans had not only lost the visible means of power; it also no longer possessed any following among the Jewish public who could have sustained it. Hence its end had irrevocably come. Yet, as referee, Pompey was in no great haste to announce his decision, and at first adopted a policy of "wait and see," before he made his decision.

PALESTINE UNDER ROMAN RULE

Each of the two contending parties which opposed each other in Judea was concerned with gaining for itself the favor of Pompey. At first it appeared that Aristobulus had better prospects of success for his cause. But when Pompey postponed the decision about Palestine, Aristobulus lost patience and sought to assure the continuation of his rule by military arrangements. Then Pompey became suspicious and advanced on Jerusalem. The Nabataeans were withdrawn as a gesture from the Romans. Aristobulus and his followers entrenched themselves in the city, but after a three-month siege their resistance was broken. Pompey entered Jerusalem and went into the temple; he even inspected the Holy of Holies. Yet he did not seize anything from the sanctuary, and he gave command that the worship might be resumed at once. The fact that a Gentile did not stop even at the Holy of Holies, to which only the high priest had access, appeared to the pious Jews a frightful desecration of the temple, which could only be conceived as God's judgment on his guilty people. In the Psalms of Solomon, which soon therafter arose in Pharisaic circles, it is said, with clear reference to the events which occurred upon Pompey's conquest of Jerusalem: "In his insolence the sinner knocked down strong walls with the ram, and thou didst not hinder it. Alien Gentiles ascended thine altar, insolently trod it with their shoes; because the sons of Jerusalem desecrated the sanctuary of the Lord, they defiled God's sacrifice in godlessness" (Ps. of Sol. 2:1-3). The lament was followed with the prayer: "Let it suffice, Lord, that thy hand falls upon Jerusalem in the onrush of the Gentiles" (2:22).

After the conquest of the city Pompey put matters in Palestine in order. Aristobulus, along with his two sons Alexander and Antigonus, was brought prisoner to Rome, and Hyrcanus was once again installed in the office of high priest. The boundaries were redrawn; the cities in the coastal region became independent; the Hellenistic cities in the land east of the Jordan River, which had become subject to the Hasmoneans, were combined into a free league of cities which extended from Damascus in the north to Philadelphia (the present-day Amman) in the south. This league of the so-called Decapolis—i.e., of ten cities—existed for a long time and is mentioned at various points in the New Testament (Mark 5:20; 7:31; Matt. 4:25). Samaria also was given its independence, so that the high priest had dominion only over the area which belonged immediately to the Jerusalem cultic community, Judea, the interior of Galilee, and Perea in the land east of the Jordan. Then in the year 57 B.C., the Roman provincial governor in Syria, Gabinius, divided Palestine into five adminstrative districts which were to be immediately under his control. Judea was divided into the districts of Jerusalem, Gazara, and Jericho; Galilee was apportioned to the district of Sepphoris, and Perea to the district of Amanthus. This arrangement was well thought-out and might have made possible peaceful domestic development if the civil unrest which still smoldered in the interior of the country and impulses from abroad had not produced new and grave disturbances. Aristobulus and his sons soon began to stir again, after they had escaped from Roman imprisonment and were able to return to Palestine. In Jerusalem there were many people who were dissatisfied with Hyrcanus' weak conduct of his office and therefore sympathized with Aristobulus. Still the power of Roman arms prevented him from being able to realize his aims in Palestine.

The grave disputes over rulership in the Roman realm also affected Palestine. In the struggle between Pompey and Caesar, Hyrcanus and his people supported Pompey, who held the eastern part of the realm in his hand. However, when Caesar continued to be victorious and Pompey was murdered in Egypt in 48 B.C., Hyrcanus and Antipater were able quickly and successfully to switch over to the stronger party. They sent auxiliary troops to *Caesar* in Egypt and won his favor. Caesar not only renewed the traditional rights of the cultic community of Jerusalem, but added other privileges to these as well: the city of Joppa was again added to the territory ruled by the high priest; Hyrcanus was confirmed in his office as high priest and named ethnarch and ally of the Romans; and Antipater received the rights of a hereditary Roman citizen and was installed as procurator of Judea. This meant that alongside the ancient traditional office of high priest was placed the office of governor, the purpose of which was to safeguard the interests of the Roman realm in the country. Judea was freed from the obligation to house Roman legions during the winter months. The unhindered practice of worship was assured, not only for the temple community, but also for the synagogue communities in the realm, so that from this time on, Judaism stood under the protection of the Roman state.

Through this arrangement, Antipater had gained a strong position. He arranged to share his power with his two sons by transferring to Phasael the administration of Judea, and to Herod that of Galilee. In Galilee *Herod* eliminated the nuisance of the so-called robbers, i.e., nationalistic Jewish partisans, and in that connection imposed some death penalties without first consulting the Sanhedrin in Jerusalem, with whom the supreme power in legal matters actually lay. When some called him to account for this in Jerusalem, he appeared before the Sanhedrin in the company of a bodyguard, so that no one dared to take action against him.

With the murder of Caesar, in 44 B.C., new confusion broke out in the Roman realm. Hyrcanus and Antipater first allied themselves with Caesar's murderers, but the rule of these latter did not last long. In 42 B.C., Octavian and Antony defeated them in battle at Philippi. After the victory, *Antony* assumed the government over the eastern part of the realm and lived with the Eygptian queen Cleopatra in Alexandria. Antipater fell victim to an assassin. Hyrcanus and the two sons of Antipater, Herod and Phasael, however, were confirmed in their offices by Antony. Hyrcanus continued as high priest, and Herod and Phasael ruled the country. Antony stayed constantly in Egypt, so he was not able to involve himself significantly with Syria and Palestine.

Then an attack came from the Parthians in the east, with whom *Antigonus*, the son of Aristobulus II, was allied. Previously he, like his father, had striven in vain to gain power; but this time he attained his goal. The Parthians took Hyrcanus and Phasael prisoners. Phasael killed himself, and Hyrcanus was handed over to Antigonus. The latter ordered his uncle's ears cut off, so that as a mutilated person he would be unfit for the office of high priest. Antigonus assumed this dignity in his place and was confirmed in it by the Parthians. For three years he was able with their help to rule as high priest and king of the Jews (40–37 B.C.). Hyrcanus and Phasael were eliminated, and only Herod remained.

Herod did the most clever thing he could possibly have done in this situation: he fled to the Romans and sought protection and help from them against Antigonus and the Parthians. In 40 B.C. he came to Rome and there gained confidence and advancement from Antony and Octavian. Upon the official decision of the Senate, he was named king of the Jews, though a king without a country; for in Palestine were his worst enemies, from whom he first had to wrest the country. From a base in Syria, where the Romans soon were able to drive out the Parthians, he pushed with Roman help toward Palestine, and in 37 B.C. was able to capture Jerusalem and take up his royal office. Antigonus was imprisoned and then executed. Therewith the last attempt of the Hasmoneans to gain power was shattered. Herod was in possession of the kingship and did not allow it to be disputed again.

Just as Herod had acquired his power with Roman support, so he succeeded in fortifying it with Roman help. He was crafty and ruthless, but also daring and capable when it was a matter of making decisions quickly and acting decisively. At first he was on the side of Antony, who in Egypt ruled over the eastern part of the realm, and submitted to his directions, even when they ran counter to his own interests. Thus he had to make the best of it when Antony gave to Cleopatra, at her request, the cities on the coast and Jericho. He was too clever not to realize that, under any circumstances, he had to keep the support of the Roman ruler in order to be able to assert his own position. When Antony later was defeated by Octavian, Herod was obliged to act as quickly as possible to establish a good relationship with the new ruler of the empire. He traveled to *Octavian,* who was staying on Rhodes, openly confessed to him that he had belonged up to that time to Antony's party, and as a sign of his submission laid down his crown. The word and gesture did not fail to have their effect. Octavian confirmed Herod as king of the Jews and restored to him the cities which Antony had transferred to Cleopatra. Thus Herod also gained the favor of Augustus (Octavian had assumed this surname) and was able skillfully to maintain it. The peace which came to the Roman Empire with the reign of Augustus favored Palestine also. At long last the land was free from the torment of war.

Herod purged the opponents of his regime and all those who could possibly have endangered his rule without regard for ties of friendship and family. Through his marriage with *Mariamne,* who came from the family of the Hasmoneans, he was related to the old royal family. Since he came from

Idumea, he was constantly plagued with anxiety that people did not regard him as their equal. The old Hyrcanus was murdered by him, even though the mutilations he had suffered disqualified him from holding the office of high priest. Herod himself was not of priestly lineage and therefore could not become high priest. After he had at first installed a man who was obedient to him, he finally yielded to the insistence of his mother-in-law and of the circles close to the Hasmoneans and assigned the office to his young brother-in-law Aristobulus. Yet he did not escape from the anxiety that the Hasmoneans would become dangerous to him and seek to supplant him. When Aristobulus was murdered in his bath a year later, it was no secret that the murderers were hired by Herod; yet to the public the king feigned grief over the death of the high priest. Herod's jealousy of the Hasmoneans finally became so strong that he even killed his wife Mariamne and later had their sons, Alexander and Aristobulus, murdered. He kept his affection for his firstborn son, Antipater, but shortly before his own death, sentenced him to death also, as a traitor and rebel. Suspicion governed Herod's actions; the New Testament narrative of the massacre of the infants is entirely in harmony with this picture of his character (Matt. 2:16). Herod was constantly on guard against threats to his rule from any side and did not hesitate to take vigorous, harsh, and ruthless action to eliminate them. Neither did he shrink from having anyone murdered who might possibly become a personal danger to him as an opponent of his kingship.

Herod's kingdom included not only Jews, but also Gentiles, who dwelt predominantly in the regions which had come under his rule through the generosity of Octavian. Herod did not continue the Hasmonean policy of converting Gentiles to Judaism by force, but placed Greeks and Jews side by side with equal rights, and desired as king to be a Jew to the Jews and a Greek to the Greeks. He surrounded himself with a circle of educated Hellenists and furthered the building activities in the Greek cities; baths, gymnasia, theaters, and temples were erected. The devout Jews were indignant that the Jewish king showed favor to the Greeks. Yet he also sought to conciliate the Jews by having the temple enlarged and rebuilt, so that it again took the form which it had had in the time of King Solomon. In the extensive work of building, the king took care that things were done exactly in accordance with the Law. The sanctuary was kept carefully covered, so that no one could look in. In the Diaspora also, Herod appeared as a protector of Judaism and encouraged the development of the distinctive life of the synagogue communities. In spite of this he did not succeed in gaining the approval of the devout Jews. Because of his harsh regime and the terror with which he suppressed every impulse of opposition, he remained an object of hatred for the great majority of the people.

Among the Hellenistic populace, Herod found more gratitude than among the Jews. On the site of the destroyed city of Samaria was erected a new city, which in honor of Augustus received the name of Sebaste (from the Greek sebastoc, meaning, as did the Latin augustus, "the exalted one"). On the coast a harbor was built, which was protected against filling with sand by means of moles which were built out into the sea. The city there was adorned with rich edifices and also received the name of its exalted patron: Caesarea. Strong fortifications were placed throughout the country. In Jerusalem there arose the citadel Antonia, located directly on the temple square; from here Herod could keep a constant watch over the events which took place in and at the sanctuary. The strongest fortress he built on the western shore of the Dead Sea; there the stronghold Masada stood almost impregnable on the top of the mountain. In Jericho Herod had a palace built for himself, for use in the winter. Testimonies to this building activity are still to be seen in the country today: the so-called Wailing Wall has remained from the Herodian temple structure, and the foundations of the citadel Antonia are still preserved. Excavations in Jericho, Caesarea, Masada, and other places have for the first time brought to light the full scope of the huge works. While the fortification buildings served to make his rule secure, Herod sought to enhance his reputation by giving donations to foreign cities, to have buildings erected there in his honor. In doing this he did not hesitate also to promote pagan cults, thereby following the example of Hellenistic kings who sought to make a visible display of their generosity.

Although this king did much for the country, he remained an alien to the Jews. The people did have to obey him, but the strongest influence upon the thought and behavior of the populace was exerted by the Pharisees, who nourished the hope of a change to be brought about by God, but yet did not advocate any violent revolt. Toward the end of Herod's years John the Baptist and Jesus of Nazareth were born (Matt. 2:1; Luke 1:5). Having managed by skill and cunning to assert his dominion during a long period of rule, Herod sought before his death to determine the succession to his throne. He had arranged the murder of his sons, who otherwise would have had claim to the inheritance. In the will which the king made shortly before his death, his kingdom was divided among his three sons *Archelaus, Herod Antipas,* and *Philip*: Archelaus was to become king and was to rule over Judea, Samaria, and Idumea; Antipas was to receive Galilee and Perea, which lay east of the Jordan; and Philip was to have the region east of the Jordan in the northern part of the kingdom. But this disposition could become legally effective only when the necessary confirmation had been granted in Rome. Hence after the death of Herod (4 B.C.) the three sons made the journey to the world capital, each of them with the intention of gaining as much profit as possible for himself. But the people of Jerusalem sent an embassy to Rome to petition that the rule of the Herodians be abolished and the independence of the Jerusealem cultic community be restored. Reference is made to these events in the parable in Luke 19:12, 14: "A prominent man went to a distant land to receive the royal crown for himself and then to return home. . . . But his citizens hated him and sent an embassy after him and said, 'We do not want this man to be king over us!'" Augustus did not accede to these wishes but, in essence, acted in accordance with Herod's will. Antipas and Philip were named tetrarchs, i.e., minor princes; Archelaus did not receive the title of king, but was given only the lesser one of ethnarch. Yet these distinctions in title meant nothing to the people; to them the rulers were kings, so that both Archelaus (Matt. 2:22) and Herod Antipas (Mark 6:14, 26; Matt. 14:9) are mentioned as kings in the New Testament. While the three sons of Herod were tarrying in Rome, unrest broke out in the land. Roman troops, under the command of Quintilius Varus, the governor in Syria, intervened and restored quiet and order. Nevertheless the anti-Roman attitude of the people became more intense because of the harshness and strictness of the measures taken. After the withdrawal of the troops the three princes took possession of the inheritance that had been promised to them.

Most hated by the people was *Archelaus*, who ruled so arbitrarily and with such brutal harshness (see Matt. 2:22) that the enslaved subjects once more sent an embassy to Augustus and so effectively lamented their plight that they gained a hearing. In A.D. 6 Archelaus was relieved of his office and exiled to Gaul. His territory was placed under the jurisdiction of a Roman governor, who ordered and had carried out a general census of the people in Syria and Palestine. Hence in Jesus' time Galilee and the northern part of the land east of the Jordan were under the rule of Jewish princes, while Samaria, Judea, and Idumea were ruled by the Roman governor (Luke 3:1).

The governor resided in Caesarea and went up to Jerusalem only occasionally, mostly on the high feast days of the Jews, since at those times numerous Jews came to the city as pilgrims and the probability of rebellious movements developing quickly among the assembled throngs thereby increased. In such cases it was advantageous for the governor to be physically present. The distinctive life of the cultic community and the activity of the priesthood and of the Sanhedrin were not tampered with. No images of Caesar were set up in the temple, and the Roman troops marched into the city without their banners. Since the supreme legal power was placed in the hands of the governor, the Sanhedrin could indeed regulate the affairs of the Jerusalem cultic community but could not pronounce and inflict the death penalty (John 18:31). In the citadel Antonia there was stationed only a small detachment of Roman soldiers, which was augmented at the time of the great feasts or when there was danger of disorder. Soldiers were recruited from the non-Jewish population of the country. Thus Acts 10:1 mentions a Gentile centurion, Cornelius, who served in Caesarea, the governor's seat. Paul also was taken there for examination of his case, after he had been arrested in Jerusalem (Acts 23:23, 33).

In the time of Jesus, *Pontius Pilate* held office as the Roman governor (A.D. 26–36). Philo of Alexandria reports that the conduct of his office was marked by "corruption, violence, depradations, ill treatment, offenses, numerous illegal executions, and incessant, unbearable cruelty" (*Legatio ad Caium* 302). He had no regard for the religious sensitivity of the Jews and one night caused Roman banners bearing pictures of the emperor to be brought into Jerusalem. Only when the Jews declared that they would rather die than tolerate a violation of the Law did he finally give command to remove the banners from the city. Great unrest ensued when Pilate took money from the temple treasury in order to finance an aqueduct to Jerusalem. But Pilate suppressed rising resistance with force at its first manifestation. When a Samaritan prophet had proclaimed that sacred utensils from the time of Moses were buried on Mount Gerizim and a large throng had gathered on the mountain, Pilate commanded his soldiers to deploy and arbitrarily to attack the people. Many were killed, others imprisoned, and the rest fled. The indignation of the Samaritans was so great that they turned to Vitellius, the legate in Syria, and lodged complaints about Pilate with him. They succeeded in having Pilate recalled to Rome there to account for his conduct.

The description given of Pontius Pilate in the contemporary accounts is confirmed by the New Testament. When Galilean pilgrims once wished to offer sacrifices in Jerusalem, he incited a bloodbath among them (Luke 13:1). He ordered persons suspected of revolution arrested and killed (Mark 15:7 par.; 27 par.). So hard and ruthless was he, that it is not surprising that he condemned to death on the cross, after a brief hearing, a Jew whom the Sanhedrin had handed over to him as a politically suspect person. Thus Jesus of Nazareth died outside the gates of Jerusalem, subjected by the Roman governor to the most shameful punishment known to the ancient world.

In Galilee *Herod Antipas* ruled from 4 B.C. to A.D. 39. On the Sea of Gennesaret he built himself a residence which, in honor of the reigning emperor, he named Tiberias (see John 6:1, 23; 21:1). Since the city was built on the land of a former cemetery and therefore was regarded by the Law as unclean, the law-observing Jews refused to live there. Herod Antipas did not trouble himself about this, but conducted himself instead, according to his own pleasure and desire. He was first married to a daughter of the Nabataean king, but later took as his wife Herodias, who had been the wife of his half-brother—a Herod of whom nothing is otherwise known. In so doing he came into conflict with the Law, which permitted divorce (Deut. 24:1–4) but forbade taking one's brother's wife (Lev. 18:16; 20:21). Herodias was a granddaughter of King Herod and Mariamne, the daughter of Aristobulus, who, like his mother, had been put to death by Herod. The ambitious and vain Herodias became the wife of Herod Antipas, who divorced his first wife and sent her back to her father in the Nabataean kingdom. The new marriage produced the daughter Salome. Reference is made to these events in Mark 6:17–29 par., though there Philip is erroneously named as Herodias' first husband. Mark recounts that John the Baptist had held the ruler's wrongdoing plainly before his eyes, was cast into prison, further persecuted by Herodias' intense enmity, and finally murdered.

The marriage with Herodias brought misfortune to Herod Antipas. The indignant king of the Nabataeans waged war on his former son-in-law and inflicted on him a painful defeat. Josephus relates these events and says that many Jews regarded the defeat of Herod's army as a divine dispensation; for God had required just punishment for his treatment of John the Baptist. The account continues:

Herod had had him executed, though he was a righteous man and had exhorted the Jews . . . to be baptized; baptism would be acceptable to God if it were applied, not to eliminate certain delinquencies, but to sanctify the body, since the soul is already purified by a righteous life. Since people now streamed to John the Baptist from all directions, because they felt themselves uplifted by such discourse, Herod began to fear that the influence of such a man, by whose counsel all were letting themselves be guided, could produce an uprising, and therefore he believed it to be better to render him harmless before the outbreak of such a danger than later to regret his indecisiveness if his power should be threatened. On this suspicion John was put in chains, sent to the fortress Machaerus . . . and there beheaded (*Jewish Antiquities* XVIII, 116–19).

In this presentation, it is true, the Baptist's proclamation is described in the sense of a Hellenistic sermon on virtue, but the stimulating and impressive effect of his proclamation still is strikingly maintained.

Herod Antipas was the ruler of Jesus' country. When he learned of Jesus' appearance, he thought that John the Baptist, whom he had executed, had risen from the dead (Mark 6:14–16 par.). He expressed the wish to see the miracle man himself (Luke 9:9). But Jesus called him a fox (Luke 13:32) and made his way to Jerusalem. Only in Luke's Gospel is it reported that after a preliminary hearing Pilate sent Jesus to Herod Antipas, who also had come to Jerusalem for the Passover feast, so that he too might pass judgment (Luke 23:6–16). This enlargement of the Passion narrative, however, represents a legendary expansion of the originally very brief story of Jesus' trial before the Roman governor. Just as according to Psalm 2:1–2 the kings of earth rebel and the rulers take counsel together against Yahweh and his anointed one, so according to the Lukan portrayal, the Roman ruler and the Jewish prince stand in judgment over Jesus while the raging people demand his condemnation.

In the end it became Herod Antipas' fate that his wife, Herodias, suggest that he try to persuade Caligula to bestow upon him the title of king. The prince's efforts misfired. Caligula became suspicious and had Herod Antipas exiled to Gaul (A.D. 39).

In northern Transjordania *Philip* ruled. He built himself a new residence, which he called Caesarea Philippi (see Mark 8:27 par.). The Sea of Gennesaret formed the boundary between his territory and that of Herod Antipas, a boundary which then ran northward along the Jordan River. In Capernaum there was a small border and customs station, in which there was a detachment of Antipas' men, whose commander is mentioned in Matt. 8:5–13 (and par. in Luke 7:1–10). Philip was the first Jewish ruler to have coins minted bearing the likeness of the Roman emperor. Since the populace which he governed was Jewish only in a small part, he did not need to take any account of the Jews' reluctance to produce any human likeness. Philip died in A.D. 34 without leaving behind any descendants.

For a short time Palestine once more came under the rule of a Jewish king. *Agrippa,* a grandson of King Herod, had stayed in Rome, and there had been able to gain the favor of Caligula. In A.D. 37 Caligula gave him the territory which Philip had ruled, and two years later assigned to him the land of the exiled Herod Antipas. In A.D. 41 he was also given the rule over Judea, Samaria, and Idumea, so that under his scepter the entire kingdom which his grandfather had ruled was once more united. During this period a sharp conflict threatened to break out. When Caligula demanded that his statue be erected in the temple in Jerusalem, great excitement broke out among the Jews. People already envisioned the abomination of desolation set up in the holy place (see Mark 13:14 par.). Then in A.D. 41 Caligula was murdered; and his successor, Claudius, did not insist that divine reverence be paid to him in the temple of the Jews.

Herod Agrippa represented himself as a devout Jew concerned with exact observance of the Law. For this reason he was warmly praised by the scribes and Pharisees. But he displayed this attitude only among the Jews; toward the Hellenistic population of his kingdom he appeared in a different light. Here he behaved as a Hellenistic prince, who, following the example of his grandfather, sought to enhance his reputation by erecting numerous buildings. Moreover, at the same time that he humored the Pharisees, persecuted the Christian community in Jerusalem, had James the son of Zebedee executed, and had Peter thrown in prison (Acts 12:1-3), he had himself hailed in the Hellenistic environment as a divinely sent prince and accepted the divine veneration shown to the ruler (Acts 12:21-23). When he died, the rule was not given to his son. Instead the entire country was annexed to the province of Syria and was governed by Roman procurators, who were subordinate to the governor in Syria and once again took up their official seat in Caesarea.

Some years later Agrippa II received the territory which Philip had once ruled. He was also given the right to oversee the temple in Jerusalem. He made use of this right by making appointments to the office of the high priest as it suited him, and thereby aroused the displeasure of the people of Jerusalem. He also caused offense by keeping his sister Berenice constantly with him (Acts 25:13). It was told that the brother and sister lived in an incestuous relationship.

Throughout the country hatred against the Romans grew, and it repeatedly reached the point of erupting into disorder. The band of Zealots wanted to throw off the foreign rule by the use of force, and they found growing support among the people, who saw themselves as being repeatedly tormented by the thoughtless or even malicious conduct of the Romans. Of the series of Roman procurators who were to govern Palestine in this period, two are mentioned by name in the New Testament. Beginning in A.D. 52, *Felix* occupied the office of governor. As a freedman he had climbed his way to this high positon, which he had received through the favor of the Emperor Claudius. Tacitus says of him that he "maintained the royal law with a servile disposition by means of all sorts of cruelty and greed" (*History* V. 9). The second of his wives was the Jewish princess Drusilla, the daughter of Agrippa I, whom he had wrested from her husband. As Acts 24:24 reports, Paul had to make his defense before Felix and Drusilla during his imprisonment in Caesarea. Felix was replaced—probably in the year A.D. 60, but possibly earlier—by *Porcius Festus*. Although, in contrast to his predecessors, he was a man who thought and acted in accordance with the Law, he did not succeed in reducing tensions between Jews and Romans. His time in office, which ended with his death in A.D. 62, includes the last part of the imprisonment of Paul, whose trial was to be decided in Rome (Acts 24:27 to 26:32).

THE JEWISH WAR AND THE REVOLT UNDER BAR COCHBA

The brutal conduct of the Roman occupation forces brought the Jewish people's hatred to a climax. When anti-Jewish demonstrations arose in Caesarea among the Hellenistic inhabitants, the Jews sought protection from the Romans, paid money, yet gained no assistance. Their anger over the behavior of the Romans continued. The greed of the procurator *Gessius Florus* was so boundless that in A.D. 66 he stole seventeen talents from the temple treasury. Indignant Jews derided the governor by going about in Jerusalem begging for money for the poor procurator. Gessius Florus became enraged over this and allowed his soldiers to plunder the city. He advanced two more cohorts from Caesarea and demanded that the Jews welcome the troops with ceremony. Prudent persons, especially the high priest and his followers, advised the people to yield and not to reject this demand. Thus the people were ready to submit to this profound humiliation. But when the people, following the directive, greeted the Roman soldiers, they, at the direction of the procurator, remained silent and did not return the Jews' greetings. At this there was no more restraint; the wrath of the humiliated people burst forth. The temple area was quickly occupied, and the governor had to retreat from the rebels to Caesarea. Only one cohort remained behind in Jerusalem in the strongly fortified citadel Antonia. Other than this the entire city was in the hands of the rebels.

What would happen now? Agrippa sought to persuade the Jews that armed resistance to Rome was sheer madness. The high priest, the priestly circles, and even the Pharisees urged moderation. But the raging fire could no longer be extinguished. The sacrifice which was offered daily for the Roman emperor was discontinued, and this was the signal for open revolt. Even the citadel Antonia could not withstand the onslaught of the uprising. It was seized, and so the entire city was in the hands of the Jews. The first success swept along many who at first had hesitated. Others who behaved in a suspect manner were either slain or compelled by force to join the movement. The high priest, who had attempted in vain to prevent the calamity, was murdered.

The Romans, who were taken by surprise by the rapid developments, were no longer masters of the situation. Cestius, the Roman governor in Syria, marched down with his troops. But he did not succeed in taking Jerusalem. He had to break off the campaign, and on the return march to Syria suffered a painful defeat. The jubilation of the Jews was great; the Romans had been driven from the land, and the yoke of foreign domination had been thrown off. Since a counterblow was bound to be forthcoming, people hastily prepared to defend themselves. A strike force was to be formed of partisans, and in Galilee fortifications were built. Josephus, a young priest, was sent from Jerusalem to Galilee to direct the measures which were to be taken in the northern part of the country.

The emperor Nero commissioned *Vespasian*, his ablest general, to conduct the war against the Jews. Vespasian went, with his son, Titus, to the East. He advanced from Antioch with strong forces, and Titus brought troops from Egypt. The Romans' attack was first directed against Galilee. As the powerful army advanced, the Jews were seized with fear and retreated into the fortresses, so that the open country fell into the hands of the Romans without a struggle. Josephus entrenched himself along with his people in Jotapata, but could not hold out. When after a forty-seven-day siege the Jews' resistance collapsed, the Zealots demanded that all the rebels commit suicide. Josephus rejected this demand and was able to save himself by surrendering to Vespasian and predicting that he would gain the imperial crown. Vespasian spared Josephus' life, and from that time on, Josephus remained in the Roman headquarters. Thus he became an eyewitness and later a writer of the history of the entire Jewish War. John of Gischala, the leader of the Zealots, escaped with his small band to Jerusalem. In A.D. 67 all Galilee once again found itself in the hands of the Romans.

The decision had to be made in Jerusalem, and the radical groups in the city won the upper hand. The Zealots under John of Gischala seized the temple area, and the rest of the city was occupied by Simon bar Giora. The followers of the two commanders were hostile to each other and attacked each other; opponents of the war and those who were hesitant were subjected to harsh terrorism. About this time, the original Christian community, which did not participate in the uprising, must have left the city and migrated to Pella in the land beyond the Jordan. In the meantime, the Romans waited quietly for the situation in Jerusalem to develop. When in A.D. 69 Vespasian was called by his soldiers to become emperor, he traveled to Rome and handed the direction of the war over to his son, Titus. During the Passover season in the year A.D. 70, when many pilgrims had come into the city once again, Titus marched on Jerusalem with four legions and strong auxiliary forces and surrounded the city with its inhabitants and the pilgrims. Since Jerusalem is situated on an elevation and an approach across level ground is possible only from the north, the attack was launched against the city from this side. In the face of the fearful threat, the fraternal conflict which had raged in the city up to that time was broken off in order to offer a common front of resistance to the Romans. However, against the greatly superior Roman military tactics the defenders' courage in battle and gallantry could not long hold out. Reference is made to this hopeless situation in the version of Jesus' discourse on judgment which is given in the Gospel of Luke: "But when you see Jerusalem surrounded by armies, then you will know that its desolation is near" (Luke 21:20). "For the days shall come upon you [i.e., Jerusalem], when your enemies will cast up a bank about you and surround you, and hem you in on every side, and dash you to the ground, you and your children within you, and they will not leave one stone upon another in you" (Luke 19:43–44). Jewish resistance fighters who were captured were nailed by the Romans to crosses which were set up on the banks around the city, in order thereby to terrify its defenders. In the city, however, the Zealots held the reins in their hands with inexorable strictness and compelled the populace to stand fast. People indulged in the hope that in the last hour God would intervene and rescue his people. Even if the outer court of the temple should be seized by the Gentiles and the city and the forecourt should be trampled underfoot by them, still God would not abandon to them the holy place (Rev. 11:1-2).

Yet effort and hope were in vain. The Romans broke through all three surrounding walls which encircled the city and continued to press forward against the bitter resistance of the defenders. In the final battles the temple went up in flames. Titus was just able to push his way into the Holy of Holies before it collapsed. The seven-branched candlestick and the table of shewbread were seized as trophies, to be carried later in the triumphal procession which is still commemorated by a relief on the arch of Titus in Rome. The Gospel of Matthew, in its account of the parable of the royal wedding feast, mentions the destruction of Jerusalem by fire: the king was enraged by the fact that his invitation was rejected and his servants shamefully slain, and he "sent his army, killed the murderers, and burned their city" (Matt. 22:7). The last groups of rebels who still tried to offer resistance were tracked down; John of Gischala and Simon bar Giora were captured and were taken along to Rome for the victory celebration. With the fall of the temple and the city, Judaism had lost its visible center.

Here and there resistance persisted; small groups of rebels had managed to withdraw into some fortified places. Those who held the fortress of Masada held out longest. The Romans surrounded the fortress, which is situated on a high, inaccessible mountain on the shore of the Dead Sea. Traces of the Roman siege and the outline of the Jewish fortification, which is a construction of King Herod, were recently uncovered by painstaking excavations by Israeli archaeologists. When the Jewish freedom fighters saw that their situation had become hopeless, they determined to commit suicide. The Romans, who shortly thereafter entered the fortress, found only dead bodies. Only two women, who had hid themselves along with five children in an underground water conduit, survived the end of the Jewish defense. With the fall of Masada, which occurred in A.D. 73—or perhaps not until 74—the last resistance was broken. After the victory, Vespasian ordered that Judea be separated from Syria and made into an imperial province. Its governor again held his office in Caesarea. The tenth Roman legion, which set up its camp in Jerusalem, was stationed in the country.

Judaism was able to survive the frightful catastrophe, because within it resided strong forces which made possible a new beginning. The Pharisees had stood in sharp opposition to the priesthood, which was predominantly of a

Sadducean inclination. But in the destruction of Jerusalem the Sadducees were killed. The Pharisaic movement, led by scribes, was instrumental in stimulating the reconstruction of the Jewish communities which had gathered themselves together after the catastrophe, and conferred upon these communities their distinctive mark. Along with the temple, the sacrificial cultus had also fallen. The worship of Israel's God, however could continue in the synagogues, into whose services parts of the temple liturgy now were also incorporated. In *Jabne* (Jamnia) a new Sanhedrin came together, this one composed not of priests and elders, but only of scribes. The Romans did not attack the rights which had been originally conceded to Judaism, so the synagogues continued to be under the protection of the civil authorities and the life of the communities was able to develop anew. The temple tax, which had been collected from every Jew in Palestine and in the Diaspora to defray the expenses of the cultus in Jerusalem, continued to be collected, but now had to be paid as a tax to the Romans.

In the second century A.D., Palestinian Judaism once more undertook to throw off the Roman yoke (A.D. 132–135). No connected account has been preserved of the events which occurred during the rebellion under the leadership of *Bar Cochba* (or *Bar Cosiba,* as his name appears in recently discovered texts). This second Jewish revolt had no historian. Isolated and brief references which are noted in ancient literary passages have been corroborated by discoveries which have been made in archaeological explorations in Palestine. Traces of the rebels, including letters and written records, have been discovered, so that the course of events can be reconstructed with some certainty.

Under the reign of the emperor Hadrian (A.D. 117–138) there came a sudden uprising of the Jews. It probably was prompted by two decrees which Hadrian had issued. During a tour which he undertook through the Orient in A.D. 130/131, the emperor gave instructions for erecting new buildings. In that connection he ordered a shrine for Jupiter Capitolinus to be erected on the ruins of the temple in Jerusalem. Then, in a decree, Hadrian ordered a general prohibition of castration, with which at the same time circumcision also was forbidden. That a pagan temple should be erected in the holy place and that Israel should be deprived of its sign of the covenant evoked great resentment among the Jews. As a result, the rebels undertook, through a surprise attack, to bring Judea and Jerusalem under their control. They were successful, and the offering of sacrifices was resumed, coins were minted as a sign of the newly gained independence, and people began to date events in a new era, beginning with the first year of the revolt. The leader of the rebels was hailed by Rabbi Akiba, the most highly regarded biblical scholar of that time, as the promised "son of a star" of Numbers 24:17. The messianic age appeared to be dawning. Since the Jewish Christians who lived in Palestine could not agree with the messianic claim of Bar Cochba, they were bloodily persecuted by him and his followers. Anyone who refused to renounce Jesus as the Messiah was arrested; many were executed (see Justin, *Apology* I. 31).

The Romans proceeded slowly against the rebels, who did not offer pitched battles; they were compelled to seek them in the hiding places where they had taken refuge, to surround them, starve them out, and force them to surrender. The Jewish warriors' powers of resistance began gradually to disappear. In Wadi Murabba'at several documents from the time of Bar Cochba were found, among them a letter which was written by several leaders of the rebels to Jeschua ben Gilgola, a commander at the Dead Sea fortress. In this letter it is said that the Gentiles were attacking and therefore they could not come to him. And in a document which Simon bar Cochba addresses to the same recipient, he threatens him with having his feet bound in fetters if he does not break off relations with the Galileans. Perhaps those Galileans had not been willing to take part in the uprising, or the reference pertains to some unreliable people. In any case, however, the leader of the rebels was obliged to push with full energy for unconditional obedience to his commands. In place of the rejoicing with which at first many Jews proclaimed the uprising as Israel's liberation, there appeared ever-increasing disillusionment.

When the Romans little by little closed in on the rebels, Bar Cochba entrenched himself with his faithful followers in Beth-Ter in Judea. Yet this fortress was conquered by the Romans, and Bar Cochba was slain in the battle. Therewith, the hope that he, as the Messiah, would usher in the time of salvation, was shattered. Because the unhappy turn of events unmistakably proved that Bar Cochba was not God's Anointed One, rabbinical Judaism later only rarely mentioned his name. But the charge was not made that he had blasphemed God. This accusation is not applied in Judaism to a false Messiah, but only when in the Jewish view the uniqueness of God is attacked (see John 5:18; 10:36).

On the ruins of Jerusalem a Roman colony was established, which received the name of Colonia Aelia Capitolina. There a temple was erected to Jupiter. The new city was inhabited only by non-Jews; the Jews were forbidden to set foot in it. Filled with profound grief, the Jews annually commemorated on the ninth day of the month Ab (this is the end of July or the first of August), the devastation of Jerusalem and the destruction of the temple. Beginning in the fourth century A.D., they were allowed on this day of grief to enter the city and to raise their prayers of lamentation at the wall which had been left standing from the Herodian temple.

Judaism once again had suffered the gravest losses; many scribes who had supported the rebellion were killed. Legend tells that Rabbi Akiba was frightfully tortured and his flesh raked with iron combs. But when the hour came in which the Jew is to utter the prayer "Hear, O Israel, the Lord our God is One" (Deut. 6:4), as an expression of his confession of faith, Akiba is said to have held the word One very long—as is required in prayer which is meritorious—and to have expired with this word on his lips. Thus he maintained loyalty to the Law to the very last moment of his life. The firmness with which the suffering and dying people held to the Law also strengthened the living and helped the severely smitten communities to bind themselves again to the Law and to cling to the faith of their fathers.

Charles Guignebert

Hellenistic Culture

CHARLES GUIGNEBERT (1867–1939) was for thirty years was professor of the history of
Christianity at the Sorbonne. With Alfred Loisy (d. 1940) and Maurice Goguel
(d. 1956), he formed a trio of historians whose careful and detailed scholarship was in
the vanguard of New Testament studies between World Wars I and II. His works
include *Jesus* (Eng. tr., 1950), *The Jewish World in the Time of Jesus* (Eng. tr., 1958),
and *The Christ* (Eng. tr., 1968).

Like F. C. Conybeare in England and his countryman Loisy, Guignebert defended
the historical existence of Jesus, but he was nonetheless sympathetic to the history-of-
religions approach of the Christ-myth school. His view of Christianity as a social and
intellectual movement was in advance of the ideas of his time, and his work forged the
way for such scholars as Arthur Darby Nock, Robert Pfeiffer, Marcel Simon, and
J. B. Brisson.

A first tentative analysis shows the Hellenistic world to have been the complex
and confused combination of two originally distinct worlds put in direct and
intimate contact by the conquests of Alexander and which through the centuries
had reacted on one another by endosmosis. These worlds were the Hellenic and
the oriental. The latter was made up of rather diverse elements, for Egypt, Syria,
Phrygia, Cappadocia, and the Mesopotamian lands had their own characteristics,
tendencies, and originality. On more than one occasion we shall have to take
these differences into account, but we are going to put them aside in the present
exposition, and confine ourselves to the features that are part of the whole.

It goes without saying that the combination I have mentioned was not

From *The Christ* by Charles Guignebert (Secaucus, N.J.: University Books, Inc., 1968),
pp. 132–153. Published by arrangement with Lyle Stuart.

specifically the same everywhere, that the dosage and balance of the various elements which constituted it varied according to the regions. There were some countries, even cultural centers, where the Greek influence overcame oriental resistance; in others, the contrary phenomenon occurred. Generally speaking, we may say that the Hellenic influence was dominant, and even determinative, in the *intellectual sphere*—cultural forms, philosophy, science; whereas the oriental influence was vigorously affirmed in the *spiritual sphere*, the sphere of the substance and expression of religious sentiment, aspirations toward a blessed life beyond the grave, cultic organizations. Even where the two influences combined, the specialization distinctive of each remained as a rule visible.

CULTURE

The School. The Greeks had long been interested in the intellectual life in all its forms. For them, intellectual activities were not the concern and tastes of an elite alone. General attention, open to all its possibilities was accorded to the mind. Consequently, the Greeks were in general agreement that it was fitting to prepare the child to be interested in and understand the life of the intellect, a conviction leading to the elaboration of a pedagogy, buttressed with a plan of studies and a system of instruction, that was gradually adopted in all lands of Hellenic culture. This is a fact of the greatest importance, for the identity of intentions, and methods of education, acclaimed throughout the Hellenistic world, brought about a most remarkable homogeneity of mind, though there were of course nuances. In this homogeneity lay a highly energetic spring for action, which would operate at first *against* nascent Christianity, then *within* it, and finally *for* it. The cosmological, metaphysical, and moral beliefs and postulates of the Hellenic mind's first reaction to the new religion owed a great deal more to the educational system than to the actual thinking of genuine philosophers. Eventually, Christianity would reduce these beliefs and postulates to submission, making them its own by incorporating them into its own substance. It is their propagation in the schools that explains both their widespread acceptance of their great activity.

By the word *school* I do not intend to designate only those private institutions where children were instructed under the eye of Athena, institutions whose *cursus* covered three stages, beginning with the acquisition of the rudiments under the tutelage of the *primus magister*, and ending with the definitive instructions of the professor of rhetoric, passing on the way the grammarian's ruler. I also have in mind the establishments devoted to higher education, which we would call universities, whose approximate equivalents were to be found in Athens, as well as in the great cities of the Greek Orient, such as Alexandria, Antioch, Tarsus, Rhodes— to name only the most renowned. There the masters were chosen by the municipal authorities who paid them and placed at their disposal, often with the help of generous donors or subscribers, all the necessary tools of learning, especially books.

The education provided by these schools had no doubts either of its methods or its efficacy. Wholly satisfied with itself, it was quick to scorn any individual who had remained outside its ranks: such a man was likened to a *barbarian*. Tertullian avowed that the culture of the pagans interfered with their acceptance and comprehension of the truth. It was to become a commonplace in the second century to oppose *the wisdom of the barbarians*, that is, the Jews and their heirs, the Christians, to *the philosophy of the Greeks*. In fact, Christianity at first encountered vigorous antipathy from "the professorial world." On the other hand, when it began to make conquests in that world, it derived from it much benefit for its propaganda and apologetic: the conversion of a professor or a noted intellectual became a weighty argument in itself.

One can understand, however, why the first generations of Christians, who were almost entirely the products of social milieux which were strangers to intellectual concerns, were tenaciously prejudiced against the culture of the schools. Its first error, in their opinion, was that *it was pagan*. And pagan it was in the sense that (1) some of its customs were religious practices derived from paganism; (2) it was wholly based on the study of ancient authors who were steeped in Olympic paganism.

What we would call "higher education" consisted chiefly of the examination of the philosophical problems.

Philosophy. There was at the time not *one* philosophy, but *several schools* which claimed dependence on the great masters of the past—Pythagoras, Plato, Zeno, Aristotle, Diogenes—or else sought to combine them in a more or less coherent eclecticism. The *dogmata*, that is, the basic positions attributed to the authentic old masters, served as topics for commentaries and as points of departure for the speculations of their so-called disciples. Some of these *dogmata* concerned man and his moral life, what we today call psychology and ethics. Usually, however, they soared into the realm of *metaphysics* and cosmological hypotheses. Stoicism itself, which we are wont to see as primarily a system of morals, was in that day above all else a cosmology, secondarily a theology, and last of all an ethic.

The cosmological and metaphysical views of the schools, even their opinions on theological matters, as well as certain more or less legendary *Lives* of the "Masters," especially those of Pythagoras and Plato, were to have an influence on the formation of Christian doctrine; an influence, which would finally prove pervasive, on its common philosophy; an influence on the tests and proofs to which the various dogmas would have to submit before being finally accepted as orthodox; and even an influence on the legend of the Lord. But these contaminations did not occur on first contact. The situation was different, however, in the realm of morals, which remained so important that Christianity was essentially *a way of life*. In the Pauline vocabulary, for example, a rather large number of technical terms of the Stoic ethic have been singled out, and these we shall pass in review when necessary. Does this fact mean that the Apostle sat on the benches of the University of Tarsus, where, as we know, Stoic masters were dominant? Probably not; the presence of these terms in his vocabulary can be explained by the fact that these masters were given to popular preaching. They propagated the precepts of what is known as the Cynico-Stoic diatribe, an eclectic amalgamation of certain Cynical and Stoic principles, which made a kind of pragmatism, an ethic for action, following the bent for practicality attributed to Diogenes. This diatribe had the appearance of a religion of morality, that is, it considered morals as a religion, a religion with its saints, the great men who were thought to have best realized its ideals in their lives, whose example was preached. It was a religion based on *experience*, as was its doctrine. Diogenes and Socrates, the two pragmatists par excellence, were its great authorities. Their words and deeds, which, like their appearance, had been more or less stylized, constituted the wells from which the preachers drew. They strove for a lively style in their teaching in order not to discourage anyone. But the content of their sermons was always austere and bore a strong resemblance to that in which the *Conversations* of Epictetus were steeped. In additon, there were others besides the philosophers labeled as Stoics who preached to the people in this spirit. The general tendency of the age led professors of other schools to emulate them.

All of them played the role of veritable *directors of conscience* and never tired of proclaiming their precepts in public, taking no notice of the difficulties, scorn, or even injuries they met. They were not all drawn from the ranks of professors with official functions or university reputations. Some were isolated and itinerant, called to a true vocation by personal inclinations, a fact that makes us think of the Christian missionaries. For others, preaching had become a trade, which they exercised without shame, exploiting the simple, whose confidence was gained by their long beards, their stern professional cloak, and their austere appearance. The caricatures Lucian of Samosata drew of these charlatans give us an idea of their unbridled cynicism and their insincerity. But if these men were able to put their confidence in outward trappings in order to earn their livelihood, it was because these trappings went with a widespread and highly regarded profession.

We still possess a fictionalized biography of one of these preachers, written by a certain Philostratus for the curious circle in Rome which gathered around the Syrian princess of the Septimius Severus family at the beginning of the third century, a circle which applied itself with great zeal to the study of the very problems which held the attention of the preachers of the diatribe. This biography is the *Life of Apollonius of Tyana*. The hero of the book is presented as the perfect example of the breed: he had made a vow to lead an edifying life which might serve as a model to other men. He therefore imposed special obligations on himself; and went through life as if he always walked under the eyes of Truth: even in the middle of the most frightful desert, he felt himself to be under her scrutiny. His bearing was enough to make his vocation known to passersby: it was that of his profession, and his stern countenance always reflected his grave inner meditation. He went about, impassive, disdainful of the gibes of the ignorant. But he knew how to speak up before the powerful of the world and point out to them their duty. This courage was not without risks, for it happened that a Nero or a Domitian did not understand, and became angry. He bore the tribulations their sorry anger heaped on his head with a steadfast heart, as so many insignificant contingencies. Nothing could shake him. To Nero's decree proscribing philosophy he was satisfied to reply with a line from Sophocles: "For it was not Zeus who proclaimed that decree."

Above the practical teaching of these philosophers soared a beautiful and encouraging affirmation: beyond the city of men lies a city of philosophers where great souls find their consolation. It is entered at the price of long and painful personal effort, reflection, and separation from earthly goods and attachments. It welcomes men of all lands and all conditions who deserve its rewards. In reading Lucian's description, one cannot help recalling St. Augustine and the *City of God*.

There is no need to dwell on the interest and importance such ideas have for us in relation to Christian origins. I have already said that Christianity would first of all be *a way of life*, a rule of conduct, a road to salvation. By taking the diatribe as a model, it would find antecedents, forms, and usages that would keep it from being thought odd. The ethic of the philosophers, valuable in its own right and not of necessity tied to a particular religion, could be transposed to the benefit of whatever cultic organization would accept its assumptions. Cynico-Stoic preaching would offer Christianity an ethical framework and a vocabulary. It would also prepare a bridge for penetrating straight to the heart of the daily life of the Hellenistic world, even as the metaphysic of the educational system prepared frameworks for Christianity's cosmology, and the forms that would welcome its dogmatics. Thus there was a veritable preparation for *the work of Christianity* to develop in the various directions that would become necessary as its strength increased, a preparation so effective that it is impossible to visualize how Christianity could have done without it, how it could have come to be if it had not already been.

Science. Later, the Christian faith would be presented to the Gentiles as being in its essence a *revelation*, a gnosis of salvation, and the entire Christian catechesis would be subordinated to the desire to have this assumption accepted as verified truth. In fact, it is to the point to note that Christianity would encounter no obstacles except in its customs, and no contradictions except in the beliefs, of the same order and nature and on the same plane as its own affirmations, for in that day positive science, independent of speculation, did not exist. In the era of Augustus, the scientific poem of Manilius, *The Astronomics*, reveals, in its tarrying over the most elementary notions, the ignorance it supposed its readers to be wallowing in. And the author himself commits the grossest errors. Leaf through the *Natural Questions* of Seneca; note in Lucian's writings the blunders made by persons who were considered to be more cultivated than the average man; and you will have the proof that in the epoch of its inauguration and spread throughout the Hellenistic world, Christianity would encounter no scientific vulgarization.

But in the proper sense of the term, neither was there any science. The

Stoics claimed one, but it would be imprudent to take them at their word. I have just referred to the *Natural Questions* of Seneca. Let us put it alongside Pliny the Elder's *Natural History* and see what we find. Interesting oddities, but disconnected and uncriticized; ill-verified facts taken from authorities who have not been checked, or checked only superficially—no sense that phenomena are related or linked to one another—; and idle reasoning that scarcely feels the need of checking its findings by experiments. This does not mean that accurate observations, which might be suggestive, are wholly lacking in all these works; it does however indicate the absence of a true scientific spirit from such compilations and, especially, of a feeling for the sovereignty of the verified fact. The impression obtains that Seneca gathered more or less accurate observations on natural phenomena for the sole purpose of providing pegs on which to hang his reasoning. Pliny assembled *mirabilia* to amuse himself and to satisfy his rambling curiosity, which had no other object. Were there no men who went beyond this rather puerile amateurism, men with a positivistic bent who were able to see more clearly? Possibly there were, as much in that age as in any other. But we do not know who these exceptions were, if they did exist, and their influence on the state of scientific knowledge of their contemporaries cannot be perceived. To draw attention to this deficiency is for us the essential point.

Lucian, for example, tells us of a certain Hippias, for whom he professes boundless admiration. He states that this man had reached the limits of knowledge in all fields, so that compared to him his contemporaries were only children. But we do not know what this means. Did Hippias really know more than the scholars of his time, or did he simply know all that they knew, or thought they knew? We don't know. But what is most serious is that to all appearances his contemporaries didn't know either. We have at least part of the work of one of them, the doctor Galen, who also acquired a great reputation. Observant, skilled, and sometimes ingenious and penetrating, he almost never appears in the role of a scientist, for he did not have the scientific spirit: he believed, for example, in "medical" dreams. In the realm of knowledge, the best minds were radically misguided by their faith in miracles, by their delight in, their passion for, wonders and marvels. Ordinary and quite simple phenomena neither aroused nor held their attention.

This pseudo-science, then, which was in fact an auxiliary and branch of philosophy and encumbered with morals, metaphysics, and (among the Stoics and Pythagoreans) theology, could offer no obstacle to any manifestations of religious sentiment, no more than to the formation of any doctrinal system. The so-called scientific research—whose worth escapes us—of an Apuleius did not prevent him from being a pious soul who ran from one initiation to another. His reputation as a thaumaturge far excelled his renown as a naturalist.

The positive science of that day, the one that disturbed primitive Christianity the most and ended by leaving its mark on it, was *astrology*, which must be considered in conjunction with *magic*. Both, and especially the first, which was akin to gnosis, occupied in daily life a position hard for us to conceive. The importance of the second, also considerable, lies in the fact that it spread everywhere faith in the sovereign power of the ritual gesture, of the revealed form of words, which act, solely through their own efficacy, *ex opere operato*.

Astrological books, which made a large contribution to the education of the cultivated classes, were widely circulated, and a host of charlatans carried, and applied, the science of sciences to all levels of society. These men were commonly called Chaldeans, a name more indicative of the birthplace of their practices than of their true origin. The weightiest minds took them seriously, or at least did not refuse to consider their claims. In fact, they scarcely distinguished between *astronomy* and *astrology*: faith in the horoscope was everywhere affirmed. What is important to note is the fact that astrological reflections and concerns had become commonplaces in the mentality of the time, paralleling the commonplaces of ethics: from commonplaces there was no escape. The more we study the texts which reflect the life of the Roman Empire at its zenith, the deeper becomes our impression of the astonishing importance of these speculations. In reality, they pertained not to science but to faith, but a faith whose objective assumed the apparent rigor and reassuring aspect of scientific knowledge. Sometimes it was called "mathematics" and those who practiced it were, at least in Rome, called *mathematici*. There were skeptics and foes, but not many, and they were obviously wasting their time. Astrology bordered on religion because the stars were assimilated to divinities and their courses represented a sort of cosmic drama. The great gods of Olympus themselves were finally bound to the planets.

Magic appears to have been quite different: it looks less respectable, and one might at first glance take it to have been nothing more than a collection of more or less bizarre recipes. But basically it was grounded on conceptions akin to those which claimed to justify astrology. It stemmed from two notions: that an indispensable relationship united all natural bodies, which are involved in an immense animism, and that nature is subject to an order and to laws. It is this order that magic claimed to know and teach, these laws it explained, along with the means of putting them into effect. On the one hand it was related to science; on the other, it appeared as "religion's bastard sister": it peopled the world with spirits, on which and through which it operated. An incantation was as much a prayer as a means of constraining the cosmic spirits. As a rule, the magicians were scorned, for the means they employed were often despicable and repellent. They themselves frequently came from the world of the poor and wretched, but they were nonetheless feared and heeded. One more step, and we would have entered the domain of religion, or rather, we are there already, for magic is a constitutive element of the greatest importance in many widespread and infuential cults.

RELIGION

The oriental world was very religious, that is, it was very much preoccupied with religious questions, filled with cults, practices, and superstitions of every kind, and prey to a great number of charlatans who gained a living from religion and exploited religious sentiment. The religious situation was extremely complex and confused; its currents of thought and of sentiment interconnected and combined in a manner inextricable for us, and no less so for their contemporaries. Was it not the custom of these contemporaries, which inveterate usage told them was as inevitable as it was natural, to syncretize beliefs and practices, and let each man have the illusion of erecting for himself, out of the enormous mass of religious materials on hand, the faith and cultus that suited him?

Initial examination of the principal constituents of these Hellenistic religions permits one to distinguish, to some extent, between the components derived from the *Hellenic background* and those that must be assigned to the *oriental*. But detailed studies make such a distinction more difficult, and one grows more hesitant in attempting it. Nevertheless, it is quickly apparent that what is of true interest and importance for us resides in the mixtures themselves.

The Hellenic Background. To all appearances, Olympic religion was still alive. Augustus restored it in its traditional forms as the religion of Rome. But was there a sincere, profound, and widespread faith in the great gods? One hesitates to say. Among the higher classes, belief in the purely classical divinities must have been the exception; otherwise one could not understand how the jeers of a Lucian, for example, would have been possible. On the other hand, total skepticism was certainly a luxury for intellectuals and dilettantes, and it may very well be that the traditional gods still had influence among the lowest classes and retained their confidence. Elsewhere, attempts were apparently made to adapt Olympism to matters alien to it. One of the most commonly used means for this task was theological interpretation of the myths: Pythagorean theology, more or less revised by the Platonists, and Stoic theology, whose existence I have underlined in passing, were the most widespread of these systems of adaptation, but there were others, more or less syncretistic systems. One such, for instance, is to be found in Plutarch. But I am not going to dwell on this type of theological effort, because it is not this that is important for the origins of Hellenistic Christianity; only a handful of the literate, and (if one likes to put it this way) a tiny elect of religious spirits who hoped to achieve the illusion of remaining the heirs of their ancestors, were drawn to these amalgamations. It is, however, most important to note and to retain the fact that, though it seemed to respect the fact of polytheism, this interpretation of the myths actually tended toward *henotheism*, that is, it tended to unify the multiform plurality of the gods and divine functions into a single divine will and substance. This was not true monotheism, but it explains why polytheism, simplified, and as it were, contradicted by ths curious tendency, did not offer a great a resistance to the monotheistic affirmations of

Christianity as one might have supposed.

Yet some gods, whose universal reputation rested on their reputedly indispensable specializations, still had many faithful and retained a brilliant cultus. Among them were Apollo of Delphi and Apollo of Claros, known for their oracles; Artemis of Ephesus, the inspiration and presiding deity of the Venerated Mysteries; and Asclepios, the great healer. Generally speaking, in the Orient as everywhere else, specializing gods, who were not always "high gods," but gods who, it was believed, would listen to requests for specific, everyday services, were not idle. They were especially revered by the masses, whose religion always lagged behind that of the educated.

By the side of the classical gods, great or small, ecumenical or local, demons loomed large at this time in the religious life. It goes without saying that no unfavorable meaning was attached to the word *demon*. It designated divine beings, inferior to the gods and much more numerous, who peopled the cosmos. Men believed that at least one of these demons watched over every human being. They were called *genies* when they were attached to men and *junones* when they protected women. Servius, Virgil's commentator (*In Georg.* i, 302) defined a *genie* as follows: "The Ancients called a god of nature who was attached to a place or a thing or a man, a genie." And Censorinus wrote (iii, 1): "A genie is a god under whose tutelage every man lives from the moment of his birth." In short, a demon was a local or personal divinity who played the part of a guardian angel.

It is therefore no exaggeration to say that the old religion of Olympus survived effectively only in adaptations made to order for the men of the day, and through its exceedingly brilliant and pompus cultus which stirred many people aesthetically, even if it did not retain a hold on their emotions. As we know, such long and active survival of liturgy, after its dogmas have virtually perished, is a common phenomenon in the evolution of religion.

Thaumaturgy is another means of prolonging a moribund religion, and the ancient Olympism is a case in point. Thaumaturgy was not confined to the sanctuaries of Asclepios, but cited all the gods as its authorities. It had its own representatives (e.g., the Apollonius of Tyana), divine men, merchants of the marvelous, who were often implicated in magical practices, or were frankly magicians. It is of some importance to take note of these men and the general convictions which justified them, in order to understand why the presentation of Christian truth, founded on a miracle, seemed neither abnormal nor exceptional. Though they may have contested this or that wonder, the customs and the temper of the time did not spurn recourse to miracles as an apologetic device. Similarly, the Christian argument based on prophecies found its equivalent and its groundwork, as it were, in the prevalent faith in oracles, predictions, and divinations in all their forms. It is quite remarkable that Clement of Alexandria, in his *Protreptics*, begins his refutation of paganism by a thoroughgoing attack on oracles and Mysteries. I see in this fact a proof of their influence, which far surpassed that of the official religion and its conventional rites. The Christian apologists, up to and including St. Augustine, by continuing to battle against

Olympism, give the impression that they always considered it to be their basic foe; and if we were not careful they would impose this illusion, which derives from their habit of enlarging conventional topics which they borrow from one another, instead of taking nothing but reality into account.

I shall not dwell on the cult of the emperor, which became established in the Orient in the time of Augustus, and owed its success to the old oriental custom of honoring the sovereign as a divine being. Only when we study the propagation of Christianity and its advent as an organized religion on imperial soil will it become necessary for us to take note of this cult. It will constitute a very formidable civic, if not religious, obstacle to the extension of the church.

The Oriental Background. The oriental background included many old religions which, though differing in their fables and their myths, were essentially similar, in that they all rested on depictment and interpretation of the same natural phenomena. Their gods were divinities of vegetation or astral deities—which comes down to the same thing, since the growth of vegetation and the round of the seasons are governed by the course of the sun. Owing to reciprocal borrowings and the various interpretations all the myths had undergone, it had become difficult, at the beginning of our era, to establish the initial personification of each god at the origination of his cultus. It should be noted that at that time Hellenism, in the proper meaning of the term, had not as yet conquered several considerable regions of the oriental world: the Anatolian plain, the center of Syria, a part of the nomes of Egypt. In these regions indigenous cults, whose liturgy was celebrated in the idiom of the land, retained great prestige and potent power.

Some of the most widespread of these oriental religions were centered on gods who had been men, or gods who, by one aspect of their nature, were close to men, for instance, Osiris, Adonis, Attis, Tammuz. Their worshippers were naturally inclined not to regard them as inaccessible. They were, nevertheless, powerful and beneficent deities.

These oriental religions are interesting also for their rites. Springing out of a conception of life's power and its capacity for renewal, of the fecundity of nature and its need for fecundation, they often assumed obscene forms; but a profound emotion emanated from this very sensuality. And, being accessible to diverse interpretations, they also had at their disposal the means for purification. Some of these cults, of Attis and of Isis for example, had even given rise to asceticism, which in the cult of Attis was propelled to the point of sexual mutilation.

In these lands of the Orient, which had long submitted to the tyranny of absolute monarchies, the subjects did not customarily count for anything before the God-King; he and they were not forged into a people, a nation, a city. Consequently, the religion which adapted itself to these forms of political life did not resemble the one that the Greek states and the Roman people, among whom the individual disappeared before the state and was absorbed in the city, had fashioned. Occidental religion was concerned with preservation of the collectivity, the family, and the state; the oriental religions with preservation of the individual. They were in the habit of practicing rites reputedly effective in aiding the work of the sun and vegetation, a work requisite for the preservation of life. These rites were gradually transposed and adapted to preparing men for the *true life*, the life expressed by the concept of *salvation*. Myths were born which broadened the scope of and, if I may say so, *humanized* the ancient rites.

The Admixture. At first glance, all these oriental religions seem hardly to be in accord with the Greek spirit. Yet at the price of a few changes they became more or less well adapted to it. Their concord gave birth to some quite vital combinations, capable of satisfying the complex and syncretistic spirit of the Hellenistic world. The very principle of Hellenism lay in this passion for admixture and amalgamation of often wholly divergent cultural elements. And nowhere did this passion for syncretism find better ground for its manifestation and surfeit than on religious territory. Juxtaposition of men devoid at heart of religious exclusivism invariably resulted in endosmosis. In fact, the greatest infiltration of and contamination by foreign influences occurred among the Greeks, for the eastern religions were more profound, more genuinely viable, and had a much stronger hold on the sensibilities of men.

We must also take account of a few special phenomena whose influence was apparently quite potent—the intense and contagious religious life of Phrygia; the Iranian Diaspora, which brought with it Mithra into all parts of what we call the Near East; the Syrian Diaspora, which carried Adonis and his paredra, the *Syra Dea*, into all the centers of commerce on the Mediterranean; the influence of Egypt in the economic and intellectual spheres, through which Isis and Osiris, Serapis and Hermetism found favor. All oriental people who for whatever reason sought their fortune in lands other than their own, or who simply travelled, carried with them their gods and their myths. That is why the total effect of the oriental cults appears to have been quite widespread and quite complicated.

However, in some places of the Greek world, conditions were especially favorable to the confrontation of the various religions: the great cosmopolitan cities to which all the merchants of the Mediterranean flocked, Alexandria and Antioch; the junctions of the great routes of commerce, for instance Tarsus; and the great centers of Hellenic religious life, such as Claros and Ephesus, which were linked together in the devotional life of the faithful, and where, as we study the successive modifications of the Ephesian Artemis and other gods, and glance at the curious struggle for influence between Greeks and barbarians around her sanctuary, we may watch syncretism in the process of formation.

The multiple combinations of Hellenism and Orientalism resulted, on the religious plane, in two kinds of interdependent products, which represented two steps in, or, if one prefers, two aspects of, the same phenomenon: the *Mysteries of immortality* and *Hermetism*. If one were to try to differentiate between them, by reference to what we have already said about the distinction between the Greek spirit, more inclined to speculation and reasoning, and the oriental, more given to mystical emotion and religious sensualism, one might say—taking care not to force the idea—that the Mysteries are more oriental and Hermetism is more Greek. In reality, however, it was, in both cases, the Greek spirit that fructified, clarified, organized, and rationalized the old oriental myths, even in their mystique. And Hermetism might very well have been at bottom only a philosophy, a theological explanation of the Mysteries, or of a part of them. The two termini meet [one scholars's] definition very well: "An attempt of the Hellenic genius to take the spirit of Oriental religion into its service." The Greek spirit was at work on oriental elements.

THE MYSTERIES

Greek Dualism. The Mysteries were based on the idea of immortality, on the conviction that man can know a better life beyond the grave, happier than the life he led on earth. The Greeks had arrived at this conception independently, as a consequence of a dualist anthropology. Starting with the much more ancient idea of man's *double,* which leaves the body when he dies, they eventually concluded that man is composed of two elements: one *corporeal,* extinguished by death, the other *immaterial,* which survived and was known to the philosophers as man's *soul.* The miseries and deceits of human life fortified the hope in an immortal life of the soul in a blessed realm. Understandably, in the terrible times which preceded and immediately followed the beginnings of the Christian era men dwelt on the expectation of this future, which seemed to be just compensation for the tribulations of the present.

The ancient national religions had not been favorable to, or rather had not been interested in, this hope of a beyond: they were no more concerned with the future destiny of the individual than they were with his spiritual and moral perfection as religious ends. We know that they were able to achieve a constant marshalling of energies and sentiments in the service of the city or the nation, whose prosperity and continuation constituted their real aim. Their indifference to any future life takes a very curious form in the Jewish Bible, where it is formulated several times: the dead are of no concern to Yahweh; *Sheol,* into which they have descended, is not properly a part of his domain. Whether it is Sheol and the *Rephaim* who dwell in it, or Hades and the shades which people it according to the Homeric conception, it cannot be said there was any true life in these realms. In these underground habitations, men knew only a kind of larval prolongation of their earthly existence, and for the Jews the state of the *Rephaim* seems to have been even lower than that of the shades was for the Greeks.

The conceptions of Minos, Aecus, and Rhadamanthus, influenced probably by the Egyptian belief in the judgment of the dead, were more advanced, at least in the moral sense, since these mythological characters introduced the notion of the responsibility of the living before the superior Powers. Unfortunately, this notion was never defined in a satisfactory manner, and was tied to an affabulation difficult to maintain for long. I have in mind Juvenal's verse (*Sat.* II, 143f.): "That there are somewhere Manes and an underground Kingdom, and Charon's oar and dark frogs in the abyss of the Styx, and that a single barque can suffice to take so many thousands of the dead across the water, even children no longer believe, except those who have yet to pay for their bath." The same impression is found also in Plutarch, and, of course, even more in the Epicureans, whose influence is seen in the well-known saying often used as an inscription on tombstones: "I was not, I have been, I no longer am, little does it matter to me!"

It would be a great mistake to suppose that the pagan consciousness of the first century of the Roman Empire is adequately summed up in such statements. I mention them only to make clear how inadequate were the presentations of life beyond the grave in classical Greco–Roman religion. Logically, this inadequacy led to Epicurean skepticism.

However, the Greek world had long been conscious of this inadequacy, and religious sentiment had long sought to overcome it. The Mysteries antedated, by far, the conquest of the Persian Empire by Alexander, and if possible oriental influences were already hidden under some of their Greek forms, they are very difficult, if not to uncover, at least to define. The cults of Dionysus and of Orpheus, of Demeter and Kore at Eleusis, of the Cabeiri at Samothrace, of Artemis at Ephesus, of Apollo at Claros had become, fundamentally, Mysteries, that is, they claimed to initiate one into a divine secret, the revelation and guarantee of a future life of blessedness, and into a method for assuring oneself its benefits. The origins, the stages in the evolution of these cults, the external influences that may have enriched or modified them, are all so many questions that still remain quite obscure for us, not only because the facts are remote and the texts are rare, but also because the essential thing, that is, the transformation and adaptation, often escaped the Ancients, as it does us, since every one of the various revelations claimed to possess the complete and definitive truth and to have preserved it without any alteration. Orphism, for example, which started with rude and bloody rites in which the animal, a substitute for the god, was torn apart by the teeth of the initiates, ended by becoming a kind of theology and ethical doctrine, with both expounded in an abundant literature.

All the Greek Mysteries had, apparently, several general traits in common. (1) They thought that the human soul, weighed down by the body, was incapable of finding unaided the road to salvation and that this was why instruction in the Mystery was necessary. (2) They practiced an initiation of several stages, which led from the status of child in the Mystery to that of perfect one. (3) The initiates usually passed from one stage to another by means of some liturgical rite. It may well be that Orphism was an exception, in that it was more a doctrine of salvation than a story of salvation. The difference is clearly seen in Pausanias's remark (i, 37, 4): "He who has *seen* the Eleusinian Mysteries or who has *read* the books called Orphic knows what I mean." (4) Ordinarily they had no dogmas, they told a sacred story; they gave no lessons in metaphysics, they presented a spectacle and revealed the efficacy of suitable liturgical gestures. Nor did they give instruction in morals, they demanded purification rites. The initiate's own merits, his qualities or his virtues, were not taken into consideration: he derived his salvation from the fact of his initiation alone.

These old Mysteries, which had existed in their successive forms throughout all of Greek antiquity, still maintained a considerable influence in the century which surrounds the beginning of the Christian era. This was especially true of the Mysteries at Eleusis and Claros. It is not quite certain whether Orphism still existed as an organization, as (let us say) a church, but it certainly still subsisted as a combining element in religions whose specifically non-Orphic elements were derived from the Eleusinian Mysteries from theories rightly or wrongly attributed to Pythagoras, or from obscure developments and interpretations of Dionysiac myths. Archaeological discoveries, whether very recent or quite ancient, but whose meaning has really been understood only in our day, have revealed the existence of a complete syncretistic religion, based on Pythagoreanism and Orphism, in the Greco–Roman world, especially at Rome and in Italy. It seems to have attracted a great number of distinguished minds.

The archaeological discoveries I have in mind are principally the frescoes of the Farnesina in Rome; the stucco decorations of the tombs on the Latin Way and those of the Basilica of Porta Maggiore, which together present a sort of history of the initiation and the destiny of the soul; and the eloquent decorations of the Villa Item and of the Homeric House at Pompeii. Of course, there still remain uncertainties concerning the interpretation of all these pictures and symbols. But the total impression that emerges from the ensemble leaves nothing to be desired. The wealthy men who adorned their dwellings with all these costly decorations intended them to express their urgent spiritual concern, which turned them towards the immortal destiny of the soul, at the same time that they affirmed the certainty of their hopes and their confidence in the rites their Mystery revealed to them. It seems certain that the liturgy by which their initiation was effected and their devotion sustained was interpreted with the aid of a metaphysic and a cosmology which were based on the so-called Pythagorean doctrine.

The Roman world knew a renaissance of Pythagoreanism in the last days of the Republic, but it did not restore the authentic teaching of the philosopher of Crotona. It gathered together under his name a potpourri of secret doctrines, definitive *dogmata*, and magical practices, where borrowings from Orphism and the oriental religions existed side by side with the stale remains of Etruscan rites and the speculative elements derived from the Pythagoreans and the Stoics. The whole was more or less harmonized and interpreted symbolically. What seemed to be distinctively Pythagorean in this mixture was its overall orientation towards the future life, with a tendency to asceticism and mysticism, the latter meditating on the purity requisite for the soul, and the former struggling to maintain it. For the believers in this doctrine thought that this life, being only the preparation for the one to come, ought to free itself, from the baseness in which matter involved it, by moral discipline and ascesis. It is perhaps not too great an exaggeration to say that this neo-Pythagoreanism, which found expression on the walls of buildings that are haunted by the imagery of the Mystery, attracted from all points of the intellectual horizon those men who were eager for the certainty of salvation and uncomfortable in either the official religion or in Epicurean skepticism. Was there a uniform doctrine, a detailed catechism, a teaching balanced and coherent in all its parts? Of course not. But there were manifestations of an ardent religious feeling and of an indefectible eschatological aspiration. This doctrine was widespread at Rome in the time of Cicero and Varro, who wanted to be buried according to the Pythagorean rite, and in the circle of Nigidius Figulus, *Pythagoricus et Magus*, who had no doubt sought it out in the Orient. It was influential in Alexandria, and in the second century Lucian was to echo its nearly general unpopularity, an unpopularity occasioned in all probability by the sect's seemingly aristocratic and exclusive character.

As I have said, Orphism no longer existed as an independent religion. Its ideas, however, survived to so great an extent in the religious thought of the time that it was still singularly fruitful. It should not be forgotten that the notion that the world is delivered to evil and that the body is a burden and a hindrance for the soul, whose destiny is to escape its bonds and arrive at eternal and blessed life, was spread by Orphism, which also implanted the conviction that man's efforts to win salvation were powerless without divine assistance. These two ideas were put into circulation by what I would call the dislocation of Orphism. The importance of this fact lies in its having given independent value to these conceptions, so that one could accept them and be open to their suggestions without explicit affiliation to any mystery.

What was missing in these old Mysteries was not so much emotion (which, for example, was very strong at Eleusis), as the intensity of mysticism, the practical realization in asceticism of the idea of reparation, precise comprehension of the ways and means of salvation. If, as our era draws near, the Mysteries, especially in the syncretistic combinations which had developed outside the regular organizations, still had many adherents among the wealthy classes, they apparently no longer wielded much influence among the people, although they were, in principle, quite egalitarian. We know that the initiation at Eleusis took no heed of the age, sex, social condition, or way of life of the *mystoi*. In this the Eleusinian Mysteries resembled the individualism of the oriental Mysteries, and although the Eleusinian differed from the oriental, they were in no way opposed to submitting to the latter's influence.

The Wave from the Orient at the Inception of the Christian Era. At the time we are considering, a veritable wave from the Orient combed the shores of the Greco-Roman world: Egypt with Isis, Osiris, and Serapis; Syria, with Adonis–Tammuz, Atargatis, and the Baalim; Phrygia, with Cybele, Attis, and Sabazius; Iran and Mesopotamia with Mithra, Ishtar, and the astrologists, etc.—all were manifesting their influence simultaneously. In fact, the whole of Asia Minor, imbued with the same general ideas and stirred by the same aspirations, was filling up with unequally developed and organized cults and initiations, all tending towards mystical exaltation and hope for salvation.

The origins of this religious effervescence are of course very obscure. We can see, however, that it is related to those myths which, as we have already mentioned, originally dealt with the life of the sun and of vegetation. Transposed to man and interpreted in relation to his destiny, they ended with a common doctrine, a doctrine practically invariant from one sect to another, whose general characteristics were as follows:

1. Man is a fallen being, incapable of working out by himself his salvation, which is the gift of divine grace. Some receive it, they are the elect; others do not, they are the damned.

2. There is an element in man that endures and matter that perishes. Opinions differed however on the nature of the bond that united these two aspects of man and on the essential distinction that separated them. Consequently, the survival of the human being was presented in two quite dissimilar forms: sometimes it was conceived as the installation of the immortal soul in the abode of the blessed; at other times as a reconstitution of the entire human being, his corporeal nature having been purified. Thus there was on the one hand belief in the immortality of the soul; and on the other, expectation of the resurrection of the flesh.

3. To help man in his struggle for salvation, one relies on the example, intercession, and assistance of a divine being whose office it is to save. In Greek this being was called *Soter*. The Orientals had for a long time considered their sovereigns to be terrestrial divinities and saviors; adapting this notion to serve the ends of a life beyond the grave was therefore easy. Most frequently, this intervention of a Savior took the form of a divine experience: the divine being had lived, suffered, died, and then been resurrected. The man who shared in this experience through mystical identification with the god found therein both a model and surety for his own life.

4. It was enough to discover the efficacious precepts and mystical acts which assimilated the initiate to his Savior. Each salvation Mystery had its own method, allegedly effective, for bringing about this assimilation to the sufferings, the fate, and finally the glorification of the Soter. The method was based on all-powerful rites, both realistic and mystical, which were valuable in themselves. The principal ones were related to the two most striking forms of communion among men: the bed and the table.

5. The concept was born, and growing, that a holy life, a life purified by constraint of the desires of the flesh, was a requisite, in order to prepare for the indefectible election and to merit the grace of a perfect initiation which "divinized" the *mystos*.

6. As for their initiation, men were divided into two categories: children and perfects, with stages between the two. The perfects formed a fraternity, made one in their god and bound to his service, which was conceived as absolute freedom.

7. The elect could come from any world, any social condition, any nation. That is why these various sectarian fraternities, which were practically closed

corporations, were all based on universalism, since each aspired to contain the whole of humanity. And each was administered by a specialized priesthood, because correctness in its liturgical life was thought to be paramount.

Recruitment was guaranteed by private propaganda: each initiate considered himself to be a missionary, and was encouraged and sustained by his pride in being one of the elect. What strikes us as most odd is the fact that there was no hostility among these rival organizations. The conviction each had of possessing the truth didn't cause it to excommunicate all the others. Thus, one and the same man could seek several initiations, and could simultaneously be a member of several churches, and theoretically, of all. The common background whose principal features we have just summed up favored this syncretism, of which the vast Hermetic literature is such a curious example: it seems to be the incorporation into theories and doctrines of the empirical salvationism of the Mysteries. . . .

W. F. Albright

Influences on Hellenistic Judaism

WILLIAM FOXWELL ALBRIGHT (1891–1971) was educated at Johns Hopkins University, where he received his Ph.D. in archeology and linguistices in 1916. From 1920 to 1929 he was director of the American School of Oriental Research in Jerusalem, and until 1958 professor of Semitic languages at Johns Hopkins. Though sometimes criticized for his conservatism in supporting biblical orthodoxy, Albright was recognized as one of the most accomplished orientalists of his generation. He was the first scholar outside Palestine to confirm the authenticity of the Dead Sea Scrolls in 1947. His books include *Archeology of Palestine and the Bible* (1932); *Yahweh and the Gods of Canaan* (1962); and *History, Archeology, and Christian Humanism* (1964).

Early Iranian religion was substantially identical in character and even in detail with the Aryan faith of the Rig Veda; it was a naturalistic polytheism essentially like Homeric Greek religion. At the head of the pantheon stood Ahura Mazda, "the Lord of Wisdom" (compare the Sumerian Zen, the god of the moon, whose name has the same meaning); among the most important deities were Mithra, the god of light, and the goddess of fertility, Ardvisura Anahita, "the Great Stream, the Unblemished One." This period of Iranian religion is reflected by some of the Yashts of the Avesta, which have been only lightly worked over by later Zoroastrian editors; their constant references to chariot-warriors show that their original composition must antedate the ninth century B.C. at the latest, since cavalry had replaced chariotry by that time. Somewhere in the seventh (or the sixth) century B.C. arose Spitama Zarathushtra (Zoroaster), member of an Iranian

From *From the Stone Age to Christianity* by W. F. Albright (Baltimore, Md.: Johns Hopkins University Press, 1957), pp. 276–290. Reprinted by permission of the publisher.

agricultural and cattle-breeding community in the far northeastern marches of Transoxiana, who preached a new gospel, the general nature of which is clear from the Gathas of the Avesta. It is true that the latter do not appear to have been reduced to canonical form until about the third century A.D., but they seem to have been put into writing under the Parthian kings, probably in the first century A.D. Judging from linguistic and paleographic evidence, they were transmitted orally for not less than 500, and perhaps for over 800 years. Zoroaster taught that there was only one supreme being, the good and bright Ahura Mazda, against whom stood the independent representative of the evil and dark forces of nature, Angra Mainyu (Ahriman). Ahura Mazda created five or six (later increased to seven) minor deities, called "the Beneficent Immortals" (Amesha Spentas), all of whom bore abstract names: Good Thought, Best Order (Truth), Desirable Domination, Beneficent Devotion, Holiness, Immortality, to whom a seventh, Beneficient Spirit, was later added. To oppose these, Angra Mainyu also created evil deities or spirits. Zoroaster seems to have simplified the native religious cult of the Iranians by emphasizing the sacredness of fire, of the cow, and of the haoma plant, which was used to make a fermented sacred drink. According to Zoroaster the good Ahura Mazda will ultimately prevail over the forces of evil. The old Iranian gods were in general relegated to the rank of demons (*daivas*). There must have been some form of belief in the divine judgment and the separation between the good and the evil in the next world, but it cannot be traced with certainty back to the Achaemenian period. . . .

There is no clear trace of Iranian influence on Judaism before the second century B.C., though the beginnings of this influence may well go back a century or two earlier. In the form which Iranian religion takes in all inscriptions and literary sources of the last four centuries B.C. it can hardly have possessed any appeal to the Jews as a monotheistic or aniconic system. Even in the Gathas Ahura Mazda is only the mighty head of a hierarchy of good minor deities, against whom are arrayed Angra Mainyu and his evil followers. Iranian influences must have entered into Judaism first as a result of certain features which reminded the Jews of corresponding elements in their religion. These common features may be identified in Judaism with ease: a tendency toward dualism and to the creation of a personal antagonist to God; a tendency toward the formation of an organized angelic hierarchy; developing belief in the last judgment and in rewards and punishments after death. In a number of passages in Jewish literature dating from about 400–165 B.C. we find the idea of a personal Satan developing from the original sense of an angelic plaintiff in the celestial court, where the Almighty was allegorically represented as sitting in judgment over the deeds of men (Zech. 3; Job 1; for still older conceptions see 1 Kings 22: 19 ff.), to its final sense of the chief of the invisible powers opposed to God (so partly in Jubilees). But it is not until the late second century B.C., in the Testaments of the Twelve Patriarchs, that we find characteristically dualistic conceptions: for example the spirit of error is set against the spirit of truth (Test. Jud., 20) and Beliar (Belial) is set against God (*passim*), light is opposed to darkness (*passim*), and the seven evil spirits are arrayed against the seven good spirits. This type of dualism decreased greatly in importance in later Judaism and seems, in fact, to have been rejected by orthodox rabbinic circles, though it obtained considerable popular support in still later times. In Christianity, on the other hand, the modified dualism of the Testaments of the Twelve Patriarchs achieved a signal triumph, since it offers a simpler and more intelligible solution of the problem of evil than any other ever proposed. The very fact that it was rejected by normative Judaism shows that it was foreign to Jewish tradition, and Iranian influence can hardly be denied, especially in view of the parallels which will be described below.

It is highly probable that the idea of seven archangels was taken from Iranian sources. In the earlier books of the Old Testament and the earliest apocryphal and pseudepigraphical literature there is nowhere any suggestion that certain angels formed a specially privileged group in the celestial hierarchy, nor do any angels receive personal names identical with those of human beings. In Daniel (about 165 B.C.) Michael and Gabriel appear, and in Enoch Uriel (*Orī'el*, "God is my Light") and Raphael, as well as many other names, are added. The number of the principal angels (archangels) varies from four to seven, the latter being distinctly later than the former, as is clear not only from their literary age but also from the fact that only these four have genuinely early Israelite (or Canaanite) names, after which all others have obviously been modeled. It is curious to note that all four names belong to a type which was in most active use before the tenth century B.C. and which became archaistic after the Exile. There can, therefore, be little doubt that these angelic figures have a prehistory (Israelite or pagan?) which escapes us entirely. In any case only the *idea* of seven chief angels and of their relative station was taken from Iranian sources, since the names are absolutely different in character.

The idea of the Last Judgment also has strong Jewish roots, though Iranian conceptions appear to have influenced details. Since God was believed to sit in judgment on the deeds of all mankind, and since the last Day of the Lord was an old eschatological concept in Israel, it was a natural transition to the Last Judgment. In the form in which it appears in Daniel (7:9-12) Iranian influence is most unlikely, but in Enoch (41:1 and *passim*) and elsewhere in the last century and a half before our era, we find such distinctively Iranian details as the use of the balance to weigh the deeds of men. The apocalyptic picture of the end of the world (for example Rev. 8 ff.) calls to mind many Iranian parallels, though in view of the obscurity of Zoroastrian literary chronology, it cannot be definitely shown that they antedate Sassanian times (third to seventh centuries A.D.). The idea of the destruction of the world by fire is much more likely to be derived from the astrological interpretation of the Stoic *ekpýrōsis*, the conflagration which follows a cosmic cycle. . . .

From the foregoing it appears that Iranian conceptions did not begin to influence Judaism until the last two pre-Christian centuries, and even then exerted no effect except where the ground was already fully prepared for them. When we turn to the sphere of influence which we shall term "proto-Gnostic," for lack of a better expression, the situation changes materially. Here, however, even greater caution is needed than in dealing with Iranian influences, since we are largely dependent upon fragmentary bits of information and indirect inferences. . . .

Few problems in the history of religion are so elusive as the question of proto-Gnosticism and Judeo-Gnosticism. Since the earliest literary remains of Gnosticism proper do not antedate the second century A.D. and since the earliest Gnostic known to Irenaeus and Hippolytus was Simon Magus (see Acts 8: 9 ff.) it is obvious that we cannot use Gnostic data directly in any reconstruction of Hellenistic Jewish currents of thought. However, there is now direct evidence that some of the central ideas of the Gnostic system go back into the ancient Orient. We shall, accordingly, discuss this evidence briefly, after which we shall characterize proto-Gnosticism as a movement and point out its relation to Judaism and Christianity.

The central figure of Gnostic mythology is that of Sophia (Wisdom). It is true that the Sophia appears in very different roles in different Gnostic systems and that her figure is split into two, but the standard form is that of the Lesser Sophia, who descends from the world of spirit and light into the sphere of matter, where she becomes besmirched and cannot rise. She is then raised by God or by a special emanation from Him (generally identified by the Christian Gnostics with Christ) and returns to her original place in heaven. The Lesser Sophia also received the name Achamoth (Wisdom), which identified her with the Canaanite-Hebrew hypostatized Wisdom. The latter first appears in a remarkable gnomic document which has been incorporated into the Book of Proverbs (chapters 8-9), but which is now known to be of Canaanite origin, since it swarms with words and expressions otherwise found only in such Canaanite texts as the Ugaritic tablets and the Phoenician inscriptions. In this document, whose rich pagan imagery offered no stumbling-block to orthodox Judaism, since it was interpreted quite symbolically, Wisdom is called both Hokhmah and Hakhamôth (Hokhmôth), the latter probably being a form of Phoenician origin. Wisdom here appears as the first creation of Yahweh; she was emanated (lit. "poured out") by Him before the beginning of creation; she also appears as owning a temple with seven pillars, the cosmic significance of which is clear. The original Canaanite text of Proverbs 8-9 can hardly be later than the seventh century B.C., but the glorification of wisdom has much earlier roots in Canaanite, since we read in the epic of Baal from Ugarit (about the 15th century B.C.): "And the lady Asherah of the Sea (consort of El) answered, 'The wise El has attributed to thee (O Baal) wisdom (hkmt), together with eternity of life and good fortune.'" In the recently discovered Aramaic Proverbs of Akhiqar, from about the sixth century B.C., we read: "(Wi)sdom is (from) the gods, and to the gods is she precious; for(ever) her kingdom is fixed in heav(en), for the lord of the holy ones (i.e., the gods of heaven) hath raised her." A Jewish counterpart to this is found in Enoch 42: 1-2 (second century B.C.): "Since Wisdom found no place to dwell, she received an abode in heaven; when Wisdom came to dwell among men and found no abode, she returned to her place and dwelt among the angels." Ben Sira (early second century B.C.) makes Wisdom similarly say: "I came forth from the mouth of the Highest, and like vapor I have covered the earth; I have made my abode in the heights, and my throne on a pillar of cloud (24: 3–4)." Here Wisdom is poetically likened to a breath issuing from the mouth of God and spreading until it penetrates into all recesses. In the Wisdom of Solomon (7:25) Wisdom is called "a breath of the power of God and an emanation (outflowing) of the pure effulgence of the Almighty." Finally in Philo Judeus we find that Wisdom (Sophia or Episteme) was the first emanation of God, who created the world; she became the mother of the Logos, remaining a virgin, since God does not generate in human fashion.

These passages, which may easily be increased in number, prove conclusively that the central concept and myth of the Lesser Sophia is of Canaanite-Aramean origin, going back at least to the seventh century B.C. Sophia evidently replaces an older Canaanite goddess of wisdom, like the Mesopotamian Siduri Sabitu, who is called in a text of the late second millennium, "goddess of wisdom, genius of life," and who is undoubtedly the prototype of the sibyl Sambethe, later identified with the Lesser Sophia. There is nothing essentially Hellenic about either the idea of preexistence, which was characteristic of the gods in general, or the idea of emanation, since the latter is simply a euphemistic substitute for the basic idea of creation by sexual act. All figures of early Near Eastern and Hellenic theogonies, both concrete deities and abstractions, were created by the outpouring of semen; and the concept was so simple and so capable of receiving philosophical interpretation that it was seized upon by the early Greek cosmologists, from Thales on. The idea of the descent of Wisdom to earth is probably connected with the myth of the descent of Ishtar or Anath to Hades, as clearly illustrated by later Gnostic mythology. The myth of her elevation to heaven is again transparently connected with that of the exaltation of Ishtar or Anath to be queen of heaven. Gnostic thinkers had merely to identify the eternal Wisdom with the Iranian world of good and light, and with the Stoic divine fire and creative reason. Since the author of the Wisdom of Solomon already places God over against matter in essentially Gnostic fashion, and since he considers the body as the prison of the soul, which exists before and after life, it is safe to assume that the decisive step toward a Jewish Gnosis had already been taken in the first century B.C. At all events, the elements were at hand, and by the middle of the first century A.D. they had already been fitted into the first known Gnostic system by Simon Magus. Since the latter was a younger contemporary of Philo but does not seem to have borrowed anything directly from him, we may safely suppose that both drew inspiration from a common proto-Gnostic background.

The concept of Sophia completely overshadowed that of the Logos in Jewish as well as in Gnostic thought. In early Christian thought the Logos displaced Sophia, as we know especially from the prologue to the Gospel of John. [Although] the Christian Logos concept has generally been considered to be specifically Greek . . . it is really of oriental origin [and] goes back to a dynamistic conception of the third millennium B.C., which makes the voice of a god act as a distinct entity with power of its own. Sumerian and Canaanite texts show that the divine voice or command was correctly represented by the mighty sound of thunder. Later, in Egyptian, cuneiform, and biblical literature, we find many passages where the command of a god, the word issuing from his mouth, is virtually hypostatized. For example, in Deutero-Isaiah 40:8 we read, "But the word of our God will exist for ever." In the Wisdom of Solomon, some four centuries or more later, occurs the remarkable passage (18:15): "Thy mighty Word [Logos] sprang from heaven, from the royal throne, a stern warrior, into the land devoted to destruction, bearing Thy unchanging command as a sharp sword." As Dürr has shown, with a wealth of illustration, this idea is Semitic, not Hellenic; in the Proverbs of Akhiqar from Elephantine, the word of an earthly monarch is described in terms which closely resemble the passage just quoted from the Wisdom of Solomon: "Mild is the word (millethâ) of a king, but sharper and more cutting than a two-edged sword. . . . Gentle is the tongue of a king, yet it breaks the ribs of a dragon (tannîn)." . . .

If the writer is correct in explaining the divine names of the Jewish pantheon at Elephantine in the fifth century B.C. as hypostatized aspects of Yahweh, we should have a paganizing prototype of Philonic hypostatic speculation, completely stripped of its philosophical trappings, at least a century before Alexander the Great. According to this view, the three divine names Eshem-bêth'el, Herem-bêth'el, 'Anath-bêth'el (— 'Anath-Yahu), meaning respectively "Name of the House of God" (— God), "Sacredness of the House of God," and "Sign (?) of the House of God" would reflect pure hypostatizations of deity, probably influenced by contemporary Canaanite-Aramaean theological speculation, in which Bêthe'el frequently appears as the name of a god (from the seventh to the fourth century B.C.). However this may be, it is clear that pagan theological conceptions had entered into post-exilic Jewry through the circles to which these Jews belonged, and through heretical groups like the Phrygian Jews who identified Sabazius with Hebrew Sebaoth. Of course, all such divagations were vigorously repulsed by orthodox Judaism, but as in most such cases the very intensity of the reaction produced somewhat analogous phenomena in reverse. Just as the Church Fathers, from the second century A.D. on, found it increasingly necessary to employ Greek philosophical methods and terminology to explain their views to non-Christians as well as to defend them from heretics, so Jewish thinkers of the Hellenistic age were compelled to adapt the methods and the terminology of their pagan antagonists to their own purposes, both in order to combat the latter and in order to distinguish between orthodox Judaism and the vagaries of such groups as the Essenes and the Therapeutae. Moreover, the direct evidence of Jewish writings from the period 600-200 B.C. proves that pagan Phoenician literature was then exerting a very considerable direct and indirect influence on Jewish thought, and the evidence of the Elephantine Papyri and of Tobit demonstrates that pagan Aramaic literature also began to exercise similar influence after the sixth century B.C.

It is increasingly clear that indirect pagan influences entered mainly through the compositions of eschatologists, who swarmed in Jewry during the period which began with Daniel and Enoch and which ended with the Apocalypse and 4 Esdras. The eschatologists were pneumatic souls who saw visions of the future while they were in ecstatic condition, and translated them into words with which they stirred men's imaginations and whipped them up to action. Without unfairly identifying the phenomena of ecstatic vision with ordinary dream-life, there can be no doubt that they both exhibit a divorce between conscious will and involuntary imagination, a separation which leads to unusual and often fantastic associations of ideas. At the same time, the spiritual exaltation of the visionary is undoubtedly transferred to his subconscious mental life, where it is translated into grandiose and often majestic imagery, drawn from many different sources and often quite destitute of any logical connection, though all the more powerful in its emotional effect. In practice, conventional ideas and patterns of imagery would prevent the visions of an ecstatic from assuming the pathologically bizarre forms illustrated by Thomas De Quincey and Charles Baudelaire. Through the eschatologists innumerable elements of pagan imagery and even entire myths entered into the literature of Judaism and Christianity, though it is safe to say that only an infinitesimal amount of the original mass has actually survived, since visionary excesses invariably repel sober scribes and theologians. The admission of Daniel and the Apocalypse to the Christian canon has immeasurably enriched the affective and aesthetic life of Christianity, without in the least demoralizing its theology (except in the case of certain chiliastic sects).

Among the eschatological groups we may count the enigmatic Essenes, who already formed a distinctive Jewish sect in the second century B.C.[1] . . . They rejected marriage and lived in semimonastic communities, owning everything jointly. They also rejected bloody sacrifices, though they still revered the Torah and the Temple. In place of the sacrificial system they introduced an elaborate system of sacramental meals and of lustration with water. They further possessed an extensive esoteric literature, access to which was only allowed members of the order. According to Josephus, they were interested in the virtues of plants and stones, they possessed an elaborate angelography, knowledge of which was incumbent upon the neophyte, they were rigid predestinarians, and they attached great importance to the art of predicting the future, in which they seldom made mistakes. The last three statements are particularly significant, since we can only infer from them that the Essenes, in opposition to virtually all precabalistic Jews, were believers in astrology, which harmonized just as well with their strict predestinarianism as it did with the Stoic *heimarmênê*. It is hardly likely that any extant Jewish esoteric works, from Enoch to the Qabbala, can be attributed to the Essenes, at least in their present form. It seems probable that the Essenes represent a sectarian Jewish group which had migrated from Mesopotamia to Palestine after the victory of the Maccabees. This theory would explain their interest in the virtues of plants and stones . . ., their attention to divination and astrology, their frequent lustrations (hygienically necessary in Iraq, but not in Palestine), as well as their prayer to God for sunrise, performed daily before dawn, facing eastward, since all of these points were characteristic of Mesopotamian practice. Moreover, it is easier to explain their refusal to take part in sacrificial ritual if they had come from a region so far from Jerusalem that performance of sacrifices was physically impossible at the time when their beliefs were crystallized. The relatively great ceremonial significance of lustration with water in Mesopotamian ritual has been repeatedly emphasized; and it is now known that the Euphrates was the center of a cult of water traceable in the upper Euphrates valley from about 2800 B.C. to the third century A.D., when we have a mosaic showing the river-god Euphrates with an accompanying bilingual caption in Greek and Syriac: "King (river) Euphrates." In the second century A.D. there was a Baptist sect of Gnostics whose cult of the living water of the Euphrates is thus illustrated by Hippolytus: "We are the chosen pneumatics from the living Euphrates which flows through the midst of Babylon" — "Mesopotamia is the stream of great Ocean flowing from the midst of the perfect man." . . . The concept of the water of baptism as "a fountain of water gushing forth to eternal life" (John 4:14), whose effect on the believer is such that "rivers of living water shall flow from his belly" (John 7:38) is not only genuinely oriental but is specifically Mesopotamian in origin. It is significant that the second citation is quoted by St. John from an otherwise unknown written source, which at least proves that there was a protobaptist literature which was definitely tinged with proto-Gnostic ideas.

In this milieu John the Baptist must certainly be placed, since he combined the zeal of an Israelite prophet with a true soteriological passion for saving souls from the wrath to come (Matt. 3:7), and since he united an unusually pronounced asceticism with the practice of initiating converts into the kingdom of God by baptism in the Jordan. Unfortunately, we know next to nothing of his own doctrine; and that of his alleged pupil and successor, Dositheus of Samaria, is even more obscure, though Simon Magus is said to have emerged from his school. Since John the Baptist was a prophetic evangelist who taught that repentance, confession, and baptism must precede remission of sins, it is most unlikely that John's system was itself proto-Gnostic. However, it is generally recognized that John forms the most important channel through which eschatological and soteriological ideas and practices passed from Essene or proto-Gnostic sources into Christianity. . . .

NOTE

1. Professor Albright bases his analysis of Essene beliefs on Josephus' testimony (*Antiquities* 13.5.9). The Dead Sea Scrolls, which almost certainly derive from Essene circles, had not been discovered at the time this essay was written. (Ed.)

A. Eustace Haydon

Yahweh

A. EUSTACE HAYDON was born in Brampton, Ontario, in 1880 and was educated at McMaster University and the University of Chicago (Ph.D. 1918). After serving as a pastor in Madison, Wisconsin, he joined the faculty of the University of Chicago as professor of comparative religions, a position he occupied until his retirement in 1945. He was a Leader of the Chicago Ethical Society for many years. His books on world religions include *Quest of the Ages* (1929), *Modern Trends in World Religions* (1934), and *Biography of the Gods* (1944).

When Yahweh first emerged from the shadows that veil the period of prehistory he was the tribal god of a little group of seminomads in the unpromising lands of the Negeb, south of Palestine. There was nothing about him then to suggest that he would play a significant role in the cosmic drama. Every little segment of the moving mosaic of peoples seeking or defending a heritage in the lands east of the Mediterranean had its divine protector and provider. Yahweh was only one among many. In comparison with the great gods who watched the wars of empire in the Near East during the second millennium B.C., he was an unimportant figure. His fortune was made by a happy alliance with a federation of Semitic tribes, who were destined to carve their hopes deep into the religious history of the world.

The land of Palestine knew many peoples before the Hebrews, and many gods before Yahweh. It was a highway of the ancient world over which passed restless hordes in quest of homelands and marching armies seeking the rewards of conquest and the glory of their kings. For thousands of years diverse ethnic

From *Biography of the Gods* by A. Eustace Haydon (New York: Frederick Ungar, Co., 1967), pp. 218–241. Reprinted by permission of the publisher.

stocks met and mingled their blood and their cultures in the land. The grasping arms of empire reached out over it ffom the Egyptian, Assyrian, Mitannian, and Hittite thrones. At the beginning of the twentieth century B.C., the Hurrians poured in from the north to leave their mark on the mixture. In the eighteenth century the Hyksos, "shepherd kings," with their mixed multitude flowed through on their way to lordship in Egypt and came back as an ebb tide after the defeat of their dynasty. After 2000 B.C. there are occasional references to the Habiru who were later to become Yahweh's chosen people. They were small groupings of wandering, nomad adventurers associated with the Hurrians and later with the Hyksos. The name of Yahweh had not yet found a place in the records of history.

There was no lack of gods in Palestine during the second millennium B.C. Half a hundred names have been rescued from oblivion, and excavation may discover more, but many must be lost to memory forever. Each of the many tribes and cities had its own divine friends and protectors, but the great nature forces, important for people living from the soil, had the highest rank and widest power. El, the shining, sunlit heaven was the greatest of the gods. A rival for the favor of farming folk was the great Ba'al of the storm, many-named, but best known as Hadad. His thundering voice was heard in the clouds; his weapon was the lightning and his great gift the fertilizing rain. These two gods, the all-ruling heaven and the storm rain, so often specialized as a war god, were not peculiar to Palestine. Under different names they appear in the lists of gods from the shores of the Mediterranean, through the Near East, to India. The age-old battle of the seasons, summer dying before the attack of winter, to be revived again in the spring, was represented in the north by two gods—Mot, the season of crops, and Aleyn, winter and spring waters. As Mot died by the scythe at harvest time so Aleyn, god of the waters, perished with the coming of summer and its burning sun. With only changes of names this motif of the dying and rising gods persisted for two thousand years. Associated with the gods, and effective for success in war and agriculture were the goddesses, most famous of whom were Anath, Astarte and Ashera, wife of the great Ba'al, Hadad. All these gods died long ago, but when Yahweh came to claim his kingdom they were alive and powerful, beloved of the folk and firmly rooted in the cultural life.

The northern tribes, who were later to be the more powerful part of Yahweh's people, were at home in Palestine centuries before his coming. As nomad immigrants, they began to filter into the land early in the second millennium B.C. The family of the great ancestral figure, Abraham, found a place in the wake of the Hurrian invasion in the nineteenth century. Some two centuries later other Hebrews shared the wanderings of the Hyksos. A powerful thrust led by Joshua, at the dawn of the fourteenth century, established rights of residence west of the Jordan. Under the name of Israel, the Hebrews were bound in alliance with other tribes of Canaan to defend their holdings and, during succeeding centuries, to complete the conquest. Settled as farmers and cattle raisers they advanced in wealth, power, and culture. In addition to the services of their own tribal and ancestral deities, they gladly accepted the help of the gods of their new homeland who specialized in giving fertility to field and herd. The god represented in the form of a bull, perhaps the great Hadad, was especially popular with the Israelites. Immigrants from the south, wandering priests and seers, brought to the tribes of Israel glowing reports of the mighty deeds of Yahweh, but it was more than two centuries after their settlement in the north before he claimed them as his own.

Yahweh's original home was in the south. His name, with its Arabic flavor, points to some forgotten migration from the farther south which brought him to the Negeb. There the tribe of Judah met him and was bound to him by bonds never to be broken. This tribe had a reputation for strength and aggressiveness.

> Your brothers shall praise you, O Judah;
> With your hand on the necks of your foes,
> Your father's sons shall bow down to you.
> A lion's whelp is Judah. (Gen. 49:8)

Under the leadership of Judah the other tribes of the south were united—Kenites, Simeonites, Calebites and Jeremeelites. As his people grew in number and strength, the power and importance of Yahweh were enlarged. It was with one of these groups—the Kenites—that Moses found refuge in his flight from Egypt. Brooding in discouragement over the plight of his people, he saw the vision which convinced him that Yahweh could deliver his fellow tribesmen from their Egyptian bondage. Moses' clansmen, the rescued Levites, became ardent devotees and later priests of Yahweh. The Kenite, Jethro, probably expressed the conviction of all the tribes gathered to celebrate the return of Moses when he said, "Now I know that Yahweh is greater than all other gods in that his power prevailed over them."

Jethro's speech lights up the essential quality of Yahweh in his early days. He was specialized from the beginning as a god of power. In origin he was the storm, with wind, lightning and thunder, the boisterous bringer of rain after heat and drought. Storm gods in some areas of the ancient world were honored chiefly because they brought luxurious life to pasture lands and growing crops, but very often they were transformed into gods of war. The mighty heavenly figure, with awe-inspiring voice and terrible weapons, was an ideal leader of armies. Yahweh must have been welcome in the Negeb as a raingiver but this phase of his nature was lost to sight in the glorification of his strength and power. He was pictured as a mountain-striding figure, appearing in fire and smoke, "his lightning-bolts in his right hand," in whose presence the earth trembled.

> O Yahweh when thou camest forth from Seir,
> When thou marchedst from the land of Edom,
> The earth quaked, the heavens also shook,
> The clouds, too, dripped water.

> The mountains rocked at the presence of Yahweh,
> At the presence of Yahweh, the God of Israel. (Judg. 5:4–5)

The lightning was Yahweh's arrow, the thunder was his voice. He was El-Shaddai, the mountain god, exalted and mighty. By natural right he carried the titles "Man of War" and "God of Hosts." The fighting spirit of the tribe of Judah was reflected in Yahweh and reinforced by him. The southern tribes never forgot his victory over the Egyptians. He was their defender and deliverer, the terrible destroyer of their foes. In times of need, they could confidently cry to him:

> Arise, O Yahweh, that thy foes may be scattered,
> That those who hate thee may flee before thee. (Num. 10:35)

Time after time he came rushing from the cloud-gathering mountains of the south as a Storm-god to overwhelm their enemies with the torrential rain, hail, thunder, and lightning. He had no rival in the art of war, nor as a ruthless destroyer of those who stood in the path of his people.

Yahweh began his march toward the mastery of Palestine early in the twelfth century. The federation of Judean tribes, inspired by Moses, moved northward to claim the land lying between the Negeb and the holdings of the tribes of Israel. Although these northern clans were old settlers and possessed an extensive territory, they were still ringed around with enemies. Many cultural and religious experiences separated them from the Judeans, but the two groups were drawn into an alliance by a common interest—the need for security and the desire to conquer the cities, fertile valleys and coastal plains still beyond their control. In that enterprise, the War-god of Judah played a central role.

Yahweh was an ideal divine leader for a people so long involved in warfare for the possession of their homeland. He met their need of a champion able to cut a path through hostile forces and to defend them against attack. They knew him as a god of ruthless power, terrible in his anger. He ruled his people with a firm hand and shared their attitudes toward the enemy. Within the clan he stood behind the social mores, and justice was administered in his name. He approved the tribal code whcih permitted deceit and dishonesty in dealing with the foe. To his loyal followers he was a friend to be trusted—and feared. His own southern people had had long experience and ample assurance of his kindly care. He was often angry with them, yet he loved them and could be depended upon to guard them jealously. Unlike so many gods of the early world, easily won to benevolence by priestly cunning, Yahweh kept a quality of reserve and sternness even toward his own, yet, at times, he could be persuaded to change his mind or stay his punishments by the plea of a favorite or by a pleasing offering. His ways were often unaccountable. Evil and good alike came from his hand. Vows, however rash, made to him had to be kept, regardless of the price in human suffering. The dark spirit that tortured Saul was his messenger. His holiness was fatal to Uzzah, who touched the Ark, although the motive behind the act was entirely blameless.

Saul broke faith with the Gibeonites, and the people of David's time atoned for the wrong in the anguish of three years of famine. In a burst of anger against Israel, he moved David to take a census of the people and then punished his obedience by sending three days of pestilence. Seventy thousand men died before Yahweh repented of the evil he had done.

The seers, who were his interpreters, found in these calamities signs of the good, austere and irresistible in power, who so often had come thundering from his dwellng place on the mountain heights to the help of Israel against her enemies. There was comfort and security under the protecting leadership of a god of awe-inspiring power. As an efficient War-god he dealt in death and destruction. Such a champion could arouse courage, confidence, and loyalty in the hearts of those who fought under his standard. Terror walked before him. The battle-hardened Philistines were not afraid of Israel but the presence of Yahweh on the field made them tremble.

> Their gods have come to them to the camp. . . . Alas for us!
> Who shall deliver us from the power of these majestic gods?
> These are the gods who struck down the Eygptians. . . . (1 Sam. 4:7-8)

To men hedged about by hostility a god of power was essential. Yahweh justified his early reputation when David led his people through stormy and war-scarred years to victory and peace.

When Judah ruled all Palestine, Yahweh was enthroned as Lord of the land. The local fertility figures were not disturbed but the old high gods of heaven and storm were either merged in him or thrust into the background. The northern tribes learned to recognize in Yahweh the same God their fathers had known under other names. Among the many deities, none could compare in power and glory with the heavenly sovereign of the united kingdom.

> Give unto Yahweh, ye gods,
> Give unto him glory and praise;
> Give unto Yahweh the glory due his name,
> Worship Yahweh in holy array.
>
> The voice of Yahweh peals across the waters—
> It is the God of glory thundering,
> Yahweh thundering over the mighty waters.
> The thunder of Yahweh is overpowering,
> The thunder of Yahweh is full of majesty,
> The thunder of Yahweh crashes down the cedars,
> Yea, Yahweh crashes down the cedars of Lebanon,
> Making Lebanon leap like a calf,
> And Siryon like a wild ox.

> The thunder of Yahweh furls fiery bolts,
> The thunder of Yahweh makes the desert tremble,
> Yahwey makes the Desert of Kadesh tremble;
> The thunder of Yahweh splits the oaks,
> And strips the forest bare:
> In his temple everything calls out, Glory!
> Yahweh sits enthroned over the flood,
> He is enthroned as King forever. (Ps. 29:1-10)

On the field of battle, the supremacy of Yahweh was never doubted. The first serious challenge to his status came when his people began to learn and love the arts of peace. The northern tribes had long ago learned from their Canaanite neighbors that good crops and prosperity depended upon the performance of the proper seasonal ceremonies; that the local gods of the land, the Ba'alim, were the generous givers of the goods of life for tillers of the soil. These deities were specialists in agricultural fertility. Yahweh had no experience in farming. His glory had been won in the hard, rough life of the desert days and the stormy years of strife. Thus he faced the test of practical usefulness under changed conditions. The attractiveness of the new culture and the growing desires of the people weighted the scales on the side of the Ba'alim. In such a battle for supremacy the god of the conquering people must assume the duties of the native deities and so displace them, or await a slow death from a disease always fatal to a god—uselessness—as his people are captured by the gods of the land who minister to new cultural interests.

The early prophets played an important part in determining the outcome of the divine conflict in Palestine. They were fiercely loyal to Yahweh and represented him as hostile to all rivals. With their voices echoing in the countryside there was no danger that Israel would be allowed to forget him. At the same time, the prophets slowed up the process of assimilation of Yahweh to the culture of the land. They set their faces against the new civilization and demanded devotion to the simpler ideals of the nomadic life. They were supported by groups like the Rechabites, who remained stubbornly opposed to settled agricultural living. Most of the people, however, followed their practical interests and fell into the yearly rhythm of farming folk with the seasonal ceremonies addressed to fertility gods. Thus they were compelled to combine two loyalties— a recognition of Yahweh, their powerful champion in battle, and a devotion to the Ba'alim as the source of immediate values. The agricultural rites were accepted as necessary to guarantee fertility and material wealth, yet at no time was there any hesitation in acknowledging Yahweh as peculiarly Israel's God, supreme in affairs of state, their leader and defender in all relations with other peoples.

In making use of the services of other gods who were better qualified than he to meet their new needs, the people were not conscious of any disloyalty to Yahweh. They had been accustomed to a plurality of deities. Yahweh was now recognized as the owner of the land of Palestine, but he was not yet intolerant of other, lesser gods. The *teraphim*, images of the family or household divinities, were cherished in the homes. The people were familiar with graven and molten images of many gods in all the centers of worship, even in connection with the cult of Yahweh. Solomon had built sanctuaries for the foreign deities, Chemosh and Melek. The menace of the fertility gods, former owners of the land, did not seem serious. In spite of the propaganda of the protesting prophets, Yahweh was learning the arts of agricultural life and taking on the pattern of the new culture. He was slowly replacing the local gods and assuming their powers. Titles like Ba'al and Melek, belonging to them, were applied to him. Many of the local sanctuaries of the Ba'alim passed into his possession. Even the bull cult of the oldest tribe of the north was passing into the control of Yahweh. By a natural process of assimilation he was assuming responsibility for agricultural prosperity and crowding out his rivals when political disaster checked his triumph in the north.

The rebellion of Jeroboam in the tenth century split the northern tribes apart from the house of Judah. Saul had broken his heart trying to weld these two peoples into one. After the brief span of a hundred years, under David and his illustrious son, Solomon, they were willing to meet the future on different paths. Jeroboam made the separation thorough. Not only did he break the ties which bound the Israelites to the north to the throne of David and Solomon, he led them back to their old religion, away from the temple and Yahweh. The Levites who were in the north were forced to go back to Judah and Jerusalem because Jeroboam refused to let them remain as priests of Yahweh in his domain. He set up golden bulls at Dan and Bethel, and in this form restored the god of fertilty Israel had known for centuries. The old gods apparently came back to power and Yahweh seemed to be forgotten. In reality conditions were not as dark as they appeared to be. A gloomy prophet of a later generation, lamenting his loneliness, could be assured that there were thousands of loyal Yahweh devotees who had never bowed the knee to Ba'al. The rebellion of Jeroboam was only a temporary reverse for Yahweh, not a final defeat. Judah remained faithful. The prophets assumed the task of winning Israel back to their God.

Elijah, early in the ninth century, was the most spectacular champion of Yahweh's rights to the northern kingdom. On two major issues he daringly defied the ruling monarch in the name of his God, careless of the sovereign's threats to his personal safety. Although the scripture writers heaped abuse upon his name, King Ahab was certainly friendly to Yahweh in the same manner that he recognized the value of the local gods and, as a wise statesman, made alliances with the gods of other nations. He was especially considerate of the Ba'al of Tyre, the god of his wife's people. Hundreds of official seers approved of his political wisdom, but the spokesman of Yahweh was irreconcilable. When drought threatened the land with famine, Elijah made a dramatic challenge to the Ba'alim to match their might against the power of Yahweh, won a victory over the priests of Ba'al, and vindicated the superiority of his God as a rain and fertility giver.

Not only was Yahweh jealous for his own status, but he was also unable to forgive a king's autocratic infringement of democratic rights. When Ahab, aided by his scheeming queen, Jezebel, ruthlessly removed the owner of a coveted vineyard to increase his royal holdings, the voice of Elijah thundered disapproval. In this social crisis involving injustice and a violation of the accepted mores of Israel, the resentment against Jezebel and her foreign Ba'al burst into flaming rebellion. The treacherous Jehu, driving to power through rivers of blood in his revolt against the family of Ahab, was able to enlist the Rechabites and the prophetic champions of Yahweh in support of his designs, because he identified his program with the warfare of Yahweh against the Ba'alim. Elisha's messenger anointed him for his blood-drenched campaign. Rebellion, deceit, and slaughter were as nothing when weighed against the victory of Yahweh over the older, rival deities.

As the generations passed, the embattled prophets established their God as the supreme Ba'al of the land of Palestine. Gradually he assumed all the functions of the local fertility figures, adding the farming cults to his own. Yet Yahweh, as the conservatives knew him, was too austere to be associated with some of the essential, sensual rites of the new cult. Consequently the lure of the local deities long remained to trouble the peace of the prophets. When Yahweh condescended to take up the burden of farming, drove the Ba'alim from their altars, and became himself the source of fertility, wealth, and prosperity in the land, he gained unquestioned right to supremacy not only because of his victorious power, long known to Israel, but also because of his effective usefulness in their new cultural life. The first great issue of adjustment and growth was successfully passed. Other gods had their recognized places in the sun, but from this time onward no god was able to match his might in Palestine or, without his permission, to touch the tablets of destiny of his people. Yahweh ruled as Lord of the dual kingdoms of Israel and Judah.

After the destructive storm of Jehu's rebellion had passed, several generations of peace and prosperity permitted both Israel and Judah to test the social worth of their new civilization. The prophets, who kept their love for the simpler, democratic life of the past, saw their worst fears fulfilled. With the increase of wealth came sordid evils of social maladjustment—injustice, oppression of the poor, exploitation of the lowlier classes by officials and aristocrats. Love of luxury weakened the moral fiber of the wealthy, love of money led to corruption of the courts, perversion of justice and cruel indifference to the suffering of the dispossessed. The rich grew richer and the poor sank ever more deeply into wretchedness and frustration. Worst of all, the privileged classes attributed their wealth and prosperity to the favor of Yahweh because they had been careful in the correct performance of all required rites and sacrifices. This was the philosophy beneath the fertility cults which the Israelites had learned from the farming folk who knew the ways of the gods of the land. As the giver of agricultural fertility and prosperity, Yahweh was in danger of being drawn completely into the pattern of the Ba'alim. The old deities still lingered in the countryside. In many places Yahweh was only a new name for old familiar friends of the farmers. Cults which shocked the early prophets continued, but under the new leadership of Israel's God. Although the official records ignore it, in at least one locality Yahweh, like all the other fertility figures, seems to have been provided with a wife, Anath. Under the pressure of the cultural climate, he was in danger of being firmly bound to the soil of Palestine and reduced to the character of a local Ba'al, whose favor was witnessed by his bounty and who could be managed by sacrificial technique.

Yahweh was rescued from this drift into oblivion by the great prophets of the eighth and seventh centuries. Heirs of the wandering bands of Yahweh's spokesmen of earlier times, these men had a wide outlook and deep religious vision developed by the growth of the nation and the broadening of political horizons. Inspired individually to take up the prophetic task by the call of God, they were not bound by institutional traditions or the conventions of the established priesthood. The prestige of their divine calling gave them access to the court and the private councils of the rulers. Since their burning words carried the authority of the will of Yahweh, even kings dared not challenge their freedom of speech.

These bold idealists were men immersed in the practical problems of the day. They watched the increase of injustice in social life, remembering Yahweh's relationship to the democratic tribal ideals of an earlier age. Jealousy for the God as they knew him burned like a flame in their souls. They could not close their hearts to the cry of the shepherdless poor at home, nor their eyes to the danger which threatened from beyond the border. The exploitation of the small landholders, the oppression of the poor, the arrogance and luxurious living of the rich, the smug complacency of the official classes in the presence of impending national disaster, moved them to passionate protest. The anger and anguish of the dispossessed flowed into eloquent words of warning, reinforced by the confident formula—"Thus saith Yahweh." While the ruling classes in Israel basked in the warmth of prosperity, the prophets were aware of the oncoming shadow of doom behind which moved the irresistible might of Assyria. Wrestling with these issues, they transformed their God.

They stripped away all the entanglements of sacrificial ritualism woven around him by the Ba'al cults. In forthright words Yahweh spoke through Amos:

> I hate, I spurn your feasts,
> And I take no pleasure in your festal gatherings.
> Even though you offer me burnt-offerings,
> And your cereal-offerings, I will not accept them;
> And the thank-offerings of your fatted beasts I will not look upon.
> Take away from me the noise of your songs,
> And to the melody of your lyres I will not listen.
> But let justice roll down like waters,
> And righteousness like a perennial stream. (Amos 5:21–24)

The prophets could not but believe that Yahweh was concerned with justice, not sacrifice, with righteousness rather than ritual. They identified his will with the needful social ideals. He became a just and righteous God. In his name they hurled their condemnation against the licentious rich who sold the innocent for silver, and the needy for a pair of shoes; who tramped upon the heads of the poor and thrust aside the humble from the way; who crowded the lowly householder from his ancestral acres; and who bribed judges in their own interests. The officials were so very careful in the performance of cult duty that they travelled from Dan to Beersheba lest some ceremony might be slighted. For the Ba'alim such service was essential; for Yahweh it was mere futility; since he desired mercy, not sacrifice, a listening heart not the fat of rams.

> With what shall I come before Yahweh,
> And bow myself before God most high?
> Shall I come before him with burnt offerings,
> With calves a year old?
> Will Yahweh be pleased with thousands of rams,
> With myriads of streams of oil?
> Shall I give my first-born for my transgression,.
> The fruit of my body for the sin of my soul?
> You have been told, O man, what is good,
> And what Yahweh requires of you:
> Only to do justice, and to love kindness,
> And to walk humbly with your God. (Mic. 6:6-8)

He sought only social values, actualized. The prohets made his meaning plain:

> Cease to do evil, learn to do good;
> Seek justice, restrain the oppressor:
> Uphold the rights of the orphan, defend the cause of the widow! (Isa. 1.17)

This was a very different Yahweh from the God of ruthless might whom the early prophets knew and again different from the fertility figures, lulled to social insensibility by the sensuous, sacrificial spells. The lightning of his fierce anger flamed against social evils. He was still a God of terrible power but also the embodiment of the moral attributes of the noblest, human ideal. Many gods of old were lost when, in similar social crises, they could not grow to the needful moral heights. They had no prophets so they died.

Even all Yahweh's splendid achievement of moral grandeur would not have been enough to save him, amid the storms of the following centuries, if his wise seers had not found a way to break the bonds which fettered him to the land of Palestine. Overwhelmed in the wars of empire, scores of gods have met their doom. Some of them are remembered still because their names are recorded on documents that have outlived them; others are gone, to be forever forgotten unless by chance the spade of the excavator turns up their names in some old ruin. A god who loses his land and his people fades slowly from the memory of men. Yahweh faced this threat for the first time when the northern kingdom vanished from history in 721 B.C.

During the eighth century the prophets of Israel had watched with apprehension the growing threat of Assyrian power. They saw no escape from the disaster, but they had a burning faith in Yahweh. If doom came to the people it could not be through any weakness of their God but because they had broken their covenant, turned away from him to follow the false philosophy of fertility; because the masters of Israel had turned their faces against the poor and the land groaned under the burden of social evils.

> Israel is a spreading vine;
> His fruit renders him confident;
> The more his fruit increased,
> The more altars he made;
> The more prosperous his land became,
> The finer he did make his sacred pillars.
> Their heart is false; soon must they atone;
> Their altars shall be desecrated,
> And their sacred pillars destroyed. (Hos. 10:1-)

Therefore the long-awaited "Day of Yahweh" was to be a day of darkness and desolation, not of gladness and light. The harbingers of doom, the bearers of punishment were the peoples of foreign gods.

> O Assyria, rod of my anger,
> And staff of my fury!
> Against a godless nation I send him,
> And against the people of my wrath I charge him,
> To despoil them, and prey on them,
> And to trample them down like mire of the streets. (Isa. 10:5-6)

Long and patiently Yahweh had pleaded for repentance and warned of the destruction to come—all to no avail. The king of Assyria flaunted his might as he marched to deal the death blow to Israel, but the prophets knew that Yahweh was commanding him, using him as the instrument of his purpose. Thus an unconquerable faith, interpreting an historic tragedy, lifted Yahweh to a position of authority on the world stage and gave him status above foreign gods, even while they were trampling upon Yahweh's own people.

Instead of destroying Yahweh's prestige, the loss of the northern kingdom served rather to magnify his power and moral grandeur. At the same time it broke the first link of his bondage to the land. As the first Isaiah contemplated the doom of Israel he dared to hope that whatever might befall the nation,

Yahweh would always cherish the pious, nonpolitical community of faithful ones. When, a century and a half later, Judah fell before the destructive might of Babylon, the pattern of faith, which had saved Yahweh in the earlier crisis, gave him complete emancipation from limitations to the boundaries of a political state. In this achievement the faith of the prophets was supported by other factors in Israel's experience. Yahweh had dwelt outside Palestine before he adopted them as his people. Long after the settlement in Canaan, he was consulted at his holy mountain in the south land. He had worshipers in other lands, and Elijah assumed that he had power in Syria. After 933 B.C., when Judah and Israel were separate and often at war, Yahweh, who claimed authority over both, transcended political boundaries. Moreover, he was the God of a people before he became the God of Canaan. When he rose in moral splendor over the ruins of his late earthly kingdom, he was prepared, as the God of a people, to begin his career as God of the world.

From the beginning Israel had known Yahweh as a God of power. His might was magnified when he strode onto the international stage. Always jealous of his people, he had never willingly shared their devotion with any foreign god. The legend of Moses on Sinai dramatized his sanction of the moral law. Sole master of Israel's destiny, righteous and powerful, he had been willing to let the tides of destruction overwhelm his experiment in nation-building rather than tolerate desertion to other gods or disloyalty to human values. He loved his people and punished them. After this age of suffering, Israel never doubted that Yahweh was holy and righteous, a jealous guardian of the moral law.

The brief period of the Exile and the three centuries that followed were a time of severe testing for the people of Israel. The thread of their unity was unravelled into separate strands. Only a fraction of the population followed their conquerors unwillingly to Babylon. The larger part remained in the home land. Some fled to Egypt. From Palestine, toward all points of the compass, paths were luring ever larger numbers of Jews to the Mediterranean cities, to farther Europe, through the Near East and on to the far-off Orient. Israel and Yahweh had already begun their cosmopolitan career.

The new conditions worked a significant change in Yahweh. He bowed to hear the cry of the lonely individual. When the enfoldment of national solidarity was stripped away from the people, and the temple with its great ceremonies was no more, the security which gathered everyone into a common destiny and responsibility was lost. Without the old familiar ways of communications with the august Yahweh, whose concern had not been with individuals but with the ongoing nation, solitary souls were left to wander shepherdless. Ezekiel and Jeremiah met the need by lifting the common man to a place of personal responsibility to his God. While the wanderers sought consolation in glorious dreams, Yahweh took into his care the personal destinies of lowly folk.

During many generations, discouragement and hope alternated in the hearts of the faithful. The humiliation of the Exile was followed by a glowing enthusiasm when Cyrus seemed to be an agent of Israel's God. The great king, however, was no more favorable to the Jews than to his other subject peoples. Rejoicing at the return and the rebuilding of the temple ended in disillusionment, and the deep frustration of a conquered nation made restless by the memory of a splendid dream. The later Persian rulers were loyal to Ahura Mazda and were little inclined to foster ambitions in the minds of the people of Yahweh. When Alexander the Great took the Jews under his protecting power, Israel's hope flamed up again.

As in earlier centuries, a faithful group of daring dreamers brought Yahweh triumphantly through this time of changing fortunes. Among the Babylonian exiles and in Palestine there were seers who stubbornly refused to accept defeat. Tearful lamentations over their desolate lot served only as a foil for their bold faith in the power of their God to save. Faith flowered out of frustration. To their unconquered spirits a "must be" seemed truer and more real than an "is." Although his nation was in servitude, Yahweh must be the greatest of the gods and he must be able to guarantee a future for Israel so glorious that all other deities would become mere nothings before him. The threat of other gods was very real. Yahweh had rivals not only in the great heaven gods, Zeus and Ahura Mazda, but also in the lesser local deities so comforting to the common man. Many in the Exile were captured by the glamorous gods of Babylon. The Jews who wandered to Egypt yielded to the ways of the land, worshipped Yahweh but also gods and goddesses as his companions. In Palestine the people turned to the friendly figures of the countryside, some with names as old as history and some newcomers—Hadad, Moloch, Atargatis, and the Goddess of Fortune. In this atmosphere of discouragement and frustration the later prophets molded the character of Yahweh in its classical form.

All limitations fell away from him. He became the one and only God of heaven and earth. He spread out the heavens as a tent to dwell in, gave the stars their names, and guided their wanderings. Before him all the princes of the earth were as nothing. He watched in eternal calm the wind-blown dust of human generations. All other gods were merely empty names, helpless idols, powerless and futile to help their supplicants, but they who call upon Yahweh

> Shall renew their strength,
> They shall put forth wings like eagles,
> They shall run and not be weary,
> They shall walk and not faint. (Isa. 40:31)

In their exaltation of Yahweh the prophets of this period gave to Western culture one of its basic beliefs—that a divine plan undergirds the universe, that a divine purpose runs through time. With the far-seeing eyes of hope they saw the will of Yahweh as the thread of meaning on which all the events of history were strung. At the end will be the ideal kingdom of a restored Israel. Yahweh will then make bare his almighty arm; in the eyes of all the nations. His people are now afflicted and despised but they need not fear. Yahweh's love for Israel is beyond all human love. If he causes the faithful ones to pass through the fires of affliction, it is only that as God's suffering servant they may bear the world's woe and manifest the greatness, goodness, and holiness of Yahweh to all the earth and so draw all mankind to Israel's God. When his purpose is fulfilled through the faithfulness of his people, the day of Yahweh will break in splendor on a startled world. Then all nature will smile upon man. Justice and peace will dwell on the earth. From east and west, north and south, Yahweh will call the wanderers home to Zion. There they may sit secure in the shade of vine and fig tree with no one to make them afraid ever again.

Yahweh thus became master of the world's destiny, sole God, all-powerful and wise, holding the fates of all nations in his hands but giving a special place in the cosmic plan to his chosen people.

The wise and mighty Yahweh, sole ruler of the universe, throned in the celestial heights, was not left lonely in his heavenly splendor. He was surrounded by a radiant company of angels. The seers of Israel knew of old these messengers of the divine will who appeared on earth in human form. When they were brought into contact with Babylonian and Persian mythologies and envisioned the imposing majesty of earthly courts, they delighted to picture in imagination the glory of Yahweh's heavenly palace, the lofty throne, and his innumerable celestial ministers in their graded ranks. The angelic retinue numbered many millions. They were ethereal beings, not immaterial, but of a fiery substance, blazing like light. Death could not touch them. Only the fiat of God could snap the thread of their immortal existence. This heavenly host, surrounding the throne, executed the divine will in the world. They regulated the heavenly bodies and the rhythm of nature. An angel of princely rank ruled the sea. Rain, dew, frost, snow, hail, thunder and lightning were in angelic control. Nations had their ambassadors in Yahweh's court. In the work of providence, revelation, and punishment, the angels mediated the divine decrees. The pen of the recording angel set down indelibly the deeds of mortals. Silently among his companions moved the dark angel of death. As was natural in royal courts, there was often rivalry, as angelic ministers strove to influence their royal master to favor and forgive their beloved nations and individuals. It was a glorious company who served the celestial throne. They were dear to the hearts of the men who created them. Yahweh was drawn into intimate contact with earthly affairs by these humanlike angelic messengers. If they threatened the unity of the one God of Israel, they humanized his transcendent majesty and suffused his decrees with grace and glamor.

After the mighty will of Yahweh, which controlled the course of world history, was extended to the care of human life, a problem emerged to threaten belief in his goodness and justice. Since the individual was directly responsible for his deeds, it seemed reasonable that the wicked should suffer and that the good man should be the happy man. Life, however, presented a very different picture. The wicked were seen to flourish like the green bay tree while the man of virtue and moral integrity dragged out his days in pain and desolation. Job and his friends wrestled with this problem. The difficulty was more acute because the idea of resurrection had not yet emerged and it was not possible to justify the ways of Yahweh by balancing the scales in a better world to come. Satan was there, but he was not allowed to assume in full the role of his prototype, Ahriman, to relieve the good God from embarrassment. The answer dropped a veil of human humility between the secrets of the Almighty and the probing eyes of man's reason by asserting that Yahweh's knowledge was too high for human understanding. Since man cannot know he must trust. Faith, the good physician, furnished the medicine which gave surcease from pain and rest in glowing dreams. Many another god besides Yahweh has been rescued from the unsolved problem of evil by ackowledgment of man's ignorance and the wedding of resignation to hope.

When the stimulating atmosphere of Greek thought spread over the Near East, Yahweh faced the danger that has confronted the gods of all cultures when they have fallen into the hands of the philosophers. Unlike so many others, he refused to be reduced to an abstraction. The practical sense of his people kept him vitally bound to a purposive, ongoing, historic process of which the goal was still unrealized. No timeless, ineffable abstraction could meet the needs of Israel's hope. Yet there was real danger, for a time, of a radical transformation of his nature which would have removed him from immediate contact with the human scene to a transcendent realm, shrouded in mystery, impenetrable by the power of man. The Palestinian and Alexandrian Apocrypha, the Septuagint translation of the scriptures, and the Wisdom literature all toned down or eliminated the early vigorous imagery which pictured Yahweh with human form and qualities. Thought began to strip him of attributes, and to open a vast distance between him and lowly man. As the one transcendent being, dwelling in solitary splendor, responsible to himself alone, his essence never perfectly knowable, Yahweh was moving toward the formless realm of no return, but his anchorage in history would not let him go. That he was one and transcendent no one any longer doubted, but he was also king of the heavens, creator, ruler and righteous judge, everywhere present, all-wise, touching the earth by his providence in justice, mercy, loving kindness, long suffering, and the forgiveness of sins. He was the Lord of heaven but he was at the same time the Father of his children.

The personal name, Yahweh, acquired a sanctity, a sacred power, so that only specially qualified individuals were permitted to pronounce it. In reading the scriptures, *Adonai* (Lord) was substituted for the sacred name. It was avoided in speech by the use of such expressions as God, the Almighty, the Most High, or the Holy One.

During the Hellenistic period, men of simple faith clung to the Yahweh of tradition with all his human qualities and his love for Israel, while the intellectuals continued to stress his ineffable transcendence and to tone down his meaningful attributes. When they had placed him on heights only attainable by pure thought, it was necessary to introduce a mediator. This service was performed by Wisdom, paralleling the Greek idea of the Logos. The Wisdom of God was no mere angel but the spirit of Yahweh himself, his companion in creation, the assessor at his throne, who brought God's personal presence into intimate relation with all the events of time. Thus the world was warmed by the radiant nearness of divine Wisdom, linking the earth and the awful, transcendent God. Although this mediating power was personal and in some manner distinct from God, the unity of Yahweh was so fiercely defended in Israel that there was never any danger of his falling into the Hellenistic or Christian pattern, with two persons in the one godhead.

What might have happened if Yahweh had been exposed to the full impact of Greek philosophy is illustrated by the picture of him presented by a devout Jew who was also immersed in the heritage of Athens. Philo of Alexandria was the first Jewish thinker to feel that the existence of Good needed to be proved. For Philo the philosopher, God was the first cause, a self-determining mind, his essence forever beyond human understanding. He was without qualities, beyond all the conditions of space and time, incorporeal and transcendent. For Philo the Jew, Yahweh possessed all the attributes his Jewish heritage demanded—benevolence, perfection, omnipresesnt providential care, omniscience, and goodness. Between the ultimately unknowable God and the world, he placed mediating divine powers who shared the mystery and wisdom of the Lord. Chief of these powers was the Logos, unbegotten, eternal Son of God, second in the divine hierarchy. If Judaism had followed the lead of Philo there would have been little to differentiate Yahweh from the God of the early Christians, but Israel's God remained safely guarded in the memory and hopes of his people. . . .

Part Two

Intellectual Currents and Themes

Introduction

The essays included in this section deal with the intellectual and religious dimensions of Hellenistic Judaism.

Still monotheistic in outlook, the Jews of the Diaspora were nonetheless given to speculation about the existence of subordinate deities (angels), the establishment of God's power over the kingdoms of the world in the person of his anointed delegate, the Messiah (Gk., *Christos*), and the ideological alternative, God's judgment of the world by his appointed agent, the Son of Man. Projections of the time and signs of the kingdom and discussion of the marks of the Messiah were a pastime in the rabbinical Judaism of Jesus' day. It is no wonder that his gospel of the kingdom—identical in form, apparently, with that of the hermit, John the Baptist—occasioned the belief that Jesus himself had been the chosen one of God (Matt. 26:63-64).

In the memory of the early Christian community Jesus had himself made predictions—or, more precisely, promises—about the coming of the day of the Lord. According to Mark's account, Jesus "foresaw" the destruction of the Temple (Mark 13:2-3)—doubtless already past history when the Gospel was written—and responded to his followers' questions about the time of the eschaton (end-time). A critical reading of the Gospels indicates that there was widespread concern in the Christian cult over the delay in God's judgment of the nations, coupled with concern about the delay in Jesus' reappearance *(parousia)* as the Son of Man and judge. It may seem at first glance that the disappointment of the community—the empirical disconfirmation of its hopes—would have had the immediate effect of destroying their faith. The *Kyrios* (Lord, Paul's perferred designation for Jesus) had been crucified and had not yet confirmed the beliefs of his followers by returning in glory with an army of angels. To an almost unrealized extent, the Gospels are written with this disappointment in view; not only this, but the Jesus they portray is a Jesus who offers words of comfort and consolation to a community obliged to rationalize its discomfort in the absence of vindication and to defend its faith in the heat of controversy with Jewish teachers and pagan philosophers.

The Gospels are written therefore with the hope of the community at stake: "Tell us," the disciples (speaking with the voice of the Christians of Mark's day) say to Jesus: "When will all these things happen—what signs will appear before they begin?" Speaking with the pastoral self-assurance of a second-century priest, Jesus is given to say that there will be false Messiahs, wars and rumors of wars, famines and earthquakes and general disorder (Mark 13:5-6). The elasticity of such predictions, as their longevity suffices to show, made them suitable for almost any time and provenance, and Jesus' declaration that, even though the days grew short (Mark 13:20) no one, not even the Son of Man, knew exactly the time of the end (Mark 13:32-33), enhanced the certainty that eschaton, though slow to materialize, would still be witnessed by God's elect. The delay of the Lord, the reasoning went, had been foretold by the Lord himself (Mark 13:23).

Apocalyptic thought is the ideological link between Judaism and Christianity. The latter movement, as a Jewish heresy, radicalized certain themes (for example, the divinity and preexistence of the Son of Man) that rabbinical Judaism would officially discredit. Nonetheless, the material expectations of the early Christians, their naive hope that Jesus would come again, that he would judge them as saints, that he would penalize nonbelievers for refusing the Gospel, that on the last day the dead would leave their graves and appear before God's throne—all of these beliefs have points of contact in the speculative Judaism of the first century and in scripture. To mention only the most obvious case, belief in the physical resurrection of the dead was not the teaching of the Christians only, but the official teaching of the Pharisees, whose doctrine Jesus espouses in his controversy with the Sadducean party—"those who say there is no resurrection" (Mark 12:18 ff.). Since the question of the resurrection of the dead was a major theological sticking point in first-century Judaism, one is not surprised to find a radical apocalyptic movement embracing the doctrine as a means of supporting its belief in the return of the Messiah.

T. H. Robinson

The Hope for a Messiah

THEODORE H. ROBINSON was born in 1881 and educated at the universities of Cambridge (Litt.D.) and London (D.D.). His wide-ranging interests in Near Eastern and biblical studies made him one of the most respected Old Testament scholars of his day. His works include *Palestine in General History* (1929), *The Decline and Fall of the Hebrew Kingdoms* (1930), *Hebrew Religion: Its Origin and Development* (with W. O. E. Oesterley, 1937), and commentaries on the Gospel of Matthew (1928) and the Epistle to the Hebrews (1933).

THE EARLIER STAGES OF MESSIANIC HOPE

Kingship and deity are often found in close association. There are, indeed, many early forms of religion in which the "king" is the principal god of the tribe or locality, and the welfare of the whole community is thought to be centered in him. Thus he must be protected from every form of evil, for, if disaster befall him, the whole body must suffer. It often happens that if the king grows weak or old, he is violently removed, and a younger or stronger person is installed in his place. In the higher cultures of Egypt and Mesopotamia, the theory **was** not carried to quite the extreme at which it appears among some more primitive peoples, but in Egypt the king was the son of a god, while in Babylonia he stood in a

From *Hebrew Religion: Its Origins and Development* by T. H. Robinson and W. O. E. Oesterley (London: Society for the Promotion of Christian Knowledge, 1937), pp. 375-385, 388-396. Copyright © 1937. Reprinted by permission of the publisher.

special relation to the deity. It has been supposed that a similar theory of the king as a divine being was to be found also in Israel, but direct evidence is lacking, and the intensely strong "democratic" instincts of the Hebrew people make it improbable that this view was ever seriously held. It is, however, not impossible that the king played the role of the deity in certain types of dramatic ceremonial, and the fact that he had been "anointed" made his person sacrosanct.

We are, then, not surprised to find that the king played a part in the eschatological speculation of Egypt, Assyria, and Babylonia. "Eschatology," it is true, must not be interpreted in too narrow a sense. There was no thought of a distant future; what men hoped for was an immediate return of a golden age, in which all wrong should be righted, and all pain and evil give way to happiness and well-being. We find in Egyptian literature, for instance, poems in honor of various kings, in which the singer quoted an ancient prophecy (probably fictitious), and claimed that the monarch he was celebrating was about to fulfill the ancient dream. A parallel may be found in Virgil's adulation of Augustus, and it is a natural mode of expression for a court poet. We may, then, look for similar views in ancient Israel, though they will necessarily be modified by the characteristic political and religious thought of the Hebrew people. More than once we find expressions in certain Psalms which suggest the lengths to which even an Old Testament poet could go. Thus in Psalm 2:7 ff., the king quotes a divine decree of adoption, which gives him the authority of Yahweh, and a world-wide dominion. Psalm 72 is a prayer for a monarch who is just ascending the throne, and Psalm 110 is a description of the triumph secured for a king by Yahweh.

In passages like these Psalms, however, we seldom have reference to the great and catastrophic events which we usually associate with eschatology. And when we come to consider the characteristic Jewish apocalyptic literature, we find that, in its earlier forms, there is no reference to a human ruler, or even to a human agent of Yahweh, as he recreates the world. A typical apocalypse of this early type is to be found in Isaiah 24-27, where it is Yahweh alone who wins the great triumph, and whose accession to universal power is celebrated with feasting and with song. In the strict sense of the term, the messianic hope had a long history before it met and mingled with a stream of eschatology proper, and it is the course of that history which we must endeavor to trace briefly.

The hope of a happy future is a part of the deathless inheritance of humanity. It is but seldom that matters grow to such a pitch of suffering that men believe them to be irremediable, and the worse the state of the people, the stronger becomes the conviction that God will interfere, and the more extravagant the ways in which He will set the world right. At the last extremity men come to hold that the whole universe as we know it will be dissolved, and a new heaven and a new earth created from its shattered fragments. But before this point is reached, there are many stages through which men's hopes and visions pass; most of these have a Messiah of some kind in view.

In the earlier stages of the great hope, men do not contemplate a fundamental change in the established order of things. Society will continue to exist on its present basis, and no far-reaching constitutional revolution is to be expected. The state was naturally organized, for Israel, as a monarchy, and the ideal was that of a perfect king. We have references which may go back as far as the early tenth century, but their date is doubtful and their interpretation uncertain. We find ourselves on safe ground for the first time in Isaiah, and it is to him that we can best carry back the story of the messianic idea.

In the opening verses of Isaiah 32 we have set before us the prospect of an ideal king, who shall be a refuge and a shelter for all who are in need. It is possible that the original utterance comprises only verses 1-5, for the three following verses are vague in tone, and may well have been appended by a later age. One striking result of the perfect reign is the change in human character. The rash learn prudence, the stammering become fluent, and men cease to compare folly and wisdom. We have also a distinct reference to one of the perennial requirements of oriental government: insight and honesty in the administration of justice. In the last resort, in ancient Israel, an appeal always lay to the king, and if he had the ability to see who was speaking the truth and who was not, and if he were righteous and well-disposed, then it would follow that true justice would be exercised in all grades of society. The same thought meets us, still more clearly expressed, in a later passage (Isa. 11:1 ff.), where it is said that the ideal king "shall not judge after the sight of his eyes, nor reprove after the hearing of his ears." In a society where perjury is the rule and not the exception, it is only circumstantial evidence that can be seriously considered—and that is often manufactured. Hence the perfect judge must have remarkable powers of reaching the truth, and it is not surprising to find this qualification set in the forefront.

In Isaiah 9:6–7 occurs the well-known account of the Wonderchild. He is to be endowed with more than ordinary powers, and is to stand in a special relation to Yahweh. The description is much more developed than that of chapter 32:1 ff., and, perhaps, owes something to the older conceptions of popular and courtly messianic theory. We shall probably be right in supposing that the prophet had in mind some actual king, perhaps Hezekiah or even Manasseh, and that his words were uttered on the birth of the young prince. We note here that the reign is inaugurated by sweeping triumph over an oppressor, probably, in the first instance, the Assyrians, and the new king is a mighty warrior, and sage in counsel. Other features appear. His dominion is to spread until it is universal, and it is to be of endless duration. So had Egyptian "prophets" spoken in praise of their kings, for the disappearance of the righteous sovereign might well bring about a return of the bad old customs, and failure to leave some portion of the world's surface unsubdued might mean another conquest and another oppression. Naturally, since the kings under whom Isaiah himself lived and worked were of the house of David, the ideal monarch would also be of that stock, or, at least, he would make David's own city the seat and center of his government. In no small measure the picture here presented served as a model for most of the later messianic speculation.

Davidic ancestry is asserted in another passage which may be pre-exilic, though it is at least a century later than Isaiah. In Jeremiah 23:5 f. we have another brief sketch of the coming ideal king, whose reign is to be marked by justice and prosperity for all Israel. Here, for the first time, we have the metaphor of the "branch," or "shoot" of David. It is possible that the prophet hoped to find his desires fulfilled in Zedekiah, for the coming ruler receives a name which is the reverse of that of the last king of Judah. If that be so, then the passage will belong to the time of Zedekiah's accession, for his name till that point had been Mattaniah (2 Kings 24:17). Though the prophet was to be bitterly disappointed, yet the moment after the shock of Jehoiachin's deportation would be just the situation which would arouse hope. The worst, as it seemed, had happened, and surely now a brighter future must be dawning, a future of which the king's new name appeared symbolic.

From this time onwards Davidic ancestry is one of the normal features of the Messiah. (We can hardly include in a study of Jewish messianic hope such a passage as Isaiah 45:1, where Cyrus is expressly mentioned as the Messiah.) . . . The metaphor of the "branch" is carried still further; though the tree has now been cut down, yet there remains a hidden vitality in the stump which will send out a fresh shoot and restore the life of the tree. As before, the picture is that of the perfect king, but it includes also features which are new in the prophetic messianism. There is, indeed, an apocalyptic tinge in its coloring, for, not only have we the perfect judge and the triumphant conquerer, but a new world comes into being. Nature, and not man alone, is affected by the new reign; she is no longer "red in tooth and claw." All the lust, greed, and cruelty of the nonmoral world have vanished, the carnivorous animals have ceased to eat flesh, all alike are gentle and amenable to the mildest control, and the very cobra is almost a fit plaything for the babe at the breast. Behind this vision of loveliness and peace on earth there lies a spiritual cause; "the earth shall be full of the knowledge of Yahweh, as the waters cover the sea," and, once more, it is not man alone who has this link with God, but the humbler creation also.

Other passages, coming from the same general period, do not carry us so far. Ezekiel (34:22 ff. and 37:15 ff.) holds that a time will come when all the exiles of Israel will be restored, and Judah and Israel shall be united under the leadership of a single "shepherd." An era of freedom, dominion and prosperity will then ensue, and the new "prince" will be another David—or perhaps the original David restored to earth. In the isolated verse, Isaiah 10:10, it is the universality of the messianic kingdom which is in view, and in Amos 11-12, the power of the coming scion of the restored house of David is to be manifested particularly in the punishment of Edom. We may suspect that we have here a repercussion of the events of the exilic period, during which Edomites pressed into Palestine in numbers. Micah 5:2-4 stresses the eternity and universality of the kingdom, and names Bethlehem as the place whence the Messiah derives his origin. Though the usual interpretation is that the birthplace of the Messiah is intended, the language used may mean no more than that he will be of the house of David.

We may also note the late verse Jeremiah 33:17, which, again, insists on the eternal duration of the restored dominion of the house of David.

It seems not unlikely that the identification of the coming king with a member of David's family was already current at the close of the Exile. Once, at least, within the Old Testament period, the prophetic spirit dared to acclaim as the Messiah a son of David who actually held authority in the land. One of the earliest of the governors of the restored community, appointed by the Persian court, was Zerubbabel, a grandson of Jehoiachin. His personality and his fate have been the subject of a good deal of study and speculation in recent years, but we still cannot say that much is known of him for certain. He is described as the leader of a band of returning exiles, apparently not the first to take advantage of the decree of Cyrus, and he was the builder of the second Temple. There is ground also for the suspicion that he attempted the building of the walls of Jerusalem, but the evidence, though uncertain and confused, suggests that this project was never fully carried out. We have, however, further light on him from the utterances of Haggai and of Zechariah. The book which bears the name of the former closes with a distinctly messianic passage, in which a complete overthrow of the existing political world-order is contemplated, and Zerubbabel is to be made a "signet." The word obviously implies some very close association with Yahweh, and it is possible that it was one of the less common terms in the vocabulary of messianic thought, for we read in Jeremiah 22:24 that, though Jehoiachin were the "signet" on the right hand of Yahweh, he would yet be plucked thence and handed over to Nebuchadrezzar. It is clear that there is some special significance in the word, and it is not unnatural to suppose that even the messiahship—not mere kingship, but the highest possible form of kingship—would not save Jehoiachin from his doom. In Zechariah, however, the messianic position assigned to Zerubbabel is even clearer than in Haggai. The prophet takes the old title of "branch," which, as we have seen, was used in this technical sense even before the fall of Jerusalem, and applies it to the Jewish governor. In chapter 3 we have the familiar vision in which Joshua, the high priest contemporary with Zerubbabel, was arraigned by Satan before Yahweh and acquitted. The judgment of the divine court concludes with the promise: "Behold I will bring forth my servant the branch" (Zech. 3:8). Still clearer is the reference in 6:9 ff. Two crowns of gold are made, to be set on the head of Joshua the high priest. It is generally recognized that the text is deficient here (probably deliberately mutilated), and that one crown was original, and that destined for Zerubbabel. For the passage continues: "Thus speaketh Yahweh of hosts, saying, Behold the man whose name is the branch; and he shall grow up (literally: shall branch out) out of his place, and he shall build the Temple of the Lord, and he shall bear the glory, and shall sit and rule upon his throne, and a priest shall be upon his throne; and the counsel of peace shall be between them" (Zech. 4:6). The conclusion is inevitable; the builder of the Temple was to receive a royal position, independent of foreign rulers, and was to share the government of the country with the "head of the Church," that is, the high priest. This civil authority can be none other than

Zerubbabel himself, and it is clear that the prophet looked to him for the restoration, not only of the Temple, but also of the independent Jewish state and empire.

It is in the light of this identification of Zerubabbel with the expected Messiah that we must read much of the work of Zechariah. The task is to be accomplished by superhuman means: "Not by might, nor by power, but by my spirit, saith Yahweh of hosts" (Zech. 6:12-13). Jerusalem itself is to be so safe a place that men shall live in it to great old age, and, at the same time, the streets of the city shall be full of playing children (Zech. 8:4-5). The coming prosperity shall at least balance all the affliction that the country has suffered in recent generations, and the place shall become the religious center, not only for all Jews, but for every nation on the face of the earth.

We do not know what fate befell Zerubbabel, but it is not unlikely that, in the general settlement which occupied the early years of Darius' reign, he was removed, and may have met with a violent end. But the messianic hope survived him, and Israel still looked for a deliverer, human indeed, but yet carrying with him the power of Yahweh himself. There are many passages of exilic and post-exilic date which are sometimes regarded as messianic, especially, perhaps, the "Servant Songs" in Isaiah 40-55, but it seems probable that they ought not to be so interpreted, and that their messianic significance is due to later reflection, Jewish and Christian. An exception may be made in the case of Zechariah 9:9-11, where the Messiah appears riding in triumph into Jerusalem, there to inaugurate his universal reign of peace. But, for fuller development of the conception, we must pass on to the last two centuries before Christ.

THE MESSIAN IN APOCALYPTIC

As we have already seen, the conception of the Messiah, or ideal king, for many centuries maintained an existence independent of eschatology proper. It is necessary to emphasize this point, since in common speech the term *messianic* is often applied to the ideal state in which the universal convulsions of the Apocalypse always end. We need not doubt that the thought of a Messiah lived long in Israel, or that it played its part in the *tout ensemble* of religious belief, but it was only at a comparatively late stage in pre-Christian Judaism that the two streams of thought were combined.

Apocalyptic is always the product of distress, and reaches its greatest heights only when the situation seems desperate from the human point of view. Then God *must* step in, and, in his own ways, by methods to which man's experience furnishes no parallel, destroy Evil and install Good in its place. The Persian period of Jewish history, and the first part of the Greek period (during which Palestine was under Ptolemaic rule), were a time of comparative peace and prosperity, save for such isolated incidents as the invasion of Artaxerxes Ochus. But with the passing of Palestine into the hands of the Seleucids, early in the second century B.C., there came a change. Greek modes of thought and life became popular, especially in certain quarters; factions arose, the orthodox and the liberal parties drifting ever further into mutual hostility and hatred; and Antiochus IV threw himself with passionate earnestness into the struggle. The age of persecution which ended with the Maccabean triumph inevitably provided a fresh stimulus to eschatological speculation, and the impulse was sufficiently strong to make apocalyptic the characteristic form of Jewish religious literature until the fall of the second Temple, A.D. 70.

But, once more, apocalyptic could, and did, exist apart from the messianic hope. There is no mention of a Messiah in the one pre-Maccabean Apocalypse we have—Enoch 12-36. An ideal kingdom is established, it is true, but it is God himself who dwells in the midst of his people. Similarly we find no Messiah in Enoch 91-104, 1 and 2 Maccabees, or in any of the apocryphal books except 2 (4) Esdras, and even there his figure is absent from the Apocalypse contained in chapters 3-10, which dates from about A.D. 100. No Messiah is mentioned in the Assumption of Moses, the Slavonic Enoch, 4 Maccabees, or in the Apocalypse of Baruch. Wherever, in these books, an ideal kingdom is contemplated, the king is God himself, conquering and ruling directly, without the aid of any intermediary, human or superhuman.

The one extensive piece of apocalyptic writing in the Old Testament is the Book of Daniel, and in 7:13-14 we read of one "like a son of man," i.e., of human form, who appears after the Ancient of Days has won his triumph. He comes on the clouds of heaven, approaches the Ancient of Days, and receives a royal authority which knows no limits of space or time. While it is sometimes held that he is a personificaton of Israel as a whole, it is at least possible, even probable, that he is conceived as a superhuman individual, who gathers into his own person all the powers, qualities, and functions of the ancient Messiah.

But, for the most part, even when a Messiah appears, he comes as a mere man, though with extraordinary powers and authority. In some of the many varied forms of Apocalypse he stands curiously apart from the final consummation of eschatological hopes. The old instinct, which kept asunder the conceptions of an ideal human king and a finally reconstructed world-order, is still at work, and there is hardly an instance in the post-Maccabean Jewish apocalyptic where the two are combined, though there is still room for a Messiah in a spiritual new world which shall know no end.

We thus find a tendency to develop a doctrine of a temporary messiahship, a rule on earth of the ideal king, as a penultimate stage in the apocalyptic process. It is even categorically stated that the Messiah shall die, and that his departure is the signal for the inauguration of the final stage. The duration of his reign on earth is fixed at 400 or 1000 years, and even where it is not fixed, it is assumed that it will come to an end. For Judaism had abandoned the prophetic hope of an ideal kingdom on earth, and with it the conception of an everlasting messianic reign.

Yet often the Messiah plays his part, as a human figure who is, nevertheless, in a special sense a divine agent. His character and functions, however, are variously conceived. Usually, where his ancestry is mentioned, he is of the house of David, or, at least, of the tribe of Judah, but, in one instance in the Testaments of the Twelve Patriarchs, he is a Levite—perhaps a reminiscence of the Maccabean heroes. In one passage he comes from the east; both here and in many other places he appears as a conqeuring warrior who destroys the wicked. But, at other times, he is introduced and enthroned only after the great victory has been won, and the world lies subject beneath the feet of God.

One independent and original presentation deserves special mention, that of the Similitudes of Enoch. Here the Messiah is of no human ancestry; he is not even a son of David. Among the titles applied to him is that of Son of Man; it would seem that the writer has taken it from the passage in the Book of Daniel already cited. He comes as judge of angels and of men, and is possessed in the highest degree of those qualities which the old prophets had considered indispensable in the ideal king.

With this one exception, however (though that is most important), the Messiah plays a secondary part in post-Maccabean Jewish apocalyptic. From the first he had been an earthly monarch, and, in spite of his unique capacities and powers, he had never been accorded higher rank. For the age of the apocalyptic writers, the merely human and the merely earthly were inadequate. The world as they knew it had deteriorated past all healing. They may have been remotely and dimly affected by that Greek philosophic idealism which despised all matter, or the sufferings of their present may have sufficed to drive them into a hope of an unearthly future. For, whatever be their motives, that was their ultimate ideal. The prospect of a redeemed Israel had vanished or sunk into the background, and their conception of the world to come was markedly individualistic. Losing all expectation of a restored Israel, they desired a better country, that is, a heaven.

In such a scheme the traditional figure of the Messiah could have no final place. Like all else about them, he was of the earth, earthy. True, he represented the utmost heights to which this world could attain, but the loftiest physical peaks were still immeasurably lower than that heaven toward which their eyes were turned. The utmost that even a son of David could do was in some measure to prepare the way for the eternal future. He might reign for a space on earth, exhibiting the perfect human character and creating conditions of unalloyed happiness and peace. But that was not enough; these things were but evanescent, and, when they passed, the Messiah must pass with them. It was left to Christian thought to accept, expand, and transfigure the hint dropped in the Similitudes of Enoch, and to transfer the Messiah from the realm of this life to that which is eternal in the heavens. Only so could an apocalyptic writer envisage the dual throne of God and of the Lamb, claim for his Messiah that he should reign for ever and ever, and hail Him King of kings and Lord of lords.

JEWISH ESCHATOLOGY

Eschatological thought, with its frequently accompanying apocalyptic, goes back to an early period among the Hebrews. It centered in the popular idea that a

"Day of Yahweh" would come, a day on which the national God would show his might by overcoming the enemies of his people and inaugurate a time of well-being and prosperity for them. . . .

Jewish eschatology as it came down form earlier times comprised the following themes: The belief that in the Day of Yahweh God would intervene in favor of his chosen people, and would overthrow the enemies of Israel. There was next the hope of the establishment of a new kingdom ruled over by a messianic king belonging to the house of David. Further, there was to be the ingathering of the scattered members of the race in their own land, and the conversion of the gentiles to the belief in Yahweh. These beliefs and hopes had existed in one form of another since the Exile and before; and they were intensified and came to fuller expression whenever the times became dark and perplexing.

Now if the eschatological beliefs of Judaism had had to do with these alone we should not necessarily have grounds for thinking that extraneous influences had been at work. But alongside of these beliefs we find that there are thoughts and expectations of a rather different kind. Thus, it is not for Israel exclusively that the bright future is anticipated. Although in the foreground it is the chosen people who appear, the purview is widened, and the whole world is embraced within this hope. Then, too, there is the expectation of the annihilation of the world in order that the new world of the future may take its place. Again, as regards the present world-order, it is seen to be divided up into different periods, the precise length of each of which is accurately calculated, and at the right time God will intervene in the world's history and bring about this annihilation and the creation of the new world. Further, the judgment upon Israel's enemies became the final judgment of the whole world. And finally, in connection with the end of this world and the new one to come, there appears the belief in the resurrection of the dead, and a world-wide kingdom of God.

We find therefore that with the earlier national messianic hope there are now combined expectations which are cosmological and universal. And these new thoughts do not develop organically from the old messianic prophecies; rather, they are superimposed upon, or else run parallel with, the traditional beliefs. The time-honored messianic hopes are not discarded; they continue alongside these new ideas. It is this mingling of new and old which is one of the causes of the confused and ill-balanced character of the picture of the future presented in Jewish apocalyptic, wherein we find, for example, hopes concerning this world indiscriminately mixed up with those about the world to come. There are good grounds for believing that the superimposed ideas referred to were not indigenous to Israel, but that they were absorbed by the Jewish apocalyptic thinkers, from extraneous sources. One of these extraneous sources, and so far as the present subject is concerned the most important, is to be sought in the religion of ancient Persia. . . .

PERSIAN ESCHATOLOGY AND APOCALYPTIC

It is not our purpose to deal with all the marks of Iranian influence on Jewish apocalyptic, but we shall concentrate on those points which are of importance. . . .

At the base of [Persian apocalyptic] lies the dualistic conception of the irreconcilable antagonism between the highest god, Ahura Mazda, who is all-good, and Angra Mainyu, the great spirit of evil. They are in constant conflict for the possession of the world and of mankind. The existence of the world is to last for a period of 12,000 years. The first 6,000-year-period is unimportant for our purpose; it is sufficient to say that it consisted of two eras of 3,000 years each, during the first of which all things were invisible. We get a reference to this in the Secrets of Enoch, 24:4, where God says to Enoch: "For before all were visible I alone used to go about in the invisible things." During the second of these two eras Ahura Mazda created the material, good world, and the first man.

The second 6,000 years are also divided into two eras; and it is during both of these that the conflict between Ahura Mazda and Angra Mainyu takes place. The first 3,000 years of this second great division of the world's history is the time of the complete ascendancy of Angra Mainyu, the evil spirit. But at the end of these first three thousand years there appears the figure of Zarathustra, and with him arises the hope of better things, though the conflict between the powers of good and evil continues. Then, at a certain time, occurs the miraculous birth of Shaoshyant, of the seed of Zarathustra and the virgin Hvov: he is to be the savior of the world, for his work is to be the gradual improving of mankind until it reaches perfection, when the end of the world will begin to take place. Then the dead will be raised and will be judged. Fire will come down from heaven and will burn up the earth. All men will have to pass through that fire; but some will pass through it easily, and unharmed, "as though through a milky warmth"; while others will suffer fearful torments from it; for the fire will burn up all the dross of iniquity which still clings to them. But ultimately all will be saved. And then Ahura Mazda will come forth with his angelic hosts for the final conflict against Angra Mainyu and his legions of evil spirits. Ahura Mazda will gain the victory, and the powers of evil will be annihilated. After that there will be inaugurated a life of happiness in a new world, wherein evil and sorrow and pain will find no place.

That is a very brief outline of Iranian eschatology and apocalyptic; many details have not been touched on, but what has been indicated includes all that is really fundamental.

We must now compare this with Jewish apocalyptic; and here we shall restrict ourselves to four subjects which will, however, be seen to be those of main importance, viz., (1) dualism; (2) world-epochs; (3) the judgment, and the destruction of the world by fire; (4) the resurrection of the dead. And then, finally, we shall refer to one or two other points of interest.

Dualism. Throughout Iranian eschatology and apocalyptic there lies, as we have seen, the fundamental thought of the contrast and conflict between Ahura Mazda and Angra Mainyu. The entire history of mankind is conditioned by, and is the result of, this perpetual and varying struggle; and the end of the world, with the final judgment, coincides with the triumph of the Lord of good over the powers of evil.

Dualism is foreign to Judaism, so that when dualistic conceptions occur in Jewish apocalyptic writings it is to Persian influence that we must ascribe their presence there. Thus, in a late apocalyptic passage in the book of Isaiah we have these mystical words: "And it shall come to pass in that day, that Yahweh shall punish the host of the high ones on high, and the kings of the earth upon the earth. And they shall be gathered together as prisoners into a pit, and shall be shut up in a dungeon, and after many days they shall be punished. Then the moon shall be confounded, and the sun shall be put to shame; for Yahweh Zebaoth shall reign in mount Zion and in Jerusalem, and before his ancients there shall be glory" (24:21-23). What is here referred to is seen in a number of passages in the Book of Enoch, of which two should be given: "And the Lord said unto Michael, Go, bind Semjaza and his associates . . . bind them fast for seventy generations in the valleys of the earth, till the day of their judgment and of their consummation, till the judgment that is for ever and ever is consummated. . . . Destroy all wrong from the face of the earth, and let every evil work come to an end" (10:11 ff.). Later, "There shall be the great eternal judgment, in which He will execute vengeance amongst the angels" (91:15). Similarly various other passages of this book, as well as the Book of Jubilees, the testaments of the Twelve Patriarchs, the Secrets of Enoch, and the Assumption of Moses, contain the floating apocalyptic material of earlier centuries. In all such passages that which lies behind the ideas of punishment, vengeance and judgment, is the victory of the Lord of good over the powers of evil, at the head of which stands Satan or the Devil (see especially *Testaments of the Twelve Patriarchs*, Naphthali 8, Issachar 7, Benjamin 5). In other words, we have the same dualistic conception which, as we have seen, is specifically Iranian. Particularly noticeable is the fact that the contending forces are *spiritual* powers.

Now, nobody would for a moment assert that dualistic conceptions had ever formed part of the prophetic or official Hebrew religious thought; and it is certain that orthodox Judaism would have repudiated them; so that when we find that after the Persian period they have entered into the circle of ideas in Jewish eschatology, and that they correspond with what is fundamental in Iranian belief, the conclusion is irresistible that the former was influenced by the latter. (It is also worth pointing out that Persian dualism was influenced by the earlier Babylonian Dragon-(*Tiamat*) myth, as one would naturally expect; but although this myth appears every now and again throughout the Old Testament, and must therefore have been quite familiar to Israel, there is never any hint that Hebrew religion was affected by it, as the Persian belief was.)

World-epochs. This subject, it is true, is not of much interest, but it is worth a passing notice because it belongs so closely to Iranian thought and has so clearly left its mark on Jewish apocalyptic. In the latter the idea of world-epochs occurs, for example, in the calculation that the present world-order is to last for 6,000 years: the number is strongly reminiscent of Iranian reckoning; and it would easily have lent itself to Jewish adaptation, since here it could be based on the number of days of the Creation, and according to Psalm 90: 4, a thousand years are as one day with God. Another reckoning of the duration of the world was 7,000 years, while in the Book of Enoch the time of the world's existence is divided into different periods quite in the Persian style.

This idea of world-epochs, again, is not indigenous to Jewish thought; it came from outside into Jewish apocalyptic, and it would be difficult to say where it could have come from if not from Iranian apocalyptic.

The Judgment and the Destruction of the World by Fire. Here we come to a subject of greater interest. The two ideas of judgment and of world-conflagration belong together. To be sure, prophecies of a coming judgment run through the whole of Old Testament prophetic literature; and the special idea of a world-judgment, not only that of Israel and its enemies, but of all flesh, the living and the dead, and also of angels, is to be discerned in some of the later writings of the Old Testament (see the book of Joel, Isa. 24–27, and Daniel). It is therefore not in the thought of a world-judgment, as such, that there is necessarily any connexion between Iranian and Jewish apocalyptic. The mark of the influence of the former on the latter is, however, to be seen in the consummation of the judgment, in the idea of the destruction of the world by fire. Reference was made to the fire which, according to Iranian belief, was to come down from heaven and burn up the earth; the account of this occurs in Bundehesh (30), a work of later Pahlavi literature, where it tells of a fiery stream of molten metal coming down from above and melting mountains and hills; all men, good and bad, have to pass through it. There are indications of the same conception in the earlier Gathas, the earliest part of the *Avesta*, the Zoroastrian Bible, which contains the oldest tradition. This is a conception which is peculiar to Iranian apocalyptic, so that when we find it appearing in the later phases of Jewish apocalyptic, it is only natural to ascribe its presence here to Iranian influence. A few illustrations may be given. It is first adumbrated in Zephaniah 1:14–18; 3:8. In the fourth book of the Sibylline Oracles, 173 ff., occur these words: "Then fire shall come upon the whole world . . . the whole world shall hear a rumbling and a mighty roar. And he [i.e. God] shall burn the whole earth, and consume the whole race of men, and all the cities and rivers, and the sea. He shall burn everything out, and there shall be sooty dust. . . ." A similar thought lies at the back of Daniel 7:10: "A fiery stream issued and came forth from before him: thousand thousands ministered unto him, and ten thousand times ten thousand stood before him: the judgment was set, and the books were opened." The conjunction of the fiery stream with the judgment here is significant. The judgment coming *after* the fiery stream, the point of which is the destruction of all flesh, strikes one as strange; but in the context of the passage from the Sybilline Oracles just quoted, it says that "God will clothe the bones and ashes again in human shape, and re-make men as they were before"; so that we are evidently meant to understand that the resurrection intervened between the world-conflagration and the judgment.

Again, in the extraordinary account of the end of the present world-order and of the judgment given in the Assumption of Moses 10:1–10, it is clearly as a result of the world-conflagration that it is said that "the fountains of waters shall fail, and the rivers shall dry up." Then also, in the many speculative ideas contained in Enoch 1–36, there is one which conceives of this fire as being kept in a certain place whither Enoch journeys; for he tells of how he was taken "to the fire of the west, which receives every setting of the sun"; he comes also "to a river of fire in which the fire flows like water, and discharges itself into the great sea towards the west" (17:4–5). And once more, in an eschatological passage in the Psalms of Solomon 15, the thought of the world-conflagration appears in the words of verses 6–7: "The flame of fire and the wrath against the unrighteous shall not touch him, when it goeth forth from the face of the Lord against sinners."

These passages all refer to the same event, directly or indirectly. And many authorities, though not all, are agreed that the contents of such bear on them the impress of Iranian influence. And, indeed, so far as this particular subject is concerned, the conception occurs nowhere but in Iranian and in the later Jewish apocalyptic; so that the only alternative to Iranian influence is to suppose that it arose independently in the minds of the Jewish apocalyptists. This is intrinsically improbable, for according to the traditional Jewish eschatological scheme, the earth was to be the place where the messianic kingdom would be set up.

This subject has a further interest from the fact that the idea of a world-conflagration was taken over into Christian apocalyptic. Among other passages in early Christian literature showing this there is the well-known one in 2 Peter: 3:10: "The heavenly bodies shall be dissolved with fervent heat, and the earth and the works that are therein shall be burned up."

The Resurrection. Here we come to the most important point of the whole subject, as it is also the most debatable. We have already expressed our conviction that the thought of resurrection was, at any rate, adumbrated in Isaiah 53:12, which we believe to have belonged to the exilic period. It would therefore seem at first sight to be incongruous to suppose that Jewish belief was indebted to Persia; but it must be remembered that Persian influences were at work for a considerable time before the Babylonian empire came to an end.

In any case, however, we are dealing here with the more developed forms of Jewish apocalyptic, and it will be seen that there is every reason for believing in the influence of Persian thought here.

In both Iranian and Jewish apocalyptic the resurrection is closely connected with the world-conflagration and the judgment, and the conjunction of these themes is to be found in Iranian and Jewish eschatology alone. And further, as Bousset has pointed out, in *Die Religion des Judeutums* (1926), in Jewish eschatology we have two incongruous ideas side by side: there is, in *addition* to the judgment and the general resurrection of the dead at the last day, retribution on the individual immediately after death, and therefore before the resurrection. The idea of a twofold retribution in the hereafter occurs nowhere else but in Iranian eschatology. . . .

So far, then, we have, in the briefest possible way, drawn attention to four subjects in Jewish eschatology in which, it is maintained, Persian influence is to be discerned. With the exception of world-epochs these subjects are of far-reaching importance on account of later developments both in Jewish and Christian thought.

FURTHER MARKS OF PERSIAN INFLUENCE

The subjects dealt with are far from exhausting the marks of Persian influence; a few others, of less importance, it is true, but not without interest, are worth drawing attention to, as they offer further arguments in favor of our thesis.

In various passages in the Bundehesh and in the Gathas there are indications that it is the part of Shaoshyant, the great benefactor of the human race, to take a leading part in the resurrection of the dead. In Jewish eschatology it is, as a rule, the Almighty himself who does this but there are exceptions, which are in all probability due to Persian influence. Thus, in Enoch 51:1 ff., in a passage dealing with the resurrection, the central position is taken by the Messiah, the Elect One: "And in those days shall the earth also give back that which hath been entrusted to it, and She'ol shall give back that which it hath received, and Hell shall give back that which it owes. For in those days the Elect One shall arise, and he shall choose the righteous and holy from among them; for the day hath drawn nigh that they should be saved. And the Elect One shall in those days sit upon my throne, and his mouth shall pour forth all the secrets of wisdom and counsel; for the Lord of Spirits hath given them to him, and hath glorified him." It is clear here that the Elect One (the Messiah) is thought of as the central figure at the resurrection; and this is entirely parallel to that of Shaoshyant in Persian eschatology.

Another, somewhat curious, illustration of Persian influence is connected with some rather naive ideas concerning the nature of the risen body. In Bundehesh 30:6 it is said that the risen body will be composed of the same elements as those comprised in the formation of man's original, earthly body:

> Bones from the spirit of the earth,
> Blood from water,
> Hairs from the plants,
> Life's vigor from fire.

It must surely be ultimately from this that the fuller description of man's component parts, though not, it is true, in reference to his risen body, given in the Secrets of Enoch 30:8, was taken:

> His flesh from the earth,
> His blood from the dew,
> His eyes from the sun,
> His bones from stone,
> His intelligence from the swiftness of angels and from cloud,
> His veins and his hair from the grass of the earth,
> His soul from my breath and from the wind.

To give but one other illustration: there was the strange idea that the possession of immortality would be retained by partaking of certain food which men will enjoy after the resurrection. This food, it is said in the Bundehesh 30:25, is the white haoma, and the fat of the ox Hadhayaos. This idea of food for the immortals seems to have been taken over in Jewish apocalyptic, though the nature of the food differed. In the difficult passage, Isaiah 26:19, one thing, at any rate, seems clear, and that is that the dead bodies which shall arise will partake of the dew of light. It is a far more exalted conception than the Persian one, but the thought of food for the risen is the same. According to Enoch 25: 4–5, there is in the abode of the risen a tree which has "a fragrance beyond all fragrance, and its leaves and blooms and wood wither not for ever; and its fruit is beautiful, and resembles the dates of a palm.". . .

What has been said is sufficient to show that Persian influences have left their mark on Jewish eschatology. . . .

D. S. Russell

The Resurrection of the Dead: A History

D. S. RUSSELL, general secretary of the Baptist Union of Great Britain and Ireland, was educated at Oxford University, where he was a pupil of H. Wheeler Robinson. He has written extensively on Old Testament apocryphal literature and the cultural background of later Old Testament books. *Between the Testaments* (1960) and *The Method and Message of Jewish Apocalyptic* (1964) are among his most significant works.

In very many ways the apocalyptic literature serves as a bridge between the Old Testament and the New Testament, and this is perhaps nowhere more clearly shown than in its belief concerning the life beyond death. Much of the teaching of the New Testament in this respect is inexplicable simply in terms of the Old Testament background, but it can be seen in its true light within the setting of apocalyptic thought. Of particular significance is its teaching concerning the resurrection from the dead.

According to ancient Hebrew "psychology" man's nature is the product of two factors, "the breath-soul (Heb. *nephesh*) which is the principle of life, and the complex of physical organs which this animates. Separate them, and man ceases to be, in any real sense of personality."[1] That is, man is not constituted of three "parts" called body, mind and spirit or body, soul and spirit; nor is he constituted simply of two "parts," body and soul. He is a unity of personality whose dissolution means the end of life in any true sense of that word. For a time a man, it is true, may conceivably live on in the elements of his body which possess psychical and not merely physical properties. But with the departure of his *nephesh* a man's life ebbs away and he ceases to be a living "person." What survives death is not a man's soul or spirit, but his shade or ghost, a kind of "double" of the once living man, retaining a shadowy resemblance to its once living counterpart, but bereft of that personal existence which once characterized the man.

For long centuries the belief prevailed that at death a man's shade or ghost went to Sheol, situated beneath the earth or beneath the great cosmic ocean on which the earth stood, a land of forgetfulness, darkness and despair, having no continuity with life upon the earth (see Job 10:21-22). At a later stage of Hebrew thought the belief was expressed that God's power and influence could be felt even in Sheol (Ps. 139:8), but for the most part the accepted view was that Sheol lay beyond his jurisdiction (Pss. 30:9-10; 115:17). In some passages the shade of the departed, especially if he were a man of outstanding renown like Samuel, was credited with superhuman powers and was believed to possess knowledge of the past and of the future as well (1 Sam. 28:8 ff), but for the ordinary run of men it was a land of no-return (see 2 Sam. 12:23; Job 7:9) where "the dead know nothing, neither have they any more a reward . . . there is no work or thought or knowledge or wisdom in Sheol, whither thou goest" (Eccles. 9:5, 10). All moral distinctions ceased to exist, for in Sheol "one fate comes to all, to the righteous and the wicked" (Eccles. 9:2).

Scholars have differed widely in their interpretation of such passages as Job 14:13-15 and 19:25-27 in which the writer's faith reaches out in hope for vindication beyond the bounds of human flesh, and Psalms 16, 49, 73, and 78 in which the problem of the prosperity of the wicked and the suffering of the righteous turns the psalmists' thoughts to that continuing fellowship with God at whose right hand there are "pleasures for evermore." There is certainly no clearly defined doctrine of a life beyond death encountered here, but at best only a glimmering of hope. This hope, however, was such that it could reach its logical conclusion only in a belief in a future life, and it is to the credit of the apocalyptists that they were the first to arrive at this conclusion in the doctrine of the resurrection of the dead.

THE RESURRECTION: ITS ORIGIN AND DEVELOPMENT

The Old Testament Preparation. According to the prophets of the Old Testament the hope for the future lay in the nation and in the coming kingdom which God would establish upon the earth; its glories would be shared by those righteous Israelites who were living at that time and also, some thought, by the Gentiles who would come to acknowledge Israel as the chosen people of God. This kingdom was an ever-lasting kingdom whose members would share the blessings of a ripe old age, like the patriarchs of old.

But the pious in Israel could not remain satisfied with such a belief. Already there was a growing conviction that the sense of fellowship which they enjoyed with God in this life could not surely come to an end with death, but that even in Sheol men might be able to praise him. With this there was growing up in Israel a new conception of religious individualism, associated particularly with Jeremiah, a man of deep personal religious experience. This emphasis was continued by Ezekiel who coupled with it a doctrine of individual retribution which declared that men are punished in proportion to their sin and rewarded in proportion to their righteousness during their lifetime here upon the earth. The problems raised by the contradiction between such a belief and the actual events of life are expressed in some of the Psalms and in the Book of Proverbs and find their classical expression in the Book of Job.

At long last a solution was reached which was to have a revolutionary effect on the religions both of Judaism and of Christianity. Not only would the righteous nation share in the coming messianic kingdom; the righteous individual would share in it too, for the righteous dead would be raised in resurrection and would receive due recompense from the hand of God. This synthesis of the eschatologies of the nation and of the individual was brought about by the apocalyptists whose belief in a bodily resurrection made such a fusion possible.

Its Historical Origin. Perhaps the particular point at issue which helped finally to establish this belief would be the fact of the martyrdom of many righteous in Israel. Those who had suffered martyrdom must still in some way share in the ultimate triumph of God's people when he would at last establish his kingdom on the earth. There was felt to be a lacuna unless God brought back, raised up, those who had shown themselves worthy to take part in his kingly rule. For this reason those people must have bodies; the earth must give birth to them again.

Two Old Testament passages are of particular significance in this connection—Isaiah 24-27 and Daniel 12—both of which confirm that the historical origin of the resurrection in the Old Testament is one of selection, first of the very good (see Isa. 26:19) and then of the very good and the very bad (see Dan. 12:2-3). Isaiah 24-27, which reveals certain apocalyptic characteristics, is thought to be a late addition to the Book of Isaiah, dating possibly from the third or fourth century B.C. There, we read, "Thy dead shall arise: the inhabitants of the dust shall awake and shout for joy, for a dew of lights is thy dew, and the earth shall bring to life the shades" (Isa. 26:19). Some scholars take this, like Ezekiel's vision of the valley of dry bones, to refer to a national resurrection; but if in fact it refers to the actual resurrection of men's bodies, then this is the first occurrence of such a belief in the Old Testament. It is significant that in this passage only the preeminently righteous are raised to participate in the messianic kingdom which will be established on the earth. It has been suggested that this verse may refer to the time of Artaxerxes III (358-338 B.C.), when many Jews were martyred. If this be so, we may have here the very historical event which led to the formulation of the belief in a physical resurrection from the dead.

In Daniel 12 we are on surer historical ground, for this book was compiled in 165 B.C. in the time of Antiochus IV (Epiphanes). No doubt the resurrection belief here expressed arose out of the persecution preceding the Maccabean revolt in which many Jews were martyred. There we read, "And many of them that sleep in the dust of the earth shall awake, some to everlasting life and some to everlasting contempt" (Dan. 12:2). The day of God's deliverance was near at hand when his kingdom would be established on the earth. But many in Israel had laid down their lives in faithfulness to him; surely even death could not rob them of their portion. God would raise up these martyrs so that, together with the living, they might share in the blessings of his kingdom (see also 2 Macc. 7:9, 14, 23, 36). But others among Israel's enemies had died without receiving due recompense for their wickedness. They, too, would be raised to receive the punishment that was their due. Once more the principle of selection is seen at work but now not only would the very good be raised for reward, the very bad would be raised for judgment. The shades of all other men would remain as before in the depths of dark Sheol.

Subsequent Developments. Both of these biblical conceptions of resurrection are to be found also in the extrabiblical apocalyptic books; but in the subsequent development occur many variations not all of which are clear to the reader, or even perhaps to the writers themselves.

The thought of Isaiah 24–27 is largely followed in 1 Enoch 6–36 (see also 37–71, 83–90, etc.), where only the righteous, presumably Israelites, are resurrected to take part in the messianic kingdom (25:4 ff.). The risen life is an organic development of the present life of righteousness (90:33). Here the wicked who have received punishment in this life will remain in Sheol everlastingly (22:13), but the wicked who have not received their due punishment on earth will be transferred as disembodied spirits from Sheol to Gehenna, the place of torment.

A variation on the theme of Daniel 12:2 is to be found in the Noachic Fragments in 1 Enoch where it is at least implied that the righteous will be raised to share the blessings of the living righteous in the messianic kingdom (10:7, 20), and that the wicked, or some of them (67:8), will be resurrected for judgment and will suffer in the fires of Gehenna in body and spirit (67:8–9). In the Testament of Benjamin the patriarchs rise first to share in the earthly kingdom (10:6) and then the twelve sons of Jacob, each one over his own tribe (10:7). "Then also *all* men shall rise, some unto glory and some unto shame" (10:8). This conception is still further developed in 2 Esdras, which declares that there will be a general resurrection to be followed by a judgment which will be universal and final. The souls of the righteous and the wicked, being now united with the body, will be judged; "and recompense shall follow, and the reward be made manifest" (7:35).

In certain apocryphal books, particularly the Wisdom of Solomon, the writers express a belief in the immortality of the soul and not the resurrection of the body. Among the apocalyptic writings the Book of Jubilees is of chief importance in this regard, as for example in 23:31, "And their bones will rest in the earth, and their spirits will have much joy." Jubilees in this regard, then, marks a breakaway from the firm conviction of the apocalyptic tradition.

The Resurrection and the Messianic Kingdom. The two biblical sources for belief in the resurrection, Isaiah 24–27 and Daniel 12, make it clear that the scene of the messianic kingdom is to be on this earth and that the righteous dead will be raised to take part in it. In this they are followed by several other apocalyptic writings. In 1 Enoch 6–36, for example, it is stated that Israel's enemies will be destroyed, despised Israel will be gathered together, and the city and the Temple will be rebuilt; then will follow the resurrection of the righteous to share with the living the blessings of the earth. They "shall live till they beget thousands of children, and all the days of their youth and their old age shall they complete in peace" (10:17).

But there were some who could no longer consider this present world, with all its wickedness and suffering and sorrow, as a fit and proper place for the eternal messianic kingdom. And so, in the Similitudes of Enoch (1 Enoch 37–71), for example, there is introduced the idea of a supernatural kingdom in a new heaven and a new earth, strangely united in one. "I will transform the heaven and make it an eternal blessing and light, and I will transform the earth and make it a blessing" (45:4–5). The righteous rise from the earth in resurrection to share the bliss of this kingdom which is eternal (62:13–16).

A further development is found in the Secrets of Enoch (2 Enoch), where the righteous dead rise in possession of heavenly or "spiritual" bodies to inherit a heavenly kingdom. Paradise, the final abode of the righteous, is a curious combination of the earthly and the heavenly, "between corruptibility and incorruptiblity" (8:5), wherein "all corruptible things shall pass away" (65:10). Here the earlier idea of an earthly kingdom in which the righteous are raised in their fleshy bodies is completely absent. Over against the present material world stands the glory of the new world and the "age to come."

The writer of 2 Baruch presents yet a different picture which is a compromise between the earthly and the heavenly kingdoms. What he visualizes is a temporary kingdom on earth to be followed by an eternity in heaven. Of the Messiah it is recorded, "His principate will stand for ever, until the world of corruption is at an end" (40:3). Then will come "the consummation of that which is corruptible, and the beginning of what which is not corruptible" (74:2). It is difficult to determine what part, if any, the righteous dead have in this messianic kingdom. In 30:1–2 it is stated, "When the time of the Messiah is fulfilled, he shall return in glory. Then all who have fallen asleep in hope of him shall rise again." Some scholars take this to refer to the Messiah's return at the close of the temporary kingdom, in which case the resurrection is to heavenly bliss where the righteous are transformed into the likeness of angels (51:10). Others take it as referring to the Messiah's coming to earth, in which case the resurrection is to a share in his earthly kingdom.

The writer of 2 Esdras points forward to the coming of a temporary kingdom here on this earth, to be followed by an eternity, whether on a renewed earth or in heaven itself it is hard to say. The Messiah will appear with those who have not tasted death and will dwell 400 years on the earth, at the end of which he and all men will die; for the next seven "days" the world will be turned into primaeval silence; then will take place the resurrection of all men to be brought forward for judgment at the Great Assize (see 7:29 ff.). . . .

THE NATURE OF SURVIVAL

Sheol, the Abode of Souls. The Old Testament picture of Sheol as the gloomy realm of the departed prevails in the two biblical apocalypses (Isa. 24–27 and Dan. 12), but, as has been already indicated, some very significant changes are evident even at this early stage. No longer is Sheol the eternal abode of all who have passed through death; for some it is only an intermediate state from which at last they will be removed in the resurrection to share in the glories of the messianic kingdom or to receive due punishment for their sins. In both of these passages, as in the Old Testament generally, the departed are described as shades or ghosts; but in the extrabiblical apocalyptic writings, even in some of the earliest of them, they are referred to as "souls" (see Similitudes of Enoch, Psalms of Solomon, 2 Enoch, Testament of Abraham;, 2 Esdras, 2 Baruch) or "spirits" (see Noachic Fragments of Enoch, 1 Enoch 108, Assumption of Moses, 2 Esdras, 3 Baruch), which are apparently used as synonymous terms to describe the form of man's survival after death.

This development is of the utmost significance, for now the dissolution of the personal unity of body and soul (or spirit) at death no longer meant for a man the end of real personal existence as had previously been the case. We here pass from a conception of personality *wholly* dependent on body (as had been the case in Hebrew thought) to one in terms of soul or spirit which, whatever degree of physicality it carries with it,[2] is different. The degree to which the discarnate soul or spirit is able to express personality is a matter which will be considered later; here we note that, with the rise of the resurrection belief, the conviction was forced upon the apocalyptists of a continuity of this life on earth with that in Sheol in which the departed, as conscious beings, were not altogether cut off from the fellowship of God whose jurisdiction was supreme even in Sheol itself.[3]

The souls or spirits of the departed not only experience consciousness, they are capable of emotional reactions. They cry and make lamentations, being conversant with the lawless deeds of men who are wrought on the earth (1 Enoch 9:10). More particularly they are capable of pain or pleasure in the form of punishment or reward. The most significant passage in this connection is 2 Esdras 7:[80] ff., in which the writer tells how the wicked wander in "seven ways" or degrees of torment (7:[80]) whilst the righteous rest in "seven orders" or dispensations of peace (7:[91]). Their lot is that of restlessness or repose, remorse or gratitude, fear or calm assurance. So far as their emotions or mental processes are concerned, there would seem to be very little difference between their capabilities in the life after death and those which they possessed during their life upon the earth.

But taking the literature as a whole, the reader is left with the impression that the life lived by the souls of the departed in the intermediate abode of Sheol (or of Paradise, an extension and specialization of the same idea) is not as full and complete as that lived upon the earth. This is seen especially in the limited nature of the soul's fellowship with God which can become complete only after the resurrection. It is still to some degree a "shadowy life" that is lived at this intermediate stage. The souls of the departed, deprived of their bodies, must await the resurrection for their fullest expression and realization.

Moral Distinctions in Sheol. One of the most significant features of the teaching of Daniel 12, marking an advance on the typically Old Testament outlook, is the fact that here for the first time in Hebrew thought moral distinctions appear between the righteous and the wicked in the life after death. At the resurrection the notably good and the notably bad are raised to receive their reward and punishment. These same distinctions are found also in the subsequent apocalyptic books, but in practically all of them they appear not simply at the time of the resurrection, but in that intermediate state immediately following death. The blessing of the righteous and the punishment of the wicked, based on moral judgments, are fully accomplished at the time of the final judgment, but even beforehand in Sheol there is a preliminary distribution of awards.

This fact of moral distinctions with their resulting rewards and punishments quickly led to the making of two distinct compartments or divisions in Sheol, one for the righteous and one for the wicked. This in turn led to a more pronounced and more varied distinction altering still further the topography of the life beyond, so that at length there emerged the conception of Paradise, Heaven, Hell, and Gehenna, in addition to Sheol itself.[4] In 1 Enoch 22, for example, three compartments are visualized, in Sheol, graded according to moral judgments already evident in the souls of the departed. In 1 Enoch 91–104 the writer argues strongly against the Sadducean view that in the life after death there is no difference between the fortunes of the wicked and the fortunes of the righteous. On the contrary, the wicked "shall be wretched in great tribulation, and into darkness and chains and a burning fire where there is grievous judgment, shall their spirits enter" (103:7–8); the righteous on the other hand "shall live and rejoice, neither shall their spirits perish" (103:4). The writer of the Testament of Abraham expresses the same belief in his picture of two gates through which the souls of men are driven: "This narrow gate is that of the just, which leads into life, and these that enter through it enter into Paradise. For the broad gate is that of sinners, which leads to destruction and everlasting punishment" (ch. 2; see Matt. 7:13; Luke 13:24). In 2 Baruch it is recorded that the final judgment will be intensify that which the souls of the wicked have already been experiencing in Sheol (30:4–5). To such it is said, "And now recline in anguish and rest in torment till thy last time come, in which thou wilt come again, and be tormented still more" (36:11).

It is because these moral distinctions can be made that the final judgment is possible. Every man will be judged, according to what he has done of righteousness or of wickedness, and moral values are the criterion of judgment. In 2 Enoch it is stated that on that great day all the deeds of men will be weighed in the balances: "On the day of the great judgment every weight, every measure, and every makeweight will be as in the market . . . and every one shall learn his own measure, and according to his measure shall take his reward" (44:5).

Moral Change in the Life Beyond. Some of these writers express belief in the possibility of a progressive moral change for the souls of the departed. In the Apocalypse of Moses, for example, the angels pray for the departed Adam (35:2) and the sun and the moon intercede for him (36:1). Of interest in this connection is the account given of the purification of Adam's soul (no doubt written under the influence of Greek ideas): "Then came one of the seraphim with six wings and snatched up Adam and carried him off to the Acherusian lake, and washed him thrice, in the presence of God" (37:3). Of even greater interest is the account in the Testament of Abraham which describes how the souls of the departed undergo two tests, one by the judgment of fire and one by the judgment of the balance in which a man's good deeds are weighed over against the bad. There is pointed out to the seer an intermediate class of souls whose merits and sins are equally balanced. The prayers of the righteous on behalf of such souls may mean for them an entry into salvation (ch. 14).

The majority of these writings, however, favor the view that no change is possible once a man has departed from this life; his destiny is determined both in Sheol and at the last judgment by the life which he lived upon the earth. No progress is possible for the departed soul either upwards or downwards (see 1 Enoch 22). In the words of one scholar, Sheol becomes "a place of petrified moralities and suspended graces." The position is made quite clear by the writer of 2 Baruch, "There shall not be there again . . . change of ways, nor place for prayer, nor sending of petitions, nor receiving of knowledge, nor giving of love, nor place for repentance for the soul, or supplication for offences, nor intercession of the fathers, nor prayer of the prophets, nor help of the righteous" (85:12). Repentance will be impossible, and prayers for the dead will avail nothing.

The Individual Soul and the Final Judgment. In the apocalyptic day of final judgment, as in the Old Testament Day of the Lord, the judgment of God sometimes takes the form of a judgment on the nations in a great crisis in history; but in the great majority of cases it assumes a definitely forensic character and takes the form of a Great Assize. Elsewhere the catastrophic and forensic types of judgment are confused, or else they are held side by side, the one representing a preliminary and the other the final judgment. In most cases moreover, the apocalyptists agree with the Old Testament writers, in regarding the judgment as preceding the messianic kingdom; but in a few cases they distinguish the kingdom from the "final age" so that the final judgment follows the messianic reign.

But perhaps more significant still is the fact that here the tendency toward individualization is much more strongly pronounced. Individual souls come forward for judgment. Perhaps the clearest statement of thoroughgoing individualism is to be found in 2 Esdras. There it is asked whether the righteous will be able to intercede for the ungodly on the day of judgment, "fathers for sons, sons for fathers, brothers for brothers, kinsfolk for their nearest, friends for their dearest" (7: [103]). In reply God says, "The Day of Judgment is decisive . . . for then everyone shall bear his righteousness and unrighteousness" (7: [104]–[105]). At that time intercession will be fruitless, for each one must be judged by his own merits. The individual is answerable to God, and he is answerable for himself alone.

THE RESURRECTION BELIEF AND THE NATURE
OF THE RESURRECTION BODY

The Resurrection of the Body and the Survival of Personality. We have seen that, according to the apocalyptists, the souls (or spirits) of men in Sheol were able to live an individual conscious life apart from their bodies and that in some measure at least they were able to express the personality of those who had departed from this life. But such a belief must be judged by its ultimate result and this points in almost every case to survival in the form of bodily resurrection. The souls of the departed, deprived of their bodies, were at best only "truncated personalities" who must await the resurrection for their fullest expression. As writers in the Hebrew tradition the apocalyptists believed that personality could not be expressed *ultimately* in terms of soul (or spirit) apart from body. The Greek doctrine of immortality, though it may well have influenced their thinking concerning the afterlife, could not in the end be accepted. It was utterly foreign to Hebrew mentality, for example, to regard the souls of men as "enclosed in the corporeal as though in a foreign hostile element, which survive the association with the body . . . distinct, complete and indivisible personalities . . . an independent substance that enters from beyond space and time into the material and perceptible world, and into external conjunction with the body, not into organic union with it."[5] Not the immorality of the soul but the union of soul and body in resurrection, that alone could ultimately express the survival of men's personalities in the life beyond.

The soul must be united with the body, then, in resurrection because only thus could full personality be expressed. But in addition, as we have already noted, only thus could participation in the coming kingdom be made possible.

Indeed this was the raison d'être of the resurrection from the dead, that the righteous might share in the kingdom. Some of the apocalyptic writers are consistent here and maintain that there should be no resurrection for the wicked; all such could not, therefore, share in the fellowship of God in the afterlife or participate in the messianic kingdom. They appeared "simply as disembodied souls—"naked"—in a spiritual environment without a body, without the capacity for communication with or means of expression in that environment,"[6] that is, they appeared as beings whose "personalities" were quite inadequate to respond to the experience of participation in the kingdom or of communion with God.

Other writers, however, speak of the wicked as well as the righteous being raised up. In 2 Baruch it is stated that the purpose of this was to be able thereby to recognize the departed after death (50:3-4). But there is a much more cogent reason than this: it is that they might be presented before God for judgment. If men were to be adequately punished for their sins which they had committed in the body, then it was in the body that that punishment must be borne, that is, they must be punished as men, possessing a full degree of personality, and not as truncated personalities in the form of disembodied souls. Hence it can be said of the wicked, "Their spirit is full of lust, that they may be punished in their body . . . And in proportion as the burning of their bodies becomes severe, a corresponding change shall take place in their spirit for ever and ever" (1 Enoch 67:8-9).

The Resurrection Body and Its Relation to Its Environment. Generally speaking, according as these writers thought of the kingdom on this earth or in a supramundane state, so they thought of the resurrection body as physical or spiritual in character. In those writings where the kingdom is to be established on the earth, comparatively little is said regarding the actual nature of the resurrection body, but in each case it is clearly implied that a physical body like that of men in this present life is intended (see Isaiah 26, Dan. 12, 1 Enoch 10:17). This idea is most frequently found in the earliest of these writings, but it is not confined to these. In the Sibylline Oracles we read, "Then God himself shall fashion again the bones and ashes of men, and shall raise up mortals once more as they were before" (Bk. 4, lines 181-82). This belief in a physical resurrection may perhaps be best illustrated by reference to a writing which is not classed among the apocalyptic books, but which in this respect reflects the belief expressed here. In 2 Maccabees 14:46 we read of one Razis that, "his blood now drained from him, he tore out his bowels, taking both his hands to them, and flung them at the crowds. So he died, calling on him who is the Lord of life and spirit to restore them to him again." Elsewhere the same writer tells how the third of the seven martyred brothers stretched forth his hands and said, "These I had from heaven; for his name's sake, I count them nought; from him I hope to get them back again" (7:11).

The transference of man's afterlife from earth to heaven, however, led inevitably to belief in a "spiritual" body which corresponded to its heavenly environment. In the Similitudes of Enoch, where there is a curious mingling of earth and heaven in which angels and men live together (39:4–5), "the righteous and elect . . . shall have been clothed with garments of glory. And there shall be the garments of life from the Lord of Spirits" (62:15–16). The "garments of glory," as we shall see, are the "spiritual" resurrection bodies of the righteous. At the close of the messianic kingdom, recorded in 2 Baruch, the righteous are to be raised to dwell in heaven itself (51:10). Although they are to be raised from the dust of the earth (42:8) in their physical bodies with no change in their appearance (50:2), there takes place after the judgment a gradual transformation until the physical bodies are changed into "spiritual" bodies (ch. 51; see also 2 Enoch 22:8–9).

The Relation of the Spiritual Body to the Physical Body. It is customary for the "spiritual" resurrection body to be described in several of these books under the figure of "garments" of light or glory. In 2 Enoch 22:8, for example, Michael is bidden, "Go and take Enoch out of his earthly garments . . . and put him into the garments of my glory," that is, Enoch's earthly body is to be replaced by a heavenly body, prepared beforehand, like those of the angels of God (22:9–10).

Different though they are, there is yet a curious connection between the physical body and the "spiritual" body which defies explanation. In the Apocalypse of Moses the body of Adam is buried in the earthly Paradise (38:5), and yet God says to the archangels, "Go away to Paradise in the third heaven, and strew linen clothes and cover the body of Adam, and bring oil of the 'oil of fragrance' and pour it over him" (40:2). And so "they prepared him for burial" (40:2). The connection here between the body on earth and the body in the heavenly Paradise is not made clear, but it would seem that the latter is a counterpart of the former and that it is this heavenly body which awaits the resurrection. Not only is it a counterpart of the physical body, it is coexistent with it until the day of the resurrection (2 Enoch 22:8).

Elsewhere the "spiritual" body is a transformed physical body (see 1 Enoch 108:11); the body which is buried in the earth will be raised up "a glorious body" on the day of resurrection.[7] The writer of 2 Baruch asks concerning those who are to be resurrected, "Will they then resume this form of the present, and put on these entrammelling members . . . or wilt thou perchance change these things that have been in the world as also the world?" (49:3).[8] He is told that at the resurrection the bodies of the wicked and the righteous alike will be raised with no change in their form or appearance (50:2), making possible the recognition of those who have died (50:3–4).[9] When the judgment is passed the bodies of men will be gradually transformed in a series of changes into "spiritual" bodies.

The "spiritual" body of Enoch, we are told, needs no food or anything earthly for its satisfaction (2 Enoch 56:2) and as such is like those of the angels; and yet when he returns to earth for a space of thirty days, presumably in his heavenly body (though his face had to be "frozen" so that men could behold him; see 37:2), not only is he recognized by his friends, but he even allows the whole assembly to approach and kiss him (62:2–3).[10]

The "spiritual" body, then, is not merely a symbolic body in the sense that it is representational, simply representing the earthly body but being something quite different in identity from it, having no organic relation with it; rather it may be described as constitutive, for it is constituted by body as men understand that term and has the same substructure, however much the concept is spiritualized. . . .

The apparent contradiction between the "spiritual" body as a transformed physical body and as its heavenly counterpart, coexistent with it till the day of resurrection, is partly resolved by the belief that the "spiritual" body grows *pari passu* with the physical body and that a man's righteous acts performed in the body of flesh condition the fashioning of the body in heaven. This belief is expressed explicitly in the Christian apocalyptic writings,[11] and implicitly in the Jewish.

NOTES

1. H. Wheeler Robinson, *Religious Ideas of the Old Testament* (1913), p. 83.

2. Even when the apocalyptists thought of the spirit or soul of the departed, they still had to think in terms of body, for this discarnate spirit or soul was believed to possess form or appearance. This is very different, however, from saying that it *has* a body in the sense in which it can be said of those spirits or souls which have taken part in the resurrection.

3. It is quite possible that the apocalyptists were influenced in their use of the word *soul* to describe the departed by Greek ideas of preexistence and immortality, particularly in 2 Enoch, where Alexandrian influence is evident. But it is easy to exaggerate this influence on the literature as a whole. According to Hebrew psychology, consciousness is a function not only of the body but also of the *nephesh*, which the apocalyptists came to think of in terms of "soul." It is to be noted that, although frequent use is made by Greek writers of the *psuchai* (souls) to describe discarnate things, the use of *pneumata* (spirits) in this connection is not typically Greek at all (see E. Bevan, *Symbolism and Belief* [1938], pp. 180 ff.). In certain apocalyptic writings, however, the two terms are used indiscriminately with this meaning.

4. The term *Paradise* is of Persian origin and means a garden or orchard. The Greek equivalent was used by the Septuagint to translate "the garden" of Eden. In the apocalyptic literature it signifies the abode of the spirits of the righteous. It occurs three times in the New Testament (Luke 23:43; 2 Cor. 12:4; Rev. 2:7).

The idea of Hell as a place of torment first appears in 1 Enoch 22:9–13. Closely associated with it is the term *Gehenna*, which derives from the Hebrew *Ge Hinnom* (valley of Hinnom). It is here that children were said to have been made to "pass through the fire" as a sacrifice to the god Molech (see 2 Kings 16:3; Jer. 7:31). In the apocalyptic literature the term is used to describe the place of burning torment reserved for the wicked after death (see also Matt. 5:22; 13:42).

5. E. Rohde, *Psyche* (1925), pp. 468–69, Eng. ed.

6. R. H. Charles, *Revelation*, International Critical Commentary (1920), vol. 2, pp. 193–94.

7. See 1 Cor. 15:42 ff.: "It is sown in dishonor, it is raised in glory; it is sown in weakness, it is raised in power; it is sown a natural body, it is raised a spiritual body."

8. See 1 Cor. 15:35: "How are the dead raised up? And with what body do they come?" The account of the transformation of the resurrection body in 2 Baruch 49–51 finds a striking parallel in 1 Corinthians 15.

9. See Mark 9:43 ff., which refers to the survival of physical deformities in the life after death.

10. See John 20:27 for the physical properties of the resurrection body of Jesus.

11. See Rev. 3:4: "But thou hast a few names in Sardis which did not defile their garments: and they shall walk with me in white, for they are worthy." See also 16:15.

W. O. E. Oesterley

Heaven and Hell, Angels and Demons

WILLIAM OSCAR EMIL OESTERLEY (1866-1950), a graduate of Cambridge University (Litt.D.), was a noted Hebraist, biblical scholar, and expert in comparative religions. His major works include *The Evolution of the Messianic Idea* (1908), *The Sacred Dance: A Study in Comparative Folklore* (1923). *Hebrew Religion: Its Origin and Development* (with T. H. Robinson, 1937), and *The Jews and Judaism During the Greek Period* (1941).

HEAVEN

First with regard to Heaven. Here it must be recognized at the outset that two conceptions have been combined. They are by no means always found combined in the apocalyptic literature; but that is due to the individual writers utilizing different elements of the traditions, whether indigenous or extraneous, in a haphazard manner. In the final issue they are combined. These two conceptions are those which are described as Paradise and Heaven. The former is, in the first instance, conceived of as situated somewhere on this earth—the word simply means a walled-in space, a garden—the latter lies far away, above the skies. Ultimately Paradise becomes transferred to the heavenly spheres, and is thought of as a department of Heaven. . . .

It was natural enough that the dwelling place of God—that is, Heaven—

From *Hebrew Religion: Its Origins and Development* by T. H. Robinson and W. O. E. Oesterley (London: The Society for Promoting Christian Knowledge, 1937), pp. 91-99, 194-209. Copyright © 1937. Reprinted by permission of the publisher.

125

should have been conceived of as a place wherein the divine presence dwelt alone, apart from men. One of the most vivid descriptions of this occurs in Enoch 14:17–23, where the vision of God's dwelling place is accorded to the Seer: "Its floor was of fire, and above it were lightnings and the path of the stars, and its ceiling also was flaming fire. And I looked and saw therein a lofty throne; its appearance was as crystal, and the wheels thereof as the shining sun, and there was the vision of the Cherubim. And from underneath the throne came streams of flaming fire, so that I could not look thereon. And the Great Glory [God] sat thereon, and His raiment shone more brightly than the sun, and was whiter than any snow. None of the angels could enter and behold His face by reason of the magnificence and glory; and no flesh could behold Him. The flaming fire was round about Him, and a great fire stood before Him, and none around could draw nigh Him; ten thousand times ten thousand stood before Him, yet He needed no counsellor. And the most holy ones who were nigh to Him did not leave by night nor depart from Him." The influence of Ezekiel is plainly discernible here. The obvious contradictions in the latter part are probably due, not to the Seer, but to faulty transmission. . . .

Elsewhere, it is said, in reference to the dwelling place of the Almighty, that "there is no need of any light other than that of the unspeakable splendor from the light of Thy countenance" (Apoc. of Abraham 17). Sometimes Heaven is thought of as a great building with windows and portals; its length and height none can discern; in it are stored up the stars, the rain, and the dew (Enoch 33:3, Ezra Apoc. 3:19); the Almighty has His own temple there (Test. 12 Patr.; Lev. 5:1; Enoch 71:5). In various passages different heavens are spoken of, seven altogether, and it is in the highest of them that the Almighty dwells, "far above all holiness."

Coming now to Paradise, we find a large variety of ideas attaching to it. And here it is necessary to refer, first, to one or two Old Testament passages. It is there called the Garden of God as well as the Garden of Eden. The belief was widespread that somewhere on earth, but far, far away, there was a wonderful garden in which God was wont to walk. The first man lived in it; but was expelled. Since then no man has seen it; but the view of it was granted later to the apocalyptists in vision. In Genesis 13:10 it is spoken of as the garden of Yahweh, and in Isaiah 51:3 it is said: "For Yahweh hath comforted Zion; he hath comforted all her waste places, and hath made her wilderness like Eden, and her desert like the garden of Yahweh . . ." The two are, of course, synonymous (see also Joel 2:3). But it is in the Book of Ezekiel that the most interesting passage occurs. According to Ezekiel 23:12 ff., the holy garden of God lies high up on a mountain where the anointed cherubim walk in the midst of stones of fire— probably the stars are meant. Clearly some old-world idea, of Babylonian origin, lies behind. Then, when we come to the apocalyptic literature we find that this garden has become the abode of the righteous after death; but it is still distinguished from Heaven—for example, in such a passage as Enoch 61:12: "All who sleep not above in Heaven shall bless Him; all the holy ones [the angels] in

Heaven shall bless Him; and all the elect who dwell in the Garden of life . . .";
similarly in the Apocalypse of Abraham 21: "And I saw there the Garden of
Eden and its fruits, the source of the stream issuing from it, and its trees and
their bloom, and those who have behaved righteously. And I saw therein their
foods and blessedness. And I saw there a great multitude, men and women and
children . . ." Above all, here dwell those few who never tasted of death, and
who abide there with the Son of God: "And there I saw the first fathers, and
the righteous who from the beginning dwell in that place" (Enoch 70:4); the
context implies that Enoch and Elijah are meant. But foremost among those who
dwell in this garden is "that Son of Man."

Paradise is thus distinguished from Heaven. Then we come to the final
development, according to which Paradise is thought of as Heaven itself, wherein
the Almighty and the Son of Man dwell, and whither the righteous are gathered
(Enoch 69:26 ff.):

> And there was great joy among them [the righteous],
> And they blessed and glorified and extolled;
> Because the name of that Son of Man had been revealed unto them.
> And he sat on the throne of his glory.
> And the sum of judgment was given unto the Son of Man . . .
> For that Son of Man hath appeared,
> And hath seated himself on the throne of his glory,
> And all evil shall pass away before his face,
> And the word of that Son of Man shall go forth,
> And be strong before the Lord of Spirits.

Thus, there is an earthly Paradise and a heavenly Paradise; they are distinguished
in some of the apocalypses, in others they are identified.

Regarding the conception of Heaven, we find that there is first Heaven itself;
then there is an earthly Paradise, and there is a heavenly Paradise. Ultimately, all
three are combined as the one glorious dwelling place of God far away above the
skies. The steps in the development of these conceptions are difficult to follow,
partly on account of gaps in the tradition, and partly on account of the inconsistencies and contradictions of the apocalyptic writers; but it seems certain that
Heaven, as finally conceived of, is the outcome of this combination.

HELL

As in the case of Heaven, the conception of Hell in the apocalyptic literature is
the development of preexisting ideas. It will be best to start by considering the
two Hebrew words *Sheol* (Gr., Hades) and *Ge Hinnom* (Gr., Gehenna). According
to Old Testament belief, *Sheol* was thought of as a huge hollow place under the
earth, but pictured as a city. There was no return from it; the shades of men

gathered there after they died; they dwelt in darkness, forgot all things, and their food was dust. Ge Hinnom [valley of Hinnom or of the son of Hinnom] was a valley which lay south of Jerusalem. It was a place of ill repute. In Jeremiah 7:31-32 it is said: "And they have built the high places of Topheth (the word means "fireplace"), which is in the valley of the son of Hinnom, to burn their sons and their daughters in the fire . . . Therefore, behold, the days come, saith Yahweh, that it shall no more be called Topheth, nor the valley of the son of Hinnom, but the valley of slaughter; for they shall bury in Topheth till there be no place to bury" (see also 19:6, 12, 13). On account of these evil practices Ge Hinnom came in later days to be regarded as the symbol of the place of the wicked departed in the next world, and Sheol came to be identified with it; the place of punishment in the next world received the name of the place where wicked deeds had been perpetrated on earth. We can, then, understand why, in the apocalyptic literature, Sheol is always identified with Gehenna. Thus, in Enoch 63:9-10 it is said, in reference to the confession of the wicked: "Our souls are full of unrighteous gain, but that doth not prevent us from descending form the midst thereof into the stronghold of Sheol" (= Gehenna) (Enoch 99:11, 103:7; Jubilees 7:29, 22:22). It is interesting to note that developments regarding the conceptions about Sheol are to be discerned already in the Old Testament.

In the apocalyptic books we have a considerable amount of space devoted to the abode of the wicked departed. Here is a description of what has now become Hell in the ordinary accepted sense of the word: "And I looked, and turned to another part of the earth, and saw there a deep valley with burning fire. And they brought the kings and the mighty, and began to cast them into this deep valley. And there mine eyes saw how they made these their instruments (namely), iron chains of immeasurable weight . . ." (Enoch 54:1-3). (Note here that Hell is situated on the earth—a result of mixing up Sheol with the place of punishment.) Elsewhere (in Enoch 90:26-27) it is said: "And I saw at that time how a like abyss was opened in the midst of the earth, full of fire . . . and they were all judged and found guilty, and cast into this fiery abyss, and they burned; and I saw (them) burning, and their bones burning." In the Apocalypse of Abraham 31 we read: "And I will give those who have covered me with mockery to the scorn of the Coming Age; and I have prepared them to be food for the fire of Hades [here synonymous with Gehenna], and for ceaseless flight to and fro through the air in the underworld beneath the earth." This last is a curious idea not often found (see, however, Ezra Apoc. 7:80). Presumably it is intended to express the utter restlessness of the wicked hereafter in contrast to the restful repose of the righteous, but it is also owing to the old-world idea of the spirit having wings; though how they burn ceaselessly while flying about is not explained. One more illustration of a great number (Enoch 103:5-8):

Woe to you, ye sinners, when ye have died,
If ye die in the wealth of your sins . . .

Know ye that your souls will be made to descend into
Sheol [here again symonymous with Ge Hinnom];
And ye shall be wretched in your great tribulation;
And into darkness and chains and a burning fire,
Where there is grievous judgement, shall your spirits enter . . .

Further illustrations are necessary. The apocalyptists simply revel in hell-fire for the wicked. But the idea is not originally theirs; it is borrowed . . . from Iranian eschatology.

Now, it will be readily realized what an effect these things would have had upon those who listened to the Seers; for there is no doubt that the bulk of the people believed what the Seers said, just as the Seers themselves did. If the Seers were convinced, as undoubtedly they were, that by means of visions, trances and the like, they were the recipients of divine revelations and were God's instruments for making known other things to their people, they could not do other than fulfil what they believed to be their duty. And the large amount of apocalyptic literature which has come down to us—and there is every reason to believe that it represents but a small part of what literature originally consisted— is clear evidence of the great diffusion of the teaching embodied in it.

But what must be of special interest to us is the influence which so much of the teaching of the apocalyptic literature has had upon teachers of later ages, both Jewish and Christian. Here arises especially the problem of the eschatology of the Gospels and of the New Testament generally; for it is obvious that what is written there about such things as the Second Coming, the end of the world, Heaven and Hell, must be studied in the light of what is said in the apocalyptic literature, which is, for the most part, of earlier date. . . .

That there are comparatively few references to demons in the Old Testament is due not only to the fact that the writers were not concerned with the subject, but also because the strong monotheistic teaching of prophets and psalmists drove these lower forms of belief underground, to a large extent. It is also likely that later scribal activity eliminated from . . . the biblical text some things regarding demons which were obnoxious to them. Even so, the references, direct and indirect, to demons are more numerous than is often realized. With angels it was, of course, different; to these there are plenty of references. . . .

In spite of the efforts of the best among Israel's teachers, belief in demons was never eradicated, and there is evidence in the Old Testament to show that this belief in its crassest forms appeared after the Exile, though it was not until the later Geek period that this became more fully developed. And when this did take palce it is seen to exist not merely among the lower grades of society, but in every stratum, from the highest to the lowest. . . .

In the later Greek period Judaism, as is well known, had, in comparison with the religion of the prophets and earlier psalmists, deteriorated. . . . Everywhere during the Greek period, as well as during that of imperial Rome, there was a crumblng of the religious beliefs of people. And everywhere, too, the rank growth of superstition luxuriated with uncanny vigor the belief in demons and ghosts, exorcism, magical spells, the power of a name, the tying of knots, and numerous other crazy practices, became the religious stock-in-trade of the world. It is a strange, but true, fact that belief in demons and their activity has exercised a vastly more far-reaching effect on mankind than belief in angels. Why the activity of demons should have been thought to be so much more widespread and potent than that of angels must be due to the fact that among so many the ills of life seem to loom larger than its pleasanter elements; but so it was, and yet the evidence makes it clear that angels were conceived of as the protectors of men.

ANGELS

In the preexilic literature of the Old Testament there is but little mention of angels. This is due to the fact that at one time the angels were gods—whatever may have been the case previously—and the worship of the God of Israel, always in danger of contamination in preexilic times—rendered it necessary to suppress reference to beings to whom worship had been offered in the past. An exception to this is the "angel of Yahweh"; at times this figure is not differentiated from Yahweh Himself. . . . In other passages the distinction between Yahweh and the angel is made clear, though a mysterious connection between them is postulated. . . .

The late Hellenistic and postbiblical angelology of Judaism differs from that of the Old Testament in three fundamental particulars: the doctrine of angels assumes a *systematic form*; it is from now on only that one can speak of Jewish angelology in the strict sense. Secondly, a certain number of angels receive *names*, which means that their personality becomes more definite. And thirdly, *functions* are assigned to angels in a far more express and detailed manner than ever occurs in the Old Testament; their activity among men becomes much more pronounced, they take a part in the government of the world which in the Old Testament is attributed to the Almighty. The effect of this is, as it were, to remove God farther away from the world, and to represent His will and action among men as being accomplished by angels instead of being done directly by the word of God.

At the head of the angels in the Jewish system are the seven archangels, Uriel, Raphael, Raguel, Michael, Saraqiel, Gabriel, and Jeremiel; the origin of these names is unknown, but they came from Babylonian Judaism. They are mentioned for the first time by name in Enoch 20, 90:21; Raphael, is, however, frequently mentioned in the book of Tobit, and in Tobit 12:15 "seven holy angels" are mentioned. But as supernatural beings they are originally due to Ezekiel, and he was probably indebted for the conception to Babylonian belief. Our sources, however, are not consistent here, for elsewhere (Enoch 40:2) the archangels are four in number: Michael, Raphael, Gabriel, Uriel (also called Phanuel: Enoch 40:9); they are identified with the four cherubim who are the bearers of the throne of God. This conception is also due to Ezekiel.

The most prominent among the angels, however, is Michael. He occupies a preeminent position as the angel of the people of Israel; in 1 Enoch 20:5 he is spoken of as "he that is set over the best part of mankind" (the Jews); and in Daniel 12:1 he is called "the great prince which standeth for the children of thy people," who will deliver them in the great day of judgment. Gabriel comes next in order, but there is reason to believe that he may originally have stood in the first place. Uriel, connected with the Hebrew Ur (light) rules the hosts of the stars: Raphael, as the name implies, was the angel of healing. Jeremiel is the lord of the souls awaiting the resurrection; and Phanuel, again as the name implies, is the angel of the presence, that is, of God. The other archangels play no important part.

Under these archangels there exists an innumerable company, among which there are various orders. To get some idea of their activity among men we must turn to postbiblical Jewish literature of later date. It is characteristic of the Jewish doctrine of angels that emphasis is laid on the fact that one order of the angels was created on the second day of creation; not the first day, lest it should be inferred that they took some part in the creation (Midrash Bereshith Rabba on Gen. 1:3), but, it is said elsewhere—and this further illustrates the subordinate nature of angels in the sight of God—that the angels of this order were created for a day only. Every day a new host was created, then they were absorbed by the stream of fire that issues from under the throne of God; they praise God and then disappear, to be replaced daily by new angelic creatons from the divine fire, or from the breath of god (Bereshith Rabba, 78:1). All this applies only to one order of angels; for the rabbinical teaching on this subject distinguishes between the angels who vanish and the angels who abide eternally. Of the latter there are ten orders. Their numbers are deduced from Daniel 7:10 ("ten thousand times ten thousand"), and Job 25:3, "Is there any number of his armies?", from which it is gathered that they are innumerable. Another order is that of "the angels of service"; these are they who are God's instruments and who carry out His will and His foreordanied plans for the government of the world. Attention has already been drawn to Michael as the prince and protector of Israel; in Jewish literature he is spoken of as their intercessor who pleads for the divine mercy on the people of Israel (Targ. to Ps. 137:7-8). This feeling for the need of a mediator is striking; it is far from being the only indication of its kind. Michael, therefore, apart from any other functions which he fills, is the foremost of the "angels of service." These angels are mainly occupied in protecting mortals from the attacks of demons (Midrash Debarim Rabba 4), though as we shall see later, much reliance does not seem to have been placed on angelic protection, judging from the various other means adopted for combating demons. Another function of the angels is to appear to men in dreams in order to indicate to them a duty, or some line of action, which they should take. These angelic appearances are, however, only granted to the pious and godly. Again, when, in answer to prayer, divine help is given to anyone, it is through the intermediary of angelic action that the help appears.

As to the form and appearane of the angels, according to the Midrash *Shemoth Rabba* 25, they appear sometimes as men, sometimes as women, now in a sitting posture, now standing; at other times an angel comes in the wind or in a flame of fire (here appears, thus, again the ancient Babylonian idea of the origin of angels from fire). They have wings, and can become visible or invisible at will. A curious idea is that the angels can understand and speak only the Hebrew language. It is therefore essential that prayers should be offered up in this language, otherwise the angels will not be able to carry the petitions before the Almighty, and add their own intercessions (see Tob. 12:15, where it is said that the seven holy angels "present the prayers of the saints, and go in before the glory of the Holy One"). It is commanded that prayers should only be offered up in Hebrew *(Shabath 12b)*. From this it would appear that the service of angels was thought to be restricted to Jews. . . .

DEMONS

We are concerned here mainly with the evidence about the activity of demons afforded by the rabbinical literature, but as has already been pointed out, this literature embodies an immense amount of ancient material, and there can be little doubt that it reflects the beliefs of earlier centuries on this subject. . . .

The present-day use of the word *demon* in the sense of an evil spirit is of comparatively late date; the Greek *daimon*, according to the earliest literary evidence, was used in reference to the souls of those who lived in the Golden Age (Hesiod, *Op.*, 122 ff., 251 ff.). . . . Our word *demon*, therefore, meant originally an entirely good spirit, or soul; the change came when in the early church the pagan gods and spirits were described as demons in an evil sense. But apart from these it was, of course, recognized that there were plenty of evil spirits in the sense understood from time immemorial. In the New Testament the term *demon* is applied indiscriminately to pagan gods (Acts 17:18, 1 Cor. 10:20), to bad spirits (Luke 4:33, 36), and to merely harmful spirits, without moral connotation (Matt. 9:32-33). According to the traditional belief, suffering was a mark of divine wrath for sin, that is, "possession," whether indicated by dumbness, blindness, etc., was a deserved punishment. . . .

At the head of the demons stands Asmodeus, or Asmodai; he is mentioned already in the Book of Tobit, where he is spoken of as the "evil demon," par excellence, who killed successively the seven husbands of Sarah, the daughter of Raguel (3:8, 17). The general name for demons is *Mazzikin*, meaning the destroyers or those who do damage. They are spoken of sometimes as under the leadership of Mastema, or Satan (Jubilees, 10:8-11), with whom elsewhere Asmodeus is identified; Satan, moreover, appears also as Sammael, the angel of death. The demons are also known by the name of *Shedim*; the root-meaning of the word is similar to that of *Mazzikin* (to destroy, devastate, bring ruin). They are identified with the *Se'irim* (he-goats or satyrs, lit. the "hairy ones," mentioned in Num. 32:17, Isa. 13:21) and they are dealt with in the Midrash *Wajjikra Rabba* (Lev. 17:7). They include both male and female demons, and are represented as harmful as the *Mazzikin*. A third class are the *Ruchoth* (spirits) similarly both male and female. A distinction cannot always be made between these three types of demons; but, speaking generally, it may be said that *Mazzikin* is the more inclusive term, which covers demons of every type; *Ruchoth* was originally applied to departed spirits of men. Lastly, there are the *Lilin*, or night demons, who are female, and are conspicuous for their long hair. But all these terms are used more or less indiscriminately. The various traditional ideas about them make consistent usage impossible. In addition, individual rabbis had their own conceptions about them, which they record. The most frequently mentioned, however, are the *Shedim*. According to the Midrash *Bereshith Rabba* on Genesis 7:5, while God was creating them the Sabbath dawned, with the result that only their souls were created, and they had, therefore, no bodies. In *Aboth* 5:9 and in *Sifre* 147*b* § 355 it is said that God created the evil spirits on a Friday, as implied in the passage just referred to. It is for this reason that Friday was accounted an unlucky day.

In some respects the demons are like the angels; that is, both are innumerable; it is said that every one has a thousand at his right hand and ten thousand at his left. Like the angels, again, the demons have wings, and they fly from one end of the earth to the other. But they are like men in that they eat, drink, and breed, like human mortals. Like the angels, too, they are able to change their shape. As a rule, however, they appear in human form, but they have no shadow. They differ also from men in the shape of their feet, which are hen's feet, so one can always tell the difference between a man and a demon!

The demons, as a rule, have their headquarters in ruins or anywhere where there is dirt. They are essentially unclean both in a ritual and a material sense, for which reason a Jew must say his prayers at least four feet distant from anything in the shape of dirt. Further, it is held that demons are particularly busy at night. Anyone who goes out of doors before cock-crow does so at the risk of his life. It is not quite so bad on a moonlit night, because demons do not like moonshine.

According to Jewish belief, the demons were originally the servants of God, for which reason they have a knowledge of the divine purposes on earth, and are able to foretell future events; because of this men would sometimes to go a demon to inquire about the future. This was, however, dangerous, because any contact with a demon entailed risks. But, according to *Sanhedrin* 101*a*, if a demon can be got to sit on an egg or in some oil, all danger is averted. Nevertheless, it was not much use consulting demons about anything because they always lie!

The belief was widespread that demons appeared in the form of certain animals. It was a popular idea, for example, that if, in walking along a country road a snake appeared on a man's right side, it denoted that something untoward would happen to him who was unfortunate enough to have seen it. The snake was really a demon and was letting his victim know that he had something to the detriment of his victim on hand. Again, if a hen crowed like a cock, it was held indisputably to be the act of a demon; therefore the hen was at once killed. In *Pesachim* 112b the warning is given not to stand still if one sees a bull comingout of a field, because a demon is dancing between its horns. Donkeys and gnats were also believed to be the incarnations of demons.

The belief was worldwide in ancient times that all diseases, sicknesses, and infirmities were inflictions of demons. So in Jewish demonology we find a special demon of blindness, of catalepsy, of headache, of epilepsy, of nightmare, of fear, of madness, of leprosy, of melancholy, of croup; this last was a female demon called Shibetta or Shibta, who was especially dangerous to children who did not wash their hands. . . . Not only were sicknesses and the like ascribed to the evil machinations of demons, vices also were assigned to a similar source; thus, there was a demon of quarrelsomeness, of danger, of bad temper, of destructiveness, etc. With the moral question here raised we cannot deal; we will merely remark that it is human nature to find a scapegoat.

Clearly this ubiquitous activity of demons called for means of counteraction, and this leads us to say something about the prophylactic measures adopted for warding off the bane of demonic malice. Among the many quaint expedients resorted to there can be no doubt that some were the result of experience, however faulty the reasoning; that is to say, they were not the arbitrary absurdities that they appear to us. It must be recognized that cause and effect were envisaged differently in bygone ages from what they are today. In the Book of Tobit 8:2-3, we read of Tobias burning the heart and liver of a fish on the ashes of incense, thereby scaring away the demon, who apparently objected to the smell. What suggested the expedient we do not know; but it is described in all seriousness, and was based on the "science" of those days.

The power of demons was believed to be most potent at night, but as they dislike the light they can be driven off by lighting a torch. Nevertheless, and here we see a religious element coming in, on some occasions the demons' power is entirely curtailed, even after dark. On Passover night, for example, they can do no harm because it is said in Exodus 12:42, "this is that night of the Lord to be much observed of all the children of Israel throughout their generation." Therefore also one could do something which at any other time would be very dangerous. One could even drink the four cups of wine which was customary at the Passover feast, that is to say, an even number of cups. All the world over there is an idea that to do anything involving even numbers is a direct invitation to a demon; oddly enough, however, the rabbis thought that if one got up to ten glasses, even number though it was, there was no danger (from demons). Presumably that means that even a demon fights shy of a tipsy man!

To come, however, to teetotalism: If one needs some water after dark, and one goes to the river or to a pond for it, that is very dangerous, because there is a night demon called Shabriri, who will inevitably pounce upon his victim and do him harm. But there is a sovereign remedy whereby any demoniacal nonsense of this kind can be checkmated—one has simply got to chop up the demon's name, and he is done for—thus, one calls out: "Shabriri, briri, riri, iri, ri," and the demon is harmless, and one can get pailfuls of water with impunity. The idea seems to be that since, according to more or less primitive belief, the name is identified with the bearer, if one takes the name to pieces one is dissecting the demon himself; and, of course, in that disintegrated state he is harmless. To be sure, he can always pull himself together again by joining up the pieces. But then one must simply repeat the process as occasion demands.

Another way of counteracting the various ills occasioned by demons was by biblical quotations, both uttered and written down. Traces of this occur already in some of the Psalms. Very efficacious was the reciting of the Shema (Deut. 6:4-6, 11:13-21; Num. 15:37-41) beginning: "Hear, O Israel, the Lord our God is One Lord . . ."

Again, the wearing of *tephillin* (or "phylacteries") was, as the Greek word implies, believed by Hellenistic Jews, as well as others, to act as a safeguard against demons. They were regarded as amulets; the same was the case with the wearing of Zizith, the fringes or twisted cords (Deut. 23:12): "Thou shalt make thee fringes upon the four corners of thy vesture wherewith thou coverest thyself." It is well known that one of the symbolic acts, widespread in antiquity, whereby it was sought to counteract demoniacal activity, was the tying and untying of a knot. This, on the principle of imitative magic, represented that a man who had been "bound" by a demon was by the symbolic act unbound or released. And thus, by the process of counteraction by synthesis, was developed the idea that anything twisted or knotted . . . exercised a deterrent effect on demons. Again, an effective means of protection was the fixing of a Mezuzah, or door-post symbol, at the entrance of houses, and also by the door of each room in the house. It consists of a piece of parchment made of the skin of a "clean" animal, on which are written parts of the Shema. This is encased in a metal or wooden tube and fixed on the right side of the entrance. The custom is still in vogue in the present. The practice was based on a literal interpretation of Deuteronomy 6:9: "And thou shalt write them [the commandments of the Lord] upon the doorposts of thy house and upon thy gates." The rabbis in Talmudic times attributed a protective power to the Mezuzah, especially in warding off demons.

One final point: it is interesting to note that in some isolated cases, in averting evil from demons by some act, the *intention* was in various circumstances an important part. For example, the interjection "Hada," the meaning of which is not known, was an expression used for "shooing away" a demon. Now if one pours out dirt in a street and says "Hada" with the mere intention of driving away a demon, that was regarded as a pagan custom (called "Amoritish"). But if one said "Hada" with the intention of preventing harm to a passer-by on the part of a demon, it was good and effective. In this case the magic word could only drive away a demon if it was said with the right intention. Doubtless we have here an originally pagan custom to which an ethical element has been attached.

Norman Perrin

The Kingdom of God in Jewish Thought

NORMAN PERRIN was born in Wellingborough, England, in 1920 and was educated at
the universities of Manchester, London, Berlin, and Göttingen (Th.D., 1959). He was
assistant professor at Emory University and professor of New Testament Studies at the
University of Chicago Divinity School until his death in 1976. Perrin was an important
interpreter of European trends in biblical criticism. His major works include *The Kingdom of God in the Teaching of Jesus* (1963), *Rediscovering the Teaching of Jesus* (1967),
The Promise of Bultmann (1969), and *The New Testament: An Introduction* (1973).

The roots of the symbol Kingdom of God lie in the ancient Near Eastern myth of
the kingship of God. This "was taken over by the Israelites from the Canaanites,
who had received it from the great kingdoms on the Euphrates and Tigris and
Nile, where it had been developed as early as ancient Sumerian times." In this
myth the god had acted as king in creating the world, in the course of which he
had overcome and slain the primeval monster. Further, the god continued to act
as king by annually renewing the fertility of the earth, and he showed himself to
be king of a particular people by sustaining them in their place in the world. This
myth is common to all the peoples of the ancient Near East, and elements from
one version of the myth were freely used in others. Essentially it is only the name
of the god which changes as we move from people to people. In Babylonia
Marduk is king; in Assyria, Asshur; in Ammon, Milhom; in Tyre, Melkart; in
Israel, Yahweh.

A feature of this myth of the kingship of God was that it was celebrated annually in cultic ritual. In the ancient world life was seen as a constant struggle between good and evil powers, and the world as the arena of this struggle. So each winter threatened to become a permanent blight on the fertility of the earth; and each spring was a renewal of the primeval victory of the god over the monster, as each spring the god renews the fertility of the earth against the threat of his enemies and man's. It was this that was celebrated cultically in an annual New Year festival. In the cultic ritual of this festival the god became king as he reenacted the primeval victory of creation; he acted as king as he renewed the fertility of the earth; his people experienced him as king as he entered once more into their lives.

That ancient Israel learned to think of their god in this way, and to celebrate his kingship in this way, can be seen from the so-called enthronement psalms, Psalms 47, 93, 96, 97, 98, 99, with their constant refrain, "Yahweh has become king!" a cultic avowal often mistranslated, "The Lord reigns."

> Yahweh has become king; he is robed in majesty;
>   Yahweh is robed, he is girded with strength;
> Yea, the world is established; it shall not be moved;
>   thy throne is established from of old;
>   thou art from everlasting. (Ps. 93:1-2)

> Yahweh has become king: let the earth rejoice;
>   let the many coastlands be glad!
> Clouds and the thick darkness are round about him;
>   righteousness and justice are the foundation of his throne.
>   (Ps. 97:1-2)

> Say among the nations, "Yahweh has become king!
> Yea, the world is established, it shall never be moved;
> he will judge the peoples with equity." (Ps. 96:10)

Already in the last two quotations we can see a characteristic Israelite emphasis being introduced into the myth; "righteousness and justice are the foundation of his throne" and "he will judge the peoples with equity" are reminiscent of the language of covenant traditions, and this is a reminder that major elements of Israelite theology were established among the Israelite tribes *before* they adopted the myth of the kingship of God from their Canaanite neighbors. The adoption of the myth has to date from the period of the monarchy, but already in the days of tribal confederacy (amphictyony) the (future) Israelite was confessing the Salvation History.

> My father was a wandering Aramaean. He went down into Egypt to find refuge there, few in numbers; but there he became a nation, great, mighty, and strong. The Egyptians ill-treated us, they gave us no peace and inflicted harsh slavery on us. But we called on Yahweh the God of our fathers. Yahweh heard our voice and saw our

misery, our toil and our oppression; and Yahweh brought us out of Egypt with mighty hand and outstretched arm, with great terror, and with signs and wonders. He brought us here and gave us this land, a land where milk and honey flow. Here then I bring the first fruits of the produce of the soil that you, Yahweh, have given me. (Deut. 26:5b–10 [Jer. Bible])

The conception of the Salvation History (*Heilsgeschichte*) is one introduced into the discussion of the theology of the Old Testament by Gerhard von Rad, who points out that in Deuteronomy 26:5b–9 we have what he calls a credo, a confessional summary of the activity of God on behalf of his people. Such credos are found elsewhere, for example, Deuteronomy 6:20–24, Joshua 24:2b–13, and characteristically they dwell on the activity of God on behalf of his people in a sequence of events: the migrations of the patriarchs and the promise of the land (Canaan) to them; the descent into Egypt and prosperity and oppression there; the deliverance from Egypt at the Exodus; the Red Sea miracle; the wilderness wandering; the giving of the land (Canaan, the land promised to the patriarchs). This constitutes the Salvation History, the history of God's acts of salvation on behalf of his people, and it plays a major role in the development of ancient Israelite theology, as also in the development of ancient Israelite literature, since it provides the basic structure for the pentateuchal sources J, E, and P, and hence ultimately for the Pentateuch itself.

The conception of a Salvation History, and the practice of its confessional recitation at a festival at one or more of the amphictyonic sanctuaries antedates, therefore, the myth of God as king and its celebration in the temple at Jerusalem, but the question of comparative dating is not important. What is important is that Israel inherited two traditions which concerned themselves in a very special way with the activity of God. One, the ancient Near Eastern myth, celebrated the activity of God in the act of creation, and in the annual renewal of the world; the other, the amphictyonic *Heilsgeschichte* [Salvation History] celebrated the activity of God at crucial moments in the history of His people. It was natural and inevitable that these two should be brought together.

The two traditions are brought together in various ways. In the first place, the enthronement psalms extend the act of the creation of the world by God to the act of God creating and choosing his own people, to include the fundamental thrust of the Salvation History.

> Moses, Aaron one of his priests, and Samuel
> his votary, all invoked Yahweh:
>   and he answered them.
> He talked with them in the pillar of cloud;
> they obeyed his decrees, the Law he gave them.
>   (Ps. 99:6–7 [Jer. Bible])

Then, secondly, elements from the Salvation History were interpreted in terms of characteristics of the creation myth. "The sea where the Egyptians perished becomes the primeval sea (see Exod. 15:5, 8), Egypt is turned into Rahab, the primeval dragon (see Isa. 30:7; 41:9; Ps. 87:4; 89:11). Finally, the two are brought together in literary units, as in Psalm 136.

> O give thanks to Yahweh, for he is good;
> O give thanks to the God of gods;
> O give thanks to the Lord of Lords;
> To him who alone does great wonders,
> To him who by understanding made the heavens,
> To him who spread out the earth upon the waters,
> To him who made the great lights,
> The sun to rule over the day,
> The moon and the stars rule over the night;
> To him who smote the first-born of Egypt,
> And brought Israel out from among them,
> With a strong hand and an outstretched arm;
> To him who divided the Red Sea in sunder,
> And made Israel pass through the midst of it,
> But overthrew Pharaoh and his host in the Red Sea;
> To him who led his people through the wilderness,
> To him who smote great kings,
> And slew famous kings,
> Sihon, king of the Amorites,
> And Og, king of Bashan,
> And gave their land as a heritage,
> A heritage to Israel his servant;
> It is he who remembered us in our low estate,
> And rescued us from our foes,.
> He who gives food to all flesh;
> O give thanks to the God of heaven.

*   *   *

   With the bringing together of the two originally separated entities—the myth of God as king with its emphasis on creation and renewal, and the myth of the Salvation History with its emphasis on the activity of God on behalf of his people at key moments in their history—the stage was set for the emergence of the symbol Kingdom of God. At the level of language the symbol is derived from the myth of the kingship of God, for *malkuth* (reign or kingdom) is an abstract noun formed from the root *m-l-k* (reign, be king). At the level of immediate reference, however, the symbol evokes the features of the Salvation History. What happened was that the two myths came together to form one, the myth of God who created the world and is active on behalf of his people in the history of the world, and the symbol evolved to evoke that myth. We will quote two characteristic passages to illustrate the meaning and use of Kingdom (of God) in the Old Testament.

> All thy creatures praise thee, Lord,
>   and thy servants bless thee.
> They talk of the glory of the kingdom
>   and tell of thy might,
> they proclaim to their fellows how mighty
>   are thy deeds
>   how glorious the majesty of thy kingdom.
> Thy kingdom is an everlasting kingdom,
>   and thy dominion stands for all generations.
>   (Ps. 145:10-14 [NEB])

From this we can see that to speak of the "glory of [God's] kingdom" is to speak of "his might," of his "mighty deeds." Moreover to say that the Kingdom of God is "an everlasting kingdom" is to say that God's "dominion stands for all generations." As a further definition of this the psalm continues

> In all his promises the Lord keeps faith,
>   he is unchanging in all his works;
> the Lord holds up those who stumble
>   and straightens backs which are bent.

In other words, to speak of the Kingdom of God is to speak of the mighty power of God, of his kingly activity, of the things which he does in which it becomes manifest that he is indeed king.

Moving from the meaning of the symbol to that which it evokes, we turn to the song of Moses in Exodus 15 (quoting NEB). This concludes with the cry of exaltation, "The Lord shall reign for ever and ever," and consists essentially of a recital of what are understood to be the mighty acts of God on behalf of his people, that is, the Salvation History. God has delivered his people from their captivity in Egypt and destroyed those who pursued them:

> The chariots of Pharaoh and his army
>   he has cast into the sea;
> the flower of his officers
>   are engulfed in the Red Sea.

He has guided them through the wilderness and brought them to the Promised Land:

> In thy constant love thou hast led the people
>   whom thou didst ransom;
> thou has guided them by thy strength
>   to the holy dwelling-place.

Moreover God has brought his people not only to the Promised Land but also to Mount Zion, to Jerusalem and the temple that can now be established there:

> Thou broughtest them in and didst plant them
>   in the mount that is thy possession,
> the dwelling-place, O Lord, of thy own making,
> the sanctuary, O Lord, which thy own hands prepared.

In all this God was acting as king, and it is to be expected that he will continue to act as king on behalf of his people: "The Lord shall reign for ever and ever."

In these early uses of the symbol we have a consistent myth, the myth of a God who created the world and was continually active in that world on behalf of his people, with the emphasis upon the continuing activity of God. The symbol functions by evoking the myth, and in turn the myth is effective because it interprets the historical experience of the Jewish people in the world. They knew themselves as the people who had successfully escaped from Egypt, who had settled in Canaan, who had built a temple to their God on Mount Zion. In their myth it was God who had done these things on their behalf, and by using the symbol in their songs of praise they evoke the myth and so celebrate their history as the people of God. . . .

With this understanding of things the historical destiny of the Jewish people in the world becomes an important factor in the functioning of the symbol and the effectiveness of the myth. So long as the people could celebrate their freedom as the people of God in the land God had given them they could celebrate his reign of kingdom in their temple, but in fact the freedom of the people of God in the land God had given them was a precarious historical phenomenon. Ancient Palestine was a buffer state between the two world powers centered on the fertile crescent of Mesopotamia to the north and on the river Nile to the south. His-torically speaking the ancient Israelite people were able to enter Palestine from the desert about 1100 B.C. because at that time both the power to the north and the power to the south were comparatively ineffective. In Mesopotamia Assyria was only just coming to power, and in Egypt the so-called New Empire was in decline. This international situation continued, and so David was able to establish an independent Jewish state about 1000 B.C. But the situation did not continue indefinitely. In the north Assyria came to power, and in the south Egypt revived, and so Palestine became again a buffer state between two world empires, its little independent kingdoms subject again to the control of the world powers. The Israelite kingdom had split into two at the death of Solomon in 922 B.C. and the northern kingdom eventually fell to an aggressive Assyrian king in 721 B.C., while the southern kingdom, comparatively small and out of the way, managed to survive until 587 B.C., when it fell to a new power from the north, the Babylonians.

The details of all of this are of course unimportant in a discussion of the interpretation of the biblical symbol, but what is important is the impact of these historical events upon the use of the symbol Kingdom of God with its evocation of the myth of God active as king on behalf of his people in the world. To put the matter in a very summary form, what happened was that prophets arose who interpreted these events in such a way that the myth maintained its force. The catastrophes were the judgment of God upon his people and their kings for not remaining true to him; the temporary reprieves were signs that God was still active on behalf of his people. Above all, the prophets used the ancient symbolism to express the hope for a new act of God as king on behalf of his people, an act whereby he would deliver them from their new captivity to Assyria or Babylonia as once he had delivered them from Egypt.

> For the Lord our judge, the Lord our law-giver,
> the Lord our king—he himself will save us.
> (Isa. 33:22 [NEB])

> How lovely on the mountains are the feet of the herald
> who comes to proclaim prosperity and bring good news,
>   the news of deliverance,
> calling to Zion, "Your God is king."
> ....

> The Lord has bared his holy arm in the sight of
>   all the nations,
>   and the whole world from end to end
>   shall see the deliverance of our God.
>   Away from Babylon; come out, come out. . . .
> (Isa. 52:7-11 [NEB])

The most important element in the intricate historical process is perhaps that this particular hope was in fact fulfilled. The Babylonians conquered Jerusalem and exiled many of its people to Babylon in 587 B.C. Within fifty years, in 529 B.C., Cyrus, king of the Medes and Persians, conquered Babylon and took control of all the former Babylonian territories, including Syria and Palestine. Cyrus' policy was to allow people conquered and transported by the Babylonians to return home and rebuild their temples and sanctuaries, and within a year the Jews had permission to return to Jerusalem and to rebuild their temple. Under these circumstances the Jewish prophets were able to assert their myth and claim that Cyrus was in fact the servant of their God.

> Thus says the Lord to Cyrus his anointed,
>   Cyrus whom he has taken by the hand
>
> . . . .
>
> I will give you treasures from dark vaults,
>   hoarded in secret places,
> that you may know that I am the Lord,
>   Israel's God who calls you by name.
>   (Isa. 45:1-3 [NEB])

Not only did the Jewish prophets reassert the myth, they also returned to a use of the symbolism of the Kingdom of God.

> Zion, cry out for joy;
>   raise the shout of triumph, Israel;
>   be glad, rejoice with all your heart,
>   daughter of Jerusalem.
> The Lord has rid you of your adversaries,
>   he has swept away your foes;
>   the Lord is among you as king, O Israel;
>   never again shall you fear disaster.
>   (Zeph. 3:14-15 [NEB])

"The Lord is among you as king, O Israel; never again shall you fear disaster," thus exulted the prophet Zephania as the exiled Jews returned to Jerusalem and began the tasks of rebuilding their temple and reconstructing the forms and expressions of their faith. Once again, however, the events of history called into question the validity of the myth. For two hundred years or so the Jewish people lived quietly in Jerusalem and its environs as a theocracy ruled in the name of God by the high priest. But in 333 B.C. the Persian Empire was conquered by Alexander the Great, and after his death and the establishment by his generals of their independent kingdoms, Palestine resumed its age-old status of an embattled buffer state between empires to the north and to the south. To the north was Syria, ruled by the Seleucids; to the south was, as always, Egypt, now ruled by the Ptolemies. The days of ritual independence for a small Jewish state centered on Jerusalem were over. Events resumed their ancient pattern: the Jews were first under the control of the Ptolemies and then of the Seleucids. Then there came a period of decline of both the Syrian and Egyptian powers, and the Jews achieved independence again in 164 B.C., under Judas Maccabee and his brothers. More than that, the successors of the Maccabees were able to rebuild the Jewish state to something like the size it had attained under David and Solomon. But this was due, as always, to the comparative decline of the world powers. Syria and Egypt were comparatively impotent, and Rome had not yet begun to exercise power in the eastern Mediterranean. But in 63 B.C. this situation changed, and the Roman general Pompey appeared in Palestine to regulate the affairs of the eastern Mediterranean on behalf of Rome. Roman power was irresistible, and the Jewish people again lost their independence as a result of a change in the international political situation.

After 63 B.C. the situation of the Jews in Palestine was a particularly bitter one. They had returned from their captivity in Babylon exulting in God as king who had again delivered them. They had then known almost two centuries of virtual independence only to fall prey again to Egyptians and Syrians. Under Judas Maccabee and his successors they had known another century of independence, and even a restoration of their state to something of its ancient glory. But now their situation was worse than ever. The Romans ruled in the land, and Jewish high priests, the representatives of God to the people and of the people before God, were appointed by Roman fiat. After 6 A.D. the situation worsened, for at that time the Romans began to rule Jerusalem directly by means of a Roman procurator.

Under these circumstances the Jewish people continued to evoke the ancient myth, but now the formulations have a note of intensity about them, a note almost of despairing hope. In the Assumption of Moses, an apocalyptic work written shortly before the time of Jesus, we find the symbolic language of the Kingdom of God used as follows:

> And then his [God's] kingdom shall appear
> throughout his creation,
> And then Satan shall be no more,
> And sorrow shall depart with him.
>
> . . . .
>
> For the Heavenly One will arise form his
> royal throne,
> And he will go forth form his holy habitation
> With indignation and wrath on account of his sons.
>
> . . . .
>
> For the Most High will arise, the Eternal God
> alone,
> And he will appear to punish the Gentiles
> Then thou, O Israel, shalt be happy.
>
> . . . .
>
> And God will exalt thee,
> And he will cause thee to approach the heaven
> of the stars. (Assumption of Moses 10)

Here we have the symbolic language of the Kingdom of God being used again to express the hopes of the people. The myth remains the same—that of

God as king active on behalf of his people—and the symbol remains the same—it is God's kingdom that will appear—but the formulation has changed. On the one hand, the language has grown more metaphorical: ". . . Satan shall be no more, and sorrow shall depart with him. . . ." ". . . the Heavenly One will arise from his royal throne . . . with indignation and wrath on account of his sons. . . ." On the other hand, the hope itself is coming to take a form in which the expectation is for a dramatic change in the circumstances of the Jews over against the hated Gentiles. ". . . the Most High will arise . . . he will appear to punish the Gentiles . . . Then thou, O Israel, shalt be happy . . . God will exalt thee . . . he will cause thee to approach the heaven of the stars. . . ."

This is the language of the apocalyptic, as this is the apocalyptic hope, and there is some question as to what the apocalyptic writers actually expected. It has been pointed out, above all perhaps by Amos Wilder, that apocalyptic imagery is a natural form of expression when one is in extreme circumstances, and Wilder himself has turned to it in poetry arising out of his combat experiences in the First World War. What one can say perhaps is that the extremity of the situation of the Jews under the Romans in Palestine after 63 B.C. escalated their use of language in ther expression of the characteristic hope for the activity of God on their behalf, as it also created circumstances under which they were no longer sure what they hoped for—except that it was for a deliverance like those from Egypt and Babylon in the past, but this time a permanent deliverance from all the evils of history.

One particularly prominent form of this apocalyptic hope for a deliverance from history itself is that of the hope to begin a war against Rome in which God would intervene, and which God would bring to an end by destroying the Gentiles and their Jewish collaborators or sympathizers, and by creating a world transformed, a world in which "Satan and sin will be no more." Just how widespread and realistic this particular form of the apocalyptic hope was can be seen from the fact that the Jewish people rose in revolt against Rome in 66 A.D., and again in 132; both times they began a war against Rome in which they expected God to intervene and which they expected God to bring to an end in victory for them as his people.

The people we have come to know through the Dead Sea Scrolls shared this hope. Indeed one of the Dead Sea Scrolls is a battle plan for this war against Rome, and all evil, the war in which God would intervene and which he would bring to victory on their behalf. This is the so-called War Scroll (IQM), and in it we find a use of the symbolic language of the Kingdom of God: "And to the God of Israel shall be the Kingdom, and among his people will he display might," and "Thou, O God, resplendent in the glory of thy kingdom . . . [art] in our midst as a perpetual help," (IQM 6:6 and 12:7). In both instances the symbol Kingdom of God is being used to express the hope, indeed the expectation, that God would act on behalf of his people by intervening in a war against Rome and the Roman legions. In this hope and expectation, they began the war, but the war itself, contrary to their expectation, went the way of Rome and the Roman legions.

One last use of the symbol in ancient Judaism remains to be mentioned, the the use in the Kaddish prayer, a prayer in regular use in the Jewish synagogues immediately before the time of Jesus, and for that matter still in use today. In an English translation of the ancient form, the prayer is as follows:

> Magnified and sanctified be his
>   great name in the world that he
>   has created according to his will.
> May he establish his kingdom in your
>   lifetime and in your days and in
>   the lifetime of all the house of
>   Israel, even speedily and at a
>   near time.

This is so close to a central petition of the prayer that Jesus taught his disciples:

> Hallowed be thy name,
> Thy kingdom come

that the two must be related and the most reasonable supposition is that the prayer of Jesus is a deliberate modification of the Kaddish prayer. . . .

R. Travers Herford

The Law and the Pharisees

R. TRAVERS HERFORD (1860–1950) was a distinguished interpreter of Christian origins and of the Jewish legacy of Christianity. His works include *Christianity in Talmud and Midrash* (1903), *The Pharisees* (1924), and *Talmud and Apocrypha: A Comparative Study in Jewish Social Teaching* (1933).

My purpose is to present one system of belief and practice in which the sense of obligation is brought into the closest possible connection with religion, so close that religion and morality (which is based on the sense of obligation) are inseparably blended and hardly to be distinguished; and Law, which ultimately rests on the sense of obligation, is a part of religion though not identical with it. This is that particular type of Judaism to which the name of *Pharisaism* is given. It is the development of the religion of Israel along a line which began with Ezra, continued with the Sopherim, the early scribes, was taken up by the Pharisees properly so called, and carried on by the rabbis whose teaching and ideas are recorded in the Talmud and the cognate literature. The line has continued till the present day. The system so developed has been consistent throughout in its insistence on certain main principles, whereby it has acquired the strongly marked character peculiar to itself. Since the fall of Jerusalem, A.D. 70, down to recent times, it has remained, in its essentials, the only important representation of the Jewish religion; and it would be correct to call it Pharisaism, if it were not that the name *Pharisee* came into the language at a time later than that at which

From *Judaism and Christianity* Vol. 3, edited by I. J. Rosenthal (New York: Macmillan Company, 1938; London: Sheldon Press, 1938), pp. 92–121. Reprinted by permission of the publishers.

the movement began, and passed out of common use, when the need for a distinguishing name was no longer felt. But, though the name was a temporary label, the principles of the system to which the name was attached remained consistent throughout. With this explanation, I may be allowed to use, for convenience, the name *Pharisaism* to denote the whole system developed along the lines which I have just indicated.

In this sense, Pharisaism begins with Ezra, who was indeed regarded by the Pharisees of later times as their founder and, so to speak, their patron saint. They said of him (*b. Sanh.* 21[b]) that he was worthy to have received the divine revelation from God, if Moses had not already done so. And they expressed their view of his true function by saying (*b. Succ.* 20[a]) that when that divine revelation had been forgotten in Israel, Ezra again founded it, or established it.

Whatever Ezra did, he did not make a complete breach with the past. He had behind him all the religious experience of Israel up till his own time, all the historical development of that religion, all the main ideas and beliefs which served to express it. He had no thought of breaking with these, perhaps no thought of making any innovation in them. What he did was to lay a special stress upon one factor in the religion of Israel as it had been before the captivity, a factor which had indeed been present in that religion for ages past, but which had been too little regarded or even forgotten. This was the factor of the divine revelation, believed to have been given to Moses on Sinai and by him delivered to the children of Israel. No one ever questioned that that revelation had been made; but the people who had inherited it had not been faithful in their observance of what was required of them by the terms of that revelation; and, after repeated warnings by the prophets, the calamity of the Exile was, in the view of Ezra, brought upon them as a punishment for their disobedience and a sharp reminder of their duty.

The divine revelation here referred to was recorded in the five books ascribed to Moses, and known by the name of the Torah, usually but quite wrongly called the Law. Torah never meant "law." It means "teaching," and the five books containing it were accepted as being what God had *taught* concerning His will and His nature. It was this record, as the Torah, or "the Torah of Moses," which Ezra proclaimed and whose authority he established in the Jewish community after his own return from Babylonia. Whether it was the whole Pentateuch which he proclaimed, or only the Priestly Code, does not matter for my present purpose. His proclamation of the Torah was the reminder, to those who heard him, of the divine teaching which had been neglected, the divine will which had been disobeyed, and of the urgent need of a return to the discarded obedience. If the Jews, as a community, were to have a future at all, it could only be achieved by a determined effort on their part to take to heart and put into action the divine teaching; and to do this not merely as a community but as so many individuals. The sense of obligation to do the will of God, which of course had been present in the Jewish mind for centuries, must now be intensified, so that every separate person could feel it and own its authority over himself. Here was the connection between religion and the obligation which underlies both morality and law, stressed in the most emphatic manner. Religion was the belief in, and the worship of, God. The only true service of Him was to do His will; and the authority, which created the obligation so to serve Him, was His authority.

Therefore, when Ezra secured the acceptance of the Torah by the assembled people, he pledged them to take it as the supreme authority for the guidance of their public and private life. He established it in a supremacy which it had never held up till that time. In theory to some extent it had been supreme, but in practice never. But there was a considerable difference between acknowledging a general obligation to do the will of God, and acknowledging the particular obligation to do this and that specific duty set forth in the Torah in a written precept. And Ezra's success in what he set out to do was that he really did persuade a substantial number of the people to own the authority of the Torah in the special and not merely in the general sense. He did not live to see the full accomplishment of his purpose. His view of the Torah was disputed in his own time, and for long afterwards; but it was the Torah, in the supreme position which he asserted for it, which became the ruling factor in the centuries after the fall of Jerusalem.

To have made and maintained such a claim, and to have secured the recognition of it, was to have achieved much. But Ezra himself knew well that something more was needed, some continuous protection for the position he had won. The Torah which he had established was a body of teaching, containing precepts and passages of instruction. The Torah, as the record of a divine revelation, would fail of its purpose if its contents were not made clear to the understanding of those to whom the revelation was given. When Ezra first publicly read the Torah (Neh. 8:7-8), there were at his side certain Levites who "caused the people to understand the Torah . . . and they read in the book, in the Torah of God, distinctly; and they gave the sense, so that they understood the reading." This had been, indeed, part of Ezra's plan from the time when he left Babylonia for Palestine. In Ezra 7:10 it is stated that "Ezra had set his heart to 'seek' the Torah of the Lord, and to do it, and to teach in Israel statutes and judgments," where the word translated seek should be rendered interpret or explain, according to the regular usage of the later language in reference to the Torah. For Ezra to "seek" the Torah would not be meaningful. To "interpret" it was of the utmost importance, not only for his own time but even more for later times. The Torah contained various precepts, and to the fulfillment of these precepts every Jew was individually pledged. He must therefore understand exactly what it was that he was called upon to do. He must have it explained to him by someone who was able to interpret to him the words of the Torah. Such interpretation was given, perhaps by Ezra himself, certainly by the teachers who immediately followed him and who were called the Sopherim, or scribes. The work of interpretation thus begun has never really ceased from that time to this. It might be supposed, indeed, that an interpretation once given by a competent exponent would not need to be repeated or supplemented. When such a one had declared, in reference to some precept or passage in the Torah, "this is what it means," that would seem to end the matter. If a modern scholar, interpreting a passage in some classic author, declares that it means so-and-so, he is stating what, in his opinion, the author really intended to say. But, for the Jewish interpreter, the object of his labor was to find out what this or that passage of the Torah meant to the person who was required to obey it. The difference would not be felt at first, but, in the succeeding generations after Ezra, the question addressed to the interpreter would be, "What has the Torah to say to me (or to us) now living? We are not concerned to know what it may have meant in Ezra's time. We want to know how exactly it applies to our own present life." Every Jew, so it was taught in later times, should regard himself as having been actually present at Sinai, when the Torah was delivered to Moses and accepted by all the people. When Ezra began the practice of interpretation and ensured that it should be carried on from generation to generation, he was guarding against the danger that the Torah, as an ancient sacred book, would come to be looked upon as merely an antique relic and not as a teacher able to speak to the needs of each succeeding age.

I may be attributing to Ezra a deeper insight into the significance of what he did than he really possessed; but what I have said does, I believe, correctly indicate what the interpretation of Torah really did aim at and has continued to aim at; and it serves to show why all the written material of the Talmud and Midrash is in the form of interpretation of Torah. Those whose words and names are recorded in that literature were not theologians framing a system of doctrine, or philosophers defining a body of thought, or professional moralists laying down a theory of ethics; they were teachers who tried to show to their fellow men and women what the divine revelation recorded in the Torah meant to them, what their duty was and how they could rightly fulfill it. The object of these teachers was intensely practical; it was a discipline, not a mere course of instruction, and by the method of interpretation they were able to bring the authority of the Torah to bear upon every individual conscience of those whom they could influence, in each succeeding age.

The Sopherim, then, made it their business to interpret the Torah, to explain exactly what it intended to teach to those who had accepted it. The written word of the text needed to be amplified where it was not sufficiently precise, to be more closely defined where its statements were only in general terms, to be brought to bear upon questions which were not dealt with in the original, and so on. Accordingly the oldest form which the Sopherim gave to their interpretation was that of a sort of verse-by-verse commentary on the written text of the Torah, a process known as Midrash. This method was never wholly abandoned, although a new method was introduced by the successors of the Sopherim, as I shall explain presently.

The results obtained from the interpretation of Torah by the Sopherim were of two kinds, because the subject matter with which they dealt was twofold in its contents. Part of the Torah was preceptive, consisting of precise commands—thou shalt, or thou shalt not. All the rest was nonpreceptive. Accordingly—and this is the point of connection between Torah and Law—interpretation of the preceptive part aimed at giving a clear direction how the precept in question ought to be obeyed. God had commanded Israel to do so-and-so. There must be some one exactly right way of carrying out His command, and that exactly right way, if it were not known or not certain, must be sought until it was found. It was the work of the interpreters to find it, and to state it, when found, in precise terms. Such a statement was called a *halachah*, and it served the purpose of a rule of right conduct. The word means "walking," from *halach*, to go. And, as a rule of right conduct, it was a direction indicating to a man how in a given case he should *walk* in the ways of the Lord.

The interpretation of the nonpreceptive part of the Torah had for its result no such definite statement—nothing at all events that could be regarded as a rule binding on those who received it. Its intention was to set forth what was implied in the teaching of the Torah about God, His nature and His ways, His dealings with man, and man's relation to Him. And the result so obtained was called *haggadah*, which means "declaration" and signifies that the Torah declares so-and-so. Haggadah, therefore, is the interpretation of the Torah on its nonpreceptive side. And this is the true meaning of *haggadah*; it does not mean fanciful narrative, legend, or the like, although it often took those forms. The only qualification which should be added is that the haggadah was extended so as to take in all the rest of Scripture and not the Torah alone, as its subject matter.

It is probable that of the words *halachah* and *haggadah*, *haggadah* is the older. At the beginning, when the object in view was to interpret the Torah as a whole, it was sufficient to say that the Torah "declared," so-and-so, and the result was called *haggadah*. But later, when it was found necessary to distinguish between the preceptive and the nonpreceptive parts of the Torah, the word *halachah* was introduced to indicate the results of interpretation as it affected conduct, and the word *haggadah* was restricted so as to cover only the nonpreceptive parts of the Torah. However, and whenever, these two famous words came into use—and they cannot have been later than the period of the Sopherim—they have remained ever since as technical terms of the interpretation of the Torah.

The period of the Sopherim came to an end about the year 270 B.C. Their organization as a teaching body, such as it was, ceased to function; and for nearly a century there was no authority to take its place. There was, that is, no body of persons competent to define the Halachah in any given case. This "decline and fall" of the Sopherim is almost certainly connected with the change from Persian to Greek rule, and more particularly with the fact that Judea came under the rule of either an Egyptian or a Syrian king, and was brought, for good perhaps but certainly for evil, under the influence of Hellenism. And one consequence of that change in the political condition of the Jews was that new ideas and practices were introduced or allowed to grow up, in regard to which there was no one to say whether, or how, they were related to the Torah; no one competent to discover and define a *halachah* concerning them. Yet, if this could not be done, there was danger lest the Jewish religion, as developed by the Sopherim on the lines already indicated, would, so to speak, get out of hand and gradually lose all connection with the Torah, and the Torah itself would cease to be the guide of life, and become merely an antique relic, a monument of ancient piety, whose claim to obedience was no longer recognized or acted upon.

From the point of view of those who followed the line of the Sopherim in regard to the Torah, this was a serious and pressing danger; and the means by which they met and disarmed it marks a most important change in the development of Pharisaism. In form, it was hardly more than a change in the method of interpretation of the Torah; in substance, it was a change in the essential meaning of the Torah itseslf, and it made possible the future development of Judaism, one might say, without limit. This new feature was the concept of the *unwritten Torah*, a concept whose implications were hardly recognized at first, but which proved to be of far-reaching importance for all the succeeding history of Judaism. Let me try to explain what the change was and what was involved in it.

The *halachah* was the direction that a certain precept was to be performed in a certain manner; and it was deduced by interpreting the written word of the Torah, or it was in some way connected with the text. If it had not been, it could have no claim to be received and obeyed. The Torah had been solemnly accepted, and the people pledged to obey it. Whatever was offered to them by the religious teachers must be included in the meaning of the Torah, must be a part of the Torah, shown in greater detail by the process of competent interpretation. And this process had been sufficient during the time of the Sopherim. But when, in the period after them, the new ideas and practices came in, either these must be rejected and forbidden, or else they must in some way be brought within the range of the authority of the Torah. Some of these new ideas and practices which had gradually come in were evidently good and as such ought to be recognized, but there was no support for them in the written Torah. They were not expressly mentioned in the text, and there was no method of interpetation which would establish the required connection.

The idea occurred to someone amongst the teachers of the Torah, that there must be a tradition behind these ideas and practices (though they seemed to lie outside the Torah), a tradition which would account for their being held and practiced. If that were so, then it would follow that the divine revelation was not confined to the written text of the Torah. There must be an unwritten Torah, not as the rival or even the commentary on the text, but as completing it; so that the written and unwritten together made up *the* Torah as it essentially was. This new idea appeared and began to be acted on somewhere about the year 170 B.C., and was only accepted with much hesitation, and at first by only a few of the teachers. For, of course, the new idea rested on a pure assumption, that there was a tradition, going back, as it must have done, to the time of Moses. And the teachers of Torah, whom we may now call the Pharisees, were quite aware of the weakness of their case in respect to its foundation. But they maintained it nevertheless, and justified their action in doing so by the results which they obtained from this new conception of Torah.

The immediate result was that it became possible to define a *halachah* without basing it on some text of the written Torah, or even establishing any connection with the text. The *halachah*, so defined, was vouched for by a tradition, assumed to have come down from the far-off past, and accepted on the authority of the teachers who declared it. And, by means of this concept of the unwritten Torah, these teachers were enabled to give a wider meaning to the precepts of the written Torah, being no longer tied down to the literal sense or the interpretation of it on the former lines. For the Torah was now understood to be the whole revelation, contained in the written text and the unwritten tradition taken together. And that revelation was taken to be the whole not only of what at any time was understood to be its meaning, *but of what might hereafter at any time be shown to be implied in it.* Torah was held to be the divine revelation, immeasurable and inexhaustible; and Torah, at any one time, was so much of that revelation as had come within the understanding of those to whom it had been given. All had been imparted to Moses, so it was held; and whatever might be, at any future time, unfolded as its meaning by some acute and far-seeing teacher, was contained in the Torah as Moses had received it. This conception of Torah was certainly held in the period of the Talmudic teachers, and it explains the meaning of the change made by those successors of the Sopherim who first introduced the unwritten Torah. But I think it probable that they had at first no clear perception of what they were really doing, or of the fuller meaning of Torah which was dawning on their minds. Be this as it may, the new method of defining the *halachah*, without connecting it with scripture, gave them a liberty of interpretation which they had never had before. It enabled them to modify, or even to set aside, the written word in order to bring out its real intention, or rather the real intention of God who had caused the sacred text to be written, but who had not confined His whole meaning to what was written therein. The way was thus opened for an advance from the literal meaning of the text towards a higher, and especially an ethically higher, meaning, one more in accordance with the rising moral standard of the times since the text was written. Two instances will show how this was done.

One is the famous text of the *lex talionis*, "an eye for an eye and a tooth for a tooth," etc. There is a clearly stated order that in certain cases of bodily injury a savage retaliation was to be inflicted. Those who defined the *halachah* dealing with such cases frankly abolished the written text, and made no attempt to humanize it by any artifice or interpretation. They appointed a different procedure to be followed in such cases, namely, the payment of a money fine, depending on the amount of the injury. And, in the passage in the Mishnah (M. B. *Kamma*, 8:1) where such cases are dealt with, and in the discussion of the passage in the Gemara, there is no hint that the old savage law had ever been enforced and had later been changed. There is rather the opinion that no one could ever have been so cruel and brutal as to take the written command literally. The written command became obsolete at a very early time: perhaps indeed it was never acted on. It is therefore grossly unfair to say that the principle of "an eye for an eye and a tooth for a tooth" is a principle of the Jewish religion. If it ever were so—and there is nothing to show that it was ever acted on—this had ceased to be true before Christianity appeared. Jews are no more liable to the charge than Christians are. It is by no means true that the Jewish religion can be understood by taking the written words of the Torah, or of the Old Testament as a whole, in their literal meaning.

Here is another case in which a direct command contained in the written text, not merely of the Torah but even of the Decalogue, was deliberately set aside. The Decalogue said: "Thou shalt observe the Sabbath day. . . . In it thou shalt do no manner of work,"—a command as definite and precise as words could make it. Yet this was, in certain cases, entirely disregarded and even flatly disobeyed. Those cases were such as involved danger to life. If a human life was endangered by illness or injury, then any and every law implied in the observance of the Sabbath not only *might* be but *must* be broken in order to save life. The persons in attendance on the sick or injured man were bound to do, regardless of the Sabbath, whatever was necessary to save his life, without stopping to ask permission from anyone (see b. Joma, 84^b). The Sabbath, no doubt, was a divinely appointed institution, and, as such, to be reverently observed. But a human life was more than an institution, inasmuch as a man, every man, was made in the image and likeness of God. The great truth that "the Sabbath was made for man and not man for the Sabbath" was understood by the rabbis quite independently of Jesus, and formulated by them in almost the same words. They had come to recognize and act on the principle long before the time of Jesus. Probably it goes back to the time soon after the Maccabean revolt.

These are not the only cases in which the written text of the Torah was deliberately set on one side or even flatly disobeyed. And the *halachah* which was defined in such cases was only made possible by the introduction of the concept of the unwritten Torah, whereby the connection was cut between the *halachah* and the written text.

It might seem that by the use of this concept of the unwritten Torah there would no longer be any place for, or any need of, the written Torah. But this was not the case; and those who defined the *halachah* on the lines of the unwritten Torah never understood it in that way. Thus, they never dreamed of abolishing the Sabbath, because it was expressly commanded in the Torah that it should be observed. They only said that in certain cases it must give way to a yet higher consideration, namely, the sacredness of human life. In every other case the obligation remained to observe the Sabbath. So, too, the Torah expressly sanctioned, or even commanded, divorce. Those who defined the *halachah* on the subject by no means wholly approved of divorce, or rather they were quite aware of the evils and abuses attendant on unrestricted liberty of divorce. What they did, and all that they could do, was to restrain that liberty, to make the way of divorce difficult, to secure so far as possible the rights of the divorced wife, and to discourage the reckless practice of divorce. They could not, and certainly did not, declare that divorce was in itself wrong and never under any circumstances to be allowed. Only if they had declared that, would they or could they have abolished the express teaching of the Torah on the subject; and, if they had done that, they would have virtually repudiated the Torah altogether.

These instances which I have given—and many others might be added—show that the application of the concept of the unwritten Torah made possible the development of the *halachah* in an ethical direction and not toward a mere elaboration of ritual and ceremony. Of course the *halachah* had for its object the performance of certain acts; but these were for the most part such as would serve to express a higher moral purpose, would conform to a higher moral standard, than that of the older times. For the moral standard *did* rise in the course of the centuries of Israel's history, as indeed is evident to any intelligent reader of the Old Tastament. And the Pharisees were quite aware of the fact, while at the same time they looked on the Scriptures in general and the Torah in particular as the record of what God had revealed. What they did was to lay stress on the ethically higher elements in Scripture and to leave the lower ones alone, or, where they were obliged to notice those lower elements, to explain them away by various far-fetched and fantastic devices, while maintaining at the same time the higher ethical standard which in their own reason and conscience they had come to recognize.

Indeed, one may say with truth that the whole purpose of elaborating the *halachah*, at all events after the concept of the unwritten Torah had been introduced, was to bring the Torah into accordance with the higher moral standard, as it was discerned and recognized by the teachers who defined the *halachah* in each generation. If it had been thought sufficient to do the things commanded in the Torah in their bare literal meaning, there would have been no need of any *halachah*, but there would have been a growing divergence between the Torah and the consciences of those who were pledged to obey it. The *halachah* was the means of adjustment, by which that divergence was avoided and the Torah enabled to keep its place as the supreme authority in each succeeding age, the continuous revelation of the living God, speaking to His people in the actual present and not merely in the far past. The conception of the unwritten Torah, and the *halachah* developed in accordance with it, recovered, for Judaism in general and for Pharisaism in particular, the reality of a living religion for all purposes. And nothing is further from the truth than to say that Pharisaism made the Jewish religion, the religion of the prophets, into a hard and barren formalism with no spiritual value in it. The truth rather is that the Pharisees took up the religion of the prophets and brought it to bear upon the lives of the people in a way and to an extent which the prophets had never been able to accomplish. And, paradoxical though it may sound, it is not far from the truth to say that if it had not been for the Pharisees and what they did, the prophets would never have been heard of. Be this as it may, the Pharisees certainly developed their ideas of the unwritten Torah and the *halachah* based on it with a clear and conscious reference to the teaching of the prophets.

The Pharisaic teachers were diligent students of the writings of the prophets; indeed it was due to those teachers that the prophetical books were collected and arranged in approximately their present form, so that they could be regarded as the second main division of the Scriptures, the first being, of course, the Torah. The prophetical writings were carefully read and their teaching taken to heart by those who at the same time were defining *halachah* with the help of the unwritten Torah. One result of such study was to raise the moral standard for those who meditated on their words, and this was one main reason why the *halachah* was felt to be necessary and made to serve as a means of adjusting the precepts of the Torah to the more enlightened moral sense of each succeeding age. In this way the *halachah* represented the application of the prophetic ideas to the Torah. The prophets had been teachers of righteousness, whatever else they were. The Pharisaic teachers had precisely the same object in view, and sought and found most valuable help toward attaining that object in the close study of the prophets. But the teaching of the prophets had, to all appearance, been disregarded by those to whom it had been addressed, and all their rebukes and warnings had been powerless to prevent the disaster of the Exile. This gives the clue to the work of Ezra and all his successors. A new means must be found for driving home the lesson of obedience to the divine will, as taught alike in the Torah and by the prophets; and the means which was devised and set to work was the *halachah*. And that is why the whole system of Pharisaism was a discipline and not merely a body of teaching. Those who came under the Pharisaic discipline were not allowed to get off with merely knowing what the divine will was: they were required to *do* it, and to do it in a carefully defined way. In thus establishing a discipline, the Pharisees held, and truly held, that they were carrying out the work of the prophets, and moreover doing what the prophets had never been able to do, namely, secure the actual obedience of the people to the divine will. They claimed to be the rightful successors of the prophets, and they expressed that by saying "Prophecy was taken from the prophets and given to the Wise [i.e. the Pharisaic teachers], and from these it has not been taken away" (b. B. *Bathra*, 12ª). In that acute saying more is implied than might at first appear. The *halachah*, as I have said, was the application of the ideas of the prophets to the interpretation of the Torah; and the *halachah*, developed by the help of the concept of the unwritten Torah, represented the recognition, in the minds of the Pharisaic teachers, of a higher ethical standard. In other words, they interpreted the Torah by the light of their own reason and conscience, and defined the *halachah* accordingly. The prophets had not defined *halachah*, certainly; but they spoke out of their own reason and conscience, and out of that intense conviction were able to declare "Thus saith the Lord." The Pharisaic teachers did not use that form of speech. They did not need to do so, for they had the warrant of the Torah, as the express revelation of God, for all they said. But, no less than the prophets, they felt that they had "the words of the living God"; and the *halachah* which they defined was a far more effective means than the prophets had ever found of making the divine word attended to and obeyed. To set the Pharisees in any sort of opposition to the prophets is entirely unwarranted. Pharisaism is applied prophecy, and the *halachah*, in the manner of its formation, and in the terms of Torah, represents the prophetic "freedom of speech." . . .

The interpretation of Torah took the two forms of *halachah* and *haggadah*, according as it dealt with the preceptive and the nonpreceptive portions respectively. . . . Both of these are essential elements in Pharisaism, and must be given due weight in any attempt to estimate the importance of that system. And the reason why Judaism has been called a merely legal religion, and why the word Torah has persistently been renderd by Nomos or Law, is that those who have so misjudged have taken account only of the *halachah*, which is in a sense Law, and have left out the *haggadah*, probably because they knew nothing about it. The *halachah*, which gave directions to perform certain actions, came under the notice of non-Jewish observers, at all events in its results; such observers could see that the Jew did certain things, sometimes in themselves trivial, as a religious duty; but they could not see beyond the outward act, they could not read the inward intention with which those acts were done, nor did they usually stay to ask whether there was an inward intention which would explain and justify those acts. It is out of such superficial observations that the charge of hypocrisy has been constantly brought against the Pharisees, a charge to which indeed the peculiar form of *halachah* is especially liable, but which is none the more justified on that account. I merely note this in passing, because I do not want to digress into controversial topics. My purpose throughout has been to explain as well as I can what I may call the theory of Pharisaism, the main ideas on which it was based, and by the development of which it came to be what it was. I shall devote the remainder of this essay to the discussion of certain questions which must arise in any proper study of Pharisaism: What is the real obligation of which the *halachah* is the expression? What is the relation of conscience to the Torah? In what sense and to what extent is Pharisaism a religion of law? These are, indeed, not so much separate questions as various aspects of one question, namely: How is the sense of obligation, inherent in human nature, accounted for and made effective in Pharisaism? What I have already said about *halachah* will help to provide the answer.

The entire corpus of the *halachah*, as it was gradually elaborated, codified in the Mishnah and finally embodied in the Talmud, was intended to cover the whole, and did actually cover the greater part, of the actions and relations of life, or as much as could be included of those which would commonly form part of the life of the Jew. The *halachah* was binding on every member of the community, on those at least who accepted the system. No one was bound to accept it, and no one was punished for not accepting it. Of those who did accept it, only such as did not conform to it were punished, and *that* by being subject to to disapproval more or less strongly expressed. I am not concerned at present with those who did not come under the system. For those who did, the *halachah* was, in the strict sense of the word, Law. The *halachah* was Law, the Torah was not Law. As law, the *halachah* covered the ground of both civil and criminal law, and the whole corpus of *halachah* was, in form at all events, a legal code.

So also, looked at from another point of view, the *halachah* covered the field of morality, dealing with right and wrong actions, and the obligation of conscience—in short, with the moral law in general. On the legal side and on the moral side, the *halachah* imposed, and was framed for the purpose of imposing, a considerable amount of restraint upon a man's freedom of action. But it is important to notice that neither on the legal nor on the moral side are the abstract terms used which are commonly found in legal or ethical treatises. There are no words for either "law" or "equity," though the meaning of both was well understood. There is no word for "conscience," nor for the "moral law," nor even for "religion," though again the meaning of these was perfectly familiar. Such abstract terms only became necessary when the leaders of Jewish thought began to write philosophical treatises; and they did not do so till long after the Talmud was closed. Those with whom I am concerned, the teachers who defined and developed the *halachah*, never wrote books at all, philosophical or any other. And, what is more important, they were not engaged in working out a *theory*, of ethics or of anything else. They were not in any technical sense moralists or philosophers or theologians or jurists. Teachers they certianly were; but their "colleges" or "academies" or "schools," sometimes spoken of in books on Jewish subjects written usually by non-Jewish authors, were not colleges or academies in the usual sense of the words. They were places where the teachers of Torah could gather their disciples and impress on them what the Torah was, what it meant, and what it required, all in as minute detail as they could. From first to last, from Ezra to the men who closed the Talmud about a thousand years after his time, the one and only object of the Pharisaic teachers was to interpret the Torah, and to teach it not as a body of thought, a system of doctrine, but as a guide to action, namely, the practical service of God by the doing of right actions and the refraining from wrong ones. They had no need to start from first principles and begin by inquiring into the basis of the moral law in human nature, the nature of conscience, and so on, and then connecting these up with the Torah. They began with the Torah, and needed nothing more. There they had, as they held with unquestioning conviction, the full and inexhaustible revelation of the divine will. There they were told what they should do, and they studied to learn, with more and more exact detail, how they should do it. And there they had the one and only reason for doing it, namely, that God commanded them to do it. That was the obligation, and the authority which created the obligation was His authority.

Of course the Pharisaic teachers did not invent this statement of their task, or this view of the ethical aspect of human nature. They inherited all the religious and moral experience of the ages before their time, as recorded in the scriptures. They inherited the belief that man was a free moral agent, whose service must be a voluntary choice if it were to have any moral worth. They knew of no other sanction than the will of God, as revealed in the Torah, for right action. And they could only discern what was revealed in the Torah, as the will of God, by the light of their own reason and conscience. The whole of their ideas of religion and morality were based on the recorded and inherited experience of their predecessors in Old Testament times. And the only innovation which they made was to elevate the Torah into a position of especial eminence, and to lay all the emphasis in their power upon practical obedience to its precepts. So they were not concerned with the theoretical side of morality, nor with morality as a separate subject study, nor even with religion as a separate subject of study. Religion and morality were inseparably blended in the conception of a conscious relation to God which involved the devotion of their whole mental activity to Him, in thought, belief and worship, and the obeying of His commandments in the practical conduct of life. And thus it is that, for the Pharisees, the whole of their spiritual life was conditioned by, and realized in, the conception of Torah, the full and inexhaustible revelation which God had given.

The contrast between Pharisaic Judaism and other forms of religion, notably Christianity, is usually expressed by saying that the Jew is under the constraint of an external law, while the adherents of other forms of religion are free to act according to their consciences. Whatever truth there may be in this contrast, it is certainly not the whole truth. What was the position of the Pharisee in regard to freedom of choice in his actions? Was he bound by an external law, or was he free?

That he was under an obligation to do right and to refrain from wrong goes without saying. It is so in every moral system. The obligation is the feeling of "ought," and without that there could be no morality. The obligation is a form of restraint or constraint. He who feels it owns in it a certain authority having a rightful claim to his obedience. It is not an authority which he himself has set up, or could have set up. It is in that sense an external authority. But, as he owns it in his own mind, it is an internal authority. Obviously he could not own it otherwise than in his own mind. Further, the obligation is not a compulsion. It does not force him to do the act which it points out, it merely indicates that he ought to do it, and leaves him free to choose whether or not he will do it. This is so in whatever form the sense of "ought" is recognized. It would be so if the obligation were conceived as a command, that is, a definite law, because the subject of a command is in the last resort free to choose whether he will obey it or not. A command does not become a forcible compulsion until violence is used, and then the action ceases to be moral at all.

Now the whole of the Pharisaic conception of moral action is based on the obligation to do the will of God. The obligation comes to him in the form of a command—Thou shalt, or Thou shalt not. Its authority is the authority of God. It is made known to him in the Torah; but, unless he had a mind and a conscience, he could never receive the revelation, or feel the obligation of the commands contained in it. It is not the Torah, or even the *halachah*, to which his obedience is due, or for which it is rightfully claimed. This is due to God alone, who gave the Torah as the means of *teaching* to Israel what he ought to do. To do the will of God is the end and aim of the Pharisaic discipline. The Torah teaches him what that will is and the *halachah* shows it to him in greater and greater detail. But Torah, and more particularly *halachah*, are only directions given to him *how to do* what is commanded, that will of God which it is his duty to do. In everything which he does, in obedience to the obligation which he owns, he is serving God by doing His will. Every occasion for doing so is an opportunity for service of God. And, unless he did the act commanded with the conscious purpose of serving, his act—according to the Pharisees—would have no worth, moral or religious. The theory of the *opus operatum* was definitely ruled out by the Pharisaic teachers.

Every act which the Jew owned to be a duty he represented to himself as a thing commanded, and he called it a *mitzvah*. And accordingly, every *mitzvah* was an opportunity offered to him of serving God. It might be a precept of but small range and trivial importance, and it might be anything up to the supreme and all-inclusive *mitzvah* "Thou shalt love the Lord thy God." Whatever it was, apparently great or small, it was what God willed that he should do. The Pharisee delighted in the abundance of the *mitzvoth*, and regarded them as signs of God's beneficence to His people. This is the reverse side of what is known in other connections as the "burden of the Law." What the Jew felt about it, and still in large measure feels is expressed in the term *simhah shel mitzvah*, "the joy of commandment"—a term which would never have been used if the command-ment had been felt as a burden.

The Jew, in all this, was and remained a free moral agent. If he had not been, neither Torah nor *halachah* nor *mitzvah* would have had any meaning for him, or any authority over him. But what if his conscience bid him do some act which the *halachah* told him not to do? What then? Was he in that case free to go against the *halachah*? That is a question which would naturally suggest itself to those who are not, so to speak, under the *halachah*. And the urgency of it would only be felt by those who, for whatever reason, doubted the validity of the *halachah* as a system and the wisdom of the teachers who worked it out. Within the system—that is, assuming the validity of the *halachah* and the wisdom of the teachers—the question could hardly arise, and, so far as I have read in the Talmudic literature, it never did arise. If a Jew were confronted with an occasion for doing something, and if he had in the Torah the divine command to do it, and in the *halachah* the particular direction *how* to do it, a direction given by teachers whom he trusted and who were, moreover, the accepted leaders of the whole community, then there would be nothing for conscience to urge in the opposite direction. So long as Torah, *halachah* and *mitzvah* were to him the means by which he was taught the divine will, his conscience would naturally urge him in the same direction, and he would do the act, whatever it was, with thankfulness to God for giving him the opportunity of service, and to the teachers who had shown him how he should perform that *mitzvah*, and so obey the divine will.

The word *mitzvah* is indeed one of the key words of Pharisaism. It represents what, in other systems of ethics, is expressed by the word *ought*, the fundamental sense of obligation. It is applied to every act which a man feels that he ought to do, and by the doing of which he serves God, and he does it as the fulfilment of a divine command. The *halachah* is not coextensive with *mitzvah*; for the *halachah* was only possible when the particular *mitzvah* could be defined, as in the case of negative precepts, and such positive precepts as were necessarily restricted in their range. But it was a *mitzvah* to show kindness, brotherly love, sympathy, piety, and so on. These were not definable in any *halachah*, and the attempt so to define them was never made. Instead, these were said to be "committed to the heart," meaning that they were left to the inspiration of the kind heart and the generous feeling at the moment when they were called for. The first and great commandment, "Thou shalt love the Lord thy God," and the second, which is like unto it, "Thou shalt love thy neighbor as thyself," included everything, great or small, which could be thought of as *mitzvah*, but they were never defined in a *halachah*. Which means that while the *halachah* prescribed the mode of action of a man at this point and at that, the *mitzvah* covered the whole of his life. At no point was he outside the range of the obligation to do the divine will. In everything he did, in all his waking hours, there was the opportunity to serve God.

He asked for no reason why he should do this except that it was the divine will. He did not do it for the sake of any reward. There is indeed frequent mention of reward and merit in the literature of Pharisaism, and those terms had a definite meaning; but they were never to be the motives for doing the will of God. The Torah was to be obeyed always for its own sake, *lishmah*, and for no lower reason than that. "The reward of a *mitzvah* is a *mitzvah*," said Ben Azai. A man who serves God in the doing of a *mitzvah* could hope for nothing better than to be given the opportunity to perform another. And the highest type of service is that of the man who serves God for love. Paul was not the only one to teach that love is the fulfilling of the Law. . . .

Leo Baeck

The Son of Man

LEO BAECK (1873-1956) was one of the leading Jewish social commentators of his generation. A refugee from Nazi Germany, he settled in England and devoted his time to study and writing. Among his most important works are *The Pharisees and Other Essays* (1945), *The Essence of Judaism* (1948), and *Judaism and Christianity* (Eng. tr., 1958).

The question of the meaning of the words *son of man (ben adam, bar enash)* has long been an important topic in the history of religion. There is an almost insuperable opposition between that which this term originally signified in its Hebrew and Aramaic form and that which it later came to mean in the Greek Gospels. For the attempt, which has often been made, to establish a relation between them by contending that the term assumed a new significance in the Book of Enoch and in the Fourth Book of Ezra, does not stand up under examination. Nor can it by any means be conceded under these circumstances, however popular the idea may be in some quarters, that the language and teachings of Judaism in the century before the destruction of the second temple used the expression to designate the expected Messiah.

The phrase is of ancient biblical origin. It belongs to elevated, poetic style and, through the individual, designates the species. Often it is used alternately with the other collective names for man: *ish, enosh, geber.* In the Pentateuch it occurs once, in Balaam's speech; in Joshua, Judges, Samuel, and Kings it does not occur at all. The first part of the Book of Isaiah does not contain it, probably owing to mere chance; but we do encounter it in the second part of

From *Judaism and Christianity: Selected Essays* by Leo Baeck (Philadelphia: Jewish Publications Society of America, 1961), pp. 23-38. Copyright © 1961. Reprinted by permission.

this Book, as well as in Jeremiah, Psalms, and Job. Without exception, it designates man in general, as opposed either to God or to the animals; it denotes the
human race, the human kind.[1]

In the Book of Ezekiel, the phrase has a special character; it is used by God,
often together with the pronoun *thou*, to address the prophet. Here the prophetic
style shows its manifoldness. Like Abraham and Moses before them, Samuel and
Elijah, too, had heard God address them by their names; likewise, Amos and
Jeremiah—both after having been asked by God, "What seest thou?" The other
prophets did not experiernce the call in the same way, not even Isaiah when he
heard his call in a wonderful and entirely personal manner, nor Zechariah when
he, too, was asked, "What seest thou?" Only in the Book of Daniel is the
prophet again addressed by name by the messenger of God, presumably as a fully
intended archaism.

It is entirely in accord with the whole character of Ezekiel that the poetic
expression, *son of man*, should for this prophet be the way in which the voice of
God makes its demands on him, for again and again this prophet feels seized and
hurled down by God's sublime omnipotence, and so he must always be called
and raised up again—but called not by his name, but with these words, *son of
man*, which signify to him the whole vast distance between himself and God.
The Book of Daniel adopted this phrase from Ezekiel; Daniel, too, when hum-
bled to the ground, is once addressed thus by a messenger from heaven.[2]

But in addition to this, the Book of Daniel lends our words, as well as their
synonyms, a special connotation. It tells of beings who belong to the world
above, yet look like men. In this it follows the expressions which Ezekiel used to
describe his first vision. As Ezekiel says ". . . likeness of four living creatures;
and this was their appearance: they had the likeness of a man—*demut adam*";
"upon the likeness of the throne was a likeness as the appearance of a man—
demut kemar'e adam"; Daniel, too, says, "behold, there stood before me as the
appearance of a an—*kemar'e gaber*"; "behold, one like the similitude of the sons
of men touched my lips—*kidemut bene adam*"; "there touched me again one like
the appearance of a man—*kemar'e adam*"; and then finally, in the Aramaic
section, the sentence which was to become so important in the history of religion:
"Behold, there came with the clouds of heaven one like unto a son of man—*kebar
enash*." The reference each time is not to a man, but to one who has the
appearance of a man, who looks like a man; and only after further designations
have made this quite clear, does the text say, more briefly: *man*. For example: "a
man clothed in linen, whose loins were girded with fine gold of Uphaz; his body
also was like the beryl; and his face as the appearance of lightning "; or "the
voice of a man between the banks of Ulai"; or, when the name can be given, still
more briefly, "the man Gabriel." Always a being from above is meant, one of
those with human appearance dwelling up there. It is not God, and it is not a
human being, but yet is compared with what is human. In the place where after
"the great beasts, which are four," "there came with the clouds of heaven one
like unto a son of man," something human may vibrate in the phrase: that in

which the bestial manifests its powers is here opposed by that in which the human shows what is highest in it.[3]

The style of the Book of Daniel became decisive for all subsequent apocalypses. We see this first of all in the so-called image speeches of the Book of Enoch, which are really nothing but an old *midrash* for the Book of Daniel. The Book of Daniel is here presupposed everywhere, and its words, which can be understood only by referring back to Daniel, are used throughout. Just as there, God is spoken of here, too, in an image: "the ancient of days" and "the hair of his head like pure wool"; and here, too, we read of the "son of man" and encounter references to him. And what is said about him is also the same as in Daniel. As the Book of Daniel says of him that he appears after thrones have been put there and God has sat down amid his myriads for judgment, after the books have been opened and the power been taken away from the beasts, that he may now be granted lasting dominion, so the Book of Enoch, too, says: "There I saw him who has the head of an old man, and his head was white as wool, and with him was one whose face was that of a man"; "to him, to this son of man, the conclusion of the judgment was entrusted, and he made the sinners and seducers of this world disappear from the earth and perish"; and we then encounter reference after reference to him who is "as a son of man."

It is much the same in the Fourth Book of Ezra. Even as the vision of Daniel begins with this apparition: "Behold, the four winds of the heaven broke forth upon the great sea; and four great beasts came up from the sea," and then reaches its most astonishing point in the image, "there came with the clouds of heaven one like unto a son of man," the Fourth Book of Ezra says: "A tremendous gale rose up from the sea and stirred up all its waves. I beheld how the gale brought one out of the heart of the sea who had the likeness of a man. I beheld how this man flew with the clouds of heaven." It is the same, finally, in the apocalypse of John, the Revelation of St. John the Divine. Daniel had seen one "clothed in linen, whose loins were girded with fine gold . . ., his eyes as torches of fire, and his arms and his feet like in color to burnished brass, and the voice of his words like a tremendous roaring"; and John envisages "one like unto a son of man, clothed with a garment down to the feet, and girt about the breasts with a golden girdle . . ., his eyes were as a flame of fire and his feet like unto burnished brass . . . and his voice as the roaring of many waters"; and like Daniel, he, too, sees "a bright cloud, and sitting upon the cloud one like unto a son of man."[4]

The images and words of the Book of Daniel still speak in all these books, either by being simply repeated or haggadically elaborated; nowhere is anything essential and new added to the conceptions of the Book of Daniel. It is nothing less than the apocalypse *par excellence*; and one of its important elements is the apparition of him "who is like unto a son of man and comes with the clouds of heaven and steps before God." Wherever in later works "that son of man," "this son of man," or "the son of man" is mentioned, it is the quotation from Daniel that is speaking.

In the Gospels, too, we see this clearly wherever they contain fragments out of apocalypses. When it is said here: "they shall see the son of man coming in the clouds of heaven with power and great glory," and "ye shall see the son of man sitting on the right hand of power, and coming in the clouds of heaven," one cannot fail to see that it is sentences from apocalypses, similar to that of John, that speak here, using, no less than the Revelation of St. John, the quotation from Daniel.[5]

Yet these two sentences, in which the old meaning is still evident, are over-shadowed by the many others which show time and again that the word has re-ceived a new sense in the Gospels and has become a very specific term. It is no longer the ancient apocalyptic image that appears in it; it has become an indepen-dent theological concept; it no longer serves as a parable, as testimony of a vision, but to designate something specific. It is now the phrase which unequivocally denotes the Christ of the Church; used by him, too, to designate himself.

The time when this decisive change took place can be determined. It was the time after the Apocalypse of John; for here the word occurs only as a quotation from Daniel. It was the time after Paul's epistles; for these do not contain this phrase at all—of course not as a quotation, seeing that they do not contain anything really apocalyptic, but also not as a designation of the Christ, although ·it would have to occur here in this sense if it had by that time come to be an accepted designation for him. It was the time after the Barnabas epistle; for when this epistle declares with almost impassioned brevity, "Jesus, not son of man but son of God," it is again clear that this phrase cannot yet have been an un-equivocal designation for the Christ.[6] But it was the time before the epistles of Ignatius; for when he writes to the Ephesians—and this sounds like a very emphatic objection to this sentence of Barnabas—"Jesus Christ, the son of man and son of God,"[7] then the phrase has evidently become the new concept which is to designate the essence and the name of the Christ. Thus the change in meaning clearly took place at the turn from the first to the second century. What a fixed term this expression then became quite generally, appears also from a sentence in which Rabbi Abbahu, a younger contemporary of Origen who also lived in Caesarea, turns against the Christology of the Church. When he is able to say—"If anyone says to you, 'I am God,' then he lies; 'I am the son of man,' then he will regret it; 'I shall ascend to heaven,' then he has spoken, but will not achieve it"[8]—then it is quite clear that by that time the term *son of man* referred so unequivocally to the Christ of the Church, and only to him, that in a religious controversy it could serve as the mark of recognition. The sphere, too, can be determined where this change came about. Inasmuch as in the Judaism of that time, as we know from the Targumim and the old talmudic and midrashic writings, the words *son of man* were used only for man in general and not as a name for the Messiah,[9] it can have acquired its new significance only in the Church; and this is also implied by the polemical twist of Abbahu's statement.

The long development up to this point is quite clear. Again it begins with the Book of Daniel. This book above all has such vast significance for the history of religion because we here encounter an essential change in the messianic idea.

In the thinking and the aspirations of the prophets, this idea meant a tension between the present and the future, between what existed and was still there now, and that which was becoming and yet to be. In the Book of Daniel, however, the idea signifies an opposition between the here below and the there above, between this world and the beyond. What is "to come" is here no longer a day toward which one is drawn by hope—*jammim ba'im*—but a world which opens up before one's visionary powers—*olam ha-ba'*. There the expected one, the object of longing, is a scion of the house of David who will fulfill history; here he has become the supernatural being who descends from the heavenly heights to end history. There, in the prophetic world, the line of longing is horizontal; here—and this is the essence of the apocalyptic orientation—it is vertical. Yet it is noteworthy that in the course of time the later attitude did not suppress or supplant the earlier one in the soul of the Jewish people. Both retained their place and direction, though at times they fought with each other: the son of David and the one like unto a man on the clouds of heaven. In the New Testament, too, we see how they stand next to, and opposed to, each other. While the apocalyptic orientation always gratified that impatience which wanted not to wait but to experience, as well as the desire for the miracle, the prophetic-messianic attitude derived its perennial power from the historical consciousness of the people, from its will to find the past again through the future.[10]

It is hard to say how far the beginnings of the apocalyptic idea, this intensification of the messianic idea into something supernatural, reach back. It is, however, noteworthy that this opposition of above and below is characteristic of the Alexandrian-Greek philosophy of revelation, and that the Book of Daniel, which is the first document of Palestinian-Jewish thinking to exhibit it, was written only after Palestine had for over a century been part of the Egyptian sphere of influence and culture. But whether this change in outlook had already taken place within Judaism and thus made Jewish thinking receptive for the Alexandrian influence which made possible the change, can scarcely be determined now. But however this may have been, this change has had a tremendous effect on Jewish thought: the notion of "the world to come" has ever since been a decisive idea. Everything of first-rate value is now assigned its primary and permanent place beyond this world. The Holy Scripture and the sanctuary, the people of Israel, its patriarchs and its Messiah, now belong with their beginnings and their continuance to the other world, to the ideal realm. Thus they, like every idea, are something original that was created by God before the world of becoming. They are expressly conceded pre-existence, now poetically, now conceptually. The Messiah, too, now becomes he that was from the beginning. To be sure the old messianic faith retains a goal insofar as he who is from the beginning shall appear on a day in time as the scion of David; and the particular teaching about the ideal pre-existence of the Messiah—his pre-existence in "the thoughts of God" and about his hidden name which shall one day be revealed—still leaves some room for the historical orientation; nevertheless, the Messiah has now become pre-existent, an ideal being, he that has always been with God.[11]

With this, however, he moved close to another figure, to another idea—so close that both could merge, even had to merge. The people of Israel, too, has its pre-existence like the Messiah; it, too, belongs to the other world. And in this supernatural world, Messiah and people really have no separate content, no different meaning. What else are both of them here but the genius of Israel, the ideal Israel? The dividing line which two separate words wanted to indicate disappears in the ideal realm; and in Jewish thought and poetry they often did become one. How this could come about is shown already by the seventh chapter of the Book of Daniel. Is he that "is like unto a son of man and comes with the clouds of heaven and may step before the Lord" the messiah or the people of Israel, "the people of the saints of the Most High?" Thus it is here said of him who "came with the clouds of heaven"—using words which recall the old prophesies of the Messiah—"and there was given him dominion, and glory, and a kingdom, that all the peoples, nations, and languages should serve him; his dominion is an everlasting dominion, which shall not pass away, and his kingdom that which shall not be destroyed"; and afterwards the same is here also said of the people of Israel: "the kingdom and the dominion, and the greatness of the kingdoms under the whole heaven, shall be given to the people of the saints of the Most High; their kingdom is an everlasting kingdom, and all dominions shall serve and obey them." Have not the features and traits of both merged even here? The ideal Israel or, in Daniel's language, the *sar*, the archon, the aeon of Israel has become the Messiah; and the Messiah, the ideal Israel. This is almost clearer still in the Book of Enoch. Here we encounter references to "the anointed," and he is also often called "the chosen"; and this same word is just as often used for the people of Israel. Similarly, he is called "the just,"and the people of Israel likewise, only using the plural. The king of the end of time and the people of the end of time stand there with the same predicates; and this also makes it understandable how it could later be similar in the realm of the Church with the Christ and the Church.[12] The roots, however, out of which all this developed, reach back still further, into the time before the Book of Daniel. Already the Isaiah of the Exile used the same name, *the chosen of the Lord*—this old attribute of the anointed—both for the people of Israel and for the "servant of the Lord." Nor can the old question what these words, *servant of the Lord*, mean in the speeches of this prophet, be answered in any other way: already here both the people and the man who represents the people's worth and dignity— now it is the prophet and now the Messiah—coincide in meaning.[13]

Here it should be noted how in the religious realm the attempt to express oneself becomes almost a wrestling for expressions. Everything conceptual comes only gradually. The word *Messiah* in its definite and conceptual sense thus belongs only to a later age; only the pseudepigrapha, the New Testament, the Targum, and the Mishnah have it. When the old prophesies want to speak of the ruler of the future, of the house of David in which justice will dwell and remain, then they can only proclaim this king of days to come in ever new images and comparisons: as the shoot out of the stock of Jesse, the twig out of his roots upon whom the spirit of the Lord shall rest; as the child born unto us, upon whose shoulders the government will be and whose name will be called prince of peace; as the son whose name his father shall call Immanuel, that is, "With-us-is-God"; as the righteous shoot who shall execute justice and righteousness in the land; as the one shepherd who shall feed them and be their shepherd.[14] Even of the man who belonged to a future which would come to pass in the way of this world, one could speak only in parables. How much more did this have to be so when it ws a matter of speaking to him who belonged to the beyond, to the other world, who, as the genius of the people or the messianic liberator, was full of the most abundant significance. No single word, no single designation could name him; only the image could point to him: with the clouds of heaven one had come like unto a son of man and had stepped before God. This image, in its completeness or abbreviated, as a quotation from, or as an allusion to, the Book of Daniel henceforth served to speak of him.

The sentence which provided this image entered the Greek world and the Greek language of the Church. But here the words *son of man* were no longer, as in Hebrew, a compound for simply designating a human being; here one was confronted with two words, and they meant: a son of a human being. And that which these two Greek words thus articulated soon gained a significance in the development of the Church, which led to a parting of opinions and, eventually, of convictions. The teaching of the new faith had combined the two ideas which lived among the Jewish people—the prophetic idea of the son of David and the apocalyptic one of an otherworldly being—into the doctrine of the heavenly and the human origin of the Messiah, the doctrine of the son of God who is born as a human child. But against this human birth, against this son of a human being, there now rose a radical Gnostic and Marcionite opposition. And the Church had to turn against this. As it had emphasized the conception of the son of God against Judaism, it now stressed the idea of the son of man against Gnosticism—the more emphatically, the more violent the opposition grew. In this controversy, "the son of man" became the watchword that prevailed. Where the Epistle of Barnabas still had been able to venture the sentence, "Jesus, not son of a man but son of God," Ignatius now writes to the Ephesians: "Jesus Christ, the son of a man and God." In the words of Irenaeus which follow this example, *filius dei filius hominis factus*, the Catholic Church recognized its definitive doctrine. The "son of man" thus turned from an image into a firm concept and became an essential part of the dogma. The Hellenization of our word was accomplished.[15]

In this fight against Gnosticism, which was a fight about the son of man, the Church attained a self-confidence and became the Catholic Church. To prevail, it created the canon of the New Testament. In the Gospels of the canon[16] the term *son of man* was accorded its place; and one may now understand why this phrase has here become one of the most frequent designations of Jesus and why it occasionally takes the place of the "I" when Jesus speaks of himself. It is part of the triumphant Christology of the community, and as such belongs in the Gospel of the Church. Here he is not only "as a man who comes with the clouds of heaven and steps before God," but he is the son of God who has become a son of man. The dogmatic accent here shapes the word.

Even as our term first made its way out of the ancient poetry of the Bible to the Apocalypse, it has now emerged from the Apocalypse and entered the realm of ecclesiastical concepts. Its way is a way of the history of religion.

NOTES

1. Num. 23:19; Jer. 49:18 and 49:33, 50:40, 51:43; Isa. 51:12, 56:2; Job 16:21, 25:6; Ps. 8:5, 80:18, 146:3. The Psalms very often employ the plural, *bne adam*, which we also find in Moses' song of farewell, in Joel, in Micah, in Jeremiah, and in Proverbs.

2. Ezek. 2:1 and often; 2:8 and often; Gen. 22:1; Exod. 3:4; 1 Samuel 3:10; 1 Kings 19:9 and 19:11; Amos 7:8 and 8:2; Jer. 1:11 and 24:3; Isa. 6:9; Zech. 4:2 and 6:2; Dan. 10:11–12., 12:4, 12:9, 8:17. For man in general, as opposed to the animals, and once also as opposed to God, the Book of Ezekiel employs the word *adam*.

3. Ezek. 1:5, 1:10, 1:26; Dan. 8:15, 10:16, 10:18, 7:13, 10:5, 8:6, 12:6, and 12:7.

4. Enoch 46:1ff., 71:10 ff., 42:2 ff., 48:2, 69:26 ff., 70:1, 71:17. Note also 60:10 where Enoch is addressed, after the manner of Ezekiel, "thou son of man," and 71:14 where Enoch is called the son of man who has been born for justice; here *son of man* designates simply man, after the ancient biblical manner. On the other hand, compare with this, both in the same and in the preceding chapter, 71:17 and 70:1, "that son of man" which designates, in the manner usual in this book, the one with the appearance of a man in the Book of Daniel. The only original terminology in Enoch is: son of the mother of all the living, that is, son of Havvah, Eve, after Gen. 3:20; *ben havvah* corresponds to *ben adam*. The expression of Eleazar ha-Kappar, in the middle of the second century, is the *Yalkut* for Num. 23:7, after *Midrash Yelamdenu*, may be apocryphal: "He foresaw that a man, son of a woman, would rise and make himself God and try to confuse the whole world." Else it already mirrors the Christian dogma. In the Fourth Book of Ezra, compare 13:23, after Dan. 7:2–3; and note here "this man" and, in 13, verses 5, 32, and 51: "the man risen out of the sea." This throws further light on the references in the Book of Enoch: "this son of man," "that son of man." In Revelation, see 1:13–14, after Dan. 10:5 and 7:9; compare also Revelation 1:7. For the style, compare also 5:6: "as though it had been slain."

5. Matt. 24:30 equals Mark 13:26 equals Luke 21:27; see 1. Thess. 4:15–16; Matt. 26:64 equals Mark 14:62; see Acts 8:56.

6. The Epistle of Barnabas 12:10.

7. Ignatius, Eph. 20:2.

8. Jer. Taanit II, 1 end, p. 65b near the bottom, with reference to Num. 23:19. Compare also the sentence of Eleazar ha-Kappar, cited in note 4.

9. Of the many examples, the following may be cited as especially characteristic: a sentence of Abbahu in Jer. Joma V, 3, p. 42c equals *Pessikta de-Rav Kahana*, p. 178a, "not a man—*bar nash*—but God"; further a sentence of R. Jehuda, in the middle of the second century, *Pessikta de-Rav Kahana*, 190b equals Shebuot 39b, "if one lets anybody—*bar nash*—swear"; finally the anonymous haggadic interpretation *Wayikra Rabba* for 1.2, that the meaning of *ben adam* should be "son of the just and pious."

10. Compare the Ps. of Solomon 17; Philo, *de praemiis et poenis* 16.

11. *Bereshit Rabba* I, 4, ed. Theodor, p. 6; XIV, 6, ed. Theodor, p. 130.

12. Dan. 7:9, 7:21, 22, 27; En. 52:4 (the anointed); 48:6 ff., 49:2, 50:1, 51:3 ff., 52:6 ff., 53:6, 55:4, 56:6, 58:1 ff., 61:8 ff., 62:1 ff.; see also the so-called Sixth Book of Ezra 1:53 and 1:56 (the chosen); En. 38:1 ff., 46:3 ff., 47:1, 61:13, 62:2, 71:19; see 60:2 (the just). Isa. 60:21 and Ps. 37:29,

as well as Sanhedrin X,1; *Tanhuma*, *"Hayye Sara,"* end. For "my son," Fourth Book of Ezra 13:32; see Exod. 4:22 and Ps. 2:7. An apocalyptic *haggada* of R. Meir is characteristic—*Tanhuma* "Way-yetze" II; here Jacob appears as the *sar* of the people of Israel as opposed to the *sarim* of Babel, Media, Javan, and Edom. It should also be recalled that in Philo, *de prof.* 20, *de somniis* II, 28 and 34, it is sometimes the Logos and sometimes Michael that is designated as the "high priest."

13. 2 Sam. 6:21 and 21:6; 1 Kings 11:34; Ps. 89:3 and 106:23; Isa. 43:10 and 43:20, 44:1, 45:4, 65:9, 65:15, 65:22; 52:13 ff., 61:1. It is noteworthy that the Septuagint generally translated *servant of God* with the words *pais Theou*, which also means "child" (Isa. 42:1, 49:6, 50:10, 52:13), and rarely with the word *theoulos* (49:3 and 49:5). It should also be noted how the Gospel according to Luke and the Book of Acts use the words *pais Theou* to designate Jesus (Acts 3:13, 4:27 and 4:30) as well as David (Luke 1:69) and the ideal Israel (Luke 1:54).

14. Isa. 11:1 ff., 9:5–6, 7:14–15; Jer. 23:5; Ezek. 34:23.

15. If the Epistle of Barnabas should have to be dated later, and if 16:34 should have to be interpreted in such a way that one would have to relegate the epistle to the time of Hadrian, then the quoted sentence would represent a final protest against the ecclesiastical doctrine of the son of man. The Epistle of the Hebrews could already interpret the "son of man" in Ps. 8:5 as referring to the Messiah; see 1 Cor. 15:27 and Eph. 1:22.

16. The Gospel according to Mark, too, belongs, in its canonical form, only to the last part of the first century.

Part Three

The Gospels

Introduction

It is a popular misconception that the Gospels are ancient biographies, written by eyewitnesses to the ministry of Jesus of Nazareth. The source of this opinion is a second-century bishop, Irenaeus of Lyon, who suggests in his attack on the heretics that two of the Gospels, those assigned to Matthew and John, were written by apostles of Jesus and that those assigned to Mark and Luke were written by students of apostles: Mark by a disciple of Peter at Rome, Luke by a "secretary" of Paul. The tradition linking Mark's Gospel to Peter and Matthew's to a closer follower of Jesus who had recorded his words "in the Hebrew tongue" is also attested by an early writer named Papias of Hierapolis, whose testimony, however, has perished and is only repeated piecemeal by the fourth-century writer Eusebius.

It is the conventional scholarly wisdom today that none of the present texts of the Gospels comes directly from an "eyewitness" to the teaching of Jesus, and it is extremely doubtful that any of the sayings attributed to Jesus in the Gospels were actually spoken by an historical figure. As we shall see in Part Four, it is difficult even to speak of an "historical" Jesus, given the proportions and immediacy of the myth-making process that characterizes the earliest days of the Jesus-cult. Whether or not there was an historical founder (and such is not needed, as the mystery religions testify, for the success of a cult and a coherent story about its "founder"), scholars now count it a certainty that the Gospels are compilations of "traditions" cherished by the early Christians rather than historical annals. In form, they are an odd blend of miracle stories, sayings, traditions (parables, curses, apocalyptic predictions, moral injunctions and the like), legends (the birth narratives), and myths (the story of the dying and rising god).

While it may be true, in a purely theoretical sense, that every "narrative event" (literary artifact) is unique and unrepeatable, the Gospels are, from an historian's point of view, an agglutination of common forms drawn from the stock of rabbinical wisdom, heroic tales, and the Hebrew Scripture, concocted by the cult of Christ as political, social, and religious needs warranted. To a very large degree, the life of Jesus recounted for us in the Gospels, despite the tissue of historical sequence that seems to link events to one another, is a biography of the Jesus cult, a record of their various and often conflicting understandings of who Jesus was and what he had accomplished on their behalf. Paul, whose letters are older than the Gospels by a generation, is uninterested in the historical Jesus; he knows only the Christ of the cult, the risen Lord spiritually present among the initiates: "Now you are the body of Christ, member for member; . . . If there is a natural body, there is also a spiritual body. . . . The first man was from the earth, earthy; the second man [the Christ] is from the heavens, heavenly," (1 Cor. 12:27; 15:44, 47).

The Jesus of Nazareth so superficially historicized in the Gospels is unknown to Paul, who preaches instead the "gospel" of a crucified and risen savior god (1 Cor. 1:23). In the course of time, as belief in the historical existence of the god of the cult grew in conjunction with the spread of the "gospel," stories about his birth, his teaching, the marvels wrought by his hand, the time of his return, and the circumstances of his resurrection from the dead were added to the originally simple, if circuitous "gospel" preached by the early Christian propagandists: "The Christ was raised from the dead; so how do some say that there is no resurrection of the dead? If there is no resurrection of the dead, then neither did Christ rise; and if Christ did not rise, then our preaching is worthless and your faith is worthless" (1 Cor. 15:12 ff.).

Such reasoning may have been persuasive to those already committed to the belief that the Christ had overcome death and ascended to heaven; but in the course of transmitting such a message to the unconverted masses of the Roman Empire, more details were needed: If he ascended, what had been his life on earth? Had he left any teachings that might guide the cult in its day-to-day operations? Who were his family? How could one prove to the detractors that he possessed the proper qualifications to be called the Messiah? Had he foreknown his death? Had he been seen by his followers after his resurrection, and was there a chance he would be seen again? Had his birth been an event as marvelous as his death and resurrection?

Such questions found answers available in the Hellenistic world: spirit-filled prophets (1 Cor. 14.1 ff.) would speak the "words" of the Lord even as the prophets of old had spoken with the voice of Yahweh; after a time, these sayings were taken to be the words of an historical figure and, their source forgotten, were gathered into collections—such as the one we find embedded in the Gospels of Matthew and Luke ("Q").

For these sayings it only remained for the evangelists to supply a context: narrative elaboration in the form of tales of miraculous cures and nature miracles, and appropriate passages from the Old Testament "proving" the correspondence between the "events" of Jesus' life and the prophecies.

This quantity was added in turn to what seems to have been the oldest stratum of *literary* material: the story of the death of Jesus and the bare proclamation that he had been raised again by God and seen by his followers (1 Cor. 15:1–11).

Scholarly opinion still holds (albeit not tenaciously) to the postulate of an historical figure whose life story was very soon displaced by the mythmaking activity of a cult. Some of the essays included in this section and the next reflect that hypothesis; others reflect the view that the postulation of an historical figure is unnecessary to explain the apparently "biographical" features of the Gospels. A candid appraisal of the evidence would seem to favor the latter view, but we cannot easily dismiss the possibility that an historical figure lies behind the Jesus-legend of the New Testament.

It is a truism that the historicity of events is no guarantee that they will secure a place in the memory of a social group, and nonhistoricity no guarantee that a story will not be believed, treasured, and preserved. Historical Jesus or not, the sayings and deeds of the Christ preserved in the Gospels are our fullest access to the life history of the early church.

Dennis Nineham

The Origins and Character of the Gospels

DENNIS NINEHAM was born in 1921 in Southampton, England, and graduated from Oxford University, where he studied with H. Wheeler Robinson and R. H. Lightfoot. He was fellow and chaplain of Queen's College until 1951, when he became professor of biblical and historical theology at King's College, London. From 1964 to 1969 he was Regius professor of divinity at Cambridge University and from 1969 to 1979 warden of Keble College, Oxford. Since 1980 he has been professor of theology at Bristol University. Nineham's balanced and judicious application of critical methods of the text of the New Testament has made him one of the foremost contemporary biblical scholars in Britain.

The story begins in the period immediately after the lifetime of Jesus when as yet there were no written accounts of any sort, but the tradition about him was preserved entirely by word of mouth. So far as the material in our Gospels is concerned, it was preserved during this period exclusively by Christians.[1] This is a fact of the utmost significance for the understanding of the Gospel tradition, for it means that during this period the tradition about Jesus was preserved by people to whom he was not a dead figure of the past, but a living contemporary with whom they were in constant and immediate relationship.

From them the Jesus of whose earthly life the tradition spoke was the same person whom they now knew as Lord and Son of God, and whom they believed to be sitting at God's right hand in glory, governing the universe on his behalf, and soon to come to earth again to judge and wind up the universe, and usher in

From the Introduction of D. E. Nineham, *Saint Mark* (London: Pelican Books, revised edition 1969), pp. 17–25. Copyright D. E. Nineham, 1963. Reprinted by permission of Penguin Books Ltd.

a wholly new world-order.

This last belief is particularly important; the earliest Christians confidently expected Christ's return and the complete establishment of God's kingdom within one or two generations at most, so from their point of view it was natural to regard the three stages of Christ's work, his earthly life in the past, his present lordship in heaven, and his future coming, as three acts of a single—and quite compact—drama, three stages in one continuous operation by which the salvation of man was to be secured and the kingdom of God established. And since the first Christians were all Jews, they naturally set this three-act drama against the background of the Old Testament and saw it as simply the final phase of God's age-long working towards man's salvation, of which the Old Testament revealed the earlier stages.

Since the early Christians thus believed themselves to be living in a comparatively short interim period before the end of the world, their energies were naturally concentrated on practical tasks, on bringing others to a realization of the situation and on the attempt to maintain and deepen their own relationship with the exalted Lord so that when he came to establish his kingdom finally, they would be worthy to be members of it. Consequently, they will have had little leisure, even had they had the aptitude, for antiquarian research into Christ's earthly life; nor would they have thought it worth while, seeing that they did not look forward to any posterity who might be expected to profit from the result of it.

Such interest as they had in the earthly life of Jesus was of a quite different kind; as we have seen, they understood his earthly life as one stage in the total comprehensive drama of salvation, and consequently their curiosity about it was directed not to the precise biographical details, but to the question of what contribution it made to the total action of the play; in what way exactly had Jesus' earthly life contributed to the achievement of man's salvation and the establishment of God's kingdom? In St. Paul's Epistles—all written during this period—we can watch one early Christian wrestling with this problem and concluding, on the whole, that it was the *death* of Christ—interpreted as a sacrifice for sin—which was the decisive contribution of the earthly phase of Christ's activity to the total action of the drama. Similarly, in the finished Gospels, the events surrounding Christ's *death* are treated more fully than any others and treated, as we shall see, in a way which suggests that they had been studied and pondered in the Church longer and more deeply than earlier events in the earthly life. Indeed, so far as the evidence of the Epistles goes, St. Paul shows practically no interest in any aspect of Jesus' earthly career *except* the death.[2] But then in the Epistles St. Paul was writing to convinced Christians. When trying to convert those who knew nothing of Jesus or Christianity he must surely have spoken rather differently; he must have given at least sufficient information about the earthly life to provide the answers to certain obvious questions. Who was this Jesus to whom allegiance was being demanded, and did he merit such allegiance? How had he come to his present exalted position? Had his earthly life been such as to make plausible the very high claims that were now being made on his behalf? And when converts were won, they would have further needs. They would require a living concrete picture of the one to whom they were now committed. If they were to enter into relationship with him they must be able to envisage him, his demands, his attitude towards them, the attitude he expected from them, the way he wanted them to live, and so forth.

The early Christians thus had very definite motives for preserving memories of Jesus' earthly life, but only for preserving memories of *certain special kinds*—memories which would persuade nonbelievers of his supernatural status and help converts to realize him fully as a living person and discover the implications of their discipleship to him. In the earliest period, when converts were sought exclusively among the Jews, this will have had one particular corollary. No Jew could be expected to accept the claims made for Jesus unless it could be shown that his work was all of a piece with the saving work of God outlined in the Old Testament, and that it fulfilled the expectations there set out. In this connection the Church would need memories of Jesus which showed how his life had conformed to Old Testament predictions, especially at the moments for which decisive religious significance was claimed.

It will now be clear that the circumstances in which the tradition about Jesus was preserved *exercised a strong selective influence upon the character of what was preserved*—in a negative, as well as a positive direction. Viewing the life of Jesus as they did, there were certain things about him—for example, his sinlessness or the complete truth of all he said—that the early Christians would never have dreamed of questioning, let alone attempting to prove; they would therefore have had no interest in preserving material relevant to such issues. More important, since they thought of him as essentially a supernatural figure, even in the days of his flesh, his humanity would not in itself interest them very much. They recognized it of course as the means through which his work had been accomplished, but it never occurred to them to think of him as receiving anything essential from his human environment; and so they made no attempt to trace the effects of his environment upon him or the working of his mind— what led him to the conclusions he arrived at or what influenced him in forming his plans. Indeed, if they could have understood the term at all, they would no doubt have denied that the Son of God, for all his humanity, had any "psychology" in this sort of sense at all.[3] Hence all our questionings about Jesus' self-consciousness and his understanding of himself and his mission were entirely foreign to their concern.

Two further corollaries of the early Christians' attitude need to be noticed.

They took it for granted that the heavenly Christ was continually revealing further truth about himself to his followers in various ways (see, for example, 1 Cor. 2:16, 7:40 and John 16:22 ff.); and since the Christ who was thus revealed was the same person as the Jesus of the earthly life, it was only natural that the memories of his earthly life should be interpreted, and on occasions even modified and added to, in the light of these subsequent revelations. For example, to take a rather extreme case, it is at least possible that it was only when the heavenly Christ came to be recognized as Son of God that the idea arose that he had claimed to be such, and been recognized as such, in the days of his flesh, no explicit tradition to that effect being known.

The second corollary arises from the fact that they regarded Christ's activity as the final saving act of God to which the Old Testament had pointed forward. Since the Old Testament was regarded as completely accurate down to the last detail, it followed that everything it predicted concerning this final event must have found fulfillment at some point in Christ's ministry. Hence the Old Testament could become a source of information about the events of Christ's earthly life; and to the early Christians, with their deep conviction of its inerrancy, it may well have seemed a safer guide than the fallible memories of human witnesses, however well informed. There are, as we shall see, passages in Mark where it is impossible to be certain whether a particular story rests on a tradition derived from witnesses or whether it represents a deduction from Old Testament prophecy about what "must have" happened when the Messiah came.

If the tradition of Jesus was thus influenced by the beliefs and motives of those who preserved it, its character was also determined by the particular circumstance in which it was handed down. No doubt, at first, disciples of Jesus told stories about him to audiences of all kinds, both private and public, just as need and opportunity suggested; but it appears that the tradition on which the Gospels are based was handed on during the greater part of the oral period *in the context of public and formal occasions*; that is to say, the people by whom it was passed on were preachers and teachers, speaking at meetings for public worship or addressing groups of catechumens and the like. This had at least two very important effects on the tradition.

1. The natural thing would be for the preacher or catechist to repeat *one* story, or parable, or group of sayings, at each meeting and then go on to expound its significance for his hearers. Naturally he would choose his story or parable on each occasion in accordance with the particular needs of his audience; if he thought they needed a lesson in good-neighborliness, he would tell the parable of the Good Samaritan; if he knew they were in doubt whether to pay their taxes to the Roman authorities, he might describe how the Lord had been questioned on that subject (see Mark 12:13–17), and so on. Consequently, the order in which the incidents were recounted would vary from church to church, in accordance with local needs; and there would be no compelling motive for preserving, or even remembering, the order in which they originally occurred during Jesus' lifetime. The tradition about Jesus would thus assume the form of a variety of separate stories with no fixed or generally agreed order. No doubt particular individuals or groups sometimes made collections of some of these stories, and even had them committed to writing, but their motives in doing so were always practical and led them to select stories of a particular kind and arrange them in an order which served some practical purpose. One group, for example, might collect for controversial purposes stories of Jesus' arguments with his opponents

(see Mark 2:1–3:6), another group might be led by the needs of uneducated catechumens to collect all his sayings about "stumbling" or "salt" or "watchfulness" in an order that could be easily memorized (see Mark 9:38 ff. and 13:28–37, for example); but in such cases there would be no attempt to recover, or preserve, the original *historical* order of the incidents or sayings in question.

A partial exception to the last statement must be made in favor of the Passion narrative, to which several special considerations applied. Not only were the events of Christ's death the center of the whole ministry, as we have seen, but in the interests of its missionary work the early Church was bound to have its own more or less coherent account of the last few days of Jesus' life. It claimed divine honors for a young man who had shortly before suffered capital punishment at the hands of the Romans, after due processes of Roman law, the accusers being the accredited leaders of the Jewish faith. If the Church was to have any hope of sustaining this astonishing claim in the eyes of people with a Jewish background, it must be able to show, not only that the charges on which Jesus had been condemned were false accusations, inspired by the pride and jealousy of the Jewish leaders, but also that what had happened corresponded exactly with Old Testament prophecy and was all part of God's predetermined plan for his Son. In that connection the need for a circumstantial account of Christ's last days from the Christian standpoint will fairly soon have made itself felt; and so, as we have seen, the incidents of the Passion appear to have been the first to be collected together in anything like a historical narrative. Even so the account was some time in coming into existence, and it can only be called "historical" with considerable qualifications; the aim was not an objective historical report as those words would be understood today, but a selective account, such as would support and justify the Christian understanding of Christ's death.

Before we consider the significance of all this for the Gospels, we must look briefly at the other result of the tradition's being handed down in the context of public worship and instruction. This touches the form and content of the individual units of the tradition.

2. We have seen that the various incidents and sayings were handed on in a *public* setting. This in itself would mean that all purely personal detail would be out of place; but we must also remember that the stories were normally recounted in order to form the basis of a lesson or sermon in which their particular application would be drawn out. Naturally, therefore they would be told in the way best calculated to lead on to the subsequent exposition or application; if the point to be brought out in connection with some incident was the comment Jesus made upon it, then, in the telling of the story, the comment itself would be reported in full and given prominence, while the rest of the incident would be related as briefly as possible, just the minimum being retained that was necessary to provide the Lord's words with an intelligible setting.[4] If, on the other hand, the aim was to stress the remarkable nature of some action of Jesus, as evidence of his supernatural power, then any words that might have been spoken in connection with it would be briefly reported and little emphasized, and the emphasis

would be concentrated entirely on those features of the incident which underlined its supernatural character—for example, in the case of a healing, the chronic
and deep-seated nature of the illness, the ease with which Jesus cured it, the impression of amazement made on the bystanders, and the completeness of the cure
as evidenced by the healed man's ability to run or shout or carry his own bed
(see for example, Mark 5:25-26, 9:20—22, 2:12).

What we have just been describing can have been no more than a tendency,
and it will have taken some time to make itself felt. No doubt, in the earliest days, stories about Jesus were told by his disciples with all the wealth
of detail, often strictly irrelevant detail, we associate with the eyewitness; but
as time went on, and the stories were remote and more told by local Church
leaders who had not personally known Jesus and were not even Jews with a
first-hand knowledge of Palestine, sheer ignorance of the details must have combined with the other factors just mentioned to produce increasingly "stream-
lined" versions of various incidents in which little or nothing was retained except what was of practical religious significance. And naturally, when once a
story had attained its most "economical" form in this way, there will have been
a tendency for it to become more or less stereotyped and to circulate in that
form with relatively little further change.

At this point we must take account of another consideration which modern
readers are apt to find rather surprising. People's attitude towards history in the
ancient world was often rather different from our own. If, for example, an
ancient writer was convinced that Jesus was, as a matter of fact, Christ and Son
of God, he might well tell the story of his earthly life in terms of his having
claimed, and been accorded, those titles, even though there was no explicit
tradition to that effect. Indeed he might well feel that it would be wrong to do
otherwise; for if Jesus was in fact Son of God, then any account of his earthly
life which did not make that clear would be misleading and would not convey
the true meaning of the events it professed to describe.

Probably such feelings seldom attained the level of full consciousness, but
their influence on the development of the tradition could be all the greater for
being unconscious; another, parallel influence may have worked equally uncon-
sciously. If Jesus was Son of God, it was felt, his words must have had universal
significance; they must have something to say to his followers in every time and
place. In practice, words which Jesus had spoken in early-first-century Palestine,
often in very special circumstances, did not always seem to apply without modification to the conditions of, let us say, a Hellenistic congregation some decades
later, and so it was only natural for people to feel that what he must "really"
have meant, or said, was something which had a direct lesson for them. Here
then is another factor which will have worked, largely below the conscious level,
in the direction of modifying the various units of tradition in accordance with
the circumstances and preoccupations of the various little communities scattered
over the Mediterranean world. . . .

NOTES

1. The information we possess about Jesus from non-Christian sources is exceedingly slight, though it is sufficient to establish the facts of his existence and his character as the founder of a new religious group among the Jews of the first century. See especially Suetonius, *Claudius*, 25; Tacitus, *Annals*, xv, 44; and Josephus, *Antiquities*, xviii, 63 f., conveniently collected and discussed in C. K. Barrett, *The New Testament Background*.

2. Some scholars would perhaps regard this as a rather sweeping way of putting it, but broadly speaking the point would be generally conceded.

3. One is reminded of the hyperorthodox student, described by H. J. Cadbury, who, "when asked of a certain narrative in the gospels what Jesus had in mind, replied simply that Jesus had no mind" (*The Peril of Modernizing Jesus*, p. 30).

4. A story of this kind about Jesus is usually referred to in English as a pronouncement story.

5. Such stories are usually referred to as miracle stories.

Martin Dibelius

The Synoptic Problem

MARTIN DIBELIUS (1883-1947), born in Dresden and educated at the universities of Leipzig, Tübingen, and Berlin, was from 1915 professor of New Testament at the University of Heidelberg, where he succeeded the renowned Johannes Weiss in pioneering the new method of biblical study known as *Formgeschichte* (form-criticism). His cautious application of the method, recorded in his 1919 study *Die Formgeschichte des Evangeliums* (Eng. tr., *From Tradition to Gospel*) gained him the respect of liberal and conservative scholars alike.

In general, the form-critics held to the theory that during the period when the words of Jesus were transmitted orally, they were reduced and sometimes altered to stereotyped literary patterns (forms) such as parables, apothegms, and beatitudes. On the one hand, it was argued, this patterning served as an aid to memory, a point stressed by the conservative critics who emphasized the strength of the oral tradition in first-century Palestine. The liberals countered with the observation that the forms cannot be said to have originated in the lifetime of Jesus, but can as easily be explained in terms of the literary activity of the early Christian church. They argued further that the sheer diversity of forms and the substantial differences between the synoptic Gospels and the Gospel of John invite the conclusion that the stereotyping of forms cannot be used to establish the authenticity of the words attributed by the writers to Jesus.

In spite of great differences in size and in choice of material, the Gospels of Matthew, Mark, and Luke are nevertheless so similar to one another in numerous passages, that one can print and read their texts in three parallel columns. Only by such comparison are we able to appreciate their interrelationship, which

From *A Fresh Approach to the Gospels and Early Christian Literature* by Martin Dibelius (London: Ivor Michelson and Watson, 1938), pp. 54-57.

189

even extends to the words employed. One may also grasp how a large number of differences came into being; they are to be explained partly from the style of the individual evangelist, or from the changed situations of the Christians, and the correspondingly changed conception of Jesus' sayings and doings. From the Greek appellation of such a tabular conspectus—namely, Synposis—the usual name for the three earliest evangelists is the Synoptists. The problem presented by those peculiar relationships of similiarity and difference among the Gospels themselves is called the Synoptic Problem.

The reddiest explanations of this relationship cannot explain the similarity of the material, for the Synoptists have neither copied from one another nor have they all used the same source. And so, after many trials and errors in research, a widely accepted solution was reached in the last third of the nineteenth century, which really explained the most essential peculiarities of the interrelations of the synoptic Gospels.

This solution is known as the "two-source theory," according to which Matthew and Luke used Mark and in addition a second source, "Q," now lost.

It follows, therefore, that the short Gospel of Mark is earlier than either of its two companions and is indeed their source. The dependence of Luke upon Mark can be proved by the very order of the sections, for in his presentation of Jesus' work, Luke simply followed Mark's order; if we ignored changes and omissions that can usually be understood, this fact is proved by Luke 3:1 through 6:19; 8:4 through 9:50, and 18:15 through 24:11. That part of his material which does not come from Mark and also does not connect with him, Luke has introduced in two places. To some degree, they are to be regarded as two masses of interpolations in the life of Jesus according to Mark, namely, Luke 6:20 through 8:3 and 9:51 through 18:14. Nevertheless Luke's faithfulness to Mark is occasionally very far-reaching; e.g., the three prophecies of suffering which occur in Mark 8:31, 9:30, and 10:32 as well-spaced announcements of the Passion are ruined in their equal spacing by the second interpolation, and are to be found in Luke 9:22, 9:43, and—after the second interpolation—18:31. But Luke does not think of restoring the equality of space by a freer grouping of his material, for this would compel him to remove the prophecies of suffering from their context, and that, again, would mean destroying Mark's order.

Matthew's dependence upon Mark cannot be demonstrated in the same manner. What serves in this case as a proof of the two-source theory is, first of all, the dependence in detail of the Greek text of Matthew upon that of Mark. But in the last analysis the arrangement of Matthew shows, even if not so strikingly as that of Luke, that he had Mark's Gospel before him. Granted that in the first half of his book Matthew constructed cycles out of his material (i.e., essentially out of Mark and "Q") and so described teaching, works, disciples, disputes, and parables, in relatively homogeneous sections, yet in the second half, when he described the events not yet dealt with, including the Passion, Matthew employed no independent principle of arrangement but followed the course of events as recorded in Mark 6–15.

According to the two-source theory, Matthew and Luke used what has been called the sayings-source "Q," in additon to Mark. We gain insight into this hypothesis if we take a "Synopsis" and consider the sections absent from Mark. We then find almost verbal agreement in numerous passages, from John the Baptist's preaching of repentance to the last "speeches" of Jesus. Each of the two evangelists occasionally alters a little, usually in the manner to be observed when they are editing Mark. Luke often, but Matthew rarely, improves an expression, but Matthew, when he does so, goes deeper, and usually in the direction of a legalistic Christianity. If one has regard to these pecularities, one can reconstruct the lost source from our two witnesses and this indeed in many passages.

In this way the two-source theory is better able than any other to explain the synoptic interrelationship. Of course, it does not solve the whole problem. It cannot say whence the evangelists obtained the material peculiar to each, nor anything about the question whether Mark drew from "Q" the rather infrequent speeches which he reproduces. It does not explain how Matthew and Luke came to use the same alterations of the Mark text, nor why Luke did not reproduce certain passages which he had doubtless seen (especially Mark 6:45 through 8:26). But none of this affords a reason for doubt about the two-source theory. It only falls into disrepute if one attempts to draw from it an explanation of all details of synoptic interrelationship, and underestimates the other possibilities of explanation, e.g., the influence of oral tradition, some special sources of small extent, and finally the accommodation of the Gospels to each other in the manuscripts of the New Testament.

Ernst Kaesemann

Is the Gospel Objective?

ERNST KAESEMANN, professor emeritus of New Testament at the University of Tübin-
gen, is one of the foremost New Testament scholars of his generation. A student of the
Marburg theologian and biblical critic Rudolph Bultmann, Kaesemann is a prolific
writer and an outspoken defender of the historical-critical method. His books include
Essays on New Testament Themes (1960), *New Testament Questions of Today* (1965), and
Perspectives on Paul (Eng. tr., 1969).

The Synoptic Gospels as we have them today are the product of a tradition
which was at least forty years in the process of formation and the material of
which is composed of very small units. At first it was individual sayings and
isolated stories which were handed on; later these were collected together probably for preaching purposes; this made it possible for the evangelists, in a third
and final stage, to set the appearance of Jesus on earth within a framework of
space and time. It is thus quite impossible to extract from the Gospels anything
resembling an historical sequence or even a biographical development, and all
efforts of this kind were, and remained, flights of fancy. Anything which could
be used for such a purpose belongs to the later stage of tradition, and for the
most part to the evangelists' technique of composition. But of the individual sayings and stories it must be said that from their first appearance they were used in
the service of the community's preaching and were indeed preserved for this very
reason. It was not historical but kerygmatic* interest which handed them on.

*This term refers to the preaching of the community.—*Ed.*

From this standpoint it becomes comprehensible that this tradition, or at least the overwhelming mass of it, cannot be called authentic. Only a few words of the Sermon on the Mount and of the conflict with the Pharisees, a number of parables, and some scattered material of various kinds go back with any real degree of probability to the Jesus of history. Of his deeds, we know only that he had the reputation of being a miracle-worker, that he himself referred to his power of exorcism, and that he was finally crucified under Pilate. The preaching about him has almost entirely supplanted his own preaching, as can be seen most clearly of all in the completely unhistorical Gospel of John.

The question will naturally arise: How could such a state of affairs come about? Further Easter stories come to be attached to the announcements of the Resurrection enumerated in 1 Corinthians 15, and ever more miracles came to be ascribed to him of whom it was told that he healed Peter's mother-in-law and many who were possessed with devils. Among the sayings we must distinguish various elements. First, there is secular material, previously circulating in the manner of proverbs, but now transferred to Jesus. Then the community, appealing in its internal disagreement to the Master or seeking to make his individuality more vivid, created in the so-called conflict discourses or apothegms ideal scenes for his words and deeds. Finally—and most important of all—we have to remember the part played by the prophets in early Christianity. As we can see clearly in the Revelation of John, they clothed their own epigrammatic words in the form of "I" sayings of Jesus, speaking as Spirit-filled men with the authority and in the name of the exalted Christ. When these words handed on, the distinction between the exalted and the earthly Lord quickly disappeared, more especially as primitive Christianity was not particularly interested in the latter. Thus it came about the countless "I" sayings of the Christ who revealed himself through the mouth of prophets gained entry into the Synoptic tradition as sayings of Jesus.

Three basic axioms are vital to our understanding. (1) The framework in which the individual units of the Gospel tradition are set may guarantee a connected narrative and build up, together with the logical order, a chronological order extending over much of the material and manifesting an historical interest detectable in few other pieces of tradition, but even then, it is not this historical interest but concern with the task of proclamation which has been responsible for passing on the relatively few genuine words of Jesus and combining them with the kerygmatic resources of the community—that is, for bringing the Gospels into existence. (2) The very reason why the historical facts of the life of Jesus as good as perished from the primitive Christian message was the community's awareness that its mission was one of proclamation. (3) Apart from a few fragments of the preaching and activity of Jesus which are only accessible to us through the proclamation of the community—and even then have to be separated out under very great difficulties—the Gospels are, both in form and content, documents of primitive Christian preaching, documents, therefore, of faith in the risen Lord and therefore also of Church dogma. Here and there some material may in practice go back to an earlier stage, but in principle Christian history begins with the Easter faith of the disciples. What lies behind that is only accessible now by theoretical reconstruction—and this applies above all to the Jesus of history.

Because these are the facts, it has been possible for two hundred years to paint his portrait in ever new colors and contours; because these are the facts, there is in our own time on this point nothing but a chaos of contradictory opinions and reconstructions and there will probably never be any stronger consensus on the problem. . . .

Edgar J. Goodspeed

The Original Language of the Gospels

EDGAR J. GOODSPEED (1871-1962) was born in Quincy, Illinois, of New England
stock. His father, a Baptist clergyman, was one of the founders of the University of
Chicago, where Goodspeed received his Ph.D. in 1898. From 1915, Goodspeed made
Chicago his academic home, serving as chairman of the New Testament department
there until his retirement in 1937. His books, written in a popular style without loss
of scholarly authority, include *The New Testament: An American Translation* (1923),
How to Read the Bible (1946), and *A Life of Jesus* (1950). Goodspeed was also the
author of more than two hundred papers. He received honorary degrees from Denison
University, the University of Redlands, and the University of California.

More than forty years ago an aspiring young English scholar undertook to
account for the resemblances and differences in the first three Gospels with the
theory that they had all been translated from a primitive Aramaic Gospel, the
expressions of which were understood differently. The idea was very seriously
considered and debated by the leaders of critical study, but was definitely rejected
for a number of reasons. One was that it created more difficulties than it solved,
for it made the very numerous exact identities of Greek wording among the
Gospels harder than ever to explain. Another was that there were no contemporary Aramaic documents extant with which to compare the supposed Aramaic
idioms demanded by the theory.

This scholar's method was to pick out here and there expressions in the
Greek Gospels that sounded to him like constructions used in Aramaic, the
everyday speech of the first-century Jews of Palestine, and to translate them as
best he could into that idiom. If the Aramaic he thus produced could then, by

supposing some misunderstanding or miswriting of it, be translated back into a Greek form that gave an easier meaning, or into the parallel, slightly different form given in another Gospel, the theory was considered supported.

The subjective character of this method is obvious, and it did not long continue to hold the interest of New Testament scholars. Recently, however, it has been revived in various novel forms, with much talk of new sources and new evidence. In reality, no new sources of evidence favorable to these solutions have come to light. On the contrary, all the discoveries of the past forty years have made such solutions more and more improbable. For one thing, they should of course, if sound, increase the rhetorical power of the Gospels, the Oriental vigor of their imagery; but they invariably dilute and diminish these. This in itself is enough to show that the procedure is a mistaken one. G. K. Chesterton once observed that the style of Jesus was gigantesque—full of camels leaping through needles and mountains being hurled into the sea. The effort to tame such a style and reduce it to the commonplace is plainly futile. The tamer it becomes, the more improbable it is.

But the greatest difficulty with the method was that there seemed to be no historical occasion likely to have called forth the Aramaic Gospel it assumed, especially at so early a date as claimed—50 or 52 A.D.

This is the core of the problem. How did such a Gospel come to be written? The Gospel is Christianity's contribution to literature. To credit such a creation to the most barren age of a never very productive tongue like Aramaic would seem the height of improbability.

For in the days of Jesus, the Jews of Palestine were not engaged in writing books. It is not too much to say that a Jerusalem or Galilean Jew of the time of Christ would regard writing a book in his native tongue with positive horror. Even a century before, a Jew who wrote a book felt obliged to put it under the name of some ancient worthy like Enoch, the seventh from Adam, or to claim as its author some ancient Jew of what was called the Prophetic Period, which was understood to extend from Moses to Ezra, and from which it was believed all sound books on religion must come.

This aversion to writing books was not merely negative. It was positive. They had plenty of things to say and they said them, but they would not write them. Those were the days when the famous oral amplification of the Jewish Law was being developed by such masters as Hillel and Shammai. But the Jews would not write it; they memorized it. It seemed an act of impiety to write it, for then it might seem to rival the Scripture itself.

Those days also witnessed the translation of the Hebrew Law into the Aramaic vernacular. But this too remained unwritten for generations. Indeed, it is impossible to realize the fantastic reality of the first-century Jewish attitude toward writing books.

There is a rabbinical story that about 50 A.D. Gamaliel the First, the grandson of Hillel, saw a written copy of an Aramaic translation of Job, and immediately had it destroyed. The story may not be true, but its intention is obvious; if anyone was wicked enough to write down the Targum on Job, it must be destroyed. This was the orthodox Jewish attitude toward writing books in Aramaic, in Jerusalem about the middle of the first century.

If anything could heighten the picture, it is the behavior of Jews of that very period who escaped from these narrowing walls into the great Greek world of the day. Such men wrote books freely, but they wrote them principally in Greek. There is a peculiar irony in this, that gifted Jews should have to turn to Greek as a medium of literary expression. But Philo, Paul, and Josephus tell the story. They wrote—but they wrote in Greek.

Of the Jewish Apocrypha written within a century of the life of Jesus, the great majority were composed in Greek, not Aramaic, and it seems abundantly clear that in the times of Jesus the Jews were not writing books in Aramaic; indeed, they were actually resorting to the strangest devices to avoid doing so.

Even if the Jews had been given to Aramaic composition, and contemporary Aramaic literature had been a garden instead of a desert, the early Christians could hardly have contributed to it. They were constantly overshadowed by the sense of imminent catastrophe. The messianic advent overhung them like a huge wave of fate, threatening—or promising—to break at any moment. It was their urgent task to hasten about the ancient world warning men of what was at hand. Clearly it was no time for writing books.

But within a generation of the death of Jesus, Christianity had entered the Greek world and begun to establish itself there. In that world it found a wholly different attitude to writing and publication. "If you find a saying of a certain philosopher and have no paper," ran the Greek proverb, "write it upon your garments!" The Greeks took notes, and they wrote books. They were insatiable readers. Novelty did not repel them; it attracted them. The Athenians seemed to Luke to spend all their time telling or listening to something new. Certain it is that from the time Christianity really entered the Greek world it instinctively went about recording itself in writing—first letters, and then books.

These books were copied and recopied with such zest and zeal that there are even now more manuscripts of the Greek Gospels than of any other work of literature in the world. The older of these, the Chester Beatty papyrus, is from the first half of the third century, and was actually copied only half a century after the first assembling of a New Testament. So near do our Greek documents bring us to the making of the New Testament, and so ample is the existing manuscript evidence for them. . . .

Mark's hasty and primitive Gospel was soon expanded, probably at Antioch, into the far more impressive and effective Gospel of Matthew. The terrible fate of the Jewish nation had now had time to sink into the Christian consciousness. Matthew saw in it the nation's punishment for its rejection of the Messiah, and the unmistakable shadow of the great catastrophe is on many a page of his Gospel. Indeed, the Gospel of Matthew cannot be understood without it.

Ernest Renan called Matthew the most important book in the world. Certainly it is the climax of Gospel writing, for the books that followed it were more than Gospels. Moreover, they now began to be written by Greeks. Luke's history of the beginnings of Christianity was organized in two volumes, the first of which covered the life and work of Jesus, not as a separate subject, but as an indispensable part of the whole movement. Its progress was traced from its beginnings in Palestine until Paul found it firmly established in Rome, and the book was evidently written when the movement was such a success that its future seemed assured.

Twenty years later, the necessity of restating Christianity in terms immediately intelligible to the Greek mind led to the Gospel according to John, which is more a dialogue than a Gospel, and is full of of Greek feeling from beginning to end. To further the influence of this great book, so rich alike in theology and in devotion, there were soon gathered about it the older local Gospels to form the great quartette we know. So understood, the Gospels articulate with what we know of the progress of Christianity in the Greek world.

Many years ago, a young German scholar happened to pick up a pamphlet containing some newly published Greek papyrus documents. Each transcript was signed by the man who had deciphered it, and one of these signatures caught the young scholar's eye, for it was the name of a friend of his. He became sufficiently interested to read the text of the document above the name, and immediately felt the likeness of the language to the Greek of the New Testament. He pursued the idea, read numerous other such pieces and became convinced; the Greeks of these letters, deeds, and contracts written in New Testament times by people in Egypt was just like the Greek of the New Testament.

The Greek of the New Testament had always been a good deal of a problem. It was not like classical Greek; it was not like the Greek version of the Old Testament; it was not like the literary Greek of its own day. The older learning was forced to describe it as a "Holy Ghost language," devised by Providence for the purposes of revelation. It remained for the Greek papyri, hidden in the sands of Egypt, to reveal to us its real character. It is simply the informal, colloquial Greek of its day.

Not long after the youthful Deissmann had observed the resemblance of the Greek of the papyri to that of the New Testament, two young Oxford Fellows settled down for a winter of excavation in Upper Egypt, in the camp of Professor Flinders Petrie, the distinguished Egyptologist. They were there to learn the art of excavation and to pick up any Greek papyri that might present themselves. Professor Petrie's interest was in prehistoric Egypt, and, when the site very soon proved to be as late as the Roman period of Egyptian history, he at once turned the digging over to his young friends.

There were fame and fortune for Grenfell and Hunt in those low, drab mounds of Oxyrhynchus. One day, fifteen hundred years before, the Romans had cleared out their record office and sent the old papers out to be burned. But the fire had smouldered and gone out, and the sand had covered the worthless old papers and protected them from damp, so that Grenfell's men carried them to his camp sometimes in the very baskets in which the Romans had sent them out to be burned. It was the greatest discovery of Greek papyri ever made. But what made Oxyrhynchus forever memorable was the finding there of a leaf of "Sayings of Jesus."

Three years later at Tebtunis, Grenfell and Hunt again struck it rich. They chanced upon a crocodile cemetery, and had exhumed dozens of crocodile mummies, but no papyri, when one January day a workman in vexation struck one of the mummies with his mattock and broke it open—and behold, it was wrapped in papyrus from head to tail! So were all the Tebtunis crocodiles!

With every such increase in our papyrus resources, Deissmann's brilliant discovery receives abundant confirmation. It used to be the fashion to class some five hundred New Testament words as found only in biblical or ecclesiastical Greek. Within twenty-five years after the advent of the papyri, this list had shrunk to fifty—about one per cent of the New Testament vocabulary—and it has now practically disappeared.

Many ecclesiastical constructions in New Testament Greek used to be explained as Semitisms—that is, as due to imitation of Hebrew or Aramaic idioms. But in the presence of the Greek papyri these too have rapidly dwindled until they have lost any possible literary significance. It has become clear that New Testament Greek is not a kind of ancient Yiddish, as some have supposed. The thousands of Greek papyrus documents from the very years of its origin have definitely established its right to be, and, against the protests of classicists and Semitists, have recovered for it its rightful position, of which it had long been disinherited. The Gospels were written not in muddy Greek or an awkward patois. They were, rather, masterpieces of popular literature, the first books written in popular Greek. Their rapid advance to influence is an unanswereable testimony to their clearness and force.

Their kinship with the vernacular Greek of the papyrus letters and documents becomes steadily clearer as more and more of these appear in print. It is an amazing fact that we now have definitely dated papyrus documents from every single year of the first century—not late copies, but the actual originals. If we possessed one single Aramaic text from anywhere in that century, or even a copy of one, in the language of Palestine, we should be fortunate. But none has ever been found.

Yet the Jews were in Egypt long before the Greeks, and were numerous and active there in the first century. But, like Philo, they expressed themselves in Greek, not in the Aramaic vernacular of Palestine.

We cannot connect the Gospels with Palestinian Judaism. It definitely refused the Gospel. There is no escaping that. We may wish it otherwise, but the hard fact remains. We cannot at this date alter it. Jerusalem had neither the will nor the skill to produce the Gospels. No one has ever succeeded in fitting them into its literature or its life. Appeals to Aramaic writings five hundred years earlier, as though their diction could prove something, reveal the desperateness of the endeavor. It is like seeking support for nineteenth-century English in the idiom of Wyclif.

The Greek Gospels are a convincing monument of the conquest of the Greco-Roman world by Christianity, and also of the conquest of Christianity by the Greek genius. It is no accident that these important and most telling of books arose in Greek circles and on Greek soil. Where else in antiquity could such books have arisen? Taken as a whole, the Gospels are integrated with no one place or period, but reflect clear and definite stages in the spread of the new faith among the Greeks. And the New Testament will be best understood as the literary precipitate deposited by the Christian movement when it impinged upon the Greek world.

G. A. Wells

The Character of the Gospels

G. A. WELLS is professor of Germanic languages and literature at Birkbeck College, University of London. He has written extensively on the subject of the historical Jesus: *The Jesus of the Early Christians* (1971), *Did Jesus Exist?* (1975), and *The Historical Evidence for Jesus* (1982). Wells is the foremost contemporary spokesman for the Christ-myth theory, advanced in different forms by van den Bergh van Eysinga, Kalthoff, Arthur Drews, and J. M. Robertson.

FORM-CRITICISM

Critics who treat the books of the New Testament as historical documents must accept some criterion of their trustworthiness. They must try to determine when the books were written, for what purpose, and by whom. When they have ascertained these facts, they can judge what knowledge the writer would be likely to have, how far he might be able to distinguish true from false reports, and how far he would be influenced by religious preconceptions or dogmatic purposes.

The form-critics give a theoretical answer of these questions by analyzing Gospels and Epistles into short passages (pericopes) of distinctive literary form (e.g., creeds, short sermons, etc.). Dibelius, one of the best-known exponents, believed that the Gospels were written toward the end of the first century, that their purpose was edification and their authors compilers who pieced together the statements of apostles and missionaries. Their evidence is therefore at best secondhand. In fact he seems to suppose that the statements on which the

From *Did Jesus Exist?* by G. A. Wells, pp. 70–96. First published by Elek Books in association with Pemberton Publishing and reprinted by permission of Pemberton Publishing.

evangelists relied were seldom, if ever, derived from the original disciples of Jesus, but belonged to a tradition handed on from preacher to preacher. As a result of this mode of transmission the data were reduced to stereotyped formulae and confined to points deemed of fundamental doctrinal importance. It must have been when the disciples who had known Jesus were all dead, and when their followers carried on their work, that the phraseology began to be stereotyped, since the new generation of teachers had to rely on what the first disciples had told them, and could not supplement it with recollections of their own.

The preachers would, according to Martin Dibelius, be primarily concerned to convince their audience of the following broad facts: Jesus of Nazareth, a descendant of David, having been appointed by God the promised Messiah who should judge the world and bring salvation to the righteous, had been crucified under Pontius Pilate at the instigation of the Jews. His *bona fides* was established by his "mighty works," in particular by his resurrection, which was vouched for by numerous persons. Some of these points are found in stereotyped form in the Pauline letters and others in the discourses of Peter and Paul in Acts.

Dibelius further argues that the purpose of the missionary preachers would not lead them to refer to the biographical details of Jesus' earthly career, and for that reason one would not expect them to record the miracles and discourses which form such an important part of the Gospels. Such events were no longer of any importance in comparison with the great fact of his death and resurrection. If the preachers mentioned miracles and discourses at all, it would only be by way of illustration, and usually without any attention to time and place. The evangelists, in editing the material provided by these preachers, might try to arrange these few facts and fit them into a plausible biographical sequence. As they had little but their own imagination to go on, it is not surprising that they did not all arrange them in the same way. Only when they come to the doctrinally important death and resurrection do they show any considerable degree of harmony.

By means, then, of this theory, Dibelius undertakes to explain the lack of allusions in the Epistles to the teaching and wonder-working of Jesus, the numerous discrepancies in the Gospels, and also the lack of coherence in the Gospel discourses, where Jesus passes with apparent arbitrariness from one topic to another. A good example is Mark 9:35-50, where the individual items are linked only by what theologians call "catchword connections"—a word or phrase in one seems to have reminded the evangelist of a similar word or phrase in another, independent saying, and this led him to put them together as successive utterances in a single speech. Form-critics are doubtless right in their insistence that such passages show that Jesus' sayings originally circulated independently of any connected narrative—a view which also gained support from the discovery, early this century, of three papyri at Oxyrhynchus in the Nile valley, containing a few sayings of Jesus in Greek, and of the Gospel of Thomas near Nag Hammadi in Upper Egypt in 1945. This apocryphal work consists of about 114 sayings of Jesus (including those that had been found at Oxyrhynchus), with no indication of where or under what circumstances they were pronounced. Many sayings which in the canonical Gospels appear in a definite situation are here simply stated without it. Although some scholars have argued that the Gospel of Thomas is dependent on canonical Gospels, the contary view—that it is neither compiled from them, nor constitutes one of their sources, but is an ancient independent tradition—is also strongly held.

It is also accepted today that not only Jesus' speeches but also the sequence of the events of his life familiar from the Synoptics is no part of the primary material but a creation of Mark (whose order of events is, on the whole, preserved by Matthew and Luke). For instance, Mark 1:16 reads: "And passing along by the Sea of Galilee he saw Simon and Andrew . . . ." Almost all commentators agree that the words "by the sea of Galilee" were added by Mark. They are placed quite ungrammatically in the Greek syntax (for the verb "passing along" is not normally used with the preposition "by"). Mark, then, has interpolated a reference to *place* into a report which lacked it, and he also added a reference to *time* by placing this story of the call of Simon and Andrew at the beginning of Jesus' ministry. Both place and time are, as Dennis Nineham says in his valuable commentary, "entirely St. Mark's doing." The evangelist has thus created a fictitious chronology and an apparent itinerary. The very vagueness of much of it does not inspire confidence. Jesus appears in *the* wilderness, on *the* mountain, in *the* house. In Mark 2:15 he is at a table in "his house." Commentators are not sure whether Jesus' house is meant, or where the house is. In 2:1 and 9:33 he is "at home" and "in the house" at Capernaum, as if he resided there. When the evangelist is more definite and precise, this is sometimes in the interests of a theological thesis, not from historical accuracy. If the Gospels were compiled from relatively short pericopes, originally independent of each other, it follows that each Gospel incident must to some extent be viewed in itself and not forced into harmony with others.

It seems to be the stereotyped nature of the references to Jesus in the Epistles (and to some extent even in Acts) that has suggested the form-critics' theory. But the references in the Epistles are in fact not all characterized by their verbal uniformity, but rather by a general absence of any details about the man Jesus. This is what is so hard to explain if the Jesus of the Gospels was a real historical character and the original of the Jesus Christ of Pauline doctrine. The same objection can be made to the form-critics' view of the resurrection, which, on their hypothesis, would seem to be one of the best attested facts in the life of Jesus. For, together with the Passion, it is one of the few details which the preachers always mentioned, and—according to Dibelius—with considerable agreement as to the essentials. But this is acceptable only on a narrow view of the essentials, for the Gospels agree only in that they all allege an execution under Pilate and subsequent appearances,[1] and earlier accounts of the crucifixion and resurrection do not even link these events with Pilate, or indeed with any historical setting. Another point is that, whether the form-critics are right or not, their theory does not provide a very reliable criterion of trustworthiness.

Dibelius admits that the preachers may have adapted their recollections to fit their sermons;[2] and he does not say what reason there is to trust their memory, candor, or intelligence. He also admits that the compilers may have modified and embellished the traditions they derived from the preachers. Indeed, his theory implies that this is what happened. He says that the early preachers had no occasion to refer to biographical detail. But if they alone supplied information to the compilers of the Gospels, where did the latter find their additional facts? If there was no authentic oral tradition which reproduced Jesus' teaching, then the Gospel sayings and stories about him originated in the later Church. Teeple goes so far as to accept this implication and to declare that the theory of an authentic oral tradition that moved from Jesus' "teaching to the disciples to the churches and the New Testament is one of the most serious errors in biblical scholarship." Although few other theologians would endorse this, many would agree that each evangelist is more than a mere compiler, and that he supplemented the material he received and stamped it with a theology of his own. . . .

In spite of these weaknesses, form-criticism is today widely regarded as having definitively established that Jesus really existed, in that it has traced Mark (supposedly written before A.D. 75) to preachers' formulae which were supposedly current as early as A.D. 50, this date being, it is argued, far too near Jesus' supposed actual lifetime for wholesale invention to have gone unchallenged. It would on the contrary be truer to say that what is valid in the form-critics' theory reveals that the very sections of the Gospels which used to be regarded as most likely to be a true historical record can no longer be accepted as such.

This can be illustrated from the instructions to the twelve when they are sent out to "heal the sick, raise the dead, cleanse lepers and cast out demons." They are warned that they will be persecuted during their mission, and will "not have gone through all the towns of Israel before the Son of man comes" (Matt. 10:8 and 23). The "Son of man" is a redeemer who was to come down from the clouds at the end of time to judge mankind (Mark 13:24-28). Early this century Albert Schweitzer pointed out that Jesus' prophecy was not fulfilled: the Son of man did not bring the world to an end while the disciples were on their way casting out demons. Nor were they persecuted, but returned to him unharmed (see Mark 6:30). Schweitzer's point was that, since Matthew himself shows that these prophecies were erroneous, the whole speech in which they occur must have been actually delivered by Jesus; for no evangelist would invent a speech full of prophecies and then go on to provide the evidence that they were illusory.

Form-critics have replied that Matthew 10:55 ff., so far from representing a real discourse, is—in the words of Harvey—"an artificial composition by Matthew," and includes logia which are set in quite different contexts by Mark and by Luke.[3] It is a compilation of rulings on matters of importance to Christian missionaries at the end of the first century. The instructions concern the founding of Christian communities (as is clear from Matthew 10:11 ff.) in missionary activity spread over a long period, and are not intelligible as directives given to disciples who soon return to the speaker (as the twelve are represented as doing). It is, for instance, stipulated that when they are persecuted the missionaries are not to court martyrdom, but to flee to another town and work there. The need for a ruling on such a practical problem naturally led to the conviction that the Lord had laid down what was to be done, and hence to the formulation of a Jesuine utterance. As for the coming of the Son of man, Matthew (writing at least fifty years after the supposed date of Jesus' speech) knew quite well that this had not yet occurred. It is not plausible to assume that an evangelist who manipulates his material freely would faithfully record doctrines he regarded as mistaken. Traditions which stamped Jesus as deluded would not have been uncritically preserved by evangelists who treat him with such deference that they do not allow even his enemies to reproach him directly. (His opponents criticize his disciples when speaking to him, and complain about him when speaking to his disciples or to each other, but they do not call him to account directly.)[4] It is, then, more reasonable to assume that Matthew understood Jesus' pronouncement concerning the Son of man not as a delusion, but as something acceptable. As Haenchen has noted this will be the case if we assume that he meant the speech where he placed it to include instructions not only for the particular mission of the twelve which forms its context, but also for all future missions of the Church.

Another such composition, which gives rulings on matters of concern to the Christians of the evangelist's day, can be seen in Matthew's supplement (18:15-17) to a string of Jesuine instructions taken from Mark 9:33-50. The supplement provides rules for dealing with dissensions within the Christian community or ecclesia (which did not even exist at the time when Jesus is supposed to have spoken), and it is obvious that the evangelist is here writing in the belief that practices of the Christians of his own day were ordained by Jesus. The same is true of Mark 10:12, where he rules that if a woman divorces her husband and marries another, she commits adultery. Some Gospel sayings of Jesus can be traced to the liturgical needs of Christian communities. An obvious case is the Lord's Prayer—absent from Mark, given different settings in Matthew and Luke, and expanded by Matthew so as to make it appropriate for communal worship. In Mark 7:1-23 Jesus bases an argument against the Pharisees on the Greek translation of the Old Testament, where the Hebrew original says something different which would not have supported his case. That a Palestinian Jesus should floor orthodox Jews with an argument based on a mistranslation of their scriptures is very unlikely. The whole incident is, however, perfectly intelligible if we suppose that it was fabricated in Mark's gentile Christian community, which naturally read the Old Testatment in the Greek version, and ascribed to Jesus its own understanding of these scriptures. Bornkamm designates the process with the disarming phrase, "the tendency of the word of Jesus to become contemporary." This "tendency" was at work even among the earliest Christians, whose "prophets" claimed to be spokesmen of the risen Jesus, and represented him as giving through their mouths ordinances which later Christians transferred to the historical Jesus. The tendency to anchor later doctrines and customs to his supposed lifetime played a considerable role in building up his biography.

Form-criticism, then, tends to sever the Gospel material from the historical Jesus. One can understand Leaney's comment that this result is "less welcome" to conservative Christians than the discovery which of his recorded sayings are authentic—a result with which the form-critical method has commonly been credited.

PALESTINIAN ELEMENTS

Professors Black and Jeremias have defended the authenticity of Jesus' sayings in the Gospels by giving evidence that some of these Greek logia are discernibly based on an underlying Aramaic original. In such matters we are dependent on what has been called "a small band of Aramaic experts" within the larger body of New Testament scholars, and, although the band consists of persons unlikely to propound theories disturbing to a settled orthodoxy, it is noticeable that they "often disagree, largely from uncertainty concerning the Aramaic of the first century A.D." Furthermore, as many theologians have themselves observed, "Aramaic" is not to be equated with "authentically spoken by Jesus." Against Jeremias it has been noted that an Aramaic-speaking community could as well invent "words of the Lord" as a Greek-speaking one; and that Aramaic terms and Semitisms do not even necessarily represent an early stage in the development of the tradition:

> Some Semitisms had entered the Hellenistic Greek language in general; early Christians adopted Semitisms from the Septuagint; many Christians in the first and second centuries knew Aramaic. Therefore these linguistic characteristics could appear in late Christian tradition and writing as easily as in primitive Christian tradition. In the same later period Jewish influence continued to be exerted on Christian tradition through the Old Testament and through Christians familiar with Judaism.

Jeremias has also argued that some sayings of the Gospel Jesus contain features which are not merely Aramaic, but also unique, in that they are unrepresented in the Jewish traditions of the period, and are therefore, he supposes, to be taken as proving that the sayings are genuine. For instance, Jesus in Gethsemane (Mark 14:36) addresses God with the Aramaic word *abba* (father). Mark supplies no witnesses who could have heard what was said, and also finds it necessary to put into Jesus' mouth the Greek translation of the word (making him say: "Abba, Father, all things are possible to thee"). Nevertheless, Jeremias insists that the logion is genuine since in Jewish traditions God is never addressed simply as *abba* without some additional qualifying phrase, such as is preserved in Matthew's "our father who art in heaven." To this the adequate reply has been made that Paul's references to an early Christian practice of crying "Abba,

Father" (Rom. 8:15; Gal. 4:6) show that *abba* followed by its Greek translation was a formula current in Hellenistic Christian circles, and that Mark has simply put it into Jesus' mouth. And a leading Jewish scholar (Vermes) has given evidence that *abba* was used in the prayer language of the Judaism of the day in precisely the manner in which Jeremias and other Christian scholars have declared to be "unthinkable."

A second feature which Jeremias thinks authenticates some Jesuine sayings is the way they are prefaced with "Amen, I say unto you"—for the word *amen* is, in Judaism, never used to introduce sayings. Jeremias is himself aware that on two occasions this "genuine" word has been added secondarily by Matthew to sayings in Mark which are without it. He supposes that Matthew introduced the word because he recognized it as Jesus' way of speaking. But it is also the case— as Jeremias admits—that the whole formula has frequently been deleted in the reworking and editing of the earlier Synoptic material. This must mean that the authors of the later layers of this material did not recognize the formula as genuinely Jesuine—unless we suppose that what they recognized as Jesuine was of no interest to them! Hence, as Hasler has observed, the reasons given by Jeremias for the later additions do not square with the "tendency" to deletion that he correctly observes in the later layers. Some of the thirteen sayings introduced with the formula in Mark are obviously suspect—e.g. 9:1 (on which see p. 217); and 10:27, where the reference to sacrificing all for the sake of "the gospel" suggests the standpoint of a persecuted Christian community, not the conditions in which Jesus is supposed to have lived. (Marxsen has shown that it is characteristic of Mark to impose the word *gospel* onto the material he edits.) Hasler has made a good case for regarding the amen-formula as originally a form of words used by early Christian prophets in order to introduce sayings which, they supposed, had been communicated to them supernaturally by the risen Jesus. Only at a larger stage in the development of the tradition were, on this view, both formula and sayings ascribed to the earthly Jesus; Berger, writing independently of Hasler, shows that something very like the amen-formula was already available in the Septuagint and in Jewish apocalyptic literature, where it was used to introduce and to affirm the veracity of solemn statements. Like Hasler, he finds that the formula does not go back to a historical Jesus, but originated on the lips of prophets. But he prefers to regard the early Christian prophets not as spokesmen of the risen Jesus, but as making their forecasts about the end of the world on their own accounts, and for this very reason needing the formula to validiate their utterances. In time, he argues, it was found that more effective validation was achieved by ascribing them to Jesus, just as many Old Testament traditions came to be attached to Moses as a commanding figure of the past.

TITLES

The traditional view that the canonical Gospels were written by eyewitnesses of the events recorded in them, or at least by men who had their information directly from such witnesses, is today almost universally abandoned. Haenchen notes that the Fathers of the Church could never have originated such a view if they had properly understood Luke 1:1-4, which states that the "eyewitnesses and ministers of the word delivered" their testimony orally, and that only then did "many" (not alleged to have been eyewitnesses) "draw up a narrative." Luke thus knew nothing of gospels written by apostles . . . . The eyewitnesses . . . did not write but 'only' preached."[5] Today it is recognized (e.g., by Grant) that the authors of the Gospels are entirely unknown; that Gospels and other writings used for reading in church, at first existed without any titles, and were supplied with them only when Christian communities acquired more than one Gospel and needed some means of distinguishing between them. The canon was unable to reduce the material to a single Gospel for the reason that some influential communities had long used only one and some another.[6]

The ascription of titles, insofar as its basis can be inferred at all, seems to have been a haphazard business. Beare writes in this connection of "second-century guesses." Mark, for instance, acquired its title probably because "my son Mark" is mentioned as a close associate of "Peter the apostle" who poses as the author of 1 Peter (1:1 and 5:13). This Epistle of the late first or early second century, influenced as it is by Pauline theology, introduces "Mark" as a personage familiar from the Pauline letters (Col. 4:10) in order to create the authentic Pauline atmosphere. Nonetheless, it was probably this mention of Mark in a work ascribed to Peter that originated the tradition (preserved by Papias, A.D. 140) that Mark was written by one Mark who took down the spoken recollections of Peter. This tradition was not finally discredited until the rise of form-criticism. At the beginning of this century orthodox commentators of Mark still insisted that the Gospel is a unitary composition, owing its unity to the author's dependence on the eyewitness Peter for all his information. The change in critical standpoint is at once obvious from comparison with Taylor's—also orthodox—commentary (first published in 1952), where stress is laid upon the great diversity of the traditions which Mark collected after they had already been used in the teaching and preaching of the Church.

Papias is also responsible for the ascription of the first Gospel in the canon to "Matthew," meaning presumably the Matthew named in all the synoptic lists of the twelve. But Matthew's dependence on Mark, "the Greek gospel of a nondisciple," is only one of the considerations which make this hypothesis "completely impossible." How fanciful the choice of title and author could be is equally well illustrated in the case of the third Gospel. The second-century Church, aware that the author also wrote the book now known as the Acts of the Apostles, observed that some passages in Acts refer to Paul and his companions as "we" and "us," and on this basis selected Luke (mentioned in two Epistles as a companion of Paul) as the author.[7] The fourth Gospel is quite anonymous. The tradition that it was written by the apostle John, who was identical with the "beloved disciple" mentioned in it, is unknown until the last quarter of the second century and, as Kümmel has shown, the stages which led to this view can be reconstructed. The first twenty chapters include references to a "beloved disciple," but do not name him nor represent him as the author. The final chapter 21, an appendix almost certainly by another hand, identifies this disciple as the author, but leaves him still anonymous. Later, Christians who knew all four Gospels would readily suppose that "the disciple whom Jesus loved" must be one of the three who, according to the Synoptics, are most intimate with him, namely Peter and the two sons of Zebedee, James and John. (They alone witness the transfiguration, and go forward with him to Gethsemane: Mark 9:2; 14:33.) Since the fourth Gospel names Peter in addition to the beloved disciple, and since James died early (Acts 12:2), this leaves the authorship with John.

SOURCES AND DATES

Mark. Critical theologians are agreed that Mark is the earliest extant Gospel and that Matthew and Luke used it as one of their sources and are therefore of later date.[8] Mark is clearly one of the earliest documents we have that sets Jesus' life in Pilate's Palestine, and its date is therefore of some importance.

External evidence of Mark (i.e., mention of it by other authors) is not forthcoming until the middle of the second century. Neither Ignatius (A.D. 110) nor Polycarp (who perhaps wrote as early as A.D. 120, but more probably in A.D. 135) show any knowledge of it, although it must have existed when the latter wrote, for he used Matthew, which presupposes it. Ignatius has much common ground with Matthew, and many hold that he too used this Gospel. If so, then Mark (written before Matthew) existed by A.D. 110. Köster, however, thinks that Ignatius and Matthew were both drawing independently on traditions common to their backgrounds (see below, p. 225).[9]

The long silence of external witnesses concerning Mark is not surprising; for once Matthew had become available, it would naturally be preferred, since it includes nearly all Mark's material and very much more besides. Mark, then, must be dated before Polycarp's references to Matthew. Let us see whether evidence internal to it permits a more precise dating.

Everyone must assume that the Gospels are based either on the reports of eyewitnesses or on tradition. Even Mark is today regarded as but a redaction of early traditions. The evangelist betrays in 7:31 an ignorance of Palestinian geography hardly compatible with the assumption that he lived anywhere near the country. The Christian community for which he wrote is so remote from Jewish ideas that he has laboriously to explain Jewish practices, as when he states that "the Pharisees and the Jews in general never eat without washing the hands . . . . And there are many other points on which they have a traditional rule to maintain" (7:3–4). Such passages also betray that, in Mark's day, the freedom of gentile Christian communities from the Jewish law was taken for granted, and that he therefore wrote considerably later than Paul, for whom this matter was still a burning issue.

The traditions which Mark redacted were not exclusively oral. Taylor's evidence for his use of earlier written sources includes the "literary doublet" of two miraculous feedings, of the 5,000 and of the 4,000. The story of the 5,000 is clearly pre-Marcan, since it "bears none of the signs of Mark's literary activity within the body of the narrative." That two separate incidents are involved is hard to believe, since in the second the disciples—who are represented as having recently witnessed the first—have so completely forgotten it that they think it impossible for food to be supplied to thousands in a desert place (8:4). The doublet is best explained by assuming that a tradition of one such feeding existed in two slightly different written forms, and that the evangelist incorporated both because he supposed them to refer to different incidents. Different written, and not merely different oral forms, underlie such doublets. Two oral traditions that are slightly discrepant can easily be combined into one story. But as soon as a tradition is fixed in writing, discrepancies between it and a kindred tradition can result in both these literary forms of the story being told. Another doublet is the dual reference to deceivers in a single Jesuine discourse (13:5–6 and 21–3), and "the presumption is that Mark has taken them from two different sources."

To allow time for the post-Pauline traditions (collected and arranged in a sequence by the evangelist) to have developed, a date of composition earlier than about A.D. 70 is unlikely, and it is today seldom challenged. Some commentators think that Mark 12:9 (where Jesus predicts that God will "destroy the tenants" of his vineyard because they have murdered his "beloved son") presupposes knowledge of the destruction of Jerusalem in A.D. 70. Brandon has pressed for A.D. 71 as the date of Mark's composition, although all his evidence is consistent with a later date. He argues that Mark was written at Rome—a view which is open to objection[10]—and he supposes that Jewish payment of tribute to the emperor (encouraged in Mark 12:13–17) was of vital concern to Christians in Rome about A.D. 71. But in fact injunctions to Christians to submit to the authorities and pay taxes are not indicative of any particular place or date, and are found in Rom. 13:1–7 (which, if genuine and not interpolated,[11] is pre-Marcan), as well as in epistles of the late first and early second century. The inconclusive nature of Brandon's evidence is clear also from his argument that Mark's unexplained reference (15:38) to the rending of the temple curtain presupposes that his readers knew what it was; and that he was therefore writing for citizens of Rome, who had seen it displayed (according to Josephus' account) in the triumphal procession through the city after the Roman victory in the Jewish War. It does not appear from what Brandon says that the curtain thus displayed was rent: and in any case the Gospel reference to its rending would be universally understood as signifying a catastrophic end to the Jewish cult. Mark 13 has been made the basis of many attempts to date the Gospel more precisely.

It begins with Jesus predicting the destruction of the temple at Jerusalem:

> As he came out of the temple, one of his disciples said to him, "Look, Teacher, what wonderful stones and what wonderful buildings!" And Jesus said to him, "Do you see these great buldings? There will not be left here one stone upon another that will not be thrown down."

Any observer of the strained relations between Jews and Romans might conceivably have guessed, almost at any time during the first century, that Jerusalem and its temple would be destroyed as a result of Roman action against an insurgent people. But it is nevertheless quite likely that the logion "no stone will be left upon another" first arose in a Christian community which knew of the destruction of the temple (which occurred in A.D. 70) and wanted to believe that Jesus had predicted it. The narrative frame in which this saying is placed is patently artificial. Palestinian Jews, even those living in Galilee, would have been familiar with the temple since childhood, since it was the custom to go there for the greater festivals. It is therefore naive to make one of them speak as though he were seeing it for the first time. Here we can detect the hand of Mark, writing for gentile Christians who had never seen the temple.

The next verse changes the scene. Jesus is now sitting "on the Mount of Olives opposite the temple," and is no longer accompanied by "his disciples," but only by four intimates, who ask him: "When will this be?" Luke was obviously worried both by the implausibility of the Palestinian Jew marvelling at the temple, and by this discontinuity; for he eliminated both these features by combining the two episodes into one, and by making not disciples but unspecified "people" admire the building (Luke 21:5-7). The two features eliminated by Luke do suggest that the saying "not one stone will be left upon another" was a logion that existed as an independent unit before Mark. Thus Beare concedes that the two verses in which it occurs in Mark are "a self-contained narrative, centered in the prediction; the introduction is merely a frame for the saying." This saying probably did not come into being until after the destruction of the temple, and Mark's assimilation of it, i.e., his composition of his Gospel, must have occurred still later.

Nevertheless, most scholars insist that Mark must have been written before A.D. 75[12] because 13:4 and 14 are held to imply that the end of the world is to follow shortly after the destruction of the temple. In verse 4 Jesus is asked (in response to his statement that "no stone will be left upon another"): "When will this be, and what will be the sign when these things are all to be accomplished?" The "accomplishment of all things" is a technical term in apocalyptic literature for the end of the world, and he does in fact answer the question by telling what signs will presage it. The apocalyptic discourse that follows is thus clumsily introduced by a question about "all these things," when he has in fact spoken only of the temple. The wording of 13:4 betrays, then, that the evangelist links an event of A.D. 70 with the end of the world only because he decided to use the floating logion about the temple as an introduction to an apocalyptic discourse derived from another tradition which measures time on a different scale. Beare speaks of the "glaring lack of concord" between the two.[13] The original connection between them was merely that both are concerned with some form of destruction. Such "catchword connections," as they are called in critical theology, are often the only links between individual items in speeches by Jesus. We see now the importance of the form-critics' analysis of the Gospels, which is admitted to have established that, before Mark, "the traditions about Jesus were transmitted as brief self-contained anecdotes or sayings"; and that "when they came into his hands, there was no sure indication of the order of events." Mark's location of the apocalyptic discourse on the Mount of Olives suggests that he was following a *written* tradition which already specified this locality. Otherwise he could have recorded the discourse without changing the scene from that of the previous verses, where Jesus speaks of the end of the temple.

Jerusalem is not again mentioned explicitly in Mark 13, but verse 14 is often understood as another reference to events in the city of about A.D. 70:

> When you see the desolating sacrilege set up where it ought not to be (let the reader understand), then let those who are in Judea flee to the mountains.

The corresponding passage in Matthew (24:15) explains that "the desolating sacrilege" was something mentioned in the Book of Daniel, where the phrase is used (11:31) to allude to the heathen altar which the Syrian Seleucid ruler Antiochus Epiphanes built in the temple over the altar of burnt offering in 168 B.C. The writer was a contemporary of Antiochus, but pretends to have lived centuries earlier and to prophesy the events of his reign. He refers to them in such a veiled manner that the Christian evangelists supposed that they had not yet occurred, and that Daniel's "prophecies" in fact referred to events which would come to pass in their own day and age—events which were to presage the end of the world: for according to Daniel, the sacrilege is to inaugurate a period of unprecedented distress, after which the end will come (12:1, 11-13). Mark, then, is telling his readers that some event will shortly occur which will fulfill Daniel's prophecy, and that people in Judea are then to "flee to the mountains." Why Mark, who was not writing for Jews, should wish to tell Judeans what to do at a particular moment is not at all obvious. To explain this—and also the fact that the whole chapter (immediately before the passion narrative, but quite independent of it) is devoted to a discourse by Jesus, whereas the evangelist elsewhere makes very little attempt to record his teachings—it has often been assumed that he has here incorporated an earlier Jewish document (or Christian document addressed to Jews) which interpreted Daniel's prophecy as a reference either to the Emperor Caligula's threat in A.D. 40 to have a statue of himself placed in the temple, or to some desecration accompanying the destruction of the buildings in A.D. 70.[14] But whether Mark merely assimilated the passage or wrote it himself, he certainly goes on to say in verse 24, that the world will end "in those days after that tribulation." If, then, he expected the end soon after the distress caused by the sacrilege, and if this latter refers to an incident during the rebellion of A.D. 66 to 70, then he must have written his Gospel within a few years of A.D. 70.

In *The Jesus of the Early Christians*, I did not dispute that Mark interpreted the sacrilege in this way, although I was at a loss to see how his Gospel could have existed at such an early date, as none of the Christian Epistles (in or outside of the New Testament) which are dated within the first century shows any knowledge of it, or of its material. Furthermore, Mark 13:7-10 suggests that the writer is offering an explanation as to why the end of the world did *not* come during or soon after the Jewish rebellion. He here makes Jesus urge his audience not to be alarmed when they hear of wars and rumors of wars, for such things are but the birthpangs of the new age, and the end must be preceded by a long and painful period of missionary activity during which they will be indicted in courts, flogged in synagogues, and summoned to testify to their faith before governors and kings. It may be argued that the "wars" of this passage are too vague to be construed as an allusion to the rebellion of A.D. 66 to 70. But the additional statement of verse 10 that before the end "the gospel must first be preached to all nations" is directed against expectations of an immediate end, and is hardly consonant with expecting it to come soon after the destruction of the temple.

It is of course possible to suppose that Mark has simply strung together alien traditions without noticing or caring about their contradictions. The discourse certainly does include contradictions which are best explained by "use of disparate tradition." For instance, after having explained that the end of the world will be heralded by unmistakable signs, Jesus adds that it will take men by surprise (13:7-31, 32-3). But it is surely uncharitable to suppose that Mark went about all his editorial work completely unintelligently. And as he himself couples his mention of the desolating sacrilege with an exhortation to the reader to "understand," we must assume that he intended to convey some coherent and intelligible message. In fact the apparent contradiction between verses 10 and 14 disappears if the reference to the sacrilege can be understood as an allusion to an event later than the war of A.D. 66 to 70. And this, I think, is the case.

First Maccabees, which gives a historical account of the reign of Antiochus' Epiphanes (175-164 B.C.), tells (1:54) that "the desolating sacrilege was set up on the altar"; that pagan altars were built throughout the towns of Judea, and that death was the penalty for refusal to comply with the king's decree to offer sacrifice at them. Evasion was possible only by "fleeing to the mountains" (2:28). Christians of the first century would not have suspected that the events openly reported here are the same as those prophesied in veiled manner in the Book of Daniel. But Mark's reference to the sacrilege and to the necessity of "fleeing to the mountains" when it arrives does suggest that he had the incidents of 1 Maccabees in mind. Haenchen has argued that what Mark envisaged was a future attempt by a Roman emperor to force pagan worship on Christians as Antiochus had done on his subjects. The Book of Revelation (13:12) reckons with such a possibility. The point is not baldly stated, as open criticism of the imperial power would have been dangerous not only for the author, but also for the community in which his book was used. (For this reason he sometimes [14:8] writes "Babylon" when he means "Rome.") Mark had to be equally discreet, and hints that he is giving his message in coded form by his words "let the reader understand." Haenchen decodes the message to read: as soon as preparations (e.g., the setting up of an image or altar) are seen being made for a compulsory sacrifice to a pagan god or to the emperor himself; as soon, then, as the sacrilege is seen standing "where it ought not to be," then "those in Judea," i.e., Christians, are to "flee to the mountains." Judea is named because Mark is keeping within the framework supplied by Daniel; but in reality he had in mind the whole Roman Empire. And flight is necessary because, if Christians wait until they are brought before the heathen image or altar, they will be left with a choice only between compliance or death. If Haenchen is right, Mark is looking, not back to an event of A.D. 70, but forward to a danger that has not yet materialized. And so there is no conflict between his reference to the sacrilege and his insistence that before the end "the gospel must first be preached to all nations."[15]

Haenchen is anxious to interpret Mark as envisaging future, rather than present Roman persecution, since he agrees with the great majority of theologians who date the Gospel at about A.D. 70, whereas persecution of Christians by the Roman state does not seem to have occurred at this time, but only later, in the reign of Trajan or, at the earliest, Domitian. But in fact there is much in Mark to suggest that persecution is already a reality. In 8:27–9:1 Jesus labors the need to stand firm under persecution, and 13:13 implies a situation in which the "name" of Christian, i.e., merely professing to be a Christian, is a capital offense. Now we have seen that, although it is hazardous to try to link a Christian writer's references to persecution with any particular time or place, the situation implied by Mark 13:13 is consistent with what could well have happened not infrequently from about A.D. 90. Winter correlates this passage with Pliny's mention of the *noumen Christianum* when he asked Trajan in A.D. 112 whether the "name" of Christian was sufficient evidence of the guilt of a defendant.

In Mark 13:30 Jesus says that "this generation" will live to see the end of the world. If he really said this, then he was deluded, and commentators who accept the logion as genuine try to avoid this implication by supposing him to be speaking not of the end of the world, but of the fall of Jerusalem; or by taking "this generation" to mean the people of God, which will survive until the end of time.[16] More convincing is the argument that Jesus' assurance to "this generation was put into his mouth at a time when many Christians had begun to feel uneasy because the end of the world (represented as imminent in the earliest Christian writings) had failed to occur. This militates against the view that Mark is earlier than A.D. 70, but does not exclude a date of composition twenty or thirty years later, when a few people who had been alive about A.D. 30 were still alive. In 9:1 Jesus says that only "some" of his contemporaries will experience the end. This saying has only a "catchword" connection with the preceding verses and none at all with those that follow, and has been regarded as originally a remark of an early Christian preacher which was later credited with the authority of Jesus. Mark did not think in terms of historical precision, but regarded both this logion and the statements in chapter 13 (which he himself put together from various sources to form a continuous speech) as addressed to the Christians of his own day and age. Every reader would feel that he belonged to "this generation" of 13:30.

To sum up: Mark must have been written between A.D. 70 and the date of composition of Matthew, which used it as a source. Matthew was probably not known to Ignatius (A.D. 110), but was certainly known to Polycarp, who wrote not later than A.D. 135. Scholars who date Mark in the earlier part of the period between A.D. 70 and 135 have, as internal evidence, only Mark 13 (which I consider not to the point) as support; whereas there is cogent evidence (the ignorance of the substance of Mark apparent in all the Christian epistles of the first century) in favor of a date in the middle of this period.

Matthew and Luke. Both Matthew and Luke were unknown to Clement of Rome (who wrote at the end of the first century, or a little later); Ignatius (about A.D. 110) certainly did not know Luke, and probably not Matthew either; but both Gospels are quoted by Polycarp not later than A.D. 135. Luke may have written somewhat later than Matthew—not much later, because he knew nothing of Matthew's work.[17] McNeile dates Matthew after A.D. 80, and Kilpatrick and Grant favor a date after A.D. 90.[18]

Matthew and Luke have a good deal of material in common (apart from what they took from Mark). Most theologians agree that neither evangelist could have taken this material from the other, since they both wrote quite independently, and that their Gospels overlap because they both used as sources not only Mark but a second Greek document not now extant and usually called "Q." "Q" consists mainly of sayings of Jesus, and it sets his life in first-century Palestine by associating him with John the Baptist, but makes no mention of Pilate, nor of Jesus' passion and crucifixion. It may be earlier or later than Mark, of which it is independent; but it cannot be a very early document, for it presupposes material of different provenance which it has collected and arranged by means of "catchword" connections. It has also abandoned the early Christian idea that Jesus' second coming is to occur in the immediate future. Semitisms in the Greek logia of "Q" have made the basis of arguments that it derives from an early record of authentic utterances of Jesus. But such "Palestinian" Semitisms can be explained without this hypothesis.[19]

"Q" helps us to date Matthew and Luke because each of these gospels have introduced minor variants of their own into the material taken from it, and these variants sometimes betray the standpoint or circumstances of the evangelist. For instance, in 22:7 Matthew introduces into a parable a statement of his own (absent from the Lucan parallel) that the king—the reference must be to the king of heaven—sent his troops and burned the city of those who had killed his servants. This is generally admitted to be an allusion to the destruction of Jerusalem in A.D. 70, an event which Matthew interprets as God's punishment to the Jews for slaying Jesus and his apostles.[20] Another indication that Matthew wrote after A.D. 70 is his report of Jesus' declaration to the scribes and Pharisees:

> Therefore I send you prophets and wise men and scribes, some of whom you will kill and crucify, and some you will scourge in your synagogues and persecute from town to town, that upon you may come all the righteous blood shed on earth, from the blood of the innocent Abel to the blood of Zechariah the son of Barachiah, whom you murdered between the sanctuary and the altar. Truly I say to you, all this will come upon this generation. (23:34-6)

The prophet Zechariah, the son of Berechiah, cannot be meant, for he did not suffer martyrdom. Some commentators have supposed the reference to be to Zechariah (the son of Jehoiada), who was murdered in the court of the temple (2 Chronicles 24: 20-1); for, as 2 Chronicles is placed last in the canon of Hebrew scriptures, this Zechariah is the last of the Old Testament martyrs and so—it is argued—is appropriately contrasted with Abel, the first. But it is senseless to suppose that Matthew intended to limit the guilt of the scribes and Pharisees to "canonical" murders, the last of which occurred 800 years before Jesus, when the context makes it clear that some of the victims are to be Christian missionaries "sent" by him. The reference is obviously to Zacharias (the son of Baruch), who, as Josephus tells was put to death by Jewish zealots "in the middle of the temple" in A.D. 68. This man would, in Matthew's vision, appropriately be the last of the martyrs whose blood was to "come upon" the Jews in "this generation" when Jerusalem was destroyed two years later.

That Matthew looked back over some considerable interval to A.D. 70 is suggested by his evident concern to avoid any implication there may be in Mark 13:1-4 that the destruction of the temple is connected with the end of the world. We recall that Jesus here speaks of the temple, is then asked when "all these things" will be accomplished, and replies with a discourse about the end of the world. Matthew, however, is careful to make the disciples meet his words about the temple with two distinct questions—one about the temple and the other about "the sign of your coming and of the close of the age" (24:2-3). To make quite sure that any linkage with the temple is eliminated from the eschatological discourse thus introduced, these two questions are addressed to Jesus "as he sat on the Mount of Olives"—not, as Mark has it, "as he sat on the Mount of Olives opposite the temple." Similarly, the Marcan references (13:9) to persecution by Jewish authorities have been dropped in Matthew's account (24:9-14) of the events presaging the end. Matthew envisages persecution by Jews at an earlier stage (10:17), whereas the end is to come after the annihilation of the Jewish state in A.D. 70, when only gentiles are left with the power to put Christians to death. This is clearly the situation of the evangelist's own time.[21]

Indeed, that he restricts Jewish persecution to the period of Jesus' ministry and excludes it from the more distant future which he represents Jesus as foretelling, may well point to a date of writing later than A.D. 90; for it was about then that Christians were effectively excluded from synagogues—not by formal decree, but because a curse on heretics was at that time proposed as an insertion into synagogue worship (see p. 225) and in due course put into practice. Wherever it was implemented, Christians naturally found difficulty in continuing to attend the services. Thus the "floggings in synagogues" of Matthew 10:17 are, for the Christians addressed by Matthew, a thing of the past. If they were outside the synagogue, they were no longer liable to its discipline.

At 23:13 Jesus' complaint against the Pharisees is not that they persecute, but that they prevent Jews from turning Christian. The situation here envisaged seems to be that of the evangelist's own times: "Woe to you, scribes and Pharisees, hypocrites! Because you shut the kingdom of heaven against men; for you neither enter yourselves, nor allow those who would enter to go in." That Matthew here designates as hypocrisy behavior which sprang from religious conviction is typical of his lack of detachment throughout chapter 23, where the scribes and Pharisees are repeatedly reproached as hypocrites, whether or not the reproach in question can justly be made of both groups, and whether or not the behavior criticized can justly be called hypocrisy.

This chapter 23 begins, incongruously, with Jesus' endorsement of their teaching: "The scribes and the Pharisees sit on Moses' seat; so practice and observe whatever they tell you, but not what they do; for they preach but do not practice" (verses 2–3). This logion was surely not invented by Matthew, but assimilated by him from a Jewish-Christian source. It nevertheless represents a degraded (and therefore late) tradition; for in Luke's version of the woes, the ordinary members of the Pharisaic party are carefully distinguished from their rabbinic leaders, whereas Matthew fuses the two groups throughout chapter 23, and makes "the scribes and the Pharisees sit on Moses' seat"—as if the lay members of the Pharisaic party were all authoritative exegetes of the Torah. Hare finds it incredible that Matthew should have left these opening verses standing if he had written much later that the effective application of the cursing of heretics proposed as an innovation in the synagogue liturgy about A.D. 90. But the verses are in flagrant contradiction with other material in chapter 23 (and elsewhere in the Gospel). Matthew 16:5–12 expressly condemns "the teaching of the Pharisees"; 12:33–5 tends in the same direction; and at 15:14 they are called "blind guides." If, then, the evangelist was content to allow internal contradictions to remain, we cannot suppose him to have been sensitive to rabbinic liturgical modifications. In chapter 23 itself the opening endorsement of the Pharisees' teaching is soon retracted; verse 4 designates this teaching as a "heavy burden." (A writer who really accepted it as God-given would not thus complain of its burdensomeness.) Matthew is clearly making logia which were originally independent of each other into a continuous speech. Verses 8–12 imply that Christians need no rabbis, but have direct access to God. This too negates the doctrine of the opening verses and probably reached Matthew from sectarians who made Jesus speak on these lines because they believed that all Christians were directly inspired by the holy spirit and were therefore all "brethren" who had no need of other "teachers" or "masters." Some commentators think that these verses 8–12, which stipulate that Christians have but one master, explain why Matthew allowed the contrary endorsement of rabbinic teaching in verse 3 to stand; namely because verses 8–12 show that the material assimilated as verse 3 is no longer actual. Matthew, then, "preserves a positive tradition which has been passed on to him, but at the same time he also intimates that in his community this tradition hardly functions any more." Another example of this method—incorporating a tradition and then immediately denying its truth—is John 4:1-2.

Matthew 23:38-9 (which is without Marcan parallel) clearly aims at interposing an interval between A.D. 70 and Jesus' second or final coming. Here, in Jerusalem just before his arrest, he cries: "O Jerusalem, . . . Behold your house is forsaken and desolate. For I tell; you, you will not see me again until you say, 'Blessed be he who comes in the name of the Lord.'" On this, Montefiore makes the apposite comment:

> Probably the words are not authentic. Jerusalem had fallen: Jesus had not come. Therefore the men of a later generation felt that he must have predicted that an interval would lie between the all of the city and his second coming, during which time it would remain in ruins. Hence the present verse.

Luke also records this saying, but without the word *desolate*, which is also missing in the ancient manuscript of Matthew. The logion was thus probably taken by both evangelists from "Q," where it would not have included the words *and desolate*, but expressed the idea that Wisdom, who dwelt in the temple, had "forsaken" it. Luke makes Jesus speak it before he has reached Jerusalem, and without the *again* included in Matthew's statement "you will not see me again until you say, 'Blessed be he. . . .'" Thus in Luke Jesus' words could conceivably refer to his own triumphal entry into the city. Their position is a good example of how "catchwords" guided the evangelist in his arrangement of his material: for Jesus has just said (Luke 13:33) that a prophet can perish only in "Jerusalem," and this word allows the logion about its temple to be appended.

Whether the reference is to Jesus' triumphant entry or to his final coming, other evidence shows unambiguously that Luke wrote considerably later than A.D. 70. In adapting Mark 13, Luke writes not of the "desolating sacrilege," but of "the desolation of Jerusalem," effected by the armies encompassing it. And after describing the fall of the city as the result of a siege, he makes Jesus declare—not that the end of the world will follow immediately, but that the gentiles will trample down the city until their times are fulfilled" (21:24). Then will come a time of "distress"—not, however, now for Israel but for the gentiles, and amidst convulsions of nature the Son of man will come.[22] Luke retains (21:32), as Matthew also does (24:34), the doctrine of Mark that "this generation will not pass away before all these things take place." Yet he shows signs of embarrassment in that he is nevertheless concerned to represent Jesus as declaring that the end will come later than Mark envisaged.

At the beginning of this century Schmiedel gave evidence, which so eminent a scholar as Cadbury has described as "very persuasive," that Luke not only wrote later than the fall of Jerusalem, but also that he almost certainly utilized the *Antiquities* of Josephus—a work not available before A.D. 93. A recent commentator on Luke, Professor Ellis, is able to date the Gospel earlier than A.D. 70 only by making light of this evidence and disregarding some of it.[23]

Luke alone of the Synoptics represents Jesus as applying to himself the words of Isaiah: "He has anointed me to preach good news to the poor, . . . to proclaim release to the captives and recovering of sight to the blind, to set at liberty those who are oppressed, to proclaim the acceptable year of the Lord" (4:18–19). Luke's purpose in including this emerges from comparison with 2 Cor. 6:2, where Paul quotes similar words from Isaiah about "the acceptable time" and "the day of salvation" and adds: "Behold, now is the acceptable time; now the day of salvation." Luke, however, in making Jesus, on a past occasion, identify the time of salvation with his own ministry, represents it as past. He was writing when the end of the world, regarded as imminent by Paul, had signally failed to occur; and so he had to make Jesus' earthly life not the final period of history, but an epoch of salvation which would be succeeded by the epoch of the Church (the evangelist's own time). The former epoch, of course, influences the latter. Jesus' activities on earth are the basis of the hopes of salvation entertained by the Church. But with Luke, Jesus' message is not the Marcan one (Mark 1:15) that the kingdom is near, to come shortly, but that it "is in the midst of you" (Luke 17:21), that it has come in the person of Jesus, whose life is a guarantee of our future salvation.[24] This necessity (caused by the continuing absence of any indication that the world was reaching its end) to look back to Jesus' life, as much as forward to his second coming, in order to understand the nature of the kingdom and of salvation, was a very important motive for the creation of biographical details which supplemented the meager Pauline account.

That the Synoptics were written in the order—Mark, Matthew, Luke—can also be illustrated by the statements which they represent Jesus as making at his Sanhedrin trial about the timing of the end of the world. There is no need to regard these statements as historical, as the motive for putting them into his mouth is perfectly clear. Christians of the late first century knew that the Jews refused to accept him as the Messiah; and this provided a basis for a narrative in which he tells the Jewish authorities that he is the Messiah, and has his claim rejected. Thus Mark has it that he answers the high priest's question whether he is the Messiah with the words:

"I am; and *you will see* the Son of man seated at the right hand of Power, and coming with the clouds of heaven." Then the high priest tore his garments and said . . . "You have heard this blasphemy." (14:62–4; italics mine)

Commentators point out that Jesus' words were not blasphemous, and this again makes the narrative look like legend rather than history, particularly as there is an obvious reason for the formation of such a detail.[25] The suggestion that his interrogators would live to "see" the Son of man come down from heaven to end the world embarrassed later evangelists. Matthew somewhat clumsily amended it to: "Hereafter you will see the Son of man seated at the right hand of Power, and coming on the clouds of heaven" (26:64). Luke's emendation is more radical, and is meant to exclude the suggestion that the end would come soon enough for Jesus' contemporaries to witness it. He is made to say: "From now on, the Son of man *shall be seated* at the right hand of the power of God" (22:69). The fourth Gospel does not represent him as having been brought before the Sanhedrin for trial, and so there is no parallel passage in John.

Finally, I should mention the theory of "Proto-Luke." We saw that the commonly accepted view is that both Matthew and Luke expanded Mark by supplementing it with "Q." Each includes, additionally, some material unrepresented in the other. Matthew thus consists of Marcan material, "Q" material (i.e., non-Marcan material shared with Luke and material unique to itself (and therefore called "M"). If Matthew thus consists of Mark + "Q" + "M," Luke likewise consists of Mark + "Q" + "L" (where "L" represents material unique to Luke). Now although the dependence of Luke on Mark, and hence its lateness, is hardly disputed anymore, some have urged that the Marcan material was inserted into it only at a late stage. These critics, instead of regarding Luke as an expansion of Mark, posit a "Proto-Luke" (not now extant) consisting of "Q" + "L," and hold that, when Mark became available, this Proto-Luke was expanded into Luke as we now know it by the insertion of blocks of Marcan material (and by the addition of the two opening chapters—the present Luke 1–2). The point of the theory is, of course, to authenticate some elements in the present Gospel by making them pre-Marcan and therefore supposedly early enough in their origin to have been based on eyewitness reports. The theory has, however, not found much favor. Kümmel gives reasons for dismissing it as untenable. One of these is that Luke's passion narrative (which certainly could not have come from "Q," in which all references to the passion are lacking) includes sections where Marcan phrases appear in the middle, although the sections in other respects differ considerably from Mark. Creed puts the matter as follows: "These signs of Mark are intelligible if the Lucan narrative is a recasting and expansion of the Marcan text. If, however, Luke had already written or found a full and independent non-Marcan narrative, it seems unlikely that afterwards he would have interpolated occasional sentences and verses from Mark."

Although, then, Luke expanded Mark and did not work Mark into a document already independently completed, his copy of Mark was incomplete and lacked Mark 6:45–8:26, which has no equivalent in Luke. Immediately before this section comes the miraculous feeding of five thousand with five loaves and two small fishes—a story common to both Gospels. Jesus then took leave of everyone and "went into the hills to pray" (Mark 6:46). In Luke's copy of Mark these words seem to have been followed immediately by Mark 8:27, where he "questioned" his disciples in such a way as to elicit Peter's confession that he is the Christ; for Luke, after the story of the five thousand, passes straight to Peter's confession and introduces it with the verse: "As Jesus was praying alone, the disciples were with him and he questioned them" (9:18). It is not said that they *came* to him, but that they *were* with him whilst he was alone! Haenchen calls this verse a "desperate attempt" by Luke to run together Mark 6:46 and 8:27—an attempt which is intelligible only if the intervening Marcan material had been absent in Luke's copy of Mark. And he adds that recently discovered papyri show that it is not unusual for leaves to be missing in the middle of a codex.

John. The fourth Gospel is regarded as later than the other three. It was not known to a number of early Christian writers who knew and even quoted the others. However, this silence could be due not to ignorance, but to hostility toward a Gospel which is so much at variance with the others; and even ignorance of a Gospel might be due simply to its *local* circulation. More conclusive evidence of a later date is that John shows a tendency to enhance features which the Synoptics adumbrate (for example, see *The Jesus of the Early Christians*, pp. 127-9) and that his theology is more advanced. For instance, his elimination of the idea of a literal second coming from the clouds suggests a later stage than that represented in the Synoptics. Mark 9:1 makes Jesus say that "there are some standing here who will not taste death before they see that the kingdom of God has come with power." Matthew 65:28 and Luke 9:27 give the saying with slight variations, but all three use the phrase "will not taste death." John does not record this saying, nor the context which the Synoptics give it; but he does make Jesus affirm (8:52): "If anyone keeps my word, he will never taste death." The aim is clearly to break with the Synoptic doctrine of a second coming, and to make eternal life dependent only on keeping Jesus' word. In the fourth Gospel Christ's second coming no longer means his appearance in the sky as judge, but the coming of the holy spirit into the hearts of believers.[26]

Although John is thus of later date than the Synoptics, there is little in it to suggest that the author was acquainted with them, or even with the traditions on which they are based. His independence is particularly apparent in "the peculiar character of the Jesuine discourse he puts together." This independence is understandable, for we cannot assume that, as soon as the Synoptics were written, they were available in all major Christian communities. As we saw (p. 210), it is quite likely that, in the first century, each community held by one Gospel and did not have recourse to others. John's independence of the Synoptics is not to be taken (as it is by Dodd) as implying that his Gospel is based on traditions which are more ancient than those underlying the Synoptics and therefore of great historical accuracy; for he seems to have drawn on what were more developed, more exaggerated and—in some cases—degraded forms of the traditions represented in them. Haenchen illustrates all three of these features by comparing with its synoptic parallels John's version of the story of the anointing of Jesus' feet. In

Luke 7:36-50 a harlot wets them with her tears, which she dries with her hair; then she anoints the feet with ointment. John does not leave her anonymous, but names her as Mary. This accords with his practice elsewhere. For instance, the Synoptics report, without naming the participants, that the ear of the high priest's slave was cut off; but John states that the name of the slave was Malchus, and that the one who wielded the sword was Simon Peter. These are obviously details of growing legend. Exaggeration is apparent when Mary is made to pour a whole pound of ointment onto Jesus' feet. There is no mention of her tears, and it is the ointment that she wipes away with her hair (12:3-8). An equally senseless trait, betraying John's use of a degraded tradition, is Jesus' statement (after Judas has protested that she has wasted all the oil): "Let her keep it for the day of my burial." In Mark the protest comes from some anonymous observers; Matthew ascribes it to "the disciples," while John complicates matters by making it a hypocritical comment from Judas, who wanted the perfume sold, ostensibly for the benefit of the poor, but in fact (as treasurer of the group) in order to pocket the proceeds.

John cannot be much later than the Synoptics, for a papyrus fragment of it, found in Egypt, has been dated about A.D. 125 and constitutes the earliest preserved fragment of the New Testament. Like the Synoptics it was written at a time of violent enmity between Jews and Christians—indeed the Johannine Jesus foretells that his followers will be excluded from the synagogues (16:2); and in one narrative the evangelist declares that "the Jews had already agreed that if any one should confess him [Jesus] to be the Christ he was to be put out of the synagogue" (9:22). The reference is ostensibly to conditions obtaining in Jesus' lifetime, but it seems more likely that the evangelist wrote in knowledge of the synagogue's official cursing of heretical Jews by means of an insertion into its chief prayer authorized by Rabbi Gamaliel II about A.D. 90. This gave a formal basis to whatever earlier *ad hoc* decisions against Christians there may have been. Throughout the fourth Gospel Jesus speaks of the Jewish Law as though he himself were not a Jew and had no connection with it (8:17; 15:25). For John he is no Jew, but a divine personage who existed before the Jewish nation came into being: "Before Abraham was, I am" (8:58). Dodd, who believes that the "basic tradition" from which John created his Gospel was shaped before the Jewish War of A.D. 66, nevertheless affirms that it was written after the other three, and near the year 100. Grant argues for "a date early in the second century," and notes that resistance to this view comes mainly from those who are "reluctant to abandon the possibility that John the son of Zebedee was, if not the author of the gospel, at least in some sense responsible for it."

SUMMARY

The latest of the four Gospels existed by A.D. 125 and the earliest of them was written between A.D. 70 and this date. Christian scholars have, for obvious reasons, been anxious to date Mark at the very beginning of this period of fifty-five years; but the evidence allows that it was written about the middle of this period. Probably no great interval of time separates this, the earliest of the four, from John, the latest, because (1) John is ignorant of the other three, which therefore are likely to have had a wide and extended circulation when he wrote; (2) Clement of Rome (about A.D. 96) fails to refer to any written gospel and regards as authoritative only the Old Testament and "what the Lord said." The words of the Lord which he quotes are not taken from the Synoptics and, according to Köster, represents an *earlier* layer of tradition—something analogous to "Q." Furthermore, (3) Ignatius (about A.D. 110) did not know Luke, and although he has common ground with Matthew at many points, his dependence on Matthew is by no means proven. Matthew later became the most read Gospel because it was most widely acceptable—and because it included (more so than did other Gospels) widely accepted traditions. It is with such traditions that Ignatius overlaps. Only with Polycarp (about A.D. 120-135) do we reach a writer who is really likely to have used both Matthew and Luke, which of course presuppose Mark. The effect of this evidence is to narrow the time-gap between Mark and John considerably.

NOTES

The reader is referred to Professor Wells's full documentaion and bibliography in *Did Jesus Exist?* pp. 208-220.

1. Winter's study of the narratives of the arrest, trial and crucifixion led him to comment on the great "variety of diverging and repeatedly conflicting accounts" of these events (411, pp. 5-6). And Harvey concedes that it is "impossible" to fit the Gospel resurrection accounts together into a single coherent scheme (201, p. 297).

2. Such adaptation for preaching purposes is today admitted to underlie, e.g., Mark's account (1:16-20) of the call of the first disciples. Jesus meets fishermen he has never before seen, and they "immediately left their nets and followed him" after he had said: "Follow me, and I will make you become fishers of men." Keck concedes that this story "does not report the actual process by which he acquired disciples," but was told by Christian preachers in order to inculcate in their audiences what the proper Christian response to the call of Jesus should be (245, p. 24). The parallel passage in Luke (5:1-11) tries to make the readiness of the men to drop everything and follow him more plausible by representing them as already having heard him preach, and as witnessing a miracle he works.

3. Any synopsis (such as the one by Sparks, 376) which prints corresponding Gospel passages side by side, will show of Matthew 10 that verses 5-15 conflate Mark 6:18-11 with other material, whereas Luke (9:1-6 and 10:1-6) has kept the two separate; that verses 17-22 have been taken from the apocalyptic discourse which Mark made Jesus deliver much later in his career; and that verses 24 ff. have material which occurs in various other contexts in Mark and Luke.

4. See Mark 2:16 and 24; Luke 5:30. According to Bultman (78, p. 172) Jesus is made to face criticism of his disciples rather than of himself because an early Christian community was reproached over its attitude, e.g., to fasting and keeping the sabbath, and therefore needed traditions in which he defends the behavior of his followers on these matters. But Christian communities were quite capable

of representing him as having himself set an example, and the evangelists' failure to record direct criticism of his behavior does seem due to their respect for him.

5. 191, p. 2. Luke himself is later in time than the "many" who had already written gospels. He castigates the inadequacy of these earlier Gospels when he says that he proposes to settle the truth (1:4). He does not suggest that he will do so by drawing on them; rather does he claim to institute an independent inquiry (verse 3). His prologue makes clear that, by the time he wrote, the relation of Gospels to the events recorded in them had become a problem for the Christian community (see the searching discussion by Klein, 128, pp. 206–7, 214).

6. There is, for instance, "reason to believe that only Matthew was at all widely read in Palestine; that there were Churches in Asia Minor which only used John from the very outset; that in Egypt only the [extracanonical] Gospel of the Egyptians was accepted as valid among the Gentile Christians" (115, pp. 45–6), while the Jewish Christians of Alexandria used the Gospel of the Hebrews (28, pp. 51–2).

7. See 92, p. 261 and 188, pp. 7–8. The discerning reader will find the facts admitted in Dodd's last book where he says that the author of Luke "has been identified, *from the time when the New Testament writings were first collected* [italics mine], as the Greek physician Luke who was for some years on the 'staff' of the apostle Paul, and this may be right" (135, p. 17).

8. Within the material that they have in common with Mark, Matthew and Luke agree in the sequence of the events only in so far as they agree with Mark. Where they diverge from Mark, each goes his own way. From these facts Lachmann argued in 1835 that all three evangelists copied a lost original Gospel which is best preserved by Mark. This argument from the order of events for the priority of Mark still stands (*pace* Farmer, 152, p. 66), even though the postulate of an original Gospel underlying all three has today been replaced by the view that Matthew and Luke used Mark, since, in numerous instances, the divergence of Matthew and Luke from Mark in sequence can be understandable but not the divergence of Mark from Matthew and Luke (268, pp. 46–8).

9. Ignatius does indeed say that Jesus was baptized by John "that all righteousness might be fulfilled by him." Somewhat similar words were added by Matthew to the Marcan account of Jesus' baptism, and Ignatius' phrase therefore suggests that he knew Matthew (cf. JEC, p. 171). Köster, however, thinks that Ignatius did not take the phrase directly from Matthew but from a confessional formula which was known both to him and to the evangelist (261, p. 60).

10. Clement of Alexandria (d. ca. A.D. 251) is the first clearly to link Mark with Rome. Eusebius declares that an earlier statement (not now extant) of Papias (ca. A.D. 140) confirms Clement. By about this time Peter had come to be regarded as having preached in Rome, and Mark as we saw (above, p. 210) was early associated with Peter. Again, the "Mark" mentioned in 1 Peter 5:13 is said to be with Peter in Babylon—the code name used by early Christians for Rome (cf. above, p. 216). Clement and Papias' view of the origin of Mark was surely based on nothing more than inference from these tendentious traditions (as is betrayed by Eusebius' comments; see e.g. 149, Bk. 2, ch. 15). If Mark was in fact written in Rome, it must have originated after A.D. 96, for 1 Clement, written there at about that date, shows, as Evans notes, "no sign of any knowledge of Mark" (150, pp. 6–7; cf. 261, p. 23). Schulz thinks that the Gospel may well have been written at Tyre, Sidon or in Transjordan, (361, p. 9), and Taylor finds that a case can be made for Antioch (3845, pp. 5, 32). In other words, all we can affirm with confidence is that it was written in an important and respected Christian community. This much seems to follow from the fact that, although Matthew and Luke smoothed what Trocmé has called the "grande rusticité" (394, p. 56) of Mark's style, they nevertheless respected the substance of his work sufficiently to make it the basis of their own accounts.

11. Rom. 13:1–7, which urges subservience to the authorities, and which even designates them loyal servants of God, has long been recognized as a self-contained unit independent of its context, indeed breaking the connection between the ethical admonitions which precede and follow it. Nevertheless, Kallas' reasons (244, pp. 365–74) for setting it aside as a second-century interpolation are not fully convincing.

12. A notable exception is Farmer, who thinks Mark may have been written as late as A.D. 100 or 125; but he also argues that it is later than and dependent on Matthew and Luke (152, pp. 200, 226). Trocmé proposes A.D. 85 as an upper limit for the final redaction of Mark, but he dates the

first thirteen chapters as early as A.D. 50 (394, pp. 193, 203).

13. Grässer (176, p. 155n) and others have noted that it is possible to explain this lack of concord by supposing that Mark substituted the words "all these things" for what was originally only a reference to the temple; and that he thus aimed to correct an earlier idea that the destruction of the temple would be followed directly by the end of the world, and to affirm that it was only one link in the chain of final events. If Mark was in fact correcting an earlier tradition in this way, it is probable that the need for such correction arose because the temple had already been destroyed (without bringing about the end of the world) and that Mark was therefore writing after A.D. 70.

14. Some commentators (see refs in 231, p. 215) interpret "the desolating sacrilege set up where it ought not to be" as reference to the coming of the Antichrist—a demonic figure expected before Jesus' second advent as the final persecutor of Christians, and sometimes identified with the "son of perdition" of 2 Thess. 2:1-12, who takes his seat in the temple. The roots of this conception are probably to be found in the (originally Babylonian) legend of the battle of God with a dragon-like monster—a legend of which traces are to be found in various parts of the Old Testament. One reason for linking the "desolating sacrilege" with the Antichrist is that Mark qualifies this neuter phrase with a masculine participle—lit. "set up where *he* ought not to be." Equally allowable is the rendering of the RV: "*standing* where he ought not"; and Brandon thinks that this refers to an outsider who intruded into the temple. He takes it as an allusion to Titus' entry into the innermost sanctuary in A.D. 70, when the victorious Roman troops assembled in the temple court and sacrificed to their standards, which bore the image of the emperor. He regards this verse as the evangelist's own composition, and not as incorporated from an apocalypse of slightly earlier date (66, pp. 232-3).

15. Branscomb (70, p. 233) reaches this same conclusion from slightly different premises. He notes that the pre-Christian references to the "desolating sacrilege" (in Daniel and Maccabees) link it with the temple; and he argues that Mark was editing an apocalypse which likewise mentioned the sacrilege in connection with the temple; and that, since the evangelist was writing after A.D. 70 (when the temple no longer existed), he deleted explicit mention of it and substituted the less definite statement that the sacrilege was "set up where it ought not to be."

16. The embarrassment of commentators on Mark 13:30 and its Synoptic parallels is illustrated by Dodd's argument that the passage is an example of "shortening of historical perspective." "When the profound realities underlying a situation are depicted in the dramatic form of historical prediction, the certainty and inevitability of the spiritual processes involved are expressed in terms of the immediate imminence of the event" (132, p. 55).

17. That Luke did not know Matthew is clear from his failure to include any of Matthew's additions to Mark. It is also unlikely that, if he had used Matthew, he would have broken up Jesus' discourses as given there (particularly the Sermon on the Mount), omitted some of the fragments thus formed, and scattered others throughout his own Gospel.

18. For evidence supporting the statements made in this paragraph, see JEC, pp. 165-74; 261, pp. 23-4, 61, 122; 179, p. 302; 249, pp. 6-7, 127, 131; 292, p. xxviii.

19. Even so mystical a logion from "Q" as Matthew 11:25-7 = Luke 10:21-2 is claimed by Jeremias (228) as "Palestinian," and is in fact paralleled in the Dead Sea Scrolls (see Davies, 122, pp. 136ff). Most commentators agree that it is a piece of Church writing based on a number of Old Testament quotations and put into Jesus' mouth. Here, says Vermes, "contemporary exegetical skepticism joins forces for once with common sense" (398, p. 201).

20. Rengstorf (145, pp. 116, 125) has objected that the "burning of the city" was a literary cliché common in parables concerning kings, and in historical narratives which relate the capture and destruction of a town in the briefest possible way; and also that it fails to bring out the salient events of A.D. 70. But if Matthew is in fact here using a cliché, this would explain why his allusion to these events is not more precise.

21. Cf. Walker, 402, pp. 83-4, 115. On the other hand, Matthew's adaptation of Mark's statement about the "desolating sacrilege" seems to work in precisely the opposite direction, and to link the events of A.D. 70 with the consummation. For he says not (as Mark does) that the sacrilege will be "set up where it ought not to be," but that it will be seen "standing in the holy place" (24:15). This certainly looks like a reference to the desecration of the temple at the end of the

rebellion. The evangelist adds (verses 21 and 29) that "then there will be great tribulation" and that "immediately after the tribulation of those days" the end will come. Some commentators have, however, argued that the "holy place" does not mean the temple at all. Bonnard notes that Matthew's retention of Mark's "let the reader understand" hints that there is a hidden meaning in the prediction and indicates that Christians are to interpret "the holy place" in a special way—as a veiled reference to the Church. The "desolating sacrilege" standing there would thus be a reference to idolatry, revolt or the coming of Antichrist in the Christian community (51, p. 351); cf. Hill, 207, p. 321 and Bacon's argument (11, pp. 68-9) that Matthew "makes no prediction that the Second Coming will follow 'immediately' after the *fall of Jerusalem*. He predicts (what is much more to the purpose for his readers) that it will come immediately after the worst sufferings of *the Church*."

22. The "immediately" of Matthew 24:29 has no equivalent in Luke 21:25. And Luke has also dropped the statement of Mark 13:20 (preserved in Matthew 24:22) that the days preceding the end shall be shortened for the elect's sake.

23. He will not admit that Luke's version of Jesus' speech about the fall of Jerusalem is a "prophecy after the event" (144, p. 57). While *Biblica* 348, § 16) notes that Luke 19:43 alludes to an actual incident in the destruction of Jerusalem, Ellis makes no comment on that verse, although the old commentary he is revising refers its readers to the incident as described by Josephus.

24. See Conzelmann, 105, pp. 30-1; 106, pp. 150-1. In JEC (p. 87) I wrongly asserted that Luke 12:54-6 makes Jesus take a different attitude, and encourages his audience to look forward to momentous signs which will announce the advent of the end of the world. More plausible is the argument of Klein that "the present time" in verse 56 means the situation in the Church from the death of Jesus until the time of Luke—a period characterized by divisions (verse 52). The sense of the passage is that "to judge the present time aright" one must take the Christian side (254, p. 385). There is no reference to the end, although there was in the saying which Luke was reworking. (The Matthean form, 16:26f, is clearly more eschatological).

25. Jesus' true status was the principal point of dispute between Jewish and Christian communities late in the first century. The Christians regarded him not merely as supernatural, but even as divine, and such a claim was certainly, from the Jewish standpoint, blasphemous. (Cf. John 10:33 where the Jews try to stone him "for blasphemy; because you, being a man, make yourself God.") Hence the origin of a Christian narrative in which Jews are represented as rejecting as blasphemous his affirmation of what, for Christians, constituted his true status. As Bousset observed (59, p. 51), Mark 14:64 derives from Christian dogma, not from Jewish legal ideas. Other features of the whole passage also show that it originated in a Christian community of sophisticated Christology, and that Jesus could not have said what Mark here ascribes to him.

26. John 14:16-18; 16:7 and 13. The way such contradictions are glossed over by apologists is well illustrated by Grant's statement that "in regard to Christology and eschatology, the point of view of John is somewhat different from that of the synoptic evangelists" (182, p. 154).

Part Four

The Jesus Tradition:
History, Myth, and Legend

Introduction

The seven selections that follow deal with the major components of the Jesus-tradition: birth, baptism, preaching, crucifixion, and resurrection. Although here organized in a roughly chronological fashion, this arrangement does not correspond to the order in which the materials were composed. It is likely that the legend of the dying god, based perhaps on a kernel of historical fact, was the core of the preaching of the early Christian mystery. Around this center, the life of the cult revolved. Its eucharistic celebration, wherein the death and triumph of the god were sacramentally reenacted and participation in his "resurrection" life effected (1 Cor. 11:23ff.), was almost certainly the situation out of which the later traditional materials—the mythology of the Gospels—emerged.

The content of the Gospels may thus be seen as a story used to explain and corroborate the liturgical drama or as a history of the Christ mystery. The "backward development" of the tradition, moreover, from the central narrative of the Passion, death, and resurrection of the Lord to the legends of his birth and Davidic descent, suggest that the development of the narrative history was a very gradual process. Earlier than such traditions is Paul's belief that the Christ, the son of God, was sacrificed to God on behalf of sinners (Romans 5:9ff.), and earlier even than Paul is the ritual supper of the dying god described in 1 Corinthians 11. From this passage it is clear that the nucleus of the Passion story—the betrayal of the god—and words spoken by him signifying his abiding presence in the cultus—were linked with the ritual of his death from the earliest days of the Christian movement.

In the course of time, the Gospels accumulated a variety of fairly conventional additions to the Jesus legend: that he had been a healing god, a miracle-worker on the order of Asklepios; that he had been a teacher of wisdom, able to outwit even the most astute of the Pharisees; that he had been a follower of the famous apocalyptic teacher, John the Baptist, and in a further development, that John had been merely his forerunner; that he had been born, in accordance with prophecy, in David's city of Bethlehem and of David's stock; and in a further Christological development, (one that contradicts the Davidic genealogy entirely) that he had been born of a virgin or was the very logos of God and had descended to earth to impart the knowledge of salvation to believers. The very diversity of these traditions suggests to us how little the Gospels have to do with the biography of an individual and how much with the life of the early believers in "the Way."

Charles Guignebert

The Birth of Jesus

CHARLES GUIGNEBERT (1867–1939) was for thirty years professor of the history of Christianity at the Sorbonne. Together with Alfred Loisy (d. 1940) and Maurice Goguel (d. 1956), he formed a trio of historians whose careful and detailed scholarship was in the vanguard of New Testament studies between the two world wars. His works include *Jesus* (Eng. tr., 1950), *The Jewish World in the Time of Jesus* (Eng. tr., 1958), and *The Christ* (Eng. tr., 1968). Like F. C. Conybeare in England and his countryman, the ex-Jesuit Loisy, Guignebert defended the historical existence of Jesus, but was sympathetic to the history-of-religions approach of the Christ-myth school. His view of Christianity as a social and intellectual movement was in advance of the ideas of his time, and his work forged the way for such scholars as Arthur Darby Nock, Robert Pfeiffer, and above all Marcel Simon and J. B. Brisson.

We shall not stop to discuss the wonders with which the editors of Matthew and Luke have thought fit to adorn their accounts of the Nativity. The appearance of the miraculous star, the visit of the Magi, the flight into Egypt, and the massacre of the Innocents, on the one hand; the birth in the stable, the announcement of the glad tidings to the shepherds, the presentation in the Temple, on the other, form two groups of incidents which it is futile to endeavor to blend into one, and still more futile to attempt to connect with history. They are sheer hagiography. The editors have sought to make up for their lack of knowledge by moving but fictitious narratives, founded either upon supposedly prophetic writings, or upon popularized myths or folk tales. The Apocryphal Gospels supplementing and elaborating these edifying tales increased their improbabilities, but

---

From *The Christ* by Charles Guignebert (Secaucus, N.J.: University Books, 1966), pp. 105–131. Published by arrangement with Lyle Stuart.

did not alter their essential nature, which by the deliberate intent of their authors set them outside the sphere of verifiable and probable events. Such is the fundamental character of the miraculous element in hagiography, a fact which it would be rash and ingenuous to forget.

The question of the parents of Jesus cannot be so easily dismissed. The oldest tradition believed, probably rightly, that the mother of the Master was called *Mariam*. The name of his father was *Joseph*, according to the legends at the beginning of Matthew and Luke, and two passages in John (1:45 and 6:42). But this evidence is not in itself conclusive, and it is not confirmed by Mark, who makes no mention of Joseph. The tradition reflected in the Second Gospel thus appears to have had no interest in the father of Jesus, and it has been suggested, as a means of obviating this difficulty, that he was dead when his son began his preaching. . . . Everyone today knows that Joseph was a carpenter, but it may well be that the ancient Christians were less sure of the fact than we. In Mark 6:3 the people of Nazareth, amazed at the wisdom displayed by Jesus, exclaim: "Is this, not *the carpenter, the son of Mary?*" Matthew and Luke have both altered this passage. The former (13:55) substitutes: "Is not this *the son of the carpenter?*"; and the latter (4:22): "Is this not *the son of Joseph?*" It is our opinion that the three editors all had before them an original text of Mark, which actually read "the son of the carpenter." In Aramaic, however, the expression "the son of the carpenter" means "a carpenter," just as "a son of man" is another way of saying "a man." Accordingly, Mark has correctly translated it as "the carpenter"; Matthew had failed to understand, and has simply transcribed the expression as it stands; Luke, also failing to understand, has tried to improve it by specifying the person meant by "the carpenter."

Whether the father of Jesus was called Joseph or not, and whether or not he was a carpenter or joiner, are, however, matters of small importance. The impression conveyed, and on which we may rely, is that he was a man of humble station, earning his bread by the labor of his hands. We have no means of ascertaining anything more about him, and the details of his biography and character given by the Apocrypha are completely untrustworthy. As to his ancestors, we are entirely ignorant, and the two gospel editors who have professed to trace his descent from David are not in agreement about the name of the father, one giving it as *Jacob* (Matt. 1:16), and the other as *Heli* (Luke 3:23).

We are little better informed regarding Mary. What the Synoptic Gospels say about her is insignificant, and the contradictory fantasies of the Apocrypha are worthless, except to convince us that the primitive tradition, having no reason to be interested in the mother of Jesus in herself, has amassed no accurate and trustworthy information concerning her. Her lineage is completely unknown. Some commentators have maintained that Luke connected her, as he did Joseph, with the House of David. We should say, on the contrary, that, in representing her as a relative of Elizabeth, whom he makes a descendant of Aaron, he affiliates her with the family of Aaron. In any case, since the whole of the Lucan legend regarding the relationships of the Forerunner of Jesus cannot possibly be based upon any authentic tradition, we have no choice but to give up even that shred of information concerning the ancestors of Mary. Nor do we know what became of her after the death of Jesus. In this complete absence of any genuine tradition, the imagination of the hagiographers had full scope to indulge in the most affecting or the silliest fabrications, according to their degree of literary skill. The only passages in our Synoptics which might recall a real incident with regard to the mother of Jesus, is that which shows her, incapable as she is of understanding her son, attempting to get him away from his disciples to take him home (Mark 3:20 ff.).

There is nothing surprising in the fact that the gospel tradition leaves us in ignorance concerning the parents of Christ, for even if, as is possible, the original disciples had possessed accurate and more or less detailed information about them, there would have been no reason for transmitting it to the second generation of Christians. Almost immediately after the Crucifixion, was begun that labor of faith which, absorbed in elevating Jesus more and more above humanity, must necessarily have contemned everything that tended in the opposite direction. Too many details about his earthly family, and its actual status, which was certainly not too distinguished, could not fail, at that time, to be very embarrassing. When Paul announces that he is interested only in "the crucified and glorified Christ," he gives the exact formula for the transformation of the life of Jesus in the minds of the earliest generations of Christians. At the same time, he reveals the secret of the rapidity with which authentic recollections concerning the family of the Nazarene and his life prior to his baptism were obliterated.

The glorious legend which was thus substituted for a humble reality is very old, because the reason for the subsitution is also very old. From the moment his followers believed that Jesus was the Messiah foretold by the prophets, the transformation of his life into myth began, and proceeded apace.

The legend in its growth has left in the text of the Synoptics traces of at least three of its stages, or, if the evidence of Acts be included, we may say, four:

(1) It was the belief in the resurrection which probably established, or at least defined, as we shall see later, the faith in the Messiahship of Jesus. The Apostles, having *witnessed* the Resurrection, realized that he had been glorified by God, and no longer doubted that he was "the one who was to come." These beliefs, together with their scriptural justification, that is to say, accompanied by the prophecies which were supposed to confirm them, appear in the two discourses attributed to Peter in Acts 2:22 ff., and 4:8 ff. Such an idea was not by any means inconsistent with the phenomena of a completely human existence, and it presented itself as one which could be accepted by men who had actually lived on familiar terms with the Master. But it was not designed to satisfy for long the growing faith of men who believed in Jesus without having seen him.

(2) In the account in Luke of the event of the Baptism, we read (3:22): "The Holy Ghost descended in bodily form, in the shape of a dove, upon him, and a voice came from heaven (saying): Thou art my beloved son; in thee I am well pleased." The most authoritative manuscript of the *Western* text, codex D,

236 The Origins of Christianity

gives here the variant, borrowed from Psalm 2:7: "This day I have begotten thee." This is certainly earlier than the accepted reading, for it exhibits the belief that God adopted Jesus as his son on the day of the Baptism. Thus, the whole life of the Lord, or at least his public career, is included in the Messianic period of his existence, but his birth, according to the rabbinical conception, remains that of a man amongst men, and a man of humble status. It was not long before the progress of the faith made intolerable to the "brethren" these prosaic ideas of an insensitive Judaism, and they substituted for them beliefs more worthy of their object.

(3) The first and third Gospels both contain genealogies of Jesus connecting him with King David. The belief that the Blessed of Yahweh, the Messiah, would belong to the race of the old national king was widespread in Israel towards the beginning of our era. It is possible that the current identification of "Messiah" and "Son of David" was not taken literally in the Pharisaic schools, but amongst the people it probably was, and in our Gospels it unquestionably is. From the moment when Jesus came to be regarded by his disciples as the Messiah, it thus became necessary for him to be descended from David. The parentage of the humble Galilean workman had to go back in a direct line to the king chosen of old by Yahweh. There was no question of finding out if such a relationship could be proved, or even made to appear plausible. Hagiography does not trouble itself with such details and scruples. The point was to show that the announcement of the Prophets had not been false. A hagiographer had no need of any evidence other than that of the Prophets themselves to be convinced that Jesus was a member of the house of David, and to realize his own duty, which was to embody this truth in concrete form that it might convince the skeptical.

The genealogies of Matthew and Luke represent two of these fulfillments of prophecy, and there may possibly have been others in circulation, contradictory no doubt, like the two which remain to us. But it would show lack of intelligence to apply critical methods to these reconstructions arising from credal or apologetic necessities and directed solely towards edification.

A moment's scrutiny of the genealogy of Matthew 1:1-17 will reveal its artificiality; in fact, it is naïvely admitted in the last verse:

> So all the generations from Abraham unto David are fourteen generations, and from David unto the exile into Babylon, fourteen generations, and from the exile into Babylon unto Christ, fourteen generations.

In other words, for reasons unknown to us, but probably connected with the symbolism of numbers, or with the desire for that equality of parts which the Orientals of those days regarded as a form of perfection, the genealogist, taking the pattern of his work, and the names on which he has mainly relied, from the Bible, has constructed a framework which has no historical basis and then filled it in as he thought fit. The proof is, that his second series, the one commencing with "David begat Solomon," and comprising the kings of Judah, has skipped four names. In verse 8, instead of "Joram begat Uzziah," we should have "Joram begat Ahaziah; Ahaziah begat Joash; Joash begat Amaziah; Amaziah begat Uzziah." That is to say, Joram was not the father of Uzziah, as the genealogist would have us believe, but his great-great-grandfather. Further, in verse 11 we find: "Josiah begat Jechoniah and his brethren into the exile into Babylon," that is, "at the time of the exile." In reality, Josiah had been dead for over twenty years "at the time of the exile," and he did not beget Jechoniah, who was his grandson. It is not a case of accidental forgetfulness or casual inaccuracy; the redactor has simply cut out anything that interfered with the regular pattern of the symbolic structure by which he professed to prove that Jesus had fulfilled the divine promises made to his ancestor Abraham, and had accomplished the sacred destiny of the race of David. The prosaic facts of history mattered nothing to him.

The editor of Luke was equally indifferent to them. His genealogy which is found in 3:23-38, is in reverse order. It starts with Jesus and goes right back, through David and Abraham, to Adam "(son) of God," comprising seventy-seven names, with God at one end and Jesus at the other. This figure also seems to reflect an interest in numerical symbolism. The names, from Adam to Abraham, have been taken from the Greek Bible, as is proved by the mention of Cainan (3:36), who does not appear in the Hebrew text. From Abraham to David, Luke's list, still taken from the Bible, coincides exactly with Matthew's, but after David, instead of continuing the descent through Solomon, it takes it through Nathan, another son of David, whose name is given in 2 Samuel 5:14, and is, incidentally, the only thing we know about him. Beginning with Nathan, Luke diverges from Matthew, only temporarily rejoining him with the two names, Salathiel and Zerubbabel, and then pursuing his own course again down to Joseph. From Jesus to Abraham, Luke enumerates fifty-six generations, while Matthew gives only forty. In going back to Adam, the genealogist of Luke appears to have intended to signify the universality of salvation, and by this, no less than by his use of the Greek Bible, he reveals his Hellenic origin. It is hardly necessary to add that we do not know where he, any more than Matthew, got the names which form his list after Nathan. But it is quite comprehensible why neither of them could leave out Salathiel and Zerubbabel, names which were indissolubly associated with the Return.

By slightly different means, or, rather, with slightly different materials, the two editors have succeeded in realizing the same purpose, namely, to vindicate the Messianic status of Jesus by proving that he was a member of the house of David.

The belief in this illustrious descent is unquestionably very old, since Paul already knew and accepted it (Rom. 1:3, "of the seed of David according to the flesh"), but that is no reason for believing, without further investigation, that it was correct. There are still critics, even open-minded ones, who accept the possibility of its being so, but we cannot share their opinion. The Davidic descent of Jesus is impugned, to begin with, by the mere fact that it was *necessary*, an inevitable corollary of the announcement of the Messianic status of the Nazarene. But there is a more serious argument against it. The *Ebionim*, the descendants of the ancient Judeo-Christians, apparently rejected the genealogies, and their opinion appears to be justified by the oldest tradition. In the Synoptic narrative Jesus never boasts of his ancestor David, nor do his disciples appear to have regarded him as a descendant of the great king. Neither the appeal of the blind man of Jericho: "Son of David, Jesus, have mercy upon me" (Mark 10:47), nor the Messianic acclamation on the entry into Jerusalem: "Blessed be he that cometh in the name of the Lord. Blessed be the kingdom that cometh, of our father David" (Mark 11:9-10), can have the least weight against this double silence of Jesus and his companions. The blind man is supposed to divine that the prophet passing by is the Messiah, and it is *his* name he bestows upon Jesus in calling him "Son of David." To bless the "kingdom of David," on the other hand, is simply to hail the dawn of the Messianic day.

Another, and even more important objection, is that the author of the fourth Gospel, who could not have been ignorant of the belief in the Davidic descent, does not accept it. In the seventh chapter of John, after one of the Master's sermons, the listeners exchange admiring exclamations: "This is a prophet, " say some; "This is the Christ," say others, going further, to which the objection is made:

> But can the Christ come out of Galilee? Hath not the Scripture said that Christ cometh of the race of David, and out of the village of Bethlehem whence David came? (7:40-2).

The fact that the writer of the Gospel does not refute the objection by declaring that Jesus *was* born at Bethlehem and descended from David, proves that he did not think either of these things to be true; they were not believed in his circle. In his opinion Christ was much more than the son of David, he was his Lord. The same impression is conveyed by John 8:12-14:

> Then spake Jesus again unto them, saying: "I am the light of the world. . . ." The Pharisees therefore said unto him: "Thou bearest witness unto thyself; thy witness is not true." Jesus answered and said unto them: "Though I bear witness to myself, my witness is true, for I know whence I come and whither I go. But ye do not know whence I come nor whither I go."

This shows that Jesus, or rather, the writer of the Gospel, scorned the answer, which the Pharisees would not have accepted, certainly, without proof, but which would have impressed them at once: "I am the son of David."

Enough has been said to prove that the belief in the Davidic descent of Jesus found acceptance only among the earliest Christians, and the point need not be emphasized further. Let us now turn to the genealogies and try to evaluate their evidence.

If, as has been suggested, the two editors had gone to the public archives for their lists, they would have been the same, or at least, making due allowance for carelessness and error, approximately the same. But they are not only at variance, they are irreconcilable. From David to Jesus, Luke gives forty-two names and Matthew only twenty-six, a difference of sixteen generations, which, in terms of time, allowing an average duration for each, amounts to fully four centuries. Either Luke, that is, is four centuries too long, or Matthew four centuries too short, a divergence which the most generous allowances cannot succeed in reducing to any perceptible extent. To this first difficulty is added another, if possible even more formidable, in the fact that the two genealogies, although following different lines of descent from David, both end with Joseph.

The traditional answer to these objections is that one of the two lists gives the actual members of the line of descent, the other the putative members, arrived at by the operation of the *levirate*, as was called the custom which decreed that if a man died without issue, his nearest relative should marry his widow and endow him with the posterity which he himself had not been able to provide. The difficulty is, that in this case we should have to suppose that, between David and Joseph, the levirate affected all the generations except the two, represented by Salathiel and Zerubbabel, which are common to the two lists. This implies that the generations sprung from Solomon became as a result of the levirate and second marriages, somehow intermingled with those sprung from Nathan, which is improbable, not to say absurd. The complications may, indeed, be reduced a little, but only at the cost of further completely hypothetical assumptions. Julius Africanus, who, if he did not originate the explanation in question, at least disseminated it, admits that it is without proof, but says that it is the most satisfactory one he knows of, and is supposed to go back to the "dominicals," or relatives of Jesus, who apparently claimed that it was founded on family recollections. They accounted for their inability to produce records, by the assertion that Herod had malevolently destroyed them. It is difficult to have any confidence in such evidence, which could, at best, come only from the descendants of cousins of Jesus, who no longer had any definite information about their lineage, and who were, moreover, bound to believe that it was Davidic for the very reason that it was that of the Messiah, "the son of David."

At a much later epoch, a very different explanation was devised to reconcile the two genealogies. It was maintained that that of Matthew applied to Joseph, and that of Luke to Mary. This theory is exposed to numerous objections, of which we shall note only two, which seem to us conclusive: (1) The Jews did not admit the transmission of birthright by the mother. "It was not the custom of the Scriptures," as Saint Jerome justly remarks, "to count women in their genealogies." Hence the genealogy of Mary could be of no use for the purpose of proving that her son was descended from David. (2) It is Joseph, not Mary, whose descent the genealogist of Luke professes to trace, inasmuch as even our present text reads: "And Jesus himself, at this beginning, was about thirty years old, being the son, as was supposed, of Joseph, (son) of Heli, etc." (3:23). Moreover, in 1:27, and 2:4, it is Joseph, and not Mary, whom Luke makes a descendant of David. Mary, as has already been pointed out, is, as far as Luke is concerned, a member of the house of Aaron.

Neither of these two professed explanations is valid. The two genealogies remain contradictory, resembling each other only in their common object of proving that Jesus is in fact the "son of David" expected by Israel, and in their equal indifference to historical truth and to probability. It is significant that we find in the texts no indication that the Messiahship of Jesus was ever deduced from his Davidic descent. The process was just the reverse; the Christians first believed that he was the Messiah, and then inferred that he was descended from David.

(4) The belief in the virgin birth represents a new and culminating stage of the Messianic faith, only to be superseded by the Pauline and Johannine doctrine of the Incarnation.

The selection of Jesus for his sacred mission is now taken back to his conception, or, more accurately, for the idea of *selection* is substituted that of rigid *predestination*. The child is conceived at the express command of God in order to be "the one who is to come." And for this purpose the Virign Mary is impregnated by the Holy Ghost.

How Matthew and Luke Reconcile the Davidic Descent with the Virgin Birth

It is somewhat surprising to discover that the two Gospels which relate this miracle are the very ones which contain the Davidic genealogies. Why should they have taken so much trouble to connect Joseph with David, if Jesus was not the son of Joseph? It seems probable that the comparatively late redactors whose work has come down to us felt that they could not discard a statement which controversy with the Jews had no doubt caused to become very deeply rooted in Christian apologetics. Possibly, too, they thought that the Davidic descent of the "foster father" of the Lord was a strong factor in preserving the faith of the people. In the course of time, however, copyists, less easily satisfied, began to be somewhat disturbed by the very obvious contradiction between the conclusion of the genealogies, "Joseph begat Jesus," and the story of the Virgin Birth, which was definitely intended to annul the paternity of Joseph. Accordingly, they made some very illuminating alterations in the text. The original reading of the genealogy of Matthew undoubtedly concluded with the attribution to Joseph of the *procreation* of Jesus. Our certainty of this is confirmed by a text of Epiphanius, which informs us that the heretics of the second century, such as Cerinthus and Carpocrates, made the genealogy of Matthew the basis of their claim that Jesus was in reality the son of Joseph and Mary. Eusebius attributes the same opinion, and the same defense of it, to the Ebionite Symmachus. Our accepted text of Matthew 1:16, however, employs the following form of expression: "And Jacob begat Joseph, the husband of Mary and of *her* was born Jesus called the Christ."

In other words, the editor means to imply that Joseph was only the *apparent* father of the child of his wife Mary, and he has, in fact, wiped out with one word all the work of the genealogist. In all probability this obvious emendation was not the first. Two manuscripts read: "And Jacob begat Joseph; and Joseph, to whom was married the Virgin Mary, begat Jesus," which is probably an earlier form than our own, in which the editor has simply interpolated, as a kind of supplement, the assertion of the Virgin Birth. This peculiar combination is even more naïvely and awkwardly exhibited in the following reading: "Jacob begat Joseph, the husband of Mary, of whom was born Jesus called the Christ, and Joseph begat Jesus called the Christ."

In the case of the text of Luke, we have been less fortunate, and the manuscripts do not permit us to trace the manner in which it has been altered. But that it has been, is self-evident, and sufficiently proved by the reading of 3:23: "Jesus . . . being the son, *as was supposed* of Joseph." The words "as was supposed" betray an alteration designed, as Alfred Loisy justly observes, "to abrogate the idea of natural sonship which the text of this passage originally suggested." The belief in the Virgin Birth is thus unquestionably later than the desire to establish the Davidic descent of Jesus, as Messiah.

The assertion of the Virgin Birth came, in time, to occupy the central position in Christian apologetics, as forming the great proof of the divine origin of Jesus. It afforded, at the same time, the point of departure for the multifarious ideas and speculations out of which, in the course of the centuries, has grown the majestic structure of the cult of Mary. This result certainly far outran the purpose of those hagiographers who thus transposed for the benefit of their creed, a myth that was generally current in their environment. Their intention was only to provide a conclusive argument in their controversy with the skeptical Jews, though perhaps also, in materializing their own conception of the relation between Christ and God the Father, they were instinctively seeking to invest their Lord with the same supreme privilege possessed, according to the belief of their own adherents, by all the other Lords and Saviors renowned throughout the Hellenistic Orient. Their accounts, which are obviously outside the realm of history, would not be worth pausing over, if we were only concerned with their intentions. But the serious consequences of these accounts make it necessary for us to explain their character and define their origin.

The first point to be established is that the Virgin Birth, which is definitely asserted in Matthew 1:18–25, and Luke 1:5–80, finds no echo in any other part of the New Testament. It has been maintained that this is not so, and no ingenuity has been spared to prove it, but it is a vain task. There are limits to the forced interpretation of texts. Mark has been cited, for instance, as a witness to the virginity of Mary, on the strength of 1:1: "The beginning of the Gospel of Jesus, the son of God"; and 6:3: "Is not this the carpenter, the son of Mary?" If Jesus is the son of God, it is argued, he is not the son of Joseph, and the insistence upon his mother to the exclusion of his father, further proves that, on the human side, his mother alone was concerned in his birth. Unfortunately, for this reasoning the following points must be taken into account. (1) The words, "the son of God," in the first verse of Mark, cannot possibly have belonged to the original version of the text. Almost all the great existing versions give them, it is true, but as is well known, these are far from being original. Moreover, the *Sinaitic Syriac*, which is of great authority, and the early patristic tradition represented by Irenaeus and Origen, followed by Basil and Jerome, omit the words: *son of God*. The addition must have been made as a counterpart to the avowal of the centurion in 15:39: "Truly this man was a son of God." (2) In any case, the expression "son of God" is in all probability to be interpreted in a metaphysical and not a physical sense. (3) The phrase "son of Mary" is very naturally explained by the fact that Joseph may have been dead at the time when these people of Nazareth are supposed to have significantly designated Jesus by the name of his mother. Nothing in all the rest of Mark gives the slightest support to the interpretation which it is sought to impose upon the two passages in question. Therefore, since it is difficult to believe that the editor of Mark did not know the story of the Virgin Birth, we must suppose that he did not accept it, otherwise there would be no reason for his not having simply added it to his Gospel. There are still traces which show that in *Urmarcus*, it is not at the moment of the conception of Jesus, but at that of his baptism, that the Holy Spirit entered his humanity.

John sets forth a similar but far more exalted conception. His point of view was entirely different from that of Matthew and Luke; hence, save for the object of conforming to historical reality, if that were in question, there was no reason why he should adhere to their account of the birth of Jesus. The two Synoptists attempt to prove that a child was specially created by God to be his Messiah, and that this was accomplished by a process, the miraculousness of which is of itself an infallible "sign." John, on the other hand, believed that Jesus was the incarnation of the *logos*, coeternal with God, which is a very different thing. From this point of view, Christ is not human at all. He is dependent upon neither an earthly father nor an earthly *mother*, which is the exact meaning of 1:13, if the reading of Tertullian be accepted as original: "It was not of blood, nor of the will of the flesh, nor of the will of man, but of God that he was born." To cite this passage in favor of the Virgin Birth, is grossly to misconstrue it. The incarnation of the *logos* in Jesus does not imply that the *man* Jesus was exempt from the laws of human generation, for it was at the *Baptism*, according to John, that the *logos* descended into him. John thus elevates the idea of Mark, but he preserves its framework, and, if we may so put it, all its external garb. Accordingly, he never misses an opportunity of stating that Jesus is "the son of Joseph." Far from supporting the legend of Matthew and Luke, he definitely opposes it.

We have spoken of John in his place in order to keep the four Gospels together, but in reality, between the Palestinian tradition which Matthew, Mark, and Luke are supposed substantially to reflect, and the fourth Gospel, come the Epistles of Paul, which were written during the lifetime of the apostolic generation, in contact with men who, having known Jesus and his family, could at least testify to what was said in the Master's own circle concerning the conditions of his birth. There is not the smallest reference, in the letters of the Apostle, to the Virgin Birth. What we find there is a doctrine of the incarnation of the Holy Spirit, less definite, certainly, than that of the incarnation of the *logos* in John, but as it were anticipatory, and preparatory of it. "The Lord is the Spirit" declares 2 Corinthians 3:17. Paul's actual belief is that Christ, the divine instrument in the work of creation, and in that of the reconciliation of men with the Father, preexisted with God before time was, but his incarnation in the human person of Jesus did not in any way exclude the natural and usual conditions of his birth "according to the flesh." Paul would assuredly not have encumbered himself with his doctrine of the divine Adam, coming to redeem humanity, if he had believed that the Lord was conceived by Mary "of the Spirit." In Galatians 4:4 he writes:

> When the fulness of the time was come, God sent his son, born of a woman born under the Law, to redeem all those that were under the Law.

If this verse is read without forcing its meaning, it will appear to indicate the normal birth of a Jewish child. It is perfectly clear that if the Apostle had believed in the Virgin Birth of a child, he would have written, "God sent his son, born of a virgin, instead of "born of a woman." On the other hand, he appears to have believed in the Davidic descent of Jesus, and hence in his human generation. Finally, the prologue of Romans states that Jesus Christ, our Lord, "born of the seed of David *according to the flesh* . . . has been proved to be the Son of God, in power, *according to the spirit of holiness*, by his resurrection from the dead." This simple sentence takes us back, apparently, at least, to the Christological point of view already found in Acts, in which the Messianic exaltation of Jesus still dates from the Resurrection.

Moreover, the Gospel narrative in the Synoptics themselves knows nothing of the Virgin Birth. That is to say that, omitting the two supplementary sources of Matthew and Luke, and confining ourselves to the account whose limits and general development are dictated by Mark, we shall find that not one of the incidents contained in it, in any of our three texts, alludes, even indirectly, to this outstanding miracle. If Jesus can say, in speaking of Mary, "Who is my mother?"; and if his mother and his own brothers attempt to dissuade him from his mission, it is because neither he, nor she, nor they, know anything of his conception by the Holy Ghost. Otherwise the narrative would involve us in the greatest improbabilities and embarrassments. It is , moreover, worthy of note that the text of Luke, on careful examination, reveals two editorial strata. In one (verses 26–33 and 36) there is no question of the Virgin Birth. The angel announces to Mary the birth of a son who will be the Messiah, the son of David, and he gives her as a "sign" the fact that Elizabeth, although old and barren, is yet in the sixth month of pregnancy. Verses 34–5 form a clear interpolation, which introduces the announcement of the Virgin Birth ("The Holy Ghost shall come upon thee"), and, following upon it, that of the divine paternity of Jesus ("And he shall be called the Son of God"), which is an entirely different thing from the Messianic "election" previously spoken of.

The other writings of the New Testament which happen to allude to the birth of Jesus, show that they believe him to be a descendant of David, that is to say, born according to the laws of nature.

Finally, the men who adhered to at least a portion of the original tradition long enough to be regarded as heretics in the second century, namely, the Ebionites, rejected the doctrine of the Virgin Birth. The evidence of both Justin and Epiphanius is explicit on this point.

The documents and the facts thus confirm the conclusion already dictated by the logic of the development of primitive Christology, namely, that the doctrine of the Virgin Birth represents a secondary development of the faith in Christ Jesus. The Pauline doctrine of preexistence springs from the same purpose and desire, but it takes a different form. Logically, the two conceptions are mutually exclusive and cannot be held simultaneously.

It has been asked how the idea of this particular development could have arisen. To the men of the period which produced it, certainly no violation of the laws of nature would be incredible a priori, for miracles were the familiar stock-in-trade of all magic. The production of a child by a virgin was no more improbable than the rising of a corpse from its tomb. Nevertheless, it is reasonable to suppose that, for the Virgin Birth to have had any hope of being accepted as proof in any community, the way must have been to some extent prepared for it by the influence of more or less similar beliefs.

In our opinion, Palestine could not have offered this necessary favorable environment. It is, indeed, easy to show that the old Semitic religions were familiar with the myth of the Mother Goddess, including the representation of her as the Virgin Goddess, and even with that of the virgin birth of the king, the son of God and the Savior of his people. But, apart from the fact that the virginity of Ishtar is not to be taken literally, and that, likewise, the ostensible virginity of the human mother of the king probably merely means that her son was mysteriously begotten by a god, without her human husband having any part in the affair, no trace of any of these ideas seems to have been left in Israel at the beginning of our era. The Jews certainly believed that the birth of a child destined for the work of God, might be marked by wonderful signs, for instance that this child might be conceived, against all expectation, by a barren woman; but they do not appear to have thought that the woman could still remain a virgin in the act of conception. In particular, there is no indication of their ever having held the belief that the Messiah would be born of a virgin. It has sometimes been maintained that, if they had not all attained to this conception, some of them, at least, came very close to it, if only in metaphor, for instance, in speaking of the Virgin, daughter of Sion and mother of the Messiah; it has also been asserted that such an idea "would tend to be realized as soon as the Messianic faith was concentrated upon a particular individual." This, however, is only theory based upon a dubious possibility. In reality, there is not one scrap of documentary evidence for any expectation in Israel that the birth of the Messiah would be signalized by such a miracle, and one text, at least, declares that there was no such expectation. Justin puts into the mouth of the Jew, Tryphon, the familiar statement: "For we all await the Christ, who will be a man amongst men," and makes him say, further, that, inasmuch as the Messiah will be descended from David, he will not be born of a virgin. It was God's promise to the ancient king that "he who is to come" would issue "from his seed." Are we to think that God was mocking him? It hardly seems likely that, for the purpose of confuting the Jews of Palestine, who denied the Messiahship of Jesus, the Christian apologists would have selected so un-Jewish a "sign." Only those believe it to be Jewish who are virtually bound to do so, because of their conviction that Christianity itself was essentially a purely Jewish phenomenon.

It is not in the Jewish world, nor even in the Oriental world proper, but in the Greco-Roman world that we find the most striking parallels to the story of the miraculous conception of Jesus. It is here that we find the legend of Perseus, born of Danäe, a virgin who was impregnated by a shower of gold. (A parallel which was made the most of by the Jews, and proved so embarrassing to the Christians of the second century that they were compelled to maintain that it was an invention of the Devil to confuse men and lure them from the truth.) Here, too, we find the story of Attis, whose mother, Nana, became pregnant as a result of eating a pomegranate. It was here especially that the birth of notable men—Pythagoras, Plato, Augustus himself—tended to be explained by some kind of parthenogenesis, or by the mysterious intervention of a god. It is quite conceivable that, in a community in which so many stories of this kind were current, the Christians, desirous of adducing conclusive vindication of their faith in the divinity of Jesus, naturally turned to the sign by which men bearing the divine stamp were commonly identified. There was no question, of course, of a conscious imitation of any particular story, but simply of the influence of a certain atmosphere of belief. We shall often meet with this phenomenon.

It has been held by some that the whole story of the Virgin Birth of Jesus arose from the interpretation of a supposedly prophetic passage of the Scriptures, namely, Isaiah 7:14, *according to the Greek text of the Septuagint*. This would, in any case, make the conception a Greek development. This is the occasion of the passage: Ahaz, king of Judah, fears a new attack by the allied kings of Syria and Israel, who have just failed to take Jerusalem. The prophet reassures him, and says:

> Therefore the Lord himself shall give a sign. Behold the Virgin shall conceive and give birth to a son, and thou shalt call him Emmanuel. Butter and honey shall he eat, that he may know how to refuse the evil and choose the good. But before this child shall know how to recognize good and evil, to refuse the evil and choose the good, the land whose two kings thou abhorrest shall be forsaken.

The prophet adds that the king of Assyria will be the instrument employed by

Yahweh to crush the power of Damascus and Samaria.

Considered in its context and specific purpose, the passage has no resemblance to a Messianic prophecy. The prediction has a much more immediate bearing, and it is precisely for the purpose of indicating its speedy fulfillment that the author makes his comparison. It will require only the time necessary for a child to be conceived, born, and brought to the beginning of understanding, before Yahweh will crush the enemies of Judah. It is not the birth of the child which is emphasized by the prophet, but the happy issue for which the king is waiting, and of which he may now, relying upon the comparison given him, confidently estimate the approaching date. The child in question is probably the same one referred to again by Isaiah in 8:3: "Then I went in unto the prophetess, and she conceived and bare a son."

However this may be, the general sense of the passage is unambiguous. Only by isolating from its context the announcement of the birth of the child who is to be called *Emmanuel (God with us)*, can it be given a Messianic meaning. This, to be sure, is exactly what Matthew 1:23 does, but the point is whether the Jews themselves did so at that time. There is no evidence for it in any rabbinical writing, and every probability points to the conclusion that it was the Christians who, in their search for all the prophetic utterances regarding the Messiah, discovered and gave that interpretation of this passage.

Further, the discovery could have been made only in the Greek Bible, because the Hebrew text does not contain the word *virgin (bethulah)*, but the word *young woman (haalmah)*, which ought to have been rendered into Greek by *neanis* instead of *parthenos*. Orthodox theologians have made every effort to prove that *haalmah* might mean virgin, but without success. The prophet had no thought of predicting a miracle, and the Jews, as soon as they began to attack the Christians, did not miss the opportunity of pointing out that the term to which their opponents appealed was nothing but a blunder. Possibly the first translator into Greek was responsible for it, but it is not very probable. We simply do not know when, and by whom, it was introduced into the text of the Septuagint.

Even if the Christians found it already there—which is questionable—it has still to be proved that, as has been contended, it was that which suggested to them the Virgin Birth of Christ. The main argument of Harnack is that the Christians, convinced that Christ was born of the Spirit of God, as the accounts of the Baptism must testify, must eagerly have seized upon the word *parthenos* as a means of *effectuating* this divine relationship. We cannot agree, for the reason that a mere reading of Isaiah 7:14, even in the Greek, would not give rise to the belief that the "virgin" would remain such throughout conception, and birth. The passage says nothing of that. The translator or copyist who rendered *haalmah* by the Greek *parthenos* simply meant: "a young woman will marry, conceive, and bear a child," not "a virgin will conceive and bear a child." To suggest this interpretation, the word would have to be read with such an idea in mind, in fact, with the definite belief that Mary had conceived Jesus and yet remained a virgin. Isaiah may have been regarded as conclusive prophetic witness to the miraculous sign, but it was certainly not he who suggested it.

It is, however, perhaps possible to see where it comes from. It will be observed that in Paul, John, and Mark, none of whom believes in the Virgin Birth, Jesus is characterized as the Son of God. This description of him is, accordingly, prior to the establishment of the belief in the miracle related by Matthew and Luke, and does not arise out of it. As soon as they were convinced that, not only had Jesus been raised up by God, as a man full of the Holy Spirit, to accomplish his plans, but that his birth into this life for God had been divinely predestined, and glorified by the Holy Ghost, they must have attempted to signalize and to express this special relationship between Jesus and God. They said that he was his "son," because that was the only term in human language by which they could intelligibly, if not completely and adequately, express this relation. Since the idea of the direct generation of a man by God could only appear to the Jewish mind as a monstrous absurdity, the expression was, in reality, to the Palestinians, only a manner of speaking, only a metaphor.

A critical examination of the passages in the Synoptics in which it appears, shows that Jesus never applied it to himself and that, moreover, it had not hitherto, in Israel, any Messianic significance. That is to say, the Jews did not beforehand bestow this title of Son of God upon the expected Messiah. The Messiah must have been for them not the *Son*, but the *Servant*, of God (*Ebed Yahweh*), for such was the designation of the "men of Yahweh." But on Greek soil the Christological belief found an environment very different from that of Palestine. There, the idea of the procreation of a human being by a god was current, and the relation of real sonship between Christ and God the Father could shock no one (save Jews of rigid orthodoxy, and they could not have been very numerous). On the contrary, the term *Son of God* was more likely to arouse sympathy in that quarter than the too peculiarly Jewish, too nationalistic, name of *Messiah*. Hence it was, in all probability, in the first Christian communities among the Gentiles, that the expression arose. Possibly it did so, at first, as a simple translation of the Palestinian *Ebed-Yahweh*, for the Greek word *pais* means both *servant* and *child*, and it would be an easy transition from *child* to *son*. But it soon took on the coloring of an original Christological idea, the idea which met the needs of the environment which called it forth, the idea expressed in the Epistles of Paul. It found its Pauline and Johannine justification in the doctrine of divine preexistence and of the incarnation of the Lord. The legend of the Virgin Birth is another of its justifications, sprung from a quite different intellectual environment, but analogous to the one just cited, and finding its scriptural confirmation, when the need arose to defend it in controversy, in Isaiah 7:14. Matthew and Luke represent two concrete embodiments, different in form, but similar in spirit and meaning, of the belief: "He is the Son of God. He is born of the Holy Spirit."

Their solution, which probably dates originally from about A.D. 80, prevailed and endured because there was nothing metaphysical about it, and it was in the direct line of the stages of development which had already taken place in the progress of Christology. Above all, it appealed to the popular faith. In a sense, its success is demonstrated even more by its elaboration in the Apocryphal Gospels, which found in it what they sought, than by its final incorporation in the orthodox tradition.

THE DEVELOPMENT OF THE LEGEND OF THE VIRGIN BIRTH

Our two Synoptic accounts do not, of course, exhaust the subject of the Virgin Birth. Faith and theology alike subsequently demanded more explicit statements, which were arrived at, occasionally, only at the cost of extremely embarrassing discussions.

It was asked, for instance, whether the miraculous conception had been precisely simultaneous with the Annunciation, and since the text of Luke gave not the smallest hint in either direction, the way was open for endless discussion. The very uniqueness of the Virgin Birth led to the question in what form the Holy Spirit had entered the body of Mary, in what precise manner the generation of Jesus had been accomplished. On this point, again, the silence of the writings left a clear field for hypothesis, and placed no limit upon even the most fantastic speculations. Tertullian (*Apol.*, 21) speaks of a ray of light descending into Mary, and there becoming flesh. This suggests an adaptation of the Egyptian belief according to which the cow-mother of Apis was impregnated by a ray of light falling from Heaven (Herodotus), or a moonbeam (Plutarch). In any case, it is an interesting parallel. In the fifteenth century it was even maintained that Jesus entered the womb of his mother fully formed, but this met with the opposition of the theologians.

Popular belief made its own contribution to the subject according to its lights, and its customary tendencies. Among other fantastic ideas, there evolved that of conception by the ear. This "explanation" is not met with until the fourth century, when it is found in Saint Ephraem, Saint Augustine, and Gaudentius, but its ingenuous simplicity places its date of origin much earlier. It must have been in circulation among the people for a long time before being taken into consideration by the learned. It has been suggested that this device, designed to make the conception of Jesus completely superhuman, and to place beyond dispute the virginity of his mother, may also have been of Egyptian origin, since Plutarch (*De Iside*) tells us that the idea was prevalent among the people of Egypt that cats were conceived by the ear and were born from the mouth.

The doctrine of the Virgin Birth did not fail to expose the Christian to annoying jests and calumnies. In an Apocryphal writing entitled *History of the Nativity of Mary and the Childhood of our Lord*, Joseph, returning from a journey, replies to the virgins who are attempting to cheer him with the news of the Annunciation:

> Why do you seek to deceive me and make me believe that it was the angel of the Lord who got her with child? Perhaps someone pretended to be the angel of the Lord in order to seduce her.

The foster-father, in this case, soon abandons his skepticism and recognizes the truth, but many unbelievers received the announcement of the decisive miracle in the same way.

Almost in modern times, the daring German rationalist Paulus (died 1928) again attributed the birth of Jesus to a ruse of the ambitious *Priesterfrau*, Elizabeth, who was supposed to have sent an unknown man to play the part of the angel Gabriel and deceive the simple Mary. In antiquity, Jews and pagans vied with each other in stories attacking the honor of Mary, who was represented by them as an adulteress, or even a professional prostitute. The Samaritans themselves took part in this offensive chorus. In one of their books, the *Samaritan Chronicle*, there occurs the following passage:

> In the time of Jehonathan there was put to death Jesus, the son of Myriam, son of Joseph the carpenter, *ben Hanapheth*, at Jerusalem, in the reign of Tiberius, by Pilate the governor.

The expression *ben Hanapheth*, is interpreted by Clermont-Ganneau, on the strength of an Arabic translation, as meaning "the son of the courtesan."

When the accusation became specific, and professed to name the real father of Jesus—a Roman soldier called *Panther*, or *Pandera*—it was not easy for the Christians to adduce material proof of its falsity. The main argument of Origen is that one who came to render such services to the world could not have been born in shame. So shameless an adulteress could have produced only a madman, a monster of vice and intemperance, whereas Jesus was a pattern of all the virtues. It is hardly a convincing proof. The story of Pandera, moreover, was not the only one, nor the worst, of the anti-Christian calumnies which claimed to give the details of the charge that, if Jesus was not the son of Joseph, his mother was an adulteress. An Alexandrian storyteller makes him the issue of an incestuous relationship between Mary and her own brother.

These were clumsy fabrications, no doubt inspired by malevolence and the desire to wound, but they were the inevitable price of the controversial weapon which the Christian faith derived from the legend of the Virgin Birth, the bastard product of Jewish mentality and pagan mythology.

The elaborations and proofs, of varying ingenuity, which the necessities of polemic induced the Christians to add to the assertions of the Synoptics, did not succeed in strengthening them. In spite of praiseworthy and persevering efforts, perpetually renewed, apologetic today can no longer succeed even in disguising their inconsistency.

In the last analysis, history must discard everything contained in the orthodox tradition concerning the circumstances of the birth of Jesus, and we have no choice but to conclude that we have no information on the subject. Doubtless those circumstances were quite ordinary, so much so that they attracted no attention, which would explain why, according to the oldest of the Gospel narratives (Mark 3:31-5, quoted above), the mother of Christ herself, at the very time when the memory of the decisive miracle—if such a miracle had really occurred to, and by means of, her, might have been expected to dominate her own human affection and desire—gave no sign of being in any way conscious of her son's divine destiny.

THE FIRST-BORN OF MARY

The stories of the birth of Jesus in Matthew and Luke imply that he was the first-born of his mother, since otherwise there could be no question of a virgin birth. But it is hardly necessary to observe that the fact that this assertion is necessitated by these two accounts, and vouched for only by them, means that we have no guarantee of it whatever. Neither Mark nor Paul is interested in this point, and it must, consequently, have been a matter of indifference to the original tradition. Possibly Jesus may have been the first of the children of Joseph and Mary, but we do not know.

We say "the children of Joseph and Mary," because our Synoptics have no hesitation in giving Jesus brothers and sisters. They refer to them in the most natural way in the world. We read in Mark 3:31:

> And there came his mother and his brethren, and standing without, they sent unto him, to call him, and the multitude was sitting about him, and they said unto him: Behold thy mother and thy brethren without, ask for thee.

Again, in Mark 6:2-3, the people of Nazareth are represented as saying:

> Whence hath he these things, and what wisdom is this which is given unto him? And these miracles which his hands perform? Is this not the carpenter, the son of Mary, the brother of James, and Joses, and Juda, and Simon? And are not his sisters also with us?

We need not stop to prove that the Evangelist certainly means "brothers" and "sisters," in the usual sense of the words. There is absolutely nothing to suggest that they are to be understood in any other, and such a thing would never have been thought of, if the development of the cult of Mary had not subsequently made a different interpretation necessary. Moreover, references to these "brothers" of Jesus are fairly frequent in the New Testament, and nowhere is there any ambiguity about them. It is unquestionably blood brothers which they appear to signify. Clearly, if there had been any risk of the words "brothers" and "sisters" misleading the reader so seriously, the editors of all the writings referred to would have taken some precaution against this dangerous misinterpretation.

The fact is, that the first Christians, even after the belief in the Virgin Birth was firmly established, were content with the assertion that Jesus was the first-born. Since, at that period, they were not interested in Mary on her own account, it was a matter of indifference to them that, her divine work accomplished, she should have become the wife of Joseph in a perfectly natural sense. It is to be observed, further, that the very insistence upon the term "first-born," for instance, in Luke 2:7 ("And she brought forth her first-born son"), immediately suggests the birth of younger children. Finally, we have plenty of evidence of the existence of such a belief in the Christianity of the first four centuries.

We may be inclined to wonder why neither the texts themselves nor this commonsense tradition managed to prevail. The answer is simply that there very shortly appeared Christians who could not reconcile themselves to the idea that the mother of the Lord, once her mission was accomplished, had reverted to the level of an ordinary woman. For the doctrine of the virginity of the *Christotokos*, that is to say, *the mother of the Christ*, was gradually substituted the doctrine of the perpetual virginity of Mary, until, finally, they arrived at that of Joseph himself, which appeared as early as Saint Jerome. It was the asceticism of the fourth and fifth centuries which finally established the beliefs, henceforth to become *articles of faith*, concerning the perfect and perpetual virginity of Mary. But long before this, the Christian feeling already referred to was seeking to get rid of the brothers and sisters of Jesus. As early as the second century, the *Protevangelium of James*, and according to Origen, the *Gospel of Peter*, maintained that they were the children of Joseph alone, born of his first marriage, and the husband of Mary came to be pictured as a very old man, at the time of the Nativity. Clement of Alexandria and Origen were completely confident that Christ and his mother, the former for men, and the latter for women, had set the example of perfect continence.

It remained only for the writings of the New Testament to support this conviction, and their texts were tortured in various ways until they were finally made to profess the contrary of what they believed. We shall not here embark upon an exposition of the discussions, in which the most arbitrary theories were supported by the most unverifiable assertions. They resulted very early in the three theories which it will be sufficient to recall: (1) the *Helvidian*, maintained by Helvidius in the time of Saint Jerome, which held that the "brothers" and "sisters" were children of Joseph and Mary born *after* Jesus; (2) the *Epiphanian*, sponsored by Saint Epiphanius, which declared that the brothers and sisters were the issue of a previous marriage of Joseph; (3) the *Hieronymian*, the theory of Saint Jerome, in which the brothers and sisters became cousins of Jesus, the sons and daughters of a brother of Joseph named *Clopas*, and a sister of the Virgin who also was called *Mary*. It was, of course, this last theory which the extension to Joseph of the perfect virginity of Mary finally made the choice of the faithful. It is neither better founded nor even more probable, and impartial criticism can be seen in it only a thin subterfuge, by means of which a pious elaboration, totally without historical foundation, sought to evade the limitations of the texts.

The radical critics, who profess to reduce to a myth the very existence of Jesus, have lately given the orthodox doctrine indirect and unexpected, and, on the whole, undesirable, support. They have maintained that the "brothers" and "sisters" of Jesus were no other than groups of his followers, united to each other by the bonds of the mystical fraternity. It is well known, certainly, that the earliest Christians spoke of themselves as "brethren." And when we read in Matthew 28:10, "Go and tell my brethren to go into Galilee," or in John 20:17, "Go to my brethren and tell them that I have ascended unto my Father," we are not tempted to give the word a family sense. The redactors have, in these cases, put into the mouth of Jesus the expression which they were in the habit of using among themselves. It does not follow, however, that the meaning it assumes in these two passages is necessarily to be extended to all the others, especially those in which the brothers of Jesus are called by their proper names (Mark 6:3). Naturally, since the adherents of the mythological view do not concede that Jesus actually existed, they cannot admit that he had brothers and sisters. We do not think there is much help for the orthodox position in such feats of imagination, and certainly there is none for history.

The probable conclusions which are justified by the documentary evidence, concerning the questions we have been considering, may be summed up as follows: Jesus was born somewhere in Galilee in the time of Emperor Augustus, of a humble family, which included half a dozen or more children besides himself.

Morton Scott Enslin

John the Baptist and His Followers

MORTON SCOTT ENSLIN, born in 1897 in Somerville, Massachusetts, was educated at
Harvard College (A.B. 1919) and the Harvard Divinity School (Th.D., 1924). He has
received honorary degrees from Colby College and Hebrew Union College in recognition of his scholarly contributions in the field of Christian origins. Enslin was professor
of New Testament at Crozer Theological Seminary from 1924 to 1954 and Craig
Professor of Biblical Literature at St. Lawrence University from 1955 to 1965. He is
the author of a number of distinguished books, including *The Ethics of Paul* (1930),
Christian Beginnings (1938), *The Prophet from Nazareth* (1961), and *From Jesus to
Christianity* (1964).

All four of our Gospels begin with reference to the work of John the Baptist, who
is depicted as the forerunner of Jesus, his greater successor. Of his early life we
know little or nothing. According to Luke he was born of priestly stock, and, as
was the case of many of the Old Testament worthies, in the extreme old age of
his parents. In this same account he is represented as a relation of Jesus since his
mother and Mary were related. That the story rests upon any historical foundation is most improbable. Apparently it is a consequence of the early rewriting
of the story of John to bring him into conscious subordination to Jesus. In the
Synoptic Gospels John appears spectacularly in the wilderness of Judea and in
dramatic fashion sounds a note of doom worthy of Jeremiah or Amos: "Repent
of your sins; be baptized for the remission of them. If you don't, it will be the
worse for you; a catastrophe is coming. Even now the axe is laid at the root of

the tree. Those not bearing good fruit will be hewn down." Here is an ascetic figure, living apart from men, awing those who flocked to hear him and convicting them of guilt. In Mark, the oldest of the three accounts, Jesus is represented as being one of the group which listens, and as being baptized. There is no hint of any recognition of him by John, or that it is he who is to be the "greater one" John is so eloquently proclaiming. In Matthew, however, a new and distinctly Christian note is introduced. When Jesus comes to be baptized, John at once recognizes him, and demurs at Jesus' request. "Nay," says he in substance, "it would be far more fitting for you to baptize me." "You are quite right," says Jesus, "but suffer it to be done." In the light of this obvious recognition by Jesus of his dignity the heavenly voice can no longer say—as Mark recorded it—"Thou art my beloved Son, in whom I am well pleased." Rather it proclaims to those who need the information, "This is my beloved Son." In Luke's account this process of subordinating John to Jesus is carried a step farther. Even before their births they had met. When Mary, in whom was the divinely begotten Lord, came into the presence of the pregnant Elisabeth, the latter's babe leaped in her womb, prompting words from Elisabeth which made Mary's *Magnificat* possible. In the fourth Gospel the climax is reached. John is of a truth only the voice which proclaims Jesus. The author is familiar with the story of the baptism, but recasts it. How unfitting that the divine Word should have been baptized! Rather the Baptist sees him approaching and heralds him: "Behold the Lamb of God, that taketh away the sin of the world! This is he of whom I said, After me cometh a man who is become before me: for he was before me." The dove is present, but not for Jesus. Well does the Lord, the incarnate Word of God, know his own identity. Rather the appearance is for John, the herald. "And John bare witness saying, I have beheld the Spirit descending as a dove out of heaven; and it abode upon him. And I knew him not: but he that sent me to baptize in water, he said unto me, Upon whomsoever thou shalt see the Spirit descending, and abiding upon him, the same is he that baptizeth in the Holy Spirit. And I have seen, and have borne witness that this is the Son of God."

A careful study of these four accounts leaves but little room for doubt that John the Baptist was thus transformed by Christianity from an independent preacher into the forerunner of Jesus. Nor is it improbable that his message has been similarly edited. It is to be observed that Matthew (altering the phraseology of his source, Mark) makes him utter precisely the same clarion call as did Jesus: "Repent ye; for the kingdom of heaven is at hand" (Matt. 3:2; 4:17). The special teaching of John which Luke alone records (Luke 3:10-14) is surprisingly like that later found in the mouth of Jesus (see especially, "He that hath two coats, let him impart to him that hath none; and he that hath food, let him do likewise"). The question arises whether, after all, the picture of John heralding the advent of the greater one who will baptize the nations in fire is not actually that of Jesus heralding the advent of the Son of Man, the final judge, who was expected by many Jews to perform this function.

This explanation would appear to me supported by the one passage in Josephus in which John is mentioned.

Now, some of the Jews thought that the destruction of Herod's [i.e., Antipas'] army came from God, and that very justly, as a punishment of what he did against John, who was called the Baptist; for Herod slew him, who was a good man, and commanded the Jews to exercise virtue, both as to righteousness toward one another, and piety toward God, and so to come to baptism; for that the washing [with water] would be acceptable to him, if they made use of it, not in order to the putting away of some sins, but for the purification of the body; supposing still that the soul was thoroughly purified beforehand by righteousness. Now, when many others came in crowds about him, for they were greatly moved by hearing his words, Herod, who feared lest the great influence John had over the people might put it into his power and inclination to raise a rebellion (for they seemed ready to do anything he should advise), thought it best, by putting him to death, to prevent any mischief he might cause, and not bring himself into difficulties by sparing a man who might make him repent of it when it should be too late. Accordingly he was sent a prisoner, out of Herod's suspicious temper, to Macherus, the castle I before mentioned, and was there put to death. (Antt. 18, 5, 2).

In this brief and intelligible account two points are striking: (1) the reason given for John's execution; (2) the entire absence of any mention of what in the Gospels is a highly significant note, the advent of his greater successor. There is no need of an elaborate chain of reasoning as to why Josephus, although he mentioned John, was reluctant to mention Jesus or a mysterious "greater one" whom Christians were now confident was Jesus. The simplest and most likely explanation is that this was not an actual part of John's message. Josephus is not exercising editorial privileges; he is simply recording facts.

On the basis, then, of this critical shifting of the Gospel account and of the testimony of Josephus there would seem to be little support for the modern conjecture that Jesus was started on his career through contact with the Baptist, and that he repeated the latter's message even after John's tragic death had sundered the bond of teacher and pupil. It would, accordingly, appear more probable that the paths of Jesus and John did not cross at all and that the Gospel accounts preserve little or nothing of the actual history of this enigmatic man. As the years rolled by, John, although originally quite distinct from Jesus, was gradually brought into the Christian picture, if not into the Christian fold.

Nor is the reason for this transformation of the powerful wilderness prophet into the self-abasing voice far to seek. That John the Baptist had been in the early days a distinct hindrance to the rise of Christianity and that traces of this are still to be found in the early Christian records has seemed to many New Testament critics probable. In fact, the fourth Gospel shows a clear animus against the disciples of the Baptist, and has for one of its purposes the complete and voluntary subjugation of John to Jesus, to be able to say to his followers: "Since your leader clearly recognized that our leader was the true Lamb of God, and gladly reckoned himself as but a voice to proclaim him, so you should cease your independent existence, and with us recognize and follow our common Lord." The occasional references to the disciples of John (Mark 2:18; Luke 11:1; John

3:23; 4:1) suggest that his movement had by no means come to an end at the appearance of Jesus; nor is there any sign of a defection from his camp to that of his "greater successor." It is by no means improbable that the twelve individuals, whom Paul is said to have met in Ephesus (Acts 19:1-7), who knew only the baptism of John and had never even heard of the Holy Spirit and who were accordingly rebaptized to remedy this lack, belonged to this group still in existence. The great influence that John exerted—attested alike by Josephus and the Gospels—suggests not only that the work of his preacher was no mere flash-in-the-pan, but that it might very well have tended to divert attention from the disciples of the other martyred leader. Furthermore, the famous testimony to John which Matthew and Luke attribute to Jesus—"Among them that are born of women there hath not arisen a greater than John the Baptist: *yet he that is but little in the kingdom of heaven is greater than he*—and which has never been satisfactorily explained on the basis of the traditional relationship between the two would seem to reveal a rivalry or at least a cleavage between the two groups.

Accordingly, it appears not unlikely that the incorporation of John into the Christian picture was a deliberate and studied attempt by early Christians to vanquish an embarrassing rival. The religions of antiquity provide numerous examples of a new god gradually supplanting an old and eventually being regarded as his son. The most effective way of getting rid of a rival is to align him with one's own cause. Accordingly, it would not be difficult to explain the rise of these stories, even though the tangents of Jesus and John never crossed. The story of the imprisoned Baptist sending his disciples to ask Jesus if he were the Christ would not appear to indicate a cooling of John's ardor shown in such passages as Matthew 3:14-15 and John 1:15-42 but rather to reflect an earlier, less advanced, stage in their rapprochement.

Once John was in the Christian picture it is not difficult to see how the legend of Herodias' wrath might have arisen as an explanation of his untimely end. As has already been pointed out, Josephus gives a quite different and more plausible explanation. That a Herod should have been very much disturbed by an uncouth wilderness preacher's displeasure at his nuptials is perhaps less likely than that he should have trembled with dread at the thought of an increasingly popular movement, the burden of which was the collapse of established society. Rulers are not wont to take kindly such proclamations, even though the agent of the collapse be God himself. Antipas was probably keen sighted enough to realize John's aim was not political; nonetheless, he was canny enough to realize that such a message might well serve as the spark in the powder-chest of unrest toward Rome and all her hirelings. Naturally, such an explanation of John's demise would not prove acceptable to Christians, especially to those concerned with establishing the innocency of their movement in the eyes of Rome. How much more probable that this second Elijah, staunch advocate of pure morals that he was, had perished at the hands of this more formidable modern Jezebel!

Discussion of the significance of the baptism practiced not alone by John, but by other sects in Palestine, and of their possible influence upon the externally similar rite which soon made its appearance in the Christian group, may profitably be reserved for later. The point of present importance is that the stories about him, regardless of their value for an understanding of later Christianity, would seem to throw far less light than is usually assumed upon the one who is popularly supposed to have designated and to have quickened his greater successor.

F. C. Conybeare

The True Jesus

FREDERICK C. CONYBEARE (1856–1924) was born in Surrey, England, and educated at
the Tonbridge School and University College, Oxford, where he took first-class honors
in both classical studies (1877) and in philosophy (1879). He was elected a fellow of
his college in 1880 and praelector in philosophy, positions he resigned in 1887 to
devote himself entirely to research in history, archeology, and textual criticism of the
New Testament. In the monastery of Etchmiazdin, Conybeare discovered manuscripts
attributing the last twelve verses of Mark's Gospel to the presbyter Aristion, and in the
library of the Holy Synod in Moscow his researches uncovered the sole surviving copy
of the *Key of Truth*, the theological manual of the ancient Armenian Paulician sect.
Always outspoken and controversial, Conybeare joined the Rationalist Press Association in 1904, publishing with them his classic study, *Myth, Magic, Morals: A Study
in Christian Origins* (1905). Unlike the members of the Christ-Myth School, however,
Conybeare continued to defend the historical existence of Jesus (*The Historical Christ*,
1914), without however attributing to him the founding of a church.

We can write a life of Julius Caesar or of Cicero, because we have in the first
place letters, commentaries, and other authentic documents written by them and
their friends; in the second, lives written by Plutarch and others who had in their
hands monuments of them, now lost; and in the third, masses of contemporary
coins and inscriptions. Contrast with this wealth of sources the scanty material
which remains for a portrait of Jesus of Nazareth. So slender is it, indeed, that it
seems not absurd to some critics today to deny that he ever lived. The truth is
that the Church, by fencing round this corner of history, by refusing to apply

From *Myth, Magic and Morals* by F. C. Conybeare (London: Watts and Co., 1909), pp.
139-151. Published for Rationalist Press Association, and reprinted by permission of the
Rationalist Press Association.

within it the canons by which in other fields truth is discerned from falsehood, by beatifying credulous ignorance and anathematizing scholarship and common sense, has surrounded the whole with such a nimbus of improbability that any clever schoolboy of the twentieth century is inclined to dismiss the entire New Testament as a forgery and concoction of the priest. A child of my own, at the age of twelve, was set to do as his Sunday task a map of the missionary travels of Paul, and, having completed it, brought it to me for my approval before he showed it up to his master. When I had approved it, he said to me, in his most confidential tone: "Father, did St. Paul ever really exist?" It was evident what was in his mind: Jesus was not a historical personage like Pericles or Julius Caesar; for who save a mythical hero walks on the water, chides wind and storm into silence, and feeds thousands at once upon nothing at all? Jesus had in this child's mind—and very justly too, considering the general character of what is called religious instruction—taken his place alongside of Heracles and Dionysus. But Paul seemed to him to be more in touch with reality. Had he not been shipwrecked and imprisoned, and faced other perils of land and sea? Clearly he was the only quasi-historical personage left in the divinity lessons. If he can be eliminated, the schoolboy can relegate to mythology the whole subject matter of these lessons. Such is the nemesis of creeds and orthodoxy.

We cannot, then, aspire to write a life of Jesus. Even Ernest Renan failed, and from the hands of a Farrar we merely get under this rubric a farrago of falsehood, absurdity, and charlatanry. At the best, perhaps, we can only hope to see Jesus, as it were, through the mist, ever thickening, of the opinions which the second and third generations of his followers formed of him. Between ourselves and him intervenes—earliest of our sources in point of time—Paul, with his apocalyptic preconceptions of what a Messiah had to be, with his turbid, swirling flood of obscure fancies, his epileptic ecstasy and private revelations. Next after him in order of time we have the non-Marcan document, in which we have almost certainly echoes, perhaps more than echoes, of his teaching. Nearly contemporary with this must be the saner parts of Mark's Gospel, for the greater part of that Gospel is the work of someone who was by instinct and predilection a miracle-monger. Finally, we have the fourth Gospel, hardly less fabulous than the apocryphal rigmaroles of the second and third centuries.

Discounting all that is doubtful, what have we left? I think we may take it as true that some time about the beginning of our era there was born in Nazareth, of parents whose names were Joseph and Mary, a child who was duly circumcised and named Jesus. He was not their only child, for Mark introduces his fellow townsmen as saying: "Is not this the carpenter, the son of Mary, and brother of James and Joses and Judas and Simon? And are not his sisters here with us?"

How much younger he was than John the Baptist, under whose influence he fell on reaching manhood, we do not know. Luke's story that he was but six months younger is clearly impossible. It was a sore point with the first generation of Christians that the disciples of John did not merge themselves in the following of Jesus, but remained distinct, as is recorded in Acts. It was one way of controverting them to pretend that their master John, when he baptized Jesus by way of preparing him for membership in the impending messianic kingdom, also acclaimed him as the promised Messiah. This fiction is in Luke's narrative crowned by another—namely, by the story which brings together their two mothers before their births, in order that John, a fetus of six months, might leap in his mother's womb when she saluted Mary who had conceived the day before! A more reliable tradition, and anyhow one which cannot be reconciled with Luke's story, is that which survives in many early representations on stone or in ivory of Jesus' baptism. In these he stands knee-deep in the water, a beardless stripling, while John, a bearded man of greater height and age, pours water over his head, or, setting his hand thereon, actually ordains him.

It would seem, then, as if a certain interval of time must have separated John and Jesus in the plenitude of their activities; and chapter 50 of the non-Marcan document, though obscure yet favors such a view. For in this passage Jesus uses these words, or similar: "From the days of John the Baptist until now the kingdom of heaven is taken by force, and men of violence snatch at it." We infer that the sundry patriots, carried away by John's proclamation of the impending great event which was, among other things, to bring liberation from the Gentile yoke, had tried to hurry it on by active rebellion against the Roman government. The lesson of their faith was not lost on Jesus, who, like Philo, believed that moral regeneration, repentance, nonresistance, justice and mercy, and in general a faithful observance of the laws of Jehovah, could alone bring it about. However we explain these words, they anyhow militate against the later view, which foreshortened the past and made John and Jesus full contemporaries of one another. There are no limits in "Q" of time-transition and order of events in the life of Jesus. If he really uttered these words—and he probably did, since they are so repugnant to later tradition—he must have uttered them late in his career.

That Jesus was a successful exorcist we need not doubt, nor that he worked innumerable faith cures. Josephus describes how a famous rabbi named Eliezer drew a demon out of an afflicted man through his nostrils, and how in issuing forth it tipped over a basin of water set to receive it—all this in the presence of himself and of the Roman emperor. A generation later than Jesus, Apollonius of Tyana was casting out demons in Syria wherever he went. These demons talked just as they do in Mark's narrative, and the stories of Apollonius, which are probably from the pen of his Syro-Greek disciple, Damis, read like pages out of Mark or Matthew. From the first the exorcists had a recognized position in the Church; and in the less advanced parts of Christendom the priests are still called upon to drive out by their adjurations the demons of madness and disease. The same expulsions can be daily observed in India, China, Japan, Africa—in fact, all around the globe.

Everywhere, in primitive communities, certain individuals are reputed to possess a peculiar power over demons, and in West Africa a leading medicine man is occasionally murdered by some rival anxious to possess himself of this power for his own use and profit. Accordingly, Mark relates how, when Jesus had expelled a noisy evil spirit, the crowd exclaimed, "With authority [or power] he commands even the unclean spirits, and they obey him." Elsewhere Mark notes that the people found this great difference between Jesus on the one hand, and the scribes and Pharisees on the other—namely, that he taught as one having *authority* over the spirits. It is beyond a doubt that Jesus regarded fever, epilepsy, madness, deafness, blindness, rheumatism, and all the other weaknesses to which flesh is heir, as the direct work of evil spirits. The storm wind which churned the sea or inland lake into fury is equally an evil sprite in the Gospel story. In the Vedic poems it is the same; and, indeed, we have here a commonplace of all folklore.

Jesus also regarded himself as gifted with the special power to control evil spirits; the African medicine man is credited with the same by the cowering tribesmen. It is recorded that on one occasion a hysterical woman, who suffered from a flux of blood, touched the hem of Jesus' raiment and was healed, whereon Jesus felt that power had gone out of him. In the same way napkins or wrappers, taken from the body of Paul, were found to heal sufferers among his hearers, who applied them to themselves. The annals of superstition supply a thousand parallels to these stories. The application by Jesus of his spittle to the ears or eyes of the blind or deaf can be similarly paralleled. We know from the *Natural History* of the elder Pliny, a Latin author of the first century, that the spittle of the medicine man was a sovereign remedy all round the Mediterranean. The history of Tacitus (bk. 4, ch. 81) supplies a striking parallel to the stories told of Jesus.

In the months during which Vespasian was waiting at Alexandria for the periodical return of the summer gales and settled weather at sea, many wonders occurred, which seemed to point him out as the object of the favor of heaven and of the partiality of the gods. One of the common people of Alexandria, well known for his blindness, threw himself at the emperor's knees, and implored him, with groans, to heal his infirmity. This he did by the advice of the god Serapis, whom this nation, devoted as it is to superstitions, worships more than any other divinity. He begged Vespasian that he would deign to moisten his cheeks and eye-balls with his spittle. Another with a diseased hand, at the counsel of the same god, prayed that the limb might feel the print of a Caesar's foot. At first Vespasian ridiculed and repulsed them. They persisted; and he, though on the one hand he feared the scandal of a fruitless attempt, yet, on the other, was induced, by the entreaties of the men and by the language of his flatterers, to hope for success. at last he ordered that the opinion of physicians should be taken as to whether such blindness and infirmity were within the reach of human skill. They discussed the matter from different points of view. "In the one case," they said, "the faculty of sight was not wholly destroyed, and might return, if the obstacles were removed; in the other case the limb which had fallen into a diseased condition might be restored if a healing influence were applied; such, perhaps, might be the pleasure of the gods, and the emperor might be chosen to be the minister of the divine will; at any rate, all the glory of a successful remedy would be Caesar's, while the ridicule of failure would fall on the sufferers." And so Vespasian, supposing that all things were possible to his good fortune, and that nothing was any longer past belief, with a joyful countenance, amid the intense expectation of the multitude of bystanders, accomplished what was required. The hand was instantly restored to its use, and the light of day again shone upon the blind. Persons actually present attest both facts, even now, when nothing is to be gained by falsehood.

We see that the atmosphere of Alexandria, in the first century, in no way differed from that of Galilee; there Serapis had long filled in men's minds the place which Jesus presently filled in the minds of Christians. And Vespasian might have used to those whom he healed the words constantly addressed by Jesus to those whom he healed: "Thy faith hath made thee whole." The imperial cures which Tacitus here relates—on the testimony of men who witnessed them, who were still alive in his day, and who had nothing to gain by flattering Vespasian now that another dynasty occupied the throne—resemble the faith-healings common at Lourdes, and not unheard of in English Methodist circles. That cures effected by Jesus were often due to what, in scientific phrase, we today term autosuggestion is certainly from the naïve admission made in Mark's Gospel that, in his own country, where they knew him and his kinsfolk too well to acclaim him at once as a prophet, "he could do no mighty work, because of their unbelief." The most he could effect in the midst of these critical surroundings was to "lay his hands on a few sick folk and heal them" (Mark 6:6).

There is no reason to doubt that Jesus effected many cures of this kind beyond those which Mark records. When he had succeeded in effecting a few such cures, all would forget the failures; and his fame as a healer would gather volume like a snowball, and precede him wherever he went. We cannot doubt that Mark's description of his triumphal career, though gathered long after the event from the lips of the country folk among whom his fame lingered, is substantially correct. It is as follows (Mark 6:53-6): "And when they [Jesus and his disciples] had crossed over to the land, they came unto Gennesaret, and moored to the shore. And when they were come out of the boat, straightway the people recognized him, and ran round about the whole region, and began to carry about on their beds those that were sick, wherever they heard he was. And wheresoever he entered, into villages or into cities, or into the country, they laid the sick in the public places, and besought him that they might touch if it were but the border of his garment: and as many as touched him were made whole."

And, similarly, in 3:10 we read that "he had healed many, insomuch that as many as had plagues pressed upon him that they might touch him." Jesus would have been more than human if he had not come to believe that he really possessed in his organism some peculiar power capable of counteracting disease; and, accordingly, Mark relates, as we noted above, how he turned round, when a woman had touched his garments and been healed, and asked, "Who touched my garments?" because "he perceived in himself that the power proceeding from him had gone forth." This, of course, is a touch of exaggeration on the part of the storyteller, but it nevertheless exhibits to us the sort of belief which accompanied faith healing, and still accompanies it. The power of healing, which among the peasants of Galilee marked out a man as the Messiah, is comparable to the mysterious power which in our own generation is vested in the Mikado of Japan, who, in the belief of his humble subjects, can barely nod his head without shaking the entire land. The chieftains of primitive peoples are all endowed with similar magic powers, which render them so dangerous that their names, persons, head, hair, and even nail-parings, are taboo—that is, sacrosanct and dangerous. Sir James Frazer, in *The Golden Bough*, gives examples of chiefs and princes held to be so holy or taboo that a servitor walks behind them with a spittoon reserved specially for the royal spittle, for this even is endowed with such mysterious power as to be dangerous to any whom it may touch. The spittle of a Roman emperor or of a Jewish Messiah was equally pregnant with miraculous power. Mohammed also was "so highly respected by his companions that, whenever he made the ablution, in order to say his prayers, they ran and catched the water that he had used; and, whenever he spit, they immediately licked it up, and gathered up every hair that fell from him with great superstition."

This mysterious power, as it was chiefly revealed in the expulsion of evil spirits or demons, was itself interpreted to be a spirit, though a holy or clean one. Mark preserves to us the outlines of an early dispute, in which Jesus' own mother and brethren took part, as touching the quality of the spirit within Jesus which enabled him to cast out demons. The scribes from Jerusalem said, "He hath Beelzebub," and "By the prince of the devils he casteth out the devils." No prophet can allow the quality of the spirit which moves him to be called in question; and Jesus answers the accusation in a twofold manner. First he points out that Satan would not turn upon Satan, as his accusers assumed; and in the second place he declares that "all their sins shall be forgiven to men, and also all their blasphemies; but whoso shall blaspheme against the holy spirit hath never forgiveness, but is guilty of an eternal sin." Mohammed defended himself much in the same manner and with equal vigor against those who said of him, "He hath an unclean spirit."

We have seen that in Mark's Gospel there was no immediate recognition of Jesus by his disciples as the Messiah. Their recognition of him was slow and gradual and tardy, and even to the end they seem to have expected him, like a second David, merely to expel the unclean Roman from their holy soil by a sudden display of supernatural force. How soon the conviction formed itself in Jesus' own mind that he was the "man sent from God" we do not know. Both our documents, Mark and "Q," assume that he knew himself to be such from the first; but that is improbable. It is more likely that it was his success as a healer, his evident control of evil spirits, the plaudits of the crowd, and, above all, his own followers' recognition of his supernatural role, that forced this conviction upon him towards the close of his career. There must have been an inner development of his mind and aspirations, although our earliest documents have lost all memory of it.

All, even if Jesus at the end admitted the Messiahship thrust upon himself by his enthusiastic followers, it is not clear that he admitted it except in a potential sense. He was not the present Messiah, for the moral regeneration of his countrymen was only begun. Perhaps they were right in hailing him as a prophet, as one greater than John. But the Messiah, when he came, was to come from heaven as king and judge, baptizing with fire; whereas John only baptized unto repentance with water. Now, Pilate and the priests left to Jesus no room during this life to play so stupendous a part. To carry it out he was bound to come again in glory from heaven. Little is certain about Jesus; but there is a fair certainty that, late in his career, he imbued his followers with the conviction, which he also entertained himself, that he was destined to return after death and inaugurate a reign of God upon earth.

We have described the vision which floated before the eyes even of a cultivated Jew of Alexandria like Philo—the vision of a time when the repentance and moral regeneration of the Jews would soften the hearts of the oppressors, and move them to let their captives go free. When that time arrived a supernatural presence, visible only to the faithful, would lead the liberated Jews of all the earth back into the land of promise and plenty. Jesus seems to have convinced himself and his followers that, as he was already an agent and vehicle of the divine will, so he was destined to come again, a supernatural presence, amid the clouds of heaven. That his followers, both in Galilee and in Jerusalem, were penetrated with this conviction led to great results. It was the main psychological factor in the visions they had of him after his death.

In Acts 1:6 it is recorded that they expected him to come again at once, "and restore the kingdom to Israel." He did not come, and has not come yet; and, after nearly twenty centuries of waiting, Christian belief in the second coming is grown faint and tenuous. At the same time, the future kingdom has been spiritualized; and the millennial corn and vine, with their phenomenal output of bread and wine, no longer float before the imaginations of the pious, as they did before the minds of the early generations of believers. Filled with such dreams of the future, Jesus' immediate followers could not but have confirmatory visions of him who was to come again. Like Stephen, they saw him up in heaven, where he was resposing on a throne at the right hand of a God who has a left and right, only waiting until his followers on earth had got things ready for his second advent.

The hymns of that first age, as we know from Paul and from the Book of Revelation of John (a work of 92–93 A.D.), bore the refrain Maranatha, the Aramaic equivalent of "May the Lord come." It was this belief that the Christ was waiting up in heaven for the season to fulfil itself of his second advent in glory that generated the tales of his resurrection out of the tomb and ascension into heaven after forty days—the statutory and conventional period fixed among the Jews for all unlikely and legendary episodes.

Arthur Drews

The Teaching of Jesus

ARTHUR DREWS (1865-1935) was professor in the Hochschule at Karlsruhe, Germany, from 1896 until shortly before his death. A student of the Hegelian philosopher, Eduard von Hartmann, Drews championed the theory that Christianity was a form of Gnosticism and challenged the orthodox teaching that Jesus of Nazareth had been an historical person; an idea then gaining ground in Germany, Holland, and the United States, and as a result of the new methods of investigating the Gospels (*Formgeschichte*). Drews's enduring contribution to the discussion is *Die Christus-Mythe* (*The Christ-Myth*, 2 vols., 1909-1911).

What evidence do the words of Jesus afford of his historical reality? We have already pointed out that the contents of the Gospels point to two sources—a record of the actions of Jesus and a collection of his sayings, which we obtain from the parallels in Matthew and Luke as compared with Mark. But we also pointed out how uncertain our knowledge of this collection of sayings is—so uncertain that we may justly speak of this source as "a completely unknown x."

What makes this tradition of sayings so valuable to theologians is the circumstance that they believe it brings them much nearer to Jesus than the Gospel of Mark. It is true that they cannot deny that, even if they succeeded in entirely and confidently reconstructing this tradition, of which there is as yet no question, we would still have only a book with a certain literary form or composition, arranged on the lines of literary composition. "By means of the sayings-source we do not at once reach Jesus, but the community. To put it precisely: in suitable cases we learn from the source what seemed to the community the characteristic, distinctive, and indispensable thing in Jesus."

Now, in view of the entire constitution of the so-called primitive community, that is not a great achievement. It is even less when we reflect that we are not at all sure that the traditional "words of the Lord" are the words of a single historical individual—namely, the historical Jesus. Theologians assume this; but they are again merely begging the question—a vice which infects the whole of their historical method. "Words of the Lord"—we cannot repeat it too often—are in Scripture so frequently merely words which the Lord (namely, Yahweh) gives to his followers through the "spirit" that, even granting the existence of an historical Jesus, it would be impossible to discriminate between what is due to the "spirit" in the collection and what is due to Jesus.[1] We do not know whether the collection of sayings expressly contained only the words of Jesus, or also included sayings which were on other grounds thought worthy of being admitted. We cannot say whether words which were believed to have been spoken under the influence of the "spirit" were not afterwards incorporated into the Gospels and put in the mouth of Jesus simply because the best and most important sayings *must* have come, in the opinion of the followers, from the lips of him whom they venerated as "the Lord" in the specific sense of the word.

That a good deal that is tendentious, partisan, misunderstood, and of late origin has found its way among the "words of the Lord" in the Gospels, that different phases of religious thought have found expression in them and armed themselves with the authority of the "Lord of Lords,." is admitted by all critical students. Some idea can be formed of how much breaks down in this way if one takes the trouble to strike out of the Gospels the words of Jesus which are recognized as interpolations.

But have we any guarantee of the substantial truthfulness at least of the tradition? We are referred to the form of the tradition, the deep impression of the words of the teacher in the memory of his hearers, the accurate, almost verbal, retention of detail that distinguishes the rabbinical instruction.[2] We are told that the Talmud shows the tenacity and conscientiousness of such a tradition. Granting, however, that the circumstances of the tradition were really so favorable, how came the various sayings of Jesus to be handed down to us in so many different forms as we actually have them? How can we explain that so much was lost of the words of Jesus that was certainly important, while so much that is unimportant was preserved? Yet we cannot suppose that Jesus said and preached no more than we have in the Gospels as his words. "What was a precept of the school to the pupils of the rabbis," says Weiss, "became for the disciples of Jesus a question of beatitude. The words of the master were a matter of life and death; they were the foundation of the community, and the accurate determination of the words was their most important duty." It is remarkable, however, that the ostensibly earliest Christian writings lay so little stress on the words of Jesus that Clement, James, *The Teaching of the Apostles*, etc., quote the words of the Lord without expressly describing them as sayings of Jesus; that

that Paul himself seems to know nothing of them, since, as we saw, there is not a single clear case of his referring to sayings of Jesus, even when the similarity of idea ought to have reminded him of them, or the context should have actually compelled him to quote the authority of the master for his views.

The words of Jesus played hardly any part in the early days of Christianity. . . . According to Acts, the first Christian sermon was not a repetition of the teaching of Jesus, but a discourse about Jesus, as we learn in the instances of Peter, Stephen, Philip, and Apollo (Acts 2:14; 3:12; 7:2; 8:5 and 32; 18:24). If they really believed that these sayings belonged to an historical Jesus, why have they not been more carefully preserved? How was it possible for this collection of sayings to be lost? One would think that so valuable a thing as the word of their Lord and master would have been guarded by the community as a sacred treasure, copied innumerable times, and handed on from one generation to another. Instead of this, it seems that the mere memory of the existence of such a collection was entirely lost by Christians for centuries, and it was reserved for modern critical theologians to establish the former existence of such a source. As if providence had wished to reserve this material for their learned investigations.

THE CONTROVERSIES WITH THE PHARISEES.

An attempt has recently been made to provide a proof that the "sayings of the Lord" in the Gospels really come from the historical Jesus. These sayings and teachings, it is said, these conflicts with the Pharisees, these conversations with the disciples, parables, etc., are so "unique" and "inimitable," stand so far above all the rest of ancient literature, and have so profound a personal character, that they could only come from a personality, and, indeed, from the Jesus of the Gospels. The logical defect of this deduction is obvious. No one has ever questioned that the words of Jesus in the Gospels have a thoroughly personal and individual coloring, that they convey an impression of definite historical situations, and that they reflect the feelings and thoughts of a personal inner life. But whether this was the life of a single individual, or a number of individuals in different circumstances contributed to the "sayings of the Lord" in the Gospels—whether this single personality was the Jesus of the Gospels or some prominent rabbi—is the great point in question.

The many irreconcilable contradictions that we find in the sayings of Jesus rather suggest that several persons, not one only, are behind them. And if they really belonged to one single personality, they could be traced to Jesus only *insofar as he was known to us from other sources*; in that case only should we have a right to say that one but so "unique" a person as this Jesus could have uttered such "unique" sayings. But we know this Jesus and the "uniqueness" of his inner life only from the words ascribed to him in the Gospels. Thus the argument *always runs in a circle* when one attempts to prove the "uniqueness" of Jesus from the character of his words, and the "unique" character of his words from the "uniqueness" of the Jesus of the Gospels.

Are these sayings really of such a character that they must be due to so extraordinary a personality as Jesus?

Take his conflicts with the Pharisees. The Evangelists are eager to show the superiority of their Jesus to the Pharisees and scribes in certain distinctive circumstances, and to put it in the clearest possible light. Over and over again the Pharisees approach the Savior to put him to the test or ensnare him in the coils of their rabbinical dialectic, and over and over again they retire confounded and shamed by the clearness of his mind. Yet in very many cases the way in which Jesus confounds his learned opponents is such that we hardly know which is the more surprising, the utter unsoundness and meaninglessness of his replies, or the simplicity of the Pharisees in accepting them.

Thus, for instance, the disciples pluck ears of corn on the Sabbath, and when the Pharisees reproach Jesus for this he replies: "Have ye not read what David did, when he was hungry, and they that were with him? How he entered into the house of God, and did eat the shewbread, which was not lawful for him to eat, neither for them which were with him, but only for the priets? Or have ye not read in the law, how that on the Sabbath days the priests in the temple profane the Sabbath, and are blameless?" (Matt. 12:3). As if the action of the disciples could be in any way compared with the conduct of a hungry army, to which, moreover, the Jewish law even permitted the eating of unclean food! And as if the offering of sacrifice in the temple on the Sabbath were forbidden![3]

On another occasion the Sadducees put him the captious question, to which husband a woman would belong after death who had married seven brothers in succession, and Jesus reproaches them with not knowing the law, since in the next world people would neither marry nor be given in marriage, but be like the angels in heavens, and he adds: "As touching the resurrection of the dead, have ye not read that which was spoken unto you by God, saying, I am the God of Abraham, the God of Isaac, and the God of Jacob? God is not the God of the dead, but of the living. And when the multitude heard this," the Evangelist observes, "they were astonished at his doctrine" (Matt. 22:30-3). Why were they astonished? Can they really have supposed that the words of Jesus were a refutation of the Sadducean view that there was no resurrection of the dead? That God is the God of the living does not prove that life is not extinguished at death. And what the object is of bringing in the patriarchs it is impossible to say. When, moreover, Jesus accuses the Sadducees of ignorance of the law, he clearly forgets that precisely according to the law the woman never ceases to be the wife of her first dead husband, however many husbands she may subsequently wed. How, then, could he silence the Sadducees, or "stop their mouths," as Luther puts it, with such a remark?

Another time the Pharisees ask him, as he teaches in the temple, by what authority he does this; and Jesus replies with a question about the origin of John's baptism, whether it was from heaven or from men; and when they dare not reply—for certain very improbable reasons—he answers arrogantly, "Neither tell I you by what authority I do these things" (Matt. 21:23), and thus evades their question.

The greatest victory of Jesus over the Pharisees is supposed to have been when he asked them whose son the Messiah was, and they said, the Son of David. He then said to them: "How then doth David in spirit call him Lord, saying, The Lord said unto my Lord, Sit thou on my right hand, till I make thine enemies thy footstool [Ps. 110:1]? If David then call him Lord, how is he his son?" (Matt. 22:43-5). The Gospel says that this reply so confounded the Pharisees that they dared not answer him, and put no more questions to him from that day. As a matter of fact, the reply of Jesus contains so obvious a fallacy that at the most we could only understand the behavior of the Pharisees as a re-luctance to have anything further to do with a man who answered in such a way.

Generally speaking, the Pharisees in the Gospel descriptions are anything but plausible. These zealots of the law who ask Jesus for a proof of his Messianic mission (Matt. 12:38, 16:1), while the law expressly forbids them to attach any importance to the signs and wonders of a false prophet (Deut. 13), these heads of the community who allow themselves to be called by Jesus hypocrites, blind, serpents, and generation of vipers, calmly submit to these insults before the crowd, put their hands in their pockets, plot the destruction of Jesus, and meantime allow him to teach in the temple and the synagogue—these are cer-tainly not historical personalities, especially when we observe that none of them is personally described or named, whereas the Talmud scarcely ever omits to name the persons in its record of the innumerable discussions of the rabbis with their opponents. These Pharisees who are silenced by Jesus on every occasion and quietly allow themselves to be "struck on the mouth" or instructed by him come from the Book of Job, where we read in the twenty-ninth chapter: "The princes refrained talking, and laid their hand on their mouth. The nobles held their peace, and their tongue cleaved to the roof of their mouth. When the ear heard me, then it blessed me. . . . After my words they spake not again; and my speech dropped upon them. And they waited for me as for the rain, and they opened their mouth wide as for the latter rain." That is to say, they looked forward eagerly to the words of Job, which the Evangelist has perverted into the sense that the Pharisees sought to destroy Jesus, not to be inwardly strengthened by him. In any case, we have no reason to be "surprised" at the way in which Jesus escapes the toils of his enemies. His dialectic is by no means of a high order, as anyone will perceive who compares the conflicts of Jesus and the scribes and Pharisees with the way in which Socrates confounds his opponents in the Platonc dialogues. There is no question whatever of "uniqueness" in this respect in the case of Jesus.

SAYINGS OF JESUS ON THE WEAK AND LOWLY

Among the finest characteristics of Jesus we must place, it is said, his relation to the lowly, his love of children, his sympathy with the least conspicuous objects in nature. It is assuredly a touching and amiable feature in a man like Jesus to stoop so lovingly to the weakest of the weak, to look with tender eye on the flowers of the field and the birds of heaven, to contrast their indifference to the future with man's constant concern about his own maintenance (Matt. 6:26). But this feature is not "unique," as we learn from the Talmud where we read: "Hast thou ever seen a bird or a beast of the forest that must secure its food by work? God feeds them, and they need no effort to obtain their nourishment. Yet the beast has a mind only to serve man. He, however, knows his higher vocation—namely, to serve God; does it become him, then, to care only for his bodily wants?" (*Kidushin*, 4, *Halach* 14). "Hast thou ever seen a lion bearing a burden, or a stag gathering the summer's fruits, or a wolf buying oil? Yet all these creatures are sustained, though they know no care about their food. But I, who have been created to serve my creator, must be more concerned about my nourishment."

Further, one might hold that Isaiah's description of the Savior as especially sympathetic to the weak and needy would suffice of itself to "invent" the feeling of Jesus for children and embody it in the figure of his human personality. Children were, as the Talmud shows, greatly cherished among the Jews, and the love of them is deep-rooted in the Jewish character. "Out of the mouth of babes and sucklings," says the psalmist (9:2), "has thou ordained strength [praise]"; and Jesus repeats this to the high priests and their followers, when they are indignant at the cry with which the children greet him in the temple (Matt. 21:15). In Psalm 8 (4-5) it is said: "What is man that thou art mindful of him? and the son of man that thou visitest him? For thou hast made him a little lower than the angels, and has crowned him with glory and honor." "About the Messiah," says the Talmud, "will all gather who seek in the law, especially the little ones of the world; for by the boys who still frequent school will his strength be increased" (Sohar to Exodus, fol. 4, col. 18).

From these words we understand, even from the mythic-symbolical point of view, the saying: "Suffer little children, and forbid them not, to come unto me, for of such is the kingdom of heaven" (Matt. 19:14) or the scene where Jesus calls a child, sets him in the midst of the disciples, who have asked who is the greatest in the kingdom of heaven, and says: "Verily, I say unto you, Except ye be converted, and become as little children, ye shall not enter into the kingdom of heaven. Whosoever therefore shall humble himself as this little child, the same is greatest in the kingdom of heaven" (Matt. 18:2-4). We read in the Talmud: "A young man deserves praise when he becomes [in mind] like the children" (*Tanchuma*, fol. 36, col. 4), and "Whosoever humbles himself in this life for love of the law, the same will be reckoned among the greatest in the kingdom of heaven" (*Baha Mezia*, fol. 84, col. 2). It is not clear, moreover, that the meaning of the relevant passages in the Gospels is not symbolical, and the "children" for whom Jesus cares are not, as W. B. Smith says, proselytes to the belief in Jesus. For the Talmud speaks of those who have recently joined Judaism as "children" (*Jebamoth* 22a, 48b, 976; *Necharoth* 47a). "Whoso shall *receive* one such little child *in my name* receiveth me. But whoso shall offend one of these little ones *which believe in me,* it were better for him that a millstone were hanged about his neck, and that he were drowned in the depth of the sea" (Matt. 18:5-6). . . .

Jesus says in Matthew 11:25:

> I thank thee, O Father, Lord of heaven and earth, because thou hast hid these things from the wise and prudent, and hast revealed them unto babes.
>
> Even so, Father; for so it seemed good in thy sight.
>
> All things are delivered unto me of my Father; and no man knoweth the Son, but the Father; neither knoweth any man the Father, save the Son and he to whomsoever the Son will reveal him.
>
> Come unto me, all ye that labor and are heavy laden, and I will give you rest.
>
> Take my yoke upon you, and learn of me; for I am meek and lowly in heart; and ye shall find rest unto your souls.
>
> For my yoke is easy, and my burden is light.

These words are among the finest attributed to Jesus, but they are based on literary borrowing. The place that Jesus ascribes here to himself in regard to his father is precisely the relation of Wisdom to Yahweh in the book of Wisdom (7:14, 8:3, 17:28). In the book of Jesus Sirach also it is written: "Secure wisdom, which is not bought with gold. Bend your necks under its yoke, and let your soul receive justification. Close is it to him who desires it, and whosoever gives himself to it, he findeth it. See it with your eyes; little have I labored, and have found much refreshment in it" (51:25). In fact, Wisdom itself makes Sirach speak thus: "Come unto me, ye that desire me, and sate yourselves with my fruits. For the thought of me is better than sweet honey, and the possession of me better than virgin honey. They that eat me shall ever hunger after me, and they that drink me shall ever thirst after me. He that heareth me shall not be ashamed, and they that use me shall not sin" (24:19). The idea of the supper in which the blood of the Lord is drunk and his body eaten, to purify from sin, is perceived in these words. But we fully realize that these words of Jesus were really taken from the Scriptures and put into the mouth of Jesus by the Evangelist when we find that the first conception goes back once more to the prophet Isaiah, the great source of the Gospels:

> Ho, everyone that thirsteth, come ye to the waters, and he that hath no money; come ye, buy, and eat; yea, come, buy wine and milk without money and without price.
>
> Wherefore do ye spend money for that which is not bread? and your labor for that which satisfieth not? Hearken diligently unto me, and eat ye that which is good, and let your soul delight itself in fatness.
>
> Incline your ear, and come unto me; hear, and your soul shall live; and I will make an everlasting covenent with you, even the sure mercies of David (Isa. 55:1-3).

In this sense Jesus sends away the rich young man who cannot bring himself to abandon his wealth for the sake of the kingdom of heaven: "Verily, I say unto you, That a rich man shall hardly enter into the kingdom of heaven. . . . It is easier for a camel to go through the eye of a needle than for a rich man to enter into the kingdom of God" (Matt. 19:23). This again, is a familiar saying of the rabbis, in which the man who pretended to believe some impossibility was asked: "Are you from Pombeditha [in Babylonia], where they can drive an elephant through the eye of a needle?"[4] And when Jesus says to the disciples, who ask about their reward for following him: "Everyone that hath forsaken houses, or brothers, or sisters, or father, or mother, or wife, or children, or lands, for my name's sake, shall receive an hundredfold, and shall inherit everlasting life" (Matt. 19:29), he is merely repeating the blessing of Moses (Deut. 33:9): "Who said unto his father and to his mother, I have not seen him; neither did he acknowledge his brethren, nor knew his own children. . . . bless, Lord, his substance, and accept the work of his hands." "Many that are first shall be last, and the last shall be first," Jesus continues. And the Talmud supports him, saying: "Whoso lowereth himself, him doth God exalt; whoso exalteth himself, him doth God lower; whoso seeketh greatness, from him it flees; whoso fleeth greatness, it runneth after him" (Erubim, 13b; see Baba Bathra, fol. 10, col. 3).

JESUS' BELIEF IN GOD THE FATHER

But Jesus, theologians assure us, taught a new and unheard-of conception of God, and in this especially is the "uniqueness" and unsurpassable greatness of his teaching; for such an achievement is only possible to a supreme religious genius—namely, Jesus. God as a loving father, in contrast to the wrathful and stern God of Judaism! "God and the soul, the soul and its God." Since Harnack published his Wesen des Christentums, the refrain has echoed in every chapel and in all the publications of the evangelical and liberal theological schools. They take it for granted, of course, that the "son of God," whether this is meant in the metaphysical or merely in the metaphorical sense, must have had a quite new conception of God, throwing in the shade all earlier ideas, and they talk themselves into an ecstatic admiration of Jesus' conception of God. Yet the idea of God the Father is common to all religions; and it is sheer theological prejudice to say that, when a Greek prayed to "Father Zeus" or a German to "All-father Odin," there was no corresponding sentiment in his soul, and his piety was not colored by a childlike trust in the goodness, the surpassing wisdom, and the power of God conceived as a father. Long before the time of Jesus the idea of God as the Father was quite common among the Jews. Wendt, in System der christlichen Lehre (1906), counts no less than twenty-three passages in the Old Testament in which God is conceived as Father in just the same sense as we find in Jesus.[5] Isaiah exclaims, for instance (63:16; 64:7): "Doubtless thou art our father. . . .thou, O Lord, are our father, our redeemer."

It may be urged that the Jewish Yahweh is a stern God, who visits the sins of the fathers on the children down to the third and fourth generation (Exod. 34:7). But we also read in the Old Testament: "The fathers shall not be put to death for the children, neither shall the children be put to death for the fathers" (Deut. 24:16); and, on the other hand, the idea of God as a stern, punishing father is not foreign to Jesus. And where shall we find in the words of Jesus a finer utterance on God than this: "The Lord God, merciful and gracious, long-suffering, and abundant in goodness and truth, keeping mercy for thousands, forgiving iniquity and transgression and sin" (Exod. 34:6-7)? Or where shall we find more fervent thanksgiving for God's fatherly goodness and mercy than in the psalmist (Ps. 103)?

> Bless the Lord, O my soul; and all that is within me, bless his holy name.
> Bless the Lord, O my soul; and forget not all his benefits;
> Who forgiveth all thine iniquities; who healeth all thy diseases;
> Who redeemeth thy life from destruction; who crowneth thee with loving-kindness and tender mercies;
> Who satisfieth thy mouth with good things. . . .
> The Lord is merciful and gracious, slow to anger, and plenteous in mercy.
> He will not always chide; neither will he keep his anger for ever.
> He hath not dealt with us after our sins, nor rewarded us according to our iniquities. . . .
> *Like as a father pitieth his children,* so the Lord pitieth them that fear him.
> For he knoweth our frame; he remembereth that we are dust.
> As for man, his days are as grass; as a flower of the field, so he flourisheth.
> For the wind passeth over it, and it is gone; and the place thereof shall know it no more.
> But the mercy of the Lord is from everlasting to everlasting upon them that fear him, and his righteousness unto children's children.

As regards the relation of God the Father to the individual soul, this "religious individualism," as it is called, is not peculiar to Jesus or Christianity, but a fundamental feature of all religions, and especially of the mystery-cults. In all of them the individual sought to enter into a direct personal relation to the diety, and the subjective feeling of the presence of God in them was not less strong and deep than in the case of Jesus.

In point of fact the God of Jesus is merely the God of the Old Testament, the one God of Israel (Mark 12:29), the God of Abraham, Isaac, and Jacob (Matt. 22:32). Jesus himself, as described in the Gospels, is so little conscious of teaching anything new in this respect that he makes no claim to do so. . . .

The God and Father of Jesus is the common God of the Jews. "Not a sparrow shall fall on the ground without your Father," says Jesus (Matt. 10:29); and he adds: "The very hairs of your head are all numbered." We read the same in the book of Job: "Doth not he see my ways and count all my steps?" (31:4). "Without the will of God no bird falls from heaven," says the Talmud; "how much the less shall danger threaten a man's life, unless the creator himself makes it?" (*Bereschit rabba*, 79, fol. 77, col. 4). And it is the same in *Pesikta* (fol. 18, col. 4): "Do I not number every hair of every creature?" "No man strikes here below with his finger but it is known above" (*Chulin*, 7).

Much stress has been laid on the fact that Jesus does not speak of God in general as the father of all men, but specifically as *his* father. But in Mark (8:38; 13:32) Jesus calls God not so much *his* father as the father of the Christ. It is only in Matthew and Luke that we find that intimacy and familiarity in the words of Jesus respecting his relation to God, and in John it assumes a thoroughly mystical character.[6] But that he calls God his father is, as we saw, an expression taken from the Book of Wisdom, where the wicked ate the "just," because he speaks of God as "his father" (2:16).

LOVE OF NEIGHBORS AND OF ENEMIES

We cannot, therefore, find in their conception of God the extraordinary feature that would justify us in ascribing the words of the Gospels to so extraordinary a man as Jesus. Is it in their ethical ideas?

According to Mark (12:29), Jesus answers the scribe who asks him which is the chief commandment: "Hear, O Israel; The Lord our God is one Lord: and thou shalt love the Lord thy God with all thy heart, and with all thy soul, and with all thy mind, and with all thy strength; this is the first commandment. And the second is like—namely, this: Thou shalt love thy neighbor as thyself." The words are found in the Old Testament (Deut. 6:4 and Lev. 19:19). Jesus himself is well aware that in this he is not expressing any new idea. The way in which the scribe at once agrees with him shows that he is only putting a common opinion, and this is shown also by the parallel passage, Luke 10:25, where Jesus makes the scribe quote the words as a commonplace of the law. In Matthew 22:40, Jesus adds: "On these two commandments hang all the law and the prophets." Further, we read in Tobias 4:16: "What thou dost not wish any man to do unto thee do thou not unto another"; and we find the saying in the same negative form in the Talmud: "A heathen came to Hillel and said to him: I will embrace Judaism on condition that thou teachest me the whole doctrine during the time that I stand on one leg. And Hillel said: What thou dost not like do not to thy neighbor; that is the whole doctrine. And the rest is only explanation; go thou and learn" (*Tract. Schabbath*, 31a). If this is supposed to be less than Jesus demands, we must remember that the maxim is in a negative form in the older editions of the Gospels. In this respect, therefore, the "love" which Jesus demands is merely the Old Testament love of one's neighbor.

In Matthew 5:43, however, it is said: "Ye have heard that it hath been said, Thou shalt love thy neighbor, and hate thine enemy. But I say unto you, Love your enemies, bless them that curse you, do good to them that hate you, and pray for them which despitefully use you and persecute you." Here the love of one's neighbor seems to be elevated into a command to love one's enemies. . . . If Jesus really spoke these words, he betrayed an astonishing ignorance of the Mosaic law. Where is it written that the Jews must hate their enemies? In Leviticus 19:18, where the love of one's neighbor is prescribed, it is expressly said: "Thou shalt not avenge, nor bear any grudge against the children of they people," and "Thou shalt not hate thy brother in thine heart; thou shalt not in any wise rebuke thy neighbor, and not suffer sin upon him [thou shalt freely call thy neighbor to account, that thou bear no sin on his account]." Not only towards their own people, but even towards strangers, the Jews must not be without love: "Thou shalt not oppress a stranger; for ye know the heart of a stranger, seeing that ye were strangers in the land of Egypt" (Exod. 23:9), and "The stranger that dwelleth with you shall be unto you as one born among you, and thou shalt love him as thyself" (Lev. 19:34). Even the love of enemies is commanded in the Law: "If thou meet thine enemy's ox or his ass going astray, thou shalt surely bring it back to him again. If thou see the ass of him that hateth thee lying under his burden, and wouldest forbear to help him, thou shalt surely help with him" (Exod. 23:4-5). "Rejoice not," says Proverbs (24:17), "when thine enemy falleth, and let not thine heart be glad when he stumbleth." "If thine enemy be hungry, give him bread to eat; and if he be thirsty, give him water to drink; for thou shalt heap coals of fire upon his head, and the Lord shall reward thee" (25:21-2). In Job it is represented as a crime against God to rejoice over the misfortune of one's enemy (31:29), and the psalmist boasts of having saved one who had been his enemy without cause (7:5). "Say not thou, I will recompense evil," it is said in Proverbs (20:22), "but wait on the Lord, and he shall save thee." "Let them curse, but bless thou," says the psalmist (109:28). And Jesus Sirach says: "Forgive thy neighbor the injury he has done thee; then will thy sins be forgiven thee when thou prayest" (28:1).

Not only the Old Testament but the Talmud is full of demands of love of one's enemies and examples of good feeling towards opponents. "Thou shalt not hate, not even internally" (*Menachot*, 18). "Love him that punisheth thee" (*Derech Erez Sutha*, c. 9). "How is it possible for one that fears God to hate a man and regard him as an enemy?" (*Pessachim*, 113). A rabbi used, before he went to bed, to forgive all who had injured him during the day. Another, Rabbi Josua, wished to bring the divine judgment upon a heretic who tormented him, but went to sleep, and when he awoke reflected: This sleep was a warning that the just should never call the punishment of God on the guilty (*Berachot*, 76, also 10a). "When," says the Talmud (*Sanhedrim*, 39b), "the angels wished to sing a chant of joy because the Egyptians were destroyed in the sea, God said to them: My creatures are drowned, and would ye sing?" Finally, Job says (31:13): "If I did despise the cause of my manservant or of my maidservant, when they contended with me; what then shall I do when God riseth up?. . . Did not he that made me in the womb make him? and did not one fashion us in the womb?"

The Talmud by no means restricts this love of one's enemies to members of one's own people. As man is bidden to pray to God for sinners (Sohar to Gen., fol. 67), so God says to Moses: "Israelite or Gentile, man or woman, slave or free, all are alike for you" (Jalkut, c. 20b). In accordance with this, and in agreement with Leviticus 19:9, the Talmud commands them not to prevent the Gentile poor from gleaning in the fields (Gittin, c. 5), and repeatedly represents Abraham the Israelite as a model of tolerance. The best is, however, that the words of Jesus, "Bless them that curse you, do good to them that hate you," are not found at all in the older manuscripts of the Gospels, but are found in the Talmud, where we read: "It is better to be wronged by others than to wrong" (Sanhedrim, fol. 48), and "Be rather among the persecuted than the persecutors" (Baba mezia, 93). "Where in the world," asks Weiss, "is there a Jewish writing or a Jewish community that has ever made love of one's enemy a fundamental rule of commerce? And wherever it has been put in practice—whence came the impulse, who inspired men thereto? The Talmud, or the Old Testament, or the figure of him who sealed his word on the cross?" The answer is found in the above.

It is sheer theological prejudice and perversion of history to say that Jesus was "the first" to preach love of enemies, that men owe to his example alone that love of one's neighbor has become the supreme principle of moral conduct. As if the Stoics had not preached universal love of mankind long before the time of Jesus, not merely as a passive endurance, but as an active interest in the lot of others and disinterested helpfulness on the basis of descent from a common divine Father and as members of a common humanity! As if Jesus had not violated his own command in his conduct towards the Canaanite woman (Mark 7:27), his refusal to allow the disciples to go and preach the Gospel to the Gentiles and the Samaritans (Matt. 10:5), his curse of the places that would not be converted, and his anger against the Pharisees and scribes on account of their opposition to him! It is an empty theological phrase to say that Jesus "raised the altruistic ideal to a pitch of supreme intimacy" and "destroyed in principle the barriers between peoples and sects"; it is anything but the outcome of candid religious-scientific inquiry—it is a resolute closing of one's eyes to the facts to exalt Jesus, in face of the preceding quotations from the Old Testament and the Talmud, for a merit which does not belong to him, but to them, and to maintain the fiction that love of enemies was made a "fundamental rule of trade" by Jesus in any higher sense than we find in the rest of Judaism. As long as theologians continue to praise the moral maxims of Jesus in this way at the expense of non-Christian ethics, we must decline to regard their efforts as impartial, in spite of that claim of "honorableness" which they repeat so pitifully, and however proudly they may wrap themselves in the mantle of their scientific infallibility. We do not question their subjective honor, but we do question their ability, in their atmosphere of theological hypnotism, to see things as they really are. And if they grant that the precept of love of enemies has in it nothing peculiarly characteristic of Jesus, there is an end of the proof of "uniqueness" that was based on it, and the historical reality of the Jesus of the Gospels falls to the ground.

THE SERMON ON THE MOUNT

Careful inquiry shows that the remaining moral precepts and edifying sayings of Jesus have no more title to originality than the command to love one's neighbors and enemies. Take the Sermon on the Mount, for instance, which is wanting in Mark, and was certainly never delivered in the form in which we have it; this collection of the quintessence of the ethical teaching of Jesus is a "mere compilation of existing Jewish literature," and does not contain *a single idea* that we do not otherwise find in Jewish proverbial literature. . . .

"Blessed are the poor in spirit, for theirs is the kingdom of heaven," Jesus begins the Sermon; and the psalmist (116:6) says: "The Lord preserveth the simple; I was brought low, and he helped me." "Blessed are they that mourn, for they shall be comforted," is the next sentence; and Isaiah says (66:13), "As one whom his mother comforteth, so will I comfort you," to those who mourn the loss of their country, and announces to them the glorious fulfilment of the divine promises. "Blessed are the meek, for they shall inherit the earth," is the third maxim; and Isaiah says (57:15): "I dwell in the high and holy place, with him also that is of a contrite and humble spirit, to revive the spirit of the humble, and to revive the heart of the contrite ones." "A man's pride shall bring him low," says Proverbs (29:23), "but honor shall uphold the humble in spirit." "My son," says Ecclesiasticus (3:17), "do thy work in humility; the greater thou art do thou the more humble thyself, and thou shalt find favor in the eyes of the Lord." Rabbi Jochanan says: "When a man has acquired meekness, then will he also acquire honor, wealth, and wisdom" (*Midrash Jalkut Mischle*, 22); and the psalmist says (37:11): "But the meek shall inherit the earth, and shall delight themselves in the abundance of peace."

"Blessed are they which do hunger and thirst after righteousness," Jesus continues, "for they shall be filled." "He that walketh righteously and speaketh uprightly," says Isaiah (33:15), "shall dwell on high"; and the Talmud says: "Any age in which the doctrine is not found—that is to say, in which a righteous life, conformable to the law, is not possible—lives in hunger" (*Schemot rabba*, cap. 31; see also Ps. 118:19). In Proverbs we read (21:21): "He that followeth after righteousness and mercy findeth life, righteousness, and honor." This also agrees in substance with the fifth beatitude: "Blessed are the merciful, for they shall obtain mercy." Pity and sympathy, even for animals, are urged and praised both in the Old Testament and the Talmud (Deut. 25:4; 22:6 and 10). "Blessed are the pure in heart, for they shall see God," is the sixth beatitude. "Who shall ascend into the hill of the Lord?" says the psalmist (24:3), "or who shall stand in his holy place? He that hath clean hands and a pure heart." "Blessed are the peacemakers, for they shall be called the children of God." But the psalmist also exclaims (34:14): "Seek peace, and pursue it." Indeed, peace is lifted to so lofty a position by the Talmudists that they call the Messiah himself "peace," and Isaiah has described him as above all a bringer and prince of peace. Finally, the eighth beatitude, "Blessed are they which are persecuted for righteousness' sake, for theirs is the kingdom of heaven," has an echo in the Talmud: "They who are persecuted and persecute not, who sustain ridicule and injury and themselves do no injury, are the elect of God, of whom it is said: They shine like the sun" (*Schabbeth*, 88*b*). We have already seen, moreover, that persecution because of their righteousness is a mark of the good in the Book of Wisdom, and secures heaven for them.

It is not necessary to go into other details of the Sermon on the Mount. It contains, as we said, nothing whatever beyond the common Jewish ethic, in spite of the trouble the Evangelists have taken to set up an artificial contrast between the ethic of Jesus and the Jewish morality of the time, and the effort of Christian theologians to obscure the real relation of the Christian to the Jewish ethic. Thus the prohibition of anger against one's brother (Matt. 5:22) is from Leviticus 19:17. The maxim that merely to look upon another's wife is equal to adultery (Matt. 5:28) is covered by Job 31:1 and Ecclesiasticus 9:5 and 8, and by similar strict maxims in the Talmud, such as: "Whoever regards even the little finger of a woman has already violated matrimony in his heart" (*Bereschit*, 24 and 24*a*). When Jesus insists on purity and goodness of heart before a man approaches the altar to offer sacrifice (Matt. 5:23), he is merely following Isaiah and the other prophets who place piety of heart above the external piety of sacrifices and good works. Indeed, it seems that the much-quoted maxim, that one must not resist evil, but present the other cheek to the smiter (Matt. 5:39), can be traced to Isaiah 50:6, and the description of the servant of God, who presents his back to those who beat him and his cheeks to those who plucked the hair. There is, moreover, a famous Jewish proverb: "If any demand thy ass, give him the saddle also" (*Baba kama*, 27).

Again, the advice as to almsgiving, doing good in secret (Matt. 6:1-4), praying and fasting (v. 5), and forgiving injuries (v. 14) is founded on Jewish teaching, and is echoed in similar maxims of the Old Testament and the Talmud. Isaiah demands an inward, not an external, fast (chap. 58). The preacher bids his readers avoid many words in praying (5:1; see also Eccles. 7:14). As to the "Lord's Prayer," not only are the several phrases contained in the Old Testament (see, for instance, Eccles. 28:2) and in the Talmud, but it is certain that it was not uttered by Jesus in its present form. The warning against the accumulation of earthly treasures and against the dangers of wealth (Matt. 6:19) and the counsel to look first to the kingdom of God are quite in accord with the prophets (Ecclesus. 27:1, 31:3; Eccles. 5:9 and chap. 12). The saying, "Judge not, that ye be not judged" (Matt. 7:1), runs in the Talmud: "Judge everyone as favorably as possible" (*Abot*, i, 6), and "Judge not thy neighbor until thou hast stood in his place" (*Abot*, ii, 4), and "With the measure with which a man measures shall it be meted unto him" (*Sota*, 8*b*). The saying about the beam and the mote (Matt. 7:4) is found word for word in the Talmud (*Baba bathra*, 15), and runs, in the mouth of the Rabbi Nathan: "The fault from which thou art not free blame not in another" (*Baba mezia*, 59). The sentence, "Ask, and it shall be given to you; seek, and yet shall find; knock, and it shall be opened unto you," corresponds to the words of the prophet Jeremiah (29:13): "And ye shall seek me, and find me, when ye shall search for me with all your heart," and to "The doors of prayer are never closed" of the Talmud (*Sota*, 49). Jeremiah, like Jesus, warns against false prophets, and urges to true repentance and good deeds.

In view of all this one does not see why the people should be "astonished" at the teaching of Jesus (Matt. 7:28), since all the moral principles which the Evangelists put in the so-called Sermon on the Mount had long been, as Ernest Renan says, "the small change of the synagogues." Perhaps it will be suggested that the finest sayings of Jesus which are also found in the Talmud have been taken by the latter from the Gospels. But at the time of the compilation of the Talmud the mutual hatred of the two parties was so great that a pious Jew would quite certainly not have admitted into his collection sayings which he knew to be represented by the Christians as the "words of Jesus." If it were done unwittingly, it would only show how slight the difference was from the first between the Jewish and the Christian morality; and it would be difficult to avoid the con-clusion that the Christians had taken their "words of Jesus" from the common proverbial wisdom of the Jews.

Naturally, it was only the best in the available literature that seemed to the Christians good enough to be put in the mouth of Jesus. We are, of course, dealing with a "spiritualized and intimate Judaism," a philosophy of life and deity that had, among the dispersed Jews, been permeated by the finer thought and feeling of the Greek spirit. Anyone who doubts the possibility of this must have in mind only the description of Judaism in the pages of the Gospels themselves, and take it to be an historical fact that Judaism was in the time of Jesus as fossilized and spiritless as it is described in the Gospels. Such an assumption is a sheer *petitio principii*, and runs counter to the familiar experience that, when the religious leaders of a people lapse into formalism, the stream of inner religious life runs freely in other channels, and may produce new and remarkable phenomena. Remember the ancient mystics in the time of the scholastics of the Middle Ages, or the pietists during the predominance of the driest theological rationalism.

It is usually among the laity, the secrets sects and conventicles, that the religious life pulses all the more vigorously and becomes all the deeper in pro-portion to the formalism of the official religion. Certainly, in contrast to the spirit of the Pharisees and scribes about the beginning of the second century, it is a "new spirit" that lives in the Jesus-sect, and finds expression in the words and ideas which Jesus is supposed to have uttered. But it is not a new spirit in the creative sense, since all that it contains of moral value has been derived from the great fund of Jewish proverbial wisdom, not produced by itself. They are the ideals of men who, no one knows how long before, had brooded over the writings of the prophets, especially Isaiah, lit the fire of the inner religious world from the plain and penetrating piety of the Psalms and Proverbs, absorbed their spirit, and never ceased to remain in continuous contact with the "everliving in the Scriptures." They could not, it is true, have transferred these finer flowers of

Judaism to their own garden if they had not been personally disposed to this religious intimacy. But that one single personality gave them this spirit, as theologians say, it is just as superfluous to suppose as in similar cases of the rise of a pietistic and mystic fervor among the laity by the side of the official teaching of the sect. These first Christians had not to seek the pearls—the true and eternal—in the wilderness of official knowledge of the law, as they had never expressly looked there for them. And when it is said that only a quite exceptional religious genius like Jesus could have done this, it is forgotten that the words of Jesus which have come down to us were not selected by him, but by the Evangelists, out of tradition; since they certainly represent only an insignificant part of what Jesus could have taught.

Thus, the fall of Jerusalem, the collapse of the political and national conditions of the Jewish religion, the increasingly bitter antagonism of the legal piety of the Pharisees to the Christian sectaries, and their inner conception of the Jewish faith, wholly suffice to explain not only the outburst of Messianic hope among them, but why the Christians precisely at this time—a time of the deepest humiliation and trouble—announced that the Messiah was coming immediately, and directed all their efforts to a preparation for his coming. All the lofty moral maxims and promises on which the community had long brooded, and which they may possibly have gathered into a collection of so-called "Sayings of the Lord," now sprang to the lips of the Christians, in contrast to the official legal righteousness, took the form of sayings of the expected Messiah himself, of warnings, consolations, and promises given during his earthly life, which they regarded as a condition of his coming again in splendor as the Messiah; and while the vague image of the Isaian servant of God and Savior that lived in their hearts, perhaps fed by visionary experiences, assumed the shape and features of an historical Jesus, the word and image blended involuntarily, not consciously, in their inflamed imaginations into an inseparable unity, just as religious sects are accustomed to regard the most profound and important of their rules and customs as revelations of the deity or of their supposed founder.

FURTHER PARALLEL PASSAGES

Thus we see that from the words of Jesus no proof can be drawn of his historicity; indeed, even Weiss admits that it is "possible" that "not a single word of Jesus has been preserved, and that everything has been put into his mouth." We think that we are quite justified in assuming this when we find that it would be hard to quote a single expression of Jesus that might not be taken from the Talmud or the Old Testament. To what even apparently small details this extends is seen in Matthew 8:22: "Follow me, and let the dead bury their dead." This corresponds to the command in the Talmud to postpone the burial of the body of a relative to reading in the law (Megillah, fol. 3). In fact, the peculiar expression of Jesus can only be understood when we learn that the godless living are said in the Talmud to be "dead" (*Jalkut Rubeni*, fol. 177, col. 3). Even such a saying as that in Matthew 10:40-2 and Luke 10:16 is found in the Talmud: "He who takes his neighbor into his house has the same reward as if the *Schechina* [divine spirit] itself entered his house" (*Shir hashirim rabba*, fol. 13, col. 3). "He who feeds one learned in divine things will be blessed by God and men" (*Sohar* to Gen., fol. 129, col. 512). "If ye give ear to my angel, it is as if ye hearkened unto me" (*Schemoth rabba Abschn.*, 32, fol. 131, col. 3). "If thou honorest my commandments, thou honorest me; if thou despisest them, thou despisest me in them" (*Tanchuma*, fol. 16, col. 3).

Take such a saying as that in Matthew 10:35, "I am come to set a man at variance against his father, and the daughter against her mother, and the daughter-in-law against her mother-in-law," and compare it with Micah 7:6: "For the son dishonoreth the father, the daughter riseth up against her mother, the daughter-in-law against her mother-in-law; a man's enemies are the men of his own house." The advice of Jesus as to the method of reconciliation with a brother who has offended (Matt. 18:15-17) corresponds to the procedure enjoined by Joma (fol. 87, col. 1), except that in the one case it is the injured, and in the other the injurer, who must act. "Where two or three are gathered together in my name, there am I in the midst of them" (Matt. 18:20) runs in the Talmud: "Where there are two persons, and they make not the law the subject of their discourse, is the seat of the scoffer [Ps.1:1]; but where the law is the subject of discourse, there also is the *Schechina*"—that is, the spirit of God (*Pirke Aboth*, col. 3). Jesus says in Luke 10:18: "I beheld Satan as lightning fall from heaven." In Isaiah it is similarly said of Babylon: "How art thou fallen from heaven, O Lucifier, son of the morning! how art thou cut down to the ground, which didst weaken the nations!" (14:12), and the context makes it clear how easily the words might be applied to Satan.

We have previously shown how the Talmud agrees as to the story of the coin of the taxes and the answer of Jesus to the question of the Pharisees, whether it was lawful to give tribute to Caesar or no. The story of the anointing of Jesus at Bethany has obviously grown out of Psalm 23:5 ("Thou preparest a table before me in the presence of mine enemies; thou anointest my head with oil; my cup runneth over"), and Deuteronomy 15:11 ("For the poor shall never cease out of the land"). The scene in the garden of Gethsemane is provoked by Genesis 22:3 and 5, where Abraham takes with him his son Isaac and two servants, and bids them wait and pray while he goes with Isaac to sacrifice the boy. There is also a reference to the story of Elisha, when he falls asleep under a bush as he flies before Ahab, and is twice awakened by an angel, who gives him a loaf and a vessel of water, and bids him strengthen himself for the journey. It is significant that we find here the words which occur in the Gospels: "It is enough. Take now my life, Yahweh" (Mark 14:36 and 41). Then there is the phrase: "My soul is exceeding sorrowful." "Why art thou cast down, O my soul? and why art thou disquieted in me? hope thou in God; for I shall yet praise him for the help of his countenance"; so runs Psalm 42:5, in accord with Mark 14:34.

And verses 35 and 36 suggest Ecclesiasticus (23:1 and 4): "O Lord, my Father and the author of my life, let me not fall through them [my sins]. . . . abandon me not to the attack they plan against me."

THE PARABLES OF JESUS

The parables come after the phrases of the Sermon on the Mount as the most important of the sayings of Jesus. They are so greatly esteemed, and have such a repute for "uniqueness" and unsurpassable excellence that in the opinion of many they would suffice of themselves to establish the authorship of Jesus.

All these parables deal with "the kingdom of heaven," the manner of its spread, the way to become worthy of it, and the attitude which the Jews and Gentiles assume in regard to the promise of it in the Jesus-cult. The connection with Isaiah is thus obvious.

"Go and tell this people," Yahweh bids the prophet, "Hear ye indeed, but understand not; and see ye indeed, but perceive not. Make the heart of this people fat, and make their ears heavy, and shut their eyes; lest they see with their eyes, and hear with their ears, and understand with their heart, and convert, and be healed" (6:9–10). "With stammering lips and another tongue will he speak to this people. To whom he said, This is the rest wherewith ye may cause the weary to rest; and this is the refreshing; yet they would not hear" (28:11–12). These words have had a general influence on the description of the conduct of the Jews to Jesus, but they have had the special effect of causing the Evangelists to make Jesus speak in parables (Matt. 13:13). In this way we can understand the otherwise unintelligible saying in Mark 4:12, namely, that the Savior speaks in parables to the people in order that they may *not* understand him and be converted and receive forgiveness for their sins. There is simply no question of a quotation from Isaiah. More than elsewhere we here recognize the mystery-character of the original Christianity of the [Jesus-followers] who thus reveal their dependence on Isaiah. The doctrine is communicated in parables which are unintelligible to "outsiders" and are not intended to be understood by them. Only the disciples or initiated are permitted to perceive "the mysteries of the kingdom of heaven." Hence we read in Matthew 13:34–35: "All these things spake Jesus unto the multitude in parables; and without a parable spake he not unto them; that it might be fulfilled which was spoken by the prophet, saying, I will open my mouth in parables; I will utter things which have been kept secret from the foundation of the world" (Ps. 78:2). Mark, moreover, says that he explained all to his disciples (4:34).

In these circumstances we are not surprised to find one of the chief parables, that of the sower (Matt 13:3; Luke 8:5), first among the Naassenes, the pre-Christian Gnostic sect with a close relation to Christianity. In this parable, however, we have, as W. B. Smith has shown at length, a modification and adaptation of a much older allegory in which the Gnostic teaching illustrated the sowing by God of the seed springing from the Logos which produces the world.[7] In the case of many other parables of Jesus, also, the source can be traced, and they are not reproduced as sayings of Jesus with any great improvement. Thus the parable of the merchant who exchanges all his goods for a single pearl is found in the Talmud (*Schabbat*, fol. 119, col 1), and goes back to Proverbs 8:10: "Receive my instruction, and not silver; and knowledge rather than choice gold. For wisdom is better than rubies; and all the things that may be desired are not to be compared to it." Even the parable of the net, which follows it in Matthew, seems to be inspired by the same passage in the Talmud, according to which the pearl is lost in a storm, swallowed by a fish, and recovered by the catching of the fish, and restored to its original owner, who sells it and obtains great wealth.

We read as follows in the Talmud: "God said to man: How great is thy guilt for betraying me? Thou sinnest against me, and I have patience with thee. Thy soul comes daily to me, when thou sleepest, and renders its account, and remains my debtor. Yet I give thee back thy soul, which is my property. So do thou each evening return his pledge to thy debtor." It is not difficult to see in this passage the parable of the dishonest servant (Matt. 18:23).

Again, we read in the Talmud: "To whom shall I liken the Rabbi Bon, son of Chaija? To a king that hath hired laborers, among whom was one of great power. This man did the king summon to himself, and held speech with him. And when the night fell, the hired laborers came to receive their hire. But the king gave to the favored laborer the same hire which he had given unto the others. Then they murmured and said: We have labored the whole day, and this man hath labored but two hours, yet there is given unto him the same wage that we have received. And the king sent them away, saying: This man hath done more in two hours than ye have done during the whole of the day. Even so had the Rabbi Bon done more in the study of the law in the twenty-eight years of his life than another would have done who had lived an hundred years" (*Berachoth*, fol. 5, col. 3). The parable is quite consistent and unassailable. But the biblical parallel—the parable of the workers in the vineyard—is clearly distasteful, since the king attempts to justify his conduct by a purely arbitrary feeling, and regards his lack of justice as a virtue (Matt. 20, 15). It has not been improved in the mouth of Jesus, where it is made to illustrate the theme that in the kingdom of heaven the last shall be first, and the first last; that many are called, but few chosen (20:16).

The parable of the two sons recalls the saying of the Talmud: "The just promise little, but do much" (*Baba mezia*, fol. 76, col. 2). The parable of the rebellious vine-workers is inspired by Isaiah 5:

> My well-beloved hath a vineyard in a very fruitful hill.
> And he fenced it, and gathered out the stones thereof, and planted it with the choicest vine, and built a tower in the midst of it . . . and he looked that it should bring forth grapes, and it brought forth wild grapes.
> And now, O inhabitants of Jerusalem, and men of Judah, judge, I pray you, betwixt me and my vineyard.

What could have been done more to my vineyard, that I have not done it? Wherefore, when I looked that it should bring forth grapes, brought it forth wild grapes?

And now go to: I will tell you what I will do to my vineyard. I will take away the hedge thereof, and it shall be eaten up; and break down the wall thereof, and it shall be trodden down:

And I will lay it waste . . . . For the vineyard of the Lord of hosts is the house of Israel, and the men of Judah his pleasant plant; and he looked for judgment, but behold *oppression*; for righteousness, but behold *a cry*.

The parable of the royal marriage feast runs in the Talmud: "A king held a great banquet, to which many guests were invited. They were requested to bathe, anoint themselves, and put on their festive garments, in order to appear worthily before the king. But the hour of the banquet was not definitely fixed. The more shrewd were seen walking up and down before the door of the palace about the ninth hour of the day, awaiting the moment when they should be permitted to enter. The more short-sighted thought otherwise, and each one went about his business, as on other days. Suddenly the summons was sent forth that those who were invited should come to the king's table. Then the former came in splendid garments, but the others in their soiled workday clothes, on account of the haste of the summons. The king looked with friendly eye on those who had shown themselves prepared at his invitation; but the others, who had paid less regard to the king's command and had entered the palace in unfitting garments, had to receive as their reward the displeasure of the king. Those who were successful had a place at the royal table; the unsuccessful had to witness this, and had in addition to undergo severe punishment" (*Koheleth rabba*, 9, 8. See also *Bereschit rabba*, sect. 62, fol. 60, col. 3; and *Sohar Levit.*, fol. 40, col. 158). The parable is not very happy, on account of its many improbabilities; but in the New Testament it is altogether absurd. The invitation to a banquet already prepared; the reluctance of the guests to go to the marriage feast, so that they even kill some of the servants; the blind fury of the king, who burns the town in revenge; his anger against one who is brought in from the road because he is not wearing the wedding garment, and the terrible punishment inflicted on him—all this is so unnatural, grotesque, and ridiculous that it can only be pronounced a complete perversion of the Talmud original.

The parable of the ten virgins (Matt. 25:1), which embodies the same ideas, is no better. Ten maidens going out to meet a bridgegroom at night, and some of them forgetting the oil for their lamps and being rejected by the bridgegroom for this slight negligence—these are not pictures taken from life, but untrue constuctions of a flighty imagination. The same may be said of the master in the parable of the loan of the talents (Matt. 25:14), who is angry with the servant who brings back his talent without interest, deals hardly with him, and casts him into the darkness, where there was weeping and gnashing of teeth. We may note in passing that Mattew 25:29 is a rabbinical proverb from the Talmud, where we read: "He who gathers shall have more added unto him; but he who suffers a loss, from him shall yet more be taken" (*Tikkunim in Sohar Chadash*, fol. 75, col. 4).

Of the parables in Luke, that of the lost sheep (15:4) runs as follows in the Talmud: "A muleteer drove twelve span before him, all laden with wine. One of them strayed into the yard of a Gentile. Then the driver left the others, and sought the one that had broken loose. Asked how he had ventured to leave the others for the sake of one, he answered: The others remained on the public road, where there was no danger of any man seeking to steal my property, as he would know that he was observed by so many. So it was with the other children of Jacob [besides Joseph]. They remained under the eye of their father, and were moreover older than Joseph. He, however, was left to himself in his youth. Hence the Scripture says that God took special care of him." (*Bereschit rabba*, sect. 86, fol. 84, col. 3).

The parable of the lost piece of silver (Luke 15:8) repeats and weakens the same idea, and is likewise found in the Talmud: "When a man loses a piece of gold, he lights many lamps in order to seek it. If a man takes all this trouble for the sake of temporal things, how much the more should he when there is question of treasures that keep their worth in the world to come?" (*Midrash Schir hashirim*, fol. 3, col. 2). It is also the theory of the rabbis that penitent sinners are dearer to God than the virtuous (Luke 15:10).

The parable of the unjust steward (Luke 16:1) runs as follows in the Talmud: "A king had appointed two overseers. One he chose as master of the treasure; the other he put in charge of the straw-store. After a time the latter fell under suspicion of unfaithfulness. Nevertheless he complained that he was not promoted to the post of master of the treasure. Then was he asked, in astonishment at his words: Fool, thou hast incurred suspicion in charge of the stores of straw: how couldst thou be entrusted with the treasure?" (*Jalkut Simeoni*, (sect. 1, fol. 81, col. 1). The parable is not profound; but it is not quite inconceivable as is the case with the parable in the Gospel, when it says: "And the lord commended the unjust steward," and "Make to yourselves friends of the mammon of unrighteousness. . . . He that is faithful in that which is least is faithful also in much; and he that is unjust in the least is unjust also in much. If, therefore, ye have not been faithful in the unrighteous mammon, who will commit to your trust the true riches? And if ye have not been faithful in that which is another man's, who shall give you that which is your own?" (Luke 16:8-12). One asks in astonishment how such a parable could find admission into the New Testament.

The parable of the rich man and poor Lazarus (Luke 16:20) reminds us of the Talmud story of two men who died at the same time, one of whom had lived virtuously and the other viciously, and whom a rabbi saw, the one enjoying great delight, the other painfully licking with his tongue the edge of a spring, the water of which he could not reach, (*Tractat. Chagiga*, fol. 77, col. 4, Jerusalem Talmud). We read much the same in *Midrasch Koheleth*, fol. 86, col. 14: "Of two sinners one had been converted before his death; the other remained in sin. When the latter went to hell, he marvelled to see the former companion of his evil deeds

288 The Origins of Christianity

taken into heaven. Then he heard a voice: Fool, know that thy frightful death brought thy companion to repentance; why didst thou refuse during thy life to turn thy heart to penance? To this the sinner replied: Let me do penance now. Fool, the voice cried once more, knowest thou not that eternal life is like the Sabbath? He who does not prepare his food for the Sabbath on the day of preparation [Friday], whereof will he eat on the Sabbath? He who does not penance before he dies shall have no share in eternal life." In fact, the very words of Luke 16:25 are found in the Talmud, where it is said of the godless: "Because you have no share in that life you receive your reward in this world" (Berachoth, fol. 61, col. 2).

In order to illustrate the words, "Ask, and it shall be given you; knock, and it shall be opened unto you" (Luke 11:9), Jesus tells the parable of a man who goes to a friend at midnight and asks for three loaves, which he at length receives, not from good feeling or affection, but because of his importunity. The widow also (Luke 18:1) obtains her deliverance from her adversary after long entreaty only because she was so troublesome to the judge. . . .

The comparison of the Messiah to a bridegroom (Matt. 9:15; John 3:29) and his coming to that of a thief in the night (Luke 12:39) must have been very common among the Jews, as we find it also in Revelation (3:3, and 19:7); we have seen that this was originally a Jewish work, subsequently modified in the Christian sense; perhaps it belonged to the circle of Gnostic sects from which Christianity issued. (Also compare Isa. 61:10, and Mark 2:19.)

After all this, it is impossible to say that the parables of Jesus could not be "invented" or are "unsurpassable." On the contrary, they are often defective, sometimes quite inconceivable, and are closely related to the Jewish parables both in form and content; indeed, they are in part imitations of the latter, and are at times weakened, instead of being improved, in reproduction. It is mere theological hypnotism, which more or less affects all of us, that makes so much of the parables of Jesus. . . .

The parables of the good Samaritan (Luke 10), the prodigal son (Luke 15), and the Pharisee and the publican (Luke 18) are beautiful and important. The first, however, has a parallel in a Buddhistic parable which is believed to have had some influence on the Gospel story;[8] the coincidence proves at all events that such a parable could be "invented." The parable of the good Samaritan corresponds in substance with Deuteronomy 22:1. It is in harmony with Jewish morality, but not with the command which Jesus laid on his disciples not to go to the Samaritans. Possibly it is a later invention belonging to the time when the Christian mission was extended to non-Jewish places. Both of the first two parables give ground for reflection in the fact that they are found only in Luke, not in Matthew and John. This looks as if they were not in the so-called collection of sayings. As to the parable of the Pharisee and the publican, so excellent a story may have been invented late, just as well as that of the woman taken in adultery (John 8:3). How can we say that it was impossible for any but Jesus to have told the story?

NOTES

1. Just as in the collection of sayings it is supposed to have been written, "Jesus says," etc., so in the prophets we find the words of Yahweh introduced by "A word of Yahweh," "Thus says Yahweh," etc. We have already seen that Jesus is possibly only another name for Yahweh.

2. If this be true, how is it that such an important detail as the Lord's Prayer has been handed down to us in such various forms? No one knows exactly what words Jesus used in this prayer. According to Harnack, the earliest version is: "Father, the bread for tomorrow give us today, and forgive us our sins as we forgive others, and lead us not into temptation." *Sitzungenbericht der Preussichen Akademie der Wissenschaften*, 1904, Bd. V. See Steudel in *Berliner Religionsgespräch*, "Hat Jesus gelebt?" 1910, 59f.

3. See the *Tractate Schabboth*, fol. 17, col. 1: "The operations involved in offering sacrifice are not considered as work—that is to say, as breaking the Sabbath." See also *Rosh hashana*, fol. 21, col. 2.

4. *Baha mezia*, fol. 38, col. 2; see also *Bereschit*, fol. 55, col. 2.

5. See Exod. 34:6, Deut. 8:5 and 32:6, Ps. 103.

6. Ernest Havet, *Le Christianisme et ses origines* (1884), iv, p. 37.

7. *Der vorchistliche Jesus* (1906), pp. 108-135. Moreover, we read in the first Epistle of Clement: "The sower went forth and cast all his seed on the earth. They fall dry and naked on the soil, rot, and then the care of the Lord cause them to rise again out of their corruption, and from the one many are produced, and they bring forth fruit" (24:5). We see that the parable was told in many forms. Which form comes from Jesus?

8. Pfleiderer, *Urchristentum* (1902), i, p. 447; Van den Bergh van Eysinga, *Indische Einflüsse auf evang. Erzählungen* (2nd ed. 1909) p. 57.

J. M. Robertson

The Crucifixion Legend

JOHN MACKINNON ROBERTSON (1856-1933) wrote extensively on Elizabethan literature and the authorship of Shakespeare's plays (*The Baconian Heresy: A Refutation*, 1900). An important British spokesman for the Christ-myth theory, Robertson published his conclusions in a study entitled *Christianity and Mythology* (1900) and its sequel *The Jesus Problem* (1917).

On a full survey of the data, the crucifixion remains one of the most obscure of the quasi-mythical elements in the Jesuist legend.* Here even more than elsewhere the documents are invalid, seeing that in the "Primitive Gospel" as reconstructed by conservative criticism the story of the trial and execution has confessedly no place. Whatever may have been the primary facts, the Gospel story, framed long after the alleged event, and after a Jesus memoir was already current, has no evidential value. And the trial before Pilate, the story of the two thieves, and the sayings of the cross, have all the marks of circumstantial fiction. On the other hand, there are obvious reasons for supposing that this, a datum in Paul's gospel, stands for *some* historical fact. A slain Messiah was so unlikely a basis to be *invented* for a Jewish cult that the historical presumption must be that some teacher of Messianic pretensions had really been put to death, and that his followers had carried on the movement in the faith that he would come again. When, however, we investigate the relation of the Gospels to the Epistles, and

*Robertson uses this phrase to register his belief that there was no historical Jesus of Nazareth but rather only a Jesus legend.—Ed.

From *Christianity and Mythology* by John Mackinnon Robertson (London: Watts and Co., 1900), pp. 394-422. Published for the Rationalist Press Association, and reprinted by permission of the Rationalist Press Association.

find not only that Paul's spectral Jesus has no traceable connection with the teaching "Jesus the Nazarite" or "Jesus of Nazareth," but that the Gospels themselves betray plain traces of a factitious connection of these cognomens, and that the original Jesus of the first Gospel had no cognomen at all, we see cause to suspect that the movement really originated with the Talmudic Jesus Ben Pandira, who was stoned to death and hanged on a tree, for blasphemy or heresy, on the eve of a Passover in the reign of Alexander Jannaeus (B.C. 106-79). Dr. Löw, an accomplished Hebraist, is satisfied that this Jesus was the founder of the Essene (or Jessean) sect, whose resemblances to the legendary early Christians have so greatly exercised Christian speculation. That, however, must remain a hypothesis, since the Jesus in question is little more than a historic name. His time and place are further obscured through his being identified in the Babylonian Gemara with one Ben Sotada or Stada or Satda, who by one (doubtful) clue is put in the period of Rabbi Akiba in the second century C.E. Of the Talmudic Jesus, as of Ben Stada, it is told that he was stoned and then hanged on a tree on the eve of the Passover; but Jesus is said to have been so executed at Jerusalem, and Ben Stada at Lydda. Rabbinical commentators and later Hebraists generally take the view that two historical personages are thus indicated, and that it was a rabbinical error to identify them. It seems impossible, however, to trust to the sole chronological clue in the Ben Stada story, which is bound up . . . with the name of Mary Magdala.* We must be content to say that there is a Talmudic trace of *a* Jesus who was put to death on the eve of the Passover a century or more before the time of Pontius Pilate. The question is, then, was this Jesus literally crucified? It seems certain that the expression *hanging* was frequently used in Greeek in the Roman period for crucifixion; and the early Church was content to leave standing the passages in the Acts which described Jesus as "hanged on a tree." The detail, however, remains problematical, since the Talmud expressly talks of hanging on a tree *after* stoning—that is, the hanging up of a dead body, which to crucify would be futile.

If the Jesus of Paul were really a personage put to death under Pontius Pilate, the Epistles would give us the strongest ground for accepting an actual crucifixion. We have seen that certain important passages were interpolated; but the references to a crucified Jesus are constant, and offer no sign of interpolation. But if Paul's Jesus, who has taught nothing, and done nothing but die, be really the Jesus of a hundred years before, it becomes readily intelligible that, even if he had been only hanged after stoning, he should by that time have come to figure mythically as crucified. For, as we shall see, the cross was itself a myth element peculiarly likely to be bound up with the cult of any Savior God of the period. The historic crucifixion, scourging, and subsequent slaying of Antigonus, the last Asmonean king of the Jews, by Mark Antony, would further supply the motive for the story of Jesus having been crucified with a parade of the kingly title, as

---

*For a full discussion of the rabbinical sources see R. Joseph Hoffmann, *Jesus Outside the Gospels* (Buffalo, N.Y.: Prometheus, 1984).—*Ed.*

Antigonus doubtless would be. And, historically speaking, it is probable enough that a crucified king should have had set on his head, in mockery, a crown of straw and thorns, by way of heightening his degradation. Yet again, Philo tells a singular story of how, during the reign of Caligula, King Agrippa was insulted at Alexandria by the populace, who took a lunatic named (oddly enough) Karabbas, honored and dressed him as a mock king, and hailed him "Maris," the Syrian name for king. But here, as in the case of Antigonus, possible history is overlapped by mythology, and it is necessary to take into account the latter factor.

The story of the crown of thorns, the scourging, and the kingly title, is wholly absent, like the rest of the Gospel narratives, from the letters of Paul, and may without hesitation be held to be mythical, whatever we decide to hold concerning the crucifixion. The first explanation that occurs to the student of comparative mythology is that the crown of thorns is simply the ancient nimbus of the Sun God; and this is in all probability the root-motive. But it happens that in pagan mythology there is a closer approximation to the crown of thorns than the nimbus; a missing link, so to speak, which would serve to explain the manufacture of this part of the Christist story, as we have seen so many other Christist myths to be framed out of pagan art and mystery ritual. Two of the leading Savior figures of paganism were Prometheus and Herakles, and each of these is mythologically represented as wearing a mock crown. The myth connects the two heroes. According to Athenaeus, Jupiter condemned Prometheus, when he released him from captivity, to wear in memory of that a crown of osiers and an iron ring; and the antiquarian further quotes from the lost *Prometheus Unbound* and the *Sphinx* of Aeschylus to the effect that worshippers wear a crown in honor of Prometheus, thereby symbolically representing his bondage. The crown was thus a memorial of a sacrifice undergone for the good of mankind. But it is in connection with Prometheus that such a crown is associated with Herakles. According to the old mythologists, when Herakles, seeking the golden apples of the Hesperides, came upon Prometheus and slew the eagle which tortured him, Prometheus in gratitude warned him not to seek the apples himself, but to send Atlas for them; which Herakles did, bearing the burden of the heavens the while in Atlas' place. But when Atlas got the apples he proposed to take them himself to Eurystheus (who had set the finding of them to Herakles as his eleventh labor) and leave Herakles to bear the heavens. Again Prometheus counseled his Savior to feign acquiescence, and to beg of Atlas a momentary resumption of the load while he (Herakles) made a wisp-pad for his head. Atlas consented, and of course Herakles left him with his load forever. Thus it is Herakles the Savior that wears the mock crown. This special detail is probably one of the innumerable stories concocted to explain ancient mystery-ritual, from which we can only conclude that in ritual or mystery Prometheus and Herakles were represented as crowned with osiers or weeds. It may have been that such crowns were actually worn by the initiates; and in a cult like that of Mithra, from which the Christists took their Lord's Supper, an ascetic crown of thorns would be likely enough. A symbolical crown of some sort was certainly used, on the testimony of Tertullian. In the

Magian Mithra worship, too, the sacrificial victim was crowned; and in pagan cults generally this usage prevailed. We know, too, from Athenaeus that in Egypt crowns of thorns had a special religious vogue, there being certain thorn trees about Abydos whose branches curled into garland form. Any collocation of these garlands with a religious rite could give the hint for the Gospel myth. We have it further from Herodotus that the Greeks had a story that when Herakles landed in Egypt the Egyptians crowned him with a garland and led him in procession, intending to sacrifice him to their supreme God; but when he got to the altar the hero fell upon them and slew them. Herodotus warmly repudiates this story, on the score that the Egyptians had no human sacrifices; but it points none the less to an Egyptian ritual in which a Savior-God was led as a prisoner in procession wearing a crown, probably one of those in use at Abydos. At bottom, as above suggested, the whole ritual might very well be symbolical of the ancient nimbus.

But there is the alternative explanation so ingeniously wrought out by Sir James Frazer in *The Golden Bough*. He has shown that in the ancient Babylonian festival of the Sacaea a prisoner condemned to death was dressed in the king's robes, throned, and allowed to disport himself as the king for five days, whereafter he was stripped, scourged, and crucified. This was a combination of the common practice of sacrificing criminals as scapegoats, and of the special usage of slaying a divine man by way of renewing the youth of vegetation in particular and life in general. In all of these sacrifices, as in that of criminals to Apollo in the festival of Thargelia at Athens, the victim was crowned, like the animal victim in ordinary sacrifices. Here, then, we have a likely source, not only of the tale of the mock crowning of Jesus, but of the proposed substitution of the criminal Barabbas, who in the time of Origen figured in most manuscripts as being named *Jesus Barabbas*. And in the care taken by the Greeks in the Thargelia to remove the body of the slain victim to a distance we may have the true clue to the story of the removal of the body of the crucified Christ. Given an ancient Christist ritual mystery, this might well be an integral part of it. The drink of gall, as a matter of fact, figured in the mysteries of Dêmêtêr.

Another item in the Gospel story can with still greater probability be traced to pagan myth and art. One of the subsidiary labors of Herakles was the setting up of two pillars at Gades (Cadiz) to mark the boundaries of Europe and Libya. Here the cult of Herakles combines with that of his Phœnician double, the sun god Melkarth, worshipped at Gades, of whose mythus the Samson legend in the Hebrew Bible is a variant. The two pillars (represented in the Hebrew as in the Phœnician temples) are simply ancient symbol-limits of the course of the sun in the heavens; and, as usual, we have a variety of legends in the different mythologies to explain them. In the Samson legend they occur twice, figuring in one episode as the gateposts of Gaza which the hero carries off; in another as the two pillars of the Philistine hall, between which the shorn and blinded hero sits in his captivity; Samson here being the winter sun, weak and rayless, at the end of his course, and therefore, touching at least one pillar. Now, just as Samson in one story carries the pillars, so did Herakles, as became his strength, carry his pillars to their places; even as, in the Tyrian form of the legend, he dies at the very place where he has set them up. And in ancient art he was actually represented carrying the two pillars in such a way under his arms that they form exactly a cross. Here, probably, we have the origin of the myth of Jesus carrying his own cross to the place of execution. Christian art has always represented him staggering under the load, as even Herakles stoops with the weight of his columns. Singularly enough, the three Synoptics substitute for Jesus as crossbearer one Simon, a man of Cyrene. Cyrene is in Libya, the legendary scene, as we saw, of the pillar-carrying exploit of Herakles; and Simon (Simeon) is the nearest Greek name-form to Samson—which in Greek might be read as Simson, following the Hebrew. But in Palestine Simon, or Sem, was actually a God-name, representing the ancient sun god Semesh, identified with Baal, from whose mythus that of Samson unquestionably arose; and the God Simon was especially worshipped in Samaria. That district, lying between Galilee and Judea, must needs at an early period have tended to affect the Jesuist legend, which in the fourth Gospel makes the Founder visit the region and make converts in it. What more likely than that a representation of the sun hero Simon (so recognizable by the many Jews settled in Greece), carrying his pillars crosswise, should come to figure as that of a man Simon carrying a cross? The two versions of the cross-bearing satisfy us that the story is a myth: is any hypothesis more probable than that Simon the Cyrenian's task is a variant of that of the Cyrenian Simon-Herakles?

If the cross-bearing and thorn-crown motives in the Jesuist legend be thus reducible, like so many others, to a well-established pagan type, the greater, clearly, is the likelihood that the idea of crucifixion is a mythic development on the basis of the simple hanging of the original Jesus ben Pandira, a century before the "Christian era." Not only was the cross symbol, as all scholars now admit, absolutely universal in pre-Christian times, and, as a rule, a recognized symbol of life or immortality, but the actual idea of a mystic or exemplary crucifixion was perfectly familiar in pagan theology. Obvious myth combined with real and legendary history to crystallize the conception. The crucifixion of Antigonus, king of the Jews, would alone set up an enduring impression in Syria and Egypt; and the story of the crucifixion of Cyrus, who had actually figured as a Messiah, or Christos, for the Jews in their prophetic literature, would go still further to establish the myth-motive of a crucified Messiah wherever the Jews went—that is to say, throughout the Greco-Roman empire. The legend of the prepared sacrifice of Isaac, the only-begotten son, in which the son is bound on wood, and a ram finally takes his place, would further serve the record-worshipping Jews as a forecast; as would the story of the saving of the Israelites by the outstretching of the arms of Moses. But over and above all this, a theological crucifixion-motive pervaded mythology in both the East and the West.

The mystic crucifixion, like the cross-symbol, represents rather the coincidence of a number of symbolic and mystic notions than any one in particular. That the cross is, among other things, a phallic emblem, there can be no reasonable doubt; but it is also highly probable that it was from the earliest times associated with the fire sticks, which among the Aryans in India retained a theological sacredness long after they had ceased to be necessary for household uses. In the Vedas, Agni, the fire god, is perpetually figured as a divine child born of the two *aranis*; and to represent the god as being generated by the friction of the crossed sticks would be to figure him on the cross. And this is the probable origin of various symbolic combinations of the cross with the sun: as the figuring of the deity in the Assyrian system as a cross, of which the upright is a human figure and the transverse beam a conventionalized pair of wings, a type which in Eastern Mithraic remains becomes a crucified figure; that in turn holding out with one hand a wreath or crown, which was doubtless connected with the use of a crown (of thorns?) in the Mithraic mysteries. And in the *Mihr Yasht* ritual, in the Zend Avesta, Mithra, the sun god, drives in his chariot across the heavens "with his arms lifted up towards immortality." It is a perfectly intelligible variation of the same idea which appears in the myth of Ixion, crucified on his "four-spoked fetter," as Pindar calls it. Ixion was himself, undoubtedly, in some mythology, at some time, the actual sun god, and would as such be figured outstretched at once on the fire cross and on the sun wheel. But the apparent torture of the mystic position, misunderstood by worshipers of another system, would appear as a punishment, and so we have the myth of the presumptuous guest of Olympus, who dared to aspire to the favors of the Queen of Heaven, and is first baffled by Zeus' substitution of a cloud for Hera, and then bound by Hermes, on Zeus' command, to the fiery wheel which revolves forever in Hades. How easily any such story found currency is further shown by the transference of the four-spoked-wheel motive to the bird Iünx (the wryneck) for no better reason, perhaps, than the resemblance of its name to that of Ixion, though here again we may be touching primeval Aryan mythology, for the zig-zagging lightning is in mythology a bird—eagle, hawk, or woodpecker; and certain birds were fabled to be fallen flashes of lightning. At Babylon four Iünxes were figured in gold on the canopy, or roof, of the king's throne-room, "to keep the king in memory of the goddess of vengeance," and the mages called them the "tongues of the Gods." In the Vedic hymns, again, Agni, the fire god, is a "golden-winged bird," and his thunderbolts are "well-winged ones"; while Indra, the thunderer, is "the well-winged red one"; and the sun itself and the moon are well-winged birds which fly round the tree of the sky. With all this the winged sun god of Assyrian and Egyptian art, and the winged sun angel of Christism, connect easily enough. The step to the messianic sacrifice is only a stage further.

In this crucifixion of the sun god or fire god, again, we have one of the clues of the myth of Prometheus. Despite some recent German skepticism, the connection of Prometheus, the fire-bringer or fire-stealer, with the Sanskrit *Pramantha*, or fire-generating boring-stick, and the variant word *pramāthyus* (borer or robber) seems sufficiently well made out; and the mythical chaining of Prometheus on a rock on the Caucasus, in such wise that he cannot keep the eagle of Zeus from gnawing his liver, implies the posture of crucifixion. Lucian, indeed, expressly describes him as crucified by Zeus. In one version, however, the chains of

Prometheus are passed through the middle of a column; and here we are brought in touch with the form of the suffering-savior myth in which the god is fastened to a tree. Phoroneus, son of Inachos the water god (probably = Noach = Enoch), who in Argos was revered as the fire-bringer, as Prometheus was elsewhre, had for mother the nymph Melia (the ash); and though Steinthal perhaps assumes too readily that he was figured as a bird, from the derivation of his name from the Sanskrit epithet of Agni, *bhuranyus* (rapid, darting, flying), still the Greek name of his mother connects him with the tree. And the fact that on the one hand Prometheus was said to have made men from clay, and that on the other Phoroneus was fabled by some to be the first man, brings us still further into connection with the Greco-Jewish significance of the God-Christ, who as Logos had presided over the creation of the world.

The actual use of the symbolic tree, however, is best known in connection with the widespread ascetic worship of the self-castrated god-man Attis, who was specially honored in relation to Cybele, the virgin mother, from March 22 to 27, a date pointing at once to the vernal equinox and the arrival of spring. At that season the sacred tree of Attis—a pine—was cut down, and was carried, swathed and crowned with violets, to the temple of the Great Goddess as a symbol of the lost demigod. Then he was sought for in the hills and woods with a ritual of frenzy and lamentation, which after three days was followed by jubilation on his being given out to be found again. Attis was fabled to have been changed into the pine by the goddess in punishment for his breach of chastity; but the tree seems similarly to have been identified with the nymph he loved; and Julian, telling that the symbolic tree was annually cut down "at the moment when the sun arrives at the extreme point of the equinoctial arc," states that the cutting of the tree "has nothing to do with the rites which it accompanies." These were "holy and not to be divulged," and included "the sacred and ineffable harvest of the God Gallos," that is *castratus*. Obviously the cut pine symbolized the cut phallus, the life principle of nature and humanity. We learn from the Christian Father, Julius Firmicus, who had no scruple about publishing pagan mysteries, that on the pine tree there was bound the image of a youth; and the same writer reveals that a ritual of tree and image existed also in the worship of Isis and Osiris and in the cult of the Virgin Persephonê. In the Isiac mysteries the coffin of Osiris would seem from this evidence to have been a hollowed pine tree; and in those of Persephonê the "sacred tree," after being cut, was formed into the image of a virgin, over which the worshippers lamented for forty nights, burning it on the fortieth.

Here we have the *arbor crucis*, clearly enough, along with the whole idea of suffering, mourning, resurrection, and rejoicing. Attis, risen, became "Papa," Father and Lord; as Osiris remains the Father-God, Creator and Judge of all flesh, soul of the world, and Savior of mankind. And Dionysos, on the whole the most popular of the Greco-Roman deities in the period just before Christianity, is in the same way a god of the sacred tree, a savior, and a sacrifice. One of his epithets was *Dendrites*, (pertaining to the tree); he had his sacred pillar; and in Bœotia he was called *endendros*, (in the tree). In his case the divine suffering does not seem to have been undergone in that connection; like Mithra, he *is* the victim sacrificed in his cult; and as Mithra was certainly the divine bull, and equally the divine ram or lamb, so Dionysos was the divine bull, and doubtless also the divine ram, which was most commonly sacrificed to him, as being the animal into which, in one legend, he was actually turned by Zeus in his childhood to save him from Hera. In his childhood, however, in a common story, he is actually slain by the Titans; and in various legends he suffers persecution. In his case, no doubt, his special association with the vine gave the determining bent to the symbolism of the cult; but his wooden images were made of the phallic fig-tree, and a stump of that sometimes symbolized him. In Egypt, again, all cultivated trees were sacred to Osiris. Whether or not, or in what order, these systems borrowed from one another, it is now very hard to trace; but the presence of the sacred tree = cross in so many cults proves the universality of the idea. Attis, the unsexed youth, though probably in origin a god of vegetation, finally represents the combination of sun-worship and moon-worship, and the transference to the moon god, *Deus Lunus*, of the sex attributes of the moon goddess; while his worship at the vernal equinox in connection with the Mighty Mother identifies him in one aspect with the sun, then supposed to be reunited with the earth, and so to renew vegetation. The cult was to all appearance of Asiatic origin, as was certainly that of Mithra, another composite deity, who, however, represented sun and moon in being twy-sexed, not unsexed, and who is represented in art and symbol with a crescent behind his shoulders, making, as Firmicus vehemently insists, a virtual crucifix. In his cult, too, as we gather from the monuments, there figured the sacred tree; and at the foot of this tree, on the sacred anniversary, there was sacrificed a ram, that is, a male lamb, for the sacrifice must be immaculate. Osiris, again, finally represents a great complex of myth, being at once night-sun and day-sun, moon, moisture, Nile, seed, and other principles; and Persephonê, yet again, is the buried "germinal one," whom the Mater Dolorosa seeks with lamentations, and who is finally restored to her mother for part of the year, living above as fruit and grain, and beneath as seed: whence the myth of her capture by Pluto and her queenship of Hades.

But the full mythic significance of the sacred tree in all these systems cannot here be traced. In the religion of ancient Gaul its cultus seems to have been closely connected with the cannibalistic holy communion, since the victims slain to be eaten were first crucified in the temples. Enough that it seems to have been a world-wide myth; and that in ancient Mexico, strangely enough, there was developed the closest parallel to the Christian cultus. The sacred tree was there made into a cross on which was exposed a baked-dough figure of a savior god; and this was after a time climbed for, taken down, broken up, and sacramentally eaten. The very name of the Mexican cross meant "tree of our life, or flesh." And there too the cross-figure had a special religious significance, one of the hideous rites of the system being the standing of the murderous priest in the skin of a newly-slain woman victim; with his hands spread out "like a cross," before the image of the war god.

That the cross-symbol had already many centuries before the Christian era acquired an abstract or mystical importance in Greek theology is shown by the singular proposition in the *Timaeus* of Plato, to the effect that when God had compounded the soul of the universe he divided it lengthways into two parts which he joined together "like the figure of a ⅄," and so imposed it on the world. Not only does Justin Martyr cite this in support of the doctrine of the crucifixion of the Logos, but we know that the populace of Antioch in the time of Julian, referring to the Christian reign of Constantius as the time of "*Chi* and *Kappa*," signified their favorite savior god's name by the initial letter which itself was one of the names for the cross.

That the phallic significance of the cross should connect with all its other aspects is perfectly intelligible. For primitive peoples—and in that definition we may include the populace of civilized paganism—such symbolism was in no way monstrous, being perfectly spontaneous and natural; and the raging invective of the Christian Fathers against the pagan usages proved, not the vice of the pagans, but the growth of a new sophistication and sense of sin and shame, which, rising in Greece with the ascetic and flesh-mortifying cults as it had done among Jews and Orientals, became specially associated with Christianity, the religion par excellence of salvation-buying self-abasement. As Voltaire long ago pointed out, what are to us indecent practices could not have been so to the people who invented them. It was in the nature of religious evolution that symbolism should crystallize; and long ritualistic association of the sacred tree or cross with the God's suffering and death would give it a special significance of that kind for the devout. Still, the fact remains that the vogue of the symbol was in large measure first secured by its popular emblematic meaning; and inasmuch as the cross was thus already an amulet of life-preserving virtue, Christism profited by its acceptance, and could make that the basis for a new mystico-historical doctrine, of the kind which formed the staple of ancient theology. Wherever Christism went, the cross was before it; and when it was found that the ancient symbolical rosary was tenaciously preserved along with the correlative emblem, Christism simply adopted the rosary as it had done the cross. The vitality of the popular notion has been shown by the retention of phallic ceremonial in parts of Christian France and Italy down to our own time. And in respect of at least one symbol, Christism traded from the outset on pagan usage. The bishop's crozier, or pastoral staff, had unquestionably an emblematic meaning in the Osirian cult, from which the Christians deliberately appropriated it; and here the symbolism of cross, crozier, and tree of life was, as we saw, specially bound up with the worship of a slain savior god. "The emblem became the *stauros*, or cross of Osiris, and a new source of mythology was thus laid open. To the Egyptian the cross thus became the symbol of immortality, *and the God himself was crucified to the tree which denoted his fructifying power.*" The ritual lamentation of the divine sisters, Isis and Nephthys, for Osiris is found in the temple remains of the island of Philae expressly connected with the representation of Osiris in the form of a crucifix, the God's head standing on the top of a four-barred Nilometer, faced by the mourning female figures. Here, too, he represents the Trinity, combining the attributes of Phtah-Sokari-Osiris. There need then be no perplexity for rationalist students in regard to the text in Revelation (11:8) about "the great city which spiritually is called Sodom and Egypt, where also their [in many Greek versions *our*, as in our A. V.] Lord was crucified."

Yet again, the common representation of the Hermae (figures or emblems of Hermes, god of boundaries, serving as landmarks), in the form of a cross with a head for top, would connect the cross in particular with the doctrine of the Logos or Word, Hermes being the Logos in Greek theosophy long before the Christian era. Yet further, the recognized use of the *cruz ansata* as the symbol of Venus, and the worship of it as such in her cult, would connect the emblem just as effectively with a doctrine of love. In fine, throughout the civilized world, and equally in the uncivilized, the symbol of the cross was found more or less directly associated with deity. It was built into the foundations of Egyptian temples; it is found in mosaic, with a superimposed head of Neptune, making it a crucifix, in the ruins of a Gallo-Roman villa; it was the sign by which Osiris gave eternal life to the spirits of the just; it was the hammer (= lightning) with which northern Thor (Thonr, thunder = Indra) slew the serpent and restored the slain to life. Always it meant salvation, life; often it meant the death of a God.

The instance of Neptune brings us, finally, to another fruitful source of cross-mythology. In his early Etruscan form, as Nethuns, he appears to have been a solar deity, standing for the risen sun. In any case, as a god of the underworld, ruling the sea, but meddling with the affairs of the earth, he would figure on a cross as representing his divided or overlapping power. But most clearly does the cosmological significance of the cross appear in the astronomical representation of the lamb or ram of the zodiac, which is actually that of a quasi-crucifixion of the animal by the crossing lines of the equinoctial arcs. Astronomically speaking, the back of the zodiacal sign Areis is about ten degrees in length, and the equinoctial colure, or intersecting line, would pass through it at one part or another during seven centuries. Here, then, was the lamb on the cross in astronomy, and by consequence in the religious mysteries. Melito of Sardis, arguing that "the Lord was a lamb, like the ram which Abraham saw caught in the bush," explains that the bush "represented the cross." And the killing of the Lamb at the foot of the sacred tree, above referred to, was doubtless a symbolic sacrifice of zodiacal bearing, as was the earlier slaying of the bull by Mithra. The entrance of the sun into Aries, too, was for the ancients the birthday of the world; and Aries was thus the chief of the signs, all of which were in their turn identified with the sun god. The further significance of the lamb as symbolizing purity is likewise apparent in pagan cults before Christianity. While Hermes, who as *Kriophoros*, the Ram-bearer, supplied the art-type for the good shepherd, had no special repute for purity, Apollo, who also was named *Nomios*, the pastoral, and lamb-haired, or lamb-fleeced, is repeatedly specified by Pindar (despite the countervailing legends) as "the chaste God"; and the Greek *hagnos* (chaste), would certainly be coupled with the Latin *agnus* (lamb), throughout the

Roman Empire. In Apollo's own temple of Larissa the oracle was given out by a priestess, who once a month tasted by night of the blood of a sacrificed lamb, and became possessed by the God. Here we have one more precedent for the Christian sacrament. But a ritual lament for a slain lamb is further pointed to by the Song of "Linus," a name apparently given by misunderstanding on the part of the Greeks to Adonis or some other Syrian god, who was fabled to have grown up "among the lambs" and been slain by wild dogs, and who probably figured the destruction of the fresh spring by the summer heat. And though the Jewish Passover, with its sacrificed lamb, had a different pretext, that too has clearly an astronomical basis, its date being determined by certain relations of sun and moon. Ancient mythology is a shoreless sea of dreams, of which we can only say that in their strange way they too must represent the working of constant psychological law, if we could but catch and follow the clues.

To sum up, then: the story of the crucifixion, first, *may* rest on the remote datum of an actual crucifixion of Jesus Ben Pandira, the probable Jesus of Paul, dead long before, and represented by no preserved biography or teachings whatever. But had this Jesus really been only "hanged on a tree," the factors of a crucifixion myth were strong enough to turn the hanging into a crucifixion.

Secondly, whether or not Jesus Ben Pandira was actually crucified, it was the mythic significance of crucifixion that made the early fortune of the cult, with the aid of the mythic significance of the name Jesus or Jeschu=Joshua, the ancient sun god.

Thirdly, the whole apparatus of the Gospel crucifixion is pure myth. The Last Supper, the Passion, the betrayal, the denial, the trial, the false witnesses, Pilate's wife's dream, Pilate's repudiation of responsibility, the substitution of Barabbas, the crown of thorns, the gall and vinegar, the carrying of the cross, the mocking inscription, the talk of the two thieves, the "My God, my God, why hast thou forsaken me?" (a quotation from Ps. 22:1), the "It is finished"—all these details are as truly mythical as the rending of the temple veil, the preternatural darkness, the rising of the saints from their graves, and the rising of the crucified one from the rock tomb. The nonmiraculous items are historically as unfounded as the miraculous. All alike are late accretions, probably dramatic; and to take them as history is no more reasonable then to see history in the *Bacchae* of Euripides.

THE SEAMLESS TUNIC

The account in the fourth Gospel of the parting of the God's garments among the soldiers is a good instance in little of the process of myth-making. In the Synoptics it is simply stated that the soldiers cast lots for the garments, such being doubtless the practice at executions; the "prophecy" in the Pslam 22:18 being as a matter of course kept in mind, though not cited. But in the fourth Gospel a late hand was wrought up the narrative with singular infelicity, describing the Roman soldiers as piously agreeing among themselves to fulfil the Jewish prophecy by abstaining from rending the Lord's *chiton*, or inner garment, which was "without seam, woven from the top throughout," at the same time dividing the other garments into "four parts, to every soldier a part." In order to lay stress on the seamless character of the tunic, resort is had to the absurdity of suggesting that the natural procedure of the soldiers with such a tunic would be to cut it up, thereby making it worthless. Absolute myth is set forth with the circumstantiality of an eyewitness, very likely on the strength of a dramatic representation.

Like the water-into-wine miracle, equally special to the fourth Gospel, the myth of the seamless robe is specifically pagan. In Sparta, says Pausanias concerning his own day, "every year the women weave a chiton for Apollo at Amyclae; and they call the place where they weave it Chiton." So at Elis every fifth year sixteen matrons wove a peplos or shawl for Hera, a special place being appointed for the work in this case also. The function was rated high, in some cults the robe had a mystic as well as sacred significance. Whether or not this significance was stressed in later Greece, it has entirely disappeared in the Christian myth, where the story of the seamless chiton has no point whatever.

The mystic meaning, however, is obvious enough. As Plutarch tells, the robe of the solar Osiris, unlike that of Isis, is one, whole, and indivisible, that robe being the universal light; whereas the light of the moon is variable and chequered, and the robe if Isis is accordingly so made; both robes being actually so represented in the mysteries and in the monuments. But the two symbols blend. The solar child Cyrus, like the young Joseph, is clothed in "a coat of many colors." In the Magian system, again, "Ahura Mazda, together with Mithra, Rashnu, and Spenta Armaita, puts on a garment decked with stars, and made by God in such a way that *nobody can see the ends of its parts.*" So in the Orphic and other mysteries the sun god's robe is a purple peplos—like that put on Jesus by the mocking soldiery—with a fawnskin added to symbolize the dappled night sky, and a golden cincture to mark the sun's path. Pan, yet again, wears a deerskin of many colors to represent "the all"; and for Clement of Alexandria the robe of the high priest is "the symbol of the world of sense." Nearly every god has his typic garment. Dionysos, the god of the night sun, wears the dappled deerskin as being "an image of the starlight in which he is clothed"; Attis is crowned by Cybele with a starry cap; and Sosipolis, the guardian god of Elis, is figured as a boy in a many colored cloak covered with stars.

It is probable that in the early Christian dramatic mystery most of the details of the symbolic vestures of the other cults were reproduced in the garments divided into "four parts"; and not unlikely that the whole procedure of the "gorgeous apparel" was copied in the first instance from one of the mimic cults already described. But a myth Christianized was a myth materialized; and the seamless tunic has for the Christian world become a meaningless particular, like the many-colored coat of Joseph.

THE BURIAL AND RESURRECTION

Such narratives as those of the rock-burial and resurrection of the savior-god in the Gospels are beyond all reasonable doubt simple developments of those mourning rituals which we have seen to be in use in so many ancient systems. The lost Persephonê was mourned for forty nights; the lost Attis and Adonis were sought for with lamentation, followed by rejoicing, when they were ceremonialy found; the body of the slain Osiris was searched for with lamentation; and the prepared image, when found, seems to have been further mourned over and then rejoiced over. Whatever may have been the order of the ceremony, it is certain that the burying of an image of the slain God was a regular part of it. And, above all, in the cult of Mithra is the basis of the Gospel legend apparent. There the stone image of the "God from the rock" was laid on a bier, was mourned for, was placed in his rock tomb in the sacred cave, was withdrawn from that tomb, and was liturgically rejoiced over. The early Christians who adopted the Mithraists' Lord's Supper, adopted at the same time their resurrection mystery; and the church finally made an explanatory legend out of the ritual, just as the pagans did in myths innumerable. The later authorized myth of the descent into hell is only a development or variation of the god's death and burial, and was already especially familiar in the mysteries of Dionysos, who descended to Hades to bring back his mother Semelê and carry her to heaven; and in the worship of Attis, whose "flight," "concealment," "vanishing," and "descent into the cave" are all specified by Julian as part of the mysteries of the vernal equinox. The only wonder is that, seeing the Athenians celebrated the mysteries of Dêmêtêr twice a year, the lesser mysteries at the vernal equinox and the greater at the autumnal, the Christist system did not adapt both, as the Attis worshippers seem to have done. That it did not do so is doubtless due to the greater vogue (despite the name "lesser") of the vernal celebration.

That the contradictory Christian details as to the manner of the finding of the slain god's body are to be explained by the natural variations of their special mystery-drama we have already seen. The "Maries" in particular belong to the Judaic environment. Such circumstantialities give an air of reality to the story so long as their discrepancies are ignored. But when all the phenomena are alike taken into account, the solution supplied by comparative mythology is found to meet every aspect of the problem.

THE BANQUET OF SEVEN

In a chapter which is obviously a late appendix to the fourth Gospel (John 21) we have one more addition to the resurrection myth of the Synoptics. The risen God appears to seven of his disciples by the sea of Tiberias, and after helping them to a great haul of fish, causes them to partake of a meal of fish and bread, he himself not being represented as eating. In Mark and Luke we have two different stories. Mark gives us a manifestation to the eleven "as they sat at meat"; and Luke gives the story of the "two of them" on the way to Emmaus, to whom the God gives bread, followed by his appearance to "the eleven," on which occasion he himself eats broiled fish. The narrative in Mark is in the admittedly-late appendix (16:9-20); and that in Luke also may confidently be pronounced a late compilation, in view of its giving details which the other Gospels lack. The unhistorical character of the whole set of stories is too obvious to need enforcement; but it seems possible to throw greater light on their origin than has yet been done. In all, we have stress laid on the act of eating, either by the god or those to whom he ministers; and in a religious ceremonial of eating we may look to find the origin of the various myths.

As regards the party of seven, the cue lies to hand in the Mithraic catacomb remains. The banquet of the *Septem Pii Sacerdotes*, the seven holy priests, there represented as part of the syncretic cult of Mithras-Sabazios, was in all probability a feature in the cult of Dionysos, who also was identified with Sabazios; and the Christian story is simply one more case of a myth invented to explain a ritual usage. The wide vogue of that is to be inferred from the fact that a set of seven priests figures repeatedly in the Veda; and that a group of seven rulers of sacrificial feasts existed in pagan Rome. The materials of the banquet in the catacomb painting are noteworthy. There is a pasty, a hare, a fish, an object which the Abbé Garucci calls a goose, but which is smaller than the hare, and might be a lobster; and eight cakes or muffins, red in color, each marked with a cross and four dots or punctures—exactly the cross and "four wounds" of the Christian myth, represented on the solar disc. In the Christian story we have simply bread and fish, as befitted a poor and struggling cultus and the circumstances of the Jesuist legend; but it is significant that in the supposed Christian catacomb paintings which represent a banquet of seven—and which orthodoxy supposes to represent the episode in the fourth Gospel, without a word of regard to the admittedly Mithraic remains—there are commonly *eight basketsful* of bread. This number is viewed by the Catholics as indicating that the early Christians aimed at a symbolical truth, and to that end deliberately disregarded literal accuracy; not a word being said, again of the eight cakes or crossbuns on the table of the *Septem Pii Sacerdotes*. It is a curious circumstance that in one of these "Christian" catacomb pictures the seven figures are nude. We may surmise that a picture in which one of the seven was clothed would suffice to motive the odd statement (John 21:7) that Peter, previously naked, drew a garment about him when he was about to plunge into the sea. The frequency of the subject, as compared with the ostensibly much more important Supper of the Twelve, is a sufficient proof that it rested on some broader and older basis than the solitary narrative of the fourth Gospel.

Whether the story of the meeting with the eleven does not rest on some similar ancient ceremonial, and whether the myth of the meeting on the way to Emmaus is not in turn based on some concrete fact in ancient art or hierology, we cannot at present pretend to decide. Two things only have to be borne in mind in that connection. The story of the treachery of Judas, as we have seen, is as mythical as any of the details we have been considering; and just as the number twelve is a factitious arrangement, so may the number eleven have been determined by some outside fact, and the betrayal story have been framed in consequence. As our knowledge stands, however, the probable solution seems to be that the banquet of the eleven is a late invention, which sought to supersede or outweigh the Banquet of Seven, of which the pagan origin and vogue were notorious, by a story more in harmony with the established Christian tradition. On that view, the Banquet of Seven, mythic in itself, is the occasion of the other myth.

THE ASCENSION

Of all the Christian miracles, this is perhaps the most obviously a fable born of ignorance. Only in a world living under the primitive delusion of a flat earth and a solid overarching firmament could such a fable have been framed; and it is a standing proof of the moral frailty of the religious intelligence that such a tale is still allowed to perplex and delude the simple. Orthodoxy may however be a little more ready to consent to its disappearance when the mass of Christians realize that it is one more of the standing myths of paganism. Even as Enoch and Elijah, mythic figures both, ascend to heaven in the Old Testament, so does demigod after demigod ascend to godhood in the heathen world. Krishna thus mounts through the firmament of Indra. At Byblos, after the annual mourning over the dead Adonis, he was believed to rise on the second day and mount to heaven in the presence of his worshippers. Herakles in turn rises to heaven and immortality from the funeral-pyre which in his case rounds the solar myth, the suggestion coming from the spectacle of the litten clouds of sunset. So Dionysos in one account ascends to heaven with his consort Ariadne, in others with his mother Semelê; which latter myth is supplied, in the Christian system, only after the Gospel-making period, by the doctrine and the festival of the assumption of the Virgin Mary. Such beliefs were in the ordinary way of opinion in an age in which it was quite worth while to go through the procedure of letting loose an eagle from the funeral pyre of each deceased emperor by way of demonstrating *his* ascent to heaven.

True, there were many scoffers; and it lies on the face of the Gospels, especially of the fourth, that the Gospel-makers relied for credence much more on their elaborated circumstantial stories of the risen god's reappearances than on that of his ascension, which in the Synoptics is barely alleged, and which in the fourth Gospel is not asserted at all. But Christianity rose, in an atmosphere of thickening superstition, with the decline of ancient knowledge and civilization; and the ascension myth, once set up for modern Christendom, is thus far no more expungible by the science of Copernicus and Newton than were the pellmell of pagan myths by the better knowledge of antiquity. *Absit omen.*

Be the event what it may, the general truth is such as he who runs may read. In the fourth century, the exasperated Firmicus, met at every point by pagan precedent for the legends of his gospels, could only shriek: "*Habet Diabolus Christos suos*—the Devil has *his* Christs." We have now seen in some detail that the Christs, that of Firmicus included, were all man's. The Jesuist system is only one phase in a continuous development of ancient religion, in which god after god, name after name, is associated with the same immemorial and dimly comprehended symbols. In all probability there has been no long break for many thousands of years in the celebration of the sacred birthday on Christmas Day at the Tammuzcave at Bethlehem; and only a slight variation in the dramatic ceremonial of the death of the god at Easter, which is still regularly performed at Jerusalem. Long before biblical Judaism was known, the people of Palestine shared in the universal rituals of the primeval cults of sun and moon, nature and symbol; and the successive waves of conquest, physical and mystical, have only transformed the primordial hallucination. It might well last two thousand years more after subsisting from the dawn of civilization; and it will disappear only when all hallucination alike is solved in science.

Willi Marxsen

The Resurrection

WILLI MARXSEN born in Kiel, Germany, in 1919, studied at the University of Kiel, where from 1954 he served as *Privatdozent* (private lecturer) before becoming a full professor in 1961. He is now head of the New Testament department and professor of New Testament at the University of Münster. Marxsen's most important works are *Der Evangelist Markus* (1958) and *The Resurrection of Jesus of Nazareth* (1964).

It was only in the last two centuries of the pre-Christian era that hope of a future life for the individual penetrated Judaism (probably from Zoroastrianism) in the form of hope of the resurrection of the dead. This idea was then developed in many different ways, especially in the late Jewish Apocalypses. At the end of time, either all the dead will rise, or only the righteous, or only Israel. The idea of judgment is frequently coupled with this. There is also the notion of a double resurrection, the idea of a kingdom lasting a thousand years at the beginning of which some, and at the end of which all, will rise.

Characteristic of this new development is the expectation that the flesh, or body, will be raised. The shades who have meanwhile remained in the under-world receive new life and men will be once more the same as they were during their lifetimes. At all events, the flesh (always in the sense of the body) here plays the decisive role. This is the case even if the body is not in entirely the same form as before, being now without sickness, infirmity, or physical blemish. The future world is an intact world. That is really what Matthew 11:5 is saying: that the

From *The Resurrection of Jesus of Nazareth* by Willi Marxsen, trans. by M. Kohl (Philadelphia: Fortress Press, Copyright © 1970; London: SCM Press; Gütersloh, West Germany: Gütersloh Verlagshaus, 1970), p. 72-74 and 134-137. Reprinted by permission of the publishers.

blind will see, the lame will walk, lepers will be cleansed, the deaf will hear and the dead will be raised up. This is a gathering up of expectations about the end-time. In claiming that Jesus did all these things, the intention is to say that Jesus already brings about what was expected of the end-time.

Now we know that at the time of Jesus there was a dispute about whether there was a resurrection of the dead. The Pharisees said that there was. The Sadducees denied it (Acts 23:8); and they denied it for interesting reasons. They represented a consistent orthodoxy. The doctrine of the resurrection of the dead was not a genuine Jewish teaching found in the Old Testament; it had penetrated Judaism through outside influence. The ancient heritage had been altered by what was then a modern philosophy. The Sadducees pointed out that there was no scriptural authority for the doctrine of the resurrection of the dead. Anyone who was orthodox, who was determined to adhere to "the faith of our fathers," who did not want to relinquish the Old Testament and desired "no other gospel" (and this was all true of the Sadducees) was bound to reject this teaching of "modern theology." One did not want to fall a victim to "modernism"! But the Sadducees could not hold back the tide. Expectation of the resurrection of the dead had become general among the Jews. In the second of the "Eighteen Benedictions" of the Jewish liturgy God is praised as "Thou that quickenest ('or will resurrect') the dead."

But this idea soon came under Hellenistic influence also. This is hardly surprising, for it is easy to see how Jews who brought with them a dichotomic anthropology might soon, under Hellenistic Greek influence, interpret this in a dualistic sense. The ground had already been prepared conceptually through the twofold division.

If we now ask in what sense the resurrection of the dead was understood at the time of Jesus, it is hard to find a precise answer, because ideas differed and the concept by itself does not tell one anything about the notions which it embodies. This can be clearly seen in the New Testament. Up to a point we have already noticed it in the course of our examination of the texts. There, resurrection can be understood in highly "material" terms. This is so in the stories of the empty tomb and in the passages where the risen Jesus can be touched or where he eats with, or in the presence of, his disciples. Jewish ideas undoubtedly play a part here. But running parallel to these are ideas couched in less physical terms. The risen Jesus goes through closed doors, he is taken to be a spirit. This is no longer in accord with Jewish ideas.

A further aspect comes into view when we turn to John's Gospel and look not so much at stories about the resurrection of Jesus as at what is said about the resurrection of the dead. Before the raising of Lazarus Jesus says to Martha: "Your brother will rise again." Martha, assuming the Jewish view, replies: "I know that he will rise again in the resurrection at the last day." But Jesus now corrects or modified this opinion by saying: "*I* am the resurrection and the life; he who believes in me, though he die, yet shall he live, and whoever lives and believes in me shall never die" (John 11:25-6). Even clearer, perhaps, is another saying of Jesus found in the fourth Gospel: "Truly, truly, I say to you, he who hears my word and believes him who sent me, has eternal life; he does not come into judgment, but has passed from death to life" (John 5:24). This could have been said by a Gnostic, for what is being asserted is the very thing that is rejected as false doctrine in 2 Timothy 2:18: eternal life is *here and now*. He that believes *has* eternal life and will not be judged later. To say that John did not understand this saying in a Gnostic sense is another matter. That must be proved exegetically. In our present context the point is merely to show what widely differing ideas about the resurrection are to be found in the New Testament and what the roots of these ideas are. The way in which the different ideas permeate John's Gospel is especially noticeable—how they run parallel to one another, in some cases standing side by side in a completely unrelated way. The almost Gnostic-sounding sayings we have mentioned can be matched by highly "physical" Jewish conceptions. Although Lazarus has been four days in the grave (John 11:17) so that his body is already stinking (John 11:39) he comes out of the grave in bodily form.

All this shows that it is impossible to speak of *the* New Testament view of the resurrection of the dead. If there are people (and they do exist) who think that as Christians we are bound to take over the *conceptions* of the New Testament, one must then ask—which conceptions? And since there is a variety to choose from, who is to decide which ones are to be taken over?

But perhaps the New Testament is not concerned to communicate accurate conceptions at all. Perhaps the current concepts of the time (which are, after all, quite independent of the message of the Gospel) are simply pressed into service as an aid towards formulating a statement. It would then not be particularly surprising that any given statement should avail itself of those concepts which were familiar and current. And in this case it would not be in such concepts that the specifically Christian element need be sought for. There is, after all, no specifically Christian language; the preacher simply takes the language that is available. Translation into another language does not mean a change in the message. Why should this be the case when the prevailing concepts change? We must only be sure that the message—formulated in a new language and with the help of other ideas—remains as close as possible to the original. . . .

At the beginning always stands the story of the empty tomb. I will not go into the different accounts for the moment. We have already seen that Matthew and Luke are dependent on Mark, but that the Johannine tradition (with Mary Magdalene) also has a certain connection with the tradition found in Mark. If the aim were a harmonization, the empty tomb could be said to be the first event in the sequence. Even if later narrators have modified the account (and so no longer present a correct course of events, at least as regards the details) we still have in Mark, at least, the original tradition. But even if something like a harmonization can if necessary be achieved here, insurmountable difficulties begin with the attempt at reconstructing the later course of events.

Most noticeable of all are, first, the differences as regards the places mentioned. Anyone who is aiming at a harmonization must of course make the happenings in and around Jerusalem precede those in Galilee. Then roughly the following series would emerge:

1. The appearances of Jesus to the two women at the tomb (in Matthew; in John to Mary Magdalene only). This is contradicted by Luke, not merely by the way but quite specifically; in fact, he contradicts it in two different ways. (a) The disciples on the road to Emmaus tell their still unknown companion that women had found the tomb empty and that angels had appeared to them; that other disciples had then seen the empty tomb but that *no one had seen Jesus* (Luke 24:24). This is as much as to say that the appearance of Jesus would have set their doubts at rest. Thus the appearance to the women at the tomb is expressly denied. (b) After their return to Jerusalem the story the Emmaus disciples had to tell was anticipated by the cry: "The Lord is risen indeed and has appeared to Simon," the intention being to assert the priority of the appearance to Peter. This appearance must be considered as having taken place in Jerusalem (though not at the empty tomb). At least it is supposed to have been the first. There are therefore two rival statements: the first appearance was to the women at the tomb; the first appearance was to Peter.

2. The appearance to the disciples on the road to Emmaus. Only Luke contributes this story; but since we are told that it took place in the late afternoon and evening of Easter Sunday, two hours' journey from Jerusalem, it does not directly clash with the sequence of the other Gospels. The writers could have left the story out for some reason or other.

3. The appearance to the disciples in a house in Jerusalem. Both Luke (24:36-49) and John (20:19-23) report this, but their accounts differ greatly, the only common features being the demonstration of identity and the missionary charge. Among the many differences, one of particular importance is the gift of the spirit in John, which, according to Luke, only takes place fifty days later. The would-be harmonizer will hardly be inclined to maintain that there were two different appearances. But if there was only one, who reports it correctly? Were the disciples first doubtful (Luke) or were they immediately overjoyed (John)? What were the words with which Jesus sent the disciples forth? Did Jesus breathe on them, giving them the gift of the Holy Spirit (John), or not (Luke)?

4. The appearance to Thomas a week later. Only John relates this. The problem, however, is different from that presented by the story of the Ammaus disciples (see 2 above), for we are bound to ask why the disciples remained so long in Jerusalem, although (according to Matthew) they were supposed to go to Galilee forthwith. Moreover the meeting in Galilee is evidently held out to the disciples as their *first* sight of Jesus.

5. The appearances in Galilee, (a) to the eleven disciples on the mountain in Galilee (end of Matthew's Gospel); (b) to Peter and six other disciples on the occasion of the miraculous draught of fishes (John 21). Here it would be very difficult to determine the order of events. In this connection it must be noted in the first place that Luke excludes the appearances in Galilee—again not merely by the way but quite expressly. This is shown by his deviation in 24:6 from Mark

16:7 (the pointing forward to Galilee becomes a *reminiscence* of Galilee), as well as by Jesus' command to the disciples to remain in Jerusalem until Pentecost (Luke 24:49), a command which they then, according to Luke, obey.

But now other difficulties are added. If we read the end of Matthew with an open mind we do not gather the impression that the appearance here described has been preceded by other appearances to the same group in Jerusalem. Moreover, we ask ourselves why the missionary charge has to be repeated if it has already been given in Jerusalem (see 3 above). The appearance on the occasion of the miraculous draught seems even more curious. The fact that the disciples had already (even according to John himself) received their commission to go out and preach the Gospel has absolutely no influence on the events in John 21. They go about their daily tasks as if nothing had happened.

The conclusion is inescapable: a synchronizing harmony of the different accounts proves to be impossible. Anyone who persists in the attempt must alter the texts and declare the differences to be trivialities. . . .

J. K. Elliott

The Story of the First Easter

J. K. ELLIOTT, lecturer in New Testament studies at the University of Leeds, England, is editor of *Studies in New Testament Language and Texts*. His important studies of the history of early Christianity include *Codex Sinaiticus and the Simonides Affair* (1982) and *Questioning Christian Origins* (1982).

An investigation into the career of Jesus of Nazareth cannot be based only on his birth, baptism, ministry, trial, and death. This sequence needs to be extended to take into account the claim that after his burial he left the tomb and was seen alive by various witnesses. These resurrection appearances are referred to in each of the four New Testament Gospels, and the Easter stories are all told as if they were historical events on the same basis as, say, the crucifixion.

Each Gospel dates Jesus' resurrection from the Sunday after his burial on Good Friday. We may suspect that originally, when it was announced that Jesus had been raised "after three days," all that was meant was "after a short interval," but that, as the tradition developed, this loose expression was made into a literal three-day period: the Friday of the burial, the Saturday in the tomb, and the discovery of the empty tomb some time between darkness after the Saturday and the dawn on Sunday.

The transition between the imprecise and the precise dating of Easter may be seen in the Gospels. The earliest Gospel, Mark, speaks in its Passion predictions of Jesus' being raised "after three days," whereas the parallels to these predictions in the later Gospels alter this to "on the third day" (compare Mark 10:34 with

From *Questioning Christian Origins* by J.K. Elliott (London: SCM Press, 1982), pp. 77-92. Copyright © 1982 by SCM Press. Reprinted by permission.

Luke 18:33). One reason why the resurrection was dated in this way is that the early Christians in their constant search for Old Testament prophecies that seemed to explain and predict events in Jesus' life came across Hosea 6:2 "After two days he will revive us: on the third day he will raise us up" and made this quotation influence the Easter narrative. Another Old Testament passage, explicitly quoted in Matthew's Gospel (12:40), is Jonah 1:17–2:1, which seems to require Jesus to be buried for three days on the analogy of Jonah's "burial" in the whale for that period.

Whatever the reason for this change from Mark to the later accounts, it is a matter of historic fact that the Christian church owes its foundation to the belief that Jesus Christ of Nazareth was raised from the dead on the third day after his death and burial.

Without this belief the sect of the Nazarenes would have generally died out just as the other messianic groups had disappeared. What nourished the original followers of Jesus and turned them from being frightened men at the time of their master's crucifixion into church founders and missionaries was their belief in the resurrection of Jesus.

The reality of this belief is undeniable by anyone who has read the New Testament or the history of Christianity. But whereas we can assert with conviction that the resurrection belief founded the church, we cannot readily assert as fact the resurrection itself.

The New Testament is the foundation document of the Christian faith and is full of the theological implications of the resurrection. Paul in his letters constantly reminds his readers that the church is living in the new age of the spirit because of Christ's resurrection from the dead. He preaches of a changed relationship between man and God on which man's age-old desire for eternal salvation is now pinned. The Gospels all tell of the deeds and sayings of Jesus not because these in themselves were necessarily unique, but because they are attributed to the man who was to be raised from the dead; and each Gospel ends with the message of Jesus' resurrection. Yet the strange thing is that nowhere does the New Testament attempt to discuss the nature of the resurrection, and nowhere is the happening itself described. At the beginning of the Acts of the Apostles the author feels no awkwardness in describing in a literal way the ascension of Jesus from earth to heaven. Similarly, the Gospels find suitable vocabulary with which to depict another supernatural event, namely the alleged transfiguration of Jesus when he speaks with Moses and Elijah. It is therefore strange that no New Testament author attempts to portray the moment when Jesus leaves his tomb, even though stories of raisings from the dead are found in the New Testament Gospels and in Acts, the revivification of Lazarus in the fourth Gospel being the most famous.

Later tradition was slow to describe this episode. The history of Christian art in the West does not show us many examples of the moment of resurrection. We may contrast this with the number of representations of the nativity or the crucifixion.

Although the resurrection itself is not described in the Gospels, the stories of the first Easter tell of the visit of women to Jesus' grave, the finding of the empty tomb and the appearances of the risen Jesus. The stories of the walk to Emmaus and of doubting Thomas are well known. Familiarity, though, can often dull the critical faculty. When we analyze the Easter stories critically in the sequence Mark, Matthew, Luke, John, we find inconsistencies between the accounts that make it difficult for us to accept the historicity of any one account in preference to another. This is in contrast to the stories of the Passion, which are, by and large, in close parallel in all four Gospels.

Mark's Easter story is told in chapter 16:1–8. In this passage we have the visit of the women to the tomb and the angelic messenger's proclamation that Jesus has been raised from the dead. Apart from the surprise ending to this Gospel at verse 8, a point where we might well expect to find a story in which Peter and the other disciples meet the risen Jesus in the Galilee, there are a number of other difficulties in the chapter. The motive of the women in visiting the tomb to anoint the body is unlikely, especially in the East where, if a body was to be anointed at all, it would not be done three days after death. Likewise the Jewish repugnance for tombs and ritual abhorrence for things associated with death makes the women's motive even more unlikely. Their fears about being able to enter the sealed tomb at the beginning of the story only add further weight to our arguments. In the event, of course, the resurrection itself makes their plans unnecessary; but the motive attributed to the women in Mark is even more strange when we remember that only two chapters previously Mark has told the story of the anointing of Jesus at Bethany. Whatever the original context and intention of this anointing (and it is likely to be a reminiscence of a coronation rite in which Jesus becomes the anointed one, that is, a Messiah), Mark has Jesus in the story interpret the act as an anticipatory anointing of his body for burial, thus rendering any further anointing superfluous. Both this reinterpretation by Mark of the anointing story and the way in which he introduces the Easter story probably reflect the embarrassment of the writer and the early church that at the point of death Jesus' body was not accorded the proper burial rites. The perfunctory nature of the burial, as described in the first three Gospels, is probably historic: the early church would not have invented this story, although Mark's burial story may only have been included to anticipate the forthcoming discovery of the empty tomb. The burial needs to be described to establish that Jesus really was dead, and that he was buried in an identifiable tomb, if its subsequent emptying is in any sense to be a proof of the resurrection. The women who visit the tomb on the Sunday also need to be described as eyewitnesses of this burial to counter the objection that they visited the wrong tomb.

Matthew avoids these difficulties by having the women visit the tomb merely as sightseers; and John avoids the embarrassment no doubt felt by Mark that Jesus' body needed anointing at such a late date by stating, in contradiction to the Synoptics, that Jesus' body *was* anointed by Joseph and Nicodemus at point of

316 The Origins of Christianity

death. John, embarrassed by the absence of disciples at the burial (again a detail likely to be historic), makes Joseph of Arimathea "a disciple" by way of compensation. This enhancement of Joseph of course, continued long after the fourth Gospel, in the Glastonbury legends. The only reason why Mark has the women visit the tomb is really so that they can be shown it is empty. The empty tomb in Mark's story is, in effect, intended to be proof that Jesus is risen. "See the place where they laid him," says Mark's angel to underline the statement that Jesus has been raised from the dead. But the empty-tomb tradition, to which we shall return later, is a denial of the miraculous element in the resurrection. If the empty tomb proves that Jesus was raised from the dead, then faith in the event itself is of less significance. What Mark tries to do is to depict the finding of the empty tomb as an historic event. But for various reasons, to be discussed below, the episode is unlikely to be historic.

When we return to Matthew's Gospel, we can see how the tradition behind Mark's account has been altered and dramatized. For instance, Matthew describes the tomb actually opening before the very eyes of the women (the number of whom he reduces from three to two), unlike Mark and John who say it is already open when the visitors arrive. Matthew's purpose in making this alteration is doubtless to prove that the body could not have been stolen. The opening of the tomb is also intended by Matthew to allow the women to see inside—not to allow Jesus to leave. One is left, however, with the deduction that the body was spirited out of the tomb through solid rock. But of even greater significance, especially for the subsequent development of the Easter stories in the Gospel tradition, is the introduction of the risen Jesus into the story. In the rudimentary stage in the development represented here in Matthew 28:9-10 Jesus merely repeats the message given by the angel earlier. Later in the tradition the risen Jesus is given more and more to do and say, so much so that, especially in Luke's and John's Easter accounts, the risen Jesus seems to be little changed from Jesus of Nazareth of the ministry period. In Matthew, the presence of Jesus has made the interpreting angel redundant, and by the time the story reaches John, the angels (John doubles the number) are merely guards at the tomb.

Having thus opened the way for such elaboration of the tradition and for the creation of other stories, Matthew then completes what was implicit in Mark by including a story in which Jesus is seen by the eleven disciples. Jesus here at the end of Matthew's Gospel is a rather stylized figure unlike the later portrayals in Luke's and John's Easter accounts; but we do now have a story in which Jesus is seen by his disciples in the Galilee as promised. Jesus' encounters with the disciples are the most common type of post-resurrection appearance in the New Testament; and it is significant that no neutral witnesses see the risen Jesus. In that final story (Matt. 28:16-20), which forms the climax and conclusion to Matthew's Gospel, the words attributed to Jesus summarize the whole book. In fact, all words attributed to Jesus in the resurrection stories are likely to come not from Jesus but from the evangelist. Matthew's risen Jesus speaks like Matthew, whereas in the fourth Gospel Jesus speaks like John the theologian.

When we turn to Luke's Gospel, there are certain similarities between his Easter morning narrative and the other Gospels' accounts; for example, Luke follows Mark in the motive attributed to the women's visit to the tomb; and he resembles John in having two angels; but there are differences. The number of women is greatly increased, and the statement in Luke 24:22-3 contradicts Matthew and John by denying that any women had seen Jesus at the tomb. The greatest difference in Luke, though, is that several resurrection appearances are described, and all take place in and around Jerusalem, not the Galilee. For Luke and Acts the center of the Jewish world, Jerusalem, is the hub from which Christianity spread out to the Gentile world. For Matthew and Mark the geography of Palestine has a different significance and symbolism. For them Jerusalem is the place where Jesus is killed, and the Galilee, the area where revelations take place, is identified as "Galilee of the Gentiles" (Matt. 4:15-16) leading to the worldwide mission. Luke rounds off the Easter stories more successfully than the other evangelists with the ascension story, which is a device for terminating these post-resurrection appearances.

The increased number of stories, together with the greater attempts at realism in Luke's Gospel, is continued in the fourth Gospel, which similarly has several (but different) Easter narratives. Except in the appendix to this Gospel (John 21), John follows Luke in having the appearances set in Jerusalem. Another feature of the Easter stories in this Gospel is that great stress is placed on the identification of the risen Christ as Jesus of Nazareth.

This sketch of the inconsistencies and changes in the story began with Mark. But an historical investigation into the events of the first Easter should go back further still and get behind Mark's story. The earliest written account of the post-resurrection appearances in the New Testament is of course Paul's. As the only New Testament author who claims to have seen the risen Lord, Paul's testimony is obviously of supreme importance. Paul in 1 Corinthians 15 states that the resurrection took place "according to the scriptures," that is in the Old Testament. But Paul could not quote chapter and verse. A crucified or suffering Messiah was not expected in the Old Testament; hence a resurrected Messiah was not predicted either. Paul's statement must mean that in some way Jesus was the fulfillment of Old Testament prophecy, and that, if he as Messiah was raised from the dead, then somehow and somewhere in the Old Testament such a prediction should be capable of being located. We have often seen in the New Testament how the early Christians did seem to search their Scriptures diligently to make Old Testament prophecies fit Jesus. But the resurrection seems to have baffled them, and no adequate Old Testament quotation is ever produced. Cleopas and his companion on their walk to Emmaus are told merely that biblical witnesses anticipate the resurrection.

In 1 Corinthians 15 Paul lists several people who are said to have seen Jesus after his death. This list includes an appearance to Paul himself. If the accounts of the Damascus road experience in Acts, when Paul sees a blinding light and hears the voice of Jesus, are descriptions of that appearance to Paul referred to in

1 Corinthians, then what is being referred to as a "resurrection appearance" by Paul is obviously of a different genre from the resurrection appearances dramatized in the Gospels. If Paul assumed his experience of the risen Jesus was in any sense comparable to the visions granted to the original disciples in his list (as doubtless he would), then what he thought they had experienced was radically different from what the evangelists later described. Also, unlike the Gospels, Paul does no more than provide a list. There are no details of how, where, or when the Easter encounters took place or what happened. Similarly in Paul, there is a complete silence about the empty tomb; and it is likely that Paul did not know of this tradition. In any case, he is more interested in the present reality and future significance of the resurrection than in the purely historical aspect of the event.

The material in the early chapters of the Acts of the Apostles also contains elements that, we can presume, predate the Gospel material; and in these early chapters the resurrection proclamation is remarkably similar to the primitive teaching in Paul's letters. Again, there is no mention of Jesus' empty tomb, even though Acts 2:29 shows knowledge of the existence of David's grave. In Acts, as in Paul's letters, we find only the proclamation that Jesus, who had been killed and buried, was raised from the dead. And this is the point where Mark takes up the story by developing that proclamation and using it as a vehicle for conveying much theological teaching. There is thus a development through the Gospel tradition from the basic report that Jesus is risen to fully dramatized accounts in which Jesus is seen, speaks, and acts.

From this analysis of the stories of the first Easter in the Gospels it is obvious that we cannot reconcile the accounts or make a harmony of them. The foundations on which the theological teaching on resurrection is based are different in each Gospel, which shows that the early church's belief in Jesus' resurrection did not depend on uniform teaching. The stories, however, can be summarized. The elements in common between the accounts of the first Easter morning are that, after Joseph has placed Jesus' body in a rock tomb and sealed it with a stone, one, two, three, or several women find that stone rolled away on the third day. They enter the tomb and see a young man, or two men, or an angel sitting (according to Mark and Matthew) or standing (according to Luke) in the tomb. The women are then shown the place where Jesus was laid and told he has been raised. They are then given a message to pass on to the disciples. In Luke and Matthew they do so; but in Mark they disobey this command as they are struck dumb—a symptom frequently found in biblical narratives when a person is said to be privy to a divine proclamation. So far as the remaining post-resurrection stories are concerned, there is little common ground between the details in the Gospels. The frequency and nature of the appearances and the participants and circumstances are all different. We cannot treat any of the Easter stories as historical; but we cannot doubt the paramount significance of the narratives for the evangelists; and it is of great profit to examine the motives of the authors who included them. There is no independent witness to the Easter events outside the New Testament; so one must make use of the Gospel material alone.

If the Gospels are to be seen as missionary documents, then the main purpose of the stories in them is to evoke faith. The fourth Gospel states such an aim at the end of the first draft of the Gospel (John 20:30-1: "Jesus did many other signs in the presence of his disciples which are not written in this book, but these are written that you may believe that Jesus is the Christ, the Son of God, and that believing you may have life through his name"). Before this faith could be kindled, however, doubts had to be dismissed. In fact, one of the main motifs running through the stories of Jesus' reappearances is that of doubt. As we have already stated, the resurrection of Jesus was not expected; and therefore both the disciples and subsequent generations of believers had first to be convinced of its reality. What the Gospel writers attempt to do for their contemporaries is to show that the first believers, too, had doubts, but that these were resolved. Doubting Thomas is the most famous of those who needed convincing. The patently apologetic purpose of this episode is underlined by John's postscript, where he says (20:29b) "Blessed are those who have not seen yet have believed," which included the vast bulk of John's contemporaries. The resurrection stories, in other words, are intended to be proofs that Jesus really was raised from the dead. Doubts about this among the evangelists' contemporaries were read back into the life of the immediate post-Easter church. The disciples in Luke think that talk of resurrection is nonsense; the walkers on the way to Emmaus are convinced of Jesus' presence only when he reveals himself to them in breaking the bread (presumably a characteristic and recognizable gesture); Mary in the garden thinks Jesus is the gardener. The evangelists knew that such proofs pro-vided by Jesus' reappearances on earth were not available at the time of writing; hence the reappearance stories are described as occurring rather improbably in a limited period. Luke, for instance, ends the resurrection stories with the story of Jesus' ascension, although he does not indicate the duration between Easter and ascension. It is left for the second volume in the two-part work, Luke–Acts, to specify that this interval was forty days, a number of symbolic significance in Jewish writing. The fourth Gospel, too, in Jesus' command to Mary to cease holding him as he is about to ascend to the Father similarly provides a *terminus ad quem* for the reappearances. Paul's list of resurrection appearances suggests that he, too, is aware that the appearance granted to him was not within the restricted period in which the appearances to the original disciples took place. Despite the necessary limiting of the Easter events, the purpose of these stories is clearly to provide ostensibly historic proofs of the resurrection to putative be-lievers, so that their doubts should disappear just as those of the first disciples are said to have been removed.

Another motif, particularly in the developed tradition, is the attempt to stress the corporeality of Jesus' risen body. In Matthew and the fourth Gospel we read that Jesus' body was capable of being touched: in the fourth Gospel the wounds of his recent crucifixion are visible: in Luke, Jesus eats broiled fish. There is thus a continuity between the risen Lord and Jesus of Nazareth; even Mark makes this point—his angel in 16:7 refers us back to the precrucifixion period with the words "as he told you." Such reminders of Jesus' ministry are obviously intentional. And yet at the same time there is an attempt to show that there is a difference between the two Jesuses. For instance, in some of the Easter stories Jesus passes through closed doors; he reappears and disappears at will; and he is not readily recognizable as he was during the period of his ministry.

The New Testament Gospels' Easter stories appear to reflect here two different traditions—one spiritual, one physical. The nature of Jesus' resurrected body was understandably one that troubled the earliest believers; and it is a trouble reflected not only in the Easter narratives in the Gospels but also in the earlier story where Jesus and the Sadducees are depicted as discussing the nature of the afterlife, and also in 1 Corinthians 15, where Paul attempts to describe the idea of bodily resurrection—an essentially Jewish belief—to an audience obviously reared on Hellenistic philosophical ideas about the immortality of the soul. In the Jewish environment in which Christianity began, whenever Jesus' afterlife was being spoken of, resurrection was the natural way to describe it. Coupled with this, there may well have been an attempt in the early church to counter embryonic docetic or Gnostic heresies about Jesus' body by emphasizing that after death Jesus was still body. These heresies taught that matter was essentially evil, and that it was inconceivable for the son of God to appear in a human body—either before or after death. The evangelists, on the other hand, were at pains to stress that Jesus was the "word become *flesh*" during his ministry, and that even after his death he was no mere spirit. Luke actually has the risen Jesus say he is not a spirit but has flesh and bones. The Christians' attempt in the New Testament to preserve this essentially Jewish concept of describing life after death is the reason why so many of the Easter narratives in the Gospels contain contradictions and difficulties. There is a dichotomy between a spiritualized concept of afterlife, which many of the details in the stories presuppose, and a fully physical corporeal body demanded by the tradition's background and by the evangelists' theology. One can only resolve such difficulties by isolating the separate elements and by explaining these along theological, not historical, lines.

A further *theological* point made by the Easter narratives is that Jesus in his resurrected state is visible only to those who have faith. He is seen only by those who followed him in his lifetime or who subsequently were believers. The story in Matthew of the first Easter Sunday is significant. In this story Jesus is not seen by those guarding the tomb. The guards are not permitted to see the risen Lord and consequently have to "fall asleep" just at the crucial moment when he appears. Neutral bystanders are not privy to Christophanies. The appearance is intended only for the women; and the purpose of the story is to show how their faith was evoked by an "historic" event.

The Easter narratives try to give positive proofs of the reality of Jesus' resurrection to counter objections to resurrection belief that the early Christians met in their evangelizing. Of supreme and obvious importance is the need to say that Jesus really died. The burial story in the Gospels is intended to be that proof, and is unlikely to have been told for its own sake. In the developed tradition in John's Gospel, Pilate is made to ascertain clearly the fact of Jesus' death. This detail is present because some were arguing that Jesus did not die, and that consequently resurrection can be explained away by saying that after the deposition Jesus awoke and left his tomb.

The empty tomb is intended to be further proof that Jesus is raised, albeit in this case negative proof. A literal Hebraic view of resurrection as the resuscitation of corpses is found in Matthew 27:52–3, which is a theological insertion into the crucifixion account. For Matthew, belief in the resurrection is necessarily dependent on one leaving one's tomb. If the earliest belief was that Jesus had been raised from the dead, then logically, at least to Matthew and the Jewish mind, he could no longer be in the tomb.

But this negative proof of resurrection seems to have caused as many problems as it solved. It obviously left the way open for objectors to claim that, if the tomb was empty, then the body was stolen. This is a claim that Matthew and John in their different ways attempt to disprove. In John, Mary assumes that the disappearance of Jesus' corpse is due to the disciples' having removed it. She is soon to be discouraged from holding this view by being shown the burial clothes and head-bindings still in place in the tomb, the inference being that, if his body had been stolen, then these would have gone too. We must also infer from this story that John here thought of resurrection in a spiritual way, and that Jesus was spirited out of his bindings and out of the closed tomb. In Matthew's Gospel, on the other hand, the rumor that Jesus' body was stolen is attributed to the wickedness of the Jews. The story tells how the guards, whose purpose in guarding the tomb is thwarted by the resurrection, are asked to put about the rumor that the disciples had stolen the corpse. Many of Matthew's contemporaries were probably hearing this allegation from those opposed to the Christian proclamation; hence he had to explain how such a rumor arose. We may legitimately say that the stories of the theft of Jesus' body *were* rumors put about by opponents of the Christian message, and that these followed rather than preceded the stories of the empty tomb. It is unlikely that the Gospels tried to cover up an actual theft.

The earliest disciples of Jesus did not expect his death or his resurrection. The despair of the disciples at the crucifixion is likely to be historical. It is less probably an invention of the early church; as time went by, the early church tended to accord to those who had known the earthly Jesus a place of respect and honor; and it was an embarrassment to record an episode in which the disciples of Jesus are depicted as deserting their master at his arrest. The desertion is poignantly described in the dramatic and effective legend of Peter's threefold denial of allegiance to Jesus before the maid of the high priest, which parallels the trial his master is undergoing before the high priest himself. It is unlikely that the disciples would have deserted Jesus if he had prepared them for his resurrection. Either he did not speak of resurrection to them, or else they did not understand him when he did. The former is more probable. The Gospels do include predictions on Jesus' lips that he is to rise again after his death; but these are thought by many scholars to be prophecies after the event, put there by the evangelists. It is often said in the Gospels at these points that the disciples do not understand his predictions. This is in order to explain the embarrassing desertion later. Certainly it is significant that the resurrection is represented as playing very little part in Jesus' teaching. This is particularly surprising in view of the prominence given to the resurrection in the Acts of the Apostles and in the Pauline epistles.

So far, we have seen that the Gospels' Easter narratives include what are intended to be positive and negative proofs of the resurrection, together with attempts to describe the nature of the resurrected body itself. These narratives are also useful vehicles for other theological and doctrinal teaching, some of which may be simply listed.

In John 20:23 we notice that John connects the forgiveness of sins with the presence of the risen Christ. This, too, is the purpose of the story in John 21 with its threefold declaration of forgiveness for Peter reversing the threefold denial before the crucifixion. More significantly the resurrection stories are used to indicate that the foundation of the church began with the resurrection. It is the risen Lord at the end of Matthew who sends forth his missionaries. Similarly, at the end of Luke, the mission of the church beginning at Jerusalem is initiated by a command of the risen Jesus. In Pauline theology the new life of the Christian church is connected intimately with Jesus. He is the first-fruits of those raised from the dead; but those who are *en Christo* are able to share with him in a resurrection like his. In the meantime, says Paul, the church is living in the age of the spirit directed by the risen Lord, and the Christians are told they are the new creation. John puts this more symbolically in his Easter story when the risen Lord breathes on his disciples. He is giving them the spirit of the new age, just as God in Genesis 2 inaugurated the life of man by "breathing into his nostrils the breath of life."

The Easter stories are, therefore, no mere attempts to describe allegedly historical events. Paul, as stated earlier, is more concerned with the present and future significance of resurrection for the Christians to whom he wrote his letters than with the historical details of Christ's own resurrection. Nor can the Gospels be used as historical documents for proof of the resurrection. They are theological documents, using the resurrection story to convey theological and apologetic teaching, and in this respect are not so different from Paul's teaching as a first glance might suggest.

Having dismissed the historical reliability of the Easter stories in the Gospels, we may legitimately ask if the resurrection itself did happen. An historical approach demands that we reply that the resurrection was not an event in Jesus' career comparable to his birth and death. The resurrection *was* an event, but only in the history of the church. Yet it is difficult to describe how or why belief in Jesus' resurrection began. The traditional Christian explanation would obviously say merely that the belief grew because Jesus did rise, and because the Gospels say he was seen after his death. But, as we have indicated, this view has its own difficulties. On the other hand, one hesitates to speak of resurrection experience in terms of subjective visions or hallucinations—certainly the New Testament writers do not describe it in this way; and they could have done so if they had so wished. Something like Peter's vision in Acts, or the dream sequences in the infancy narratives, could have been utilized to describe the resurrection appearances. Resurrection to the first believers was something different, and had to be described in terms appropriate to what they claimed had been a new experience. Thus it is described in a personal style, not as a vision but almost as if Jesus himself was present.

The way in which the belief began, and why it was expressed in the way it was, may be described in the following manner. Resurrection belief arose first among those who had known Jesus in his lifetime. After his death, they had a vivid and personal feeling that Jesus was in some sense still with them and was guiding them. Later generations could not, of course, think of the risen Jesus, as did those who had known him in his ministry; but even they could say, as Paul did, that they had an overwhelming and personal feeling that the spirit of Jesus was influencing them. Jesus was "risen" because his message, personality, power, and influence continued after his death. Jesus' guidance and inspiration outlived him, and for the believer he was still living. Resurrection was the natural first-century Jewish way of describing this continuing influence.

In a milieu in which views on afterlife were expressed in terms of the resurrection of individuals by some circles at least within Judaism, it is perhaps not surprising that the earliest followers of Jesus should have spoken of their master's abiding influence, continuing presence and guidance, as his resurrection. Some people thought that John the Baptist had been raised from the dead (Mark 6:14 ff.), and that Elijah's spirit lived on in Elisha (2 Kings 2:15) and legends exist in the New Testament telling of people who were raised from the dead by Jesus and, later, by Peter and Paul. All these provide the environment in which belief in Jesus' resurrection took shape and flourished. These Jewish ideas would and did find favor in the Hellenistic world outside, where stories of dying and rising gods were part of the native folk myths. Thus to talk of the resurrection of Jesus would not have seemed so strange.

We suspect that the earliest impression of Jesus' abiding power was felt after his death during the communal meals for which the followers of Jesus seem to have continued to meet. It is significant how many of the Easter narratives have a eucharistic setting. John 21 speaks of Jesus' eating with his disciples; Cleopas and his friend recognize Jesus only in the breaking of bread; the revelations to the ten in the upper room in John's Gospel, and to the ten plus Thomas a week later, seem to have a setting similar to that of the Last Supper. When they met for such meals after his death it is probable that Jesus' erstwhile colleagues reminisced about his career, and felt that in some way the memory of him was so strong that they could and did say "he is alive." Those who had known him would obviously still think of him in a corporeal way. Later generations would obviously have no such memory to work on, and would tend to have only a spiritualized image of Christ. Perhaps this is why we have the two images in the New Testament—the physical resurrected body belonging to the earliest tradition and the spiritualized risen Lord, emanating from those predominantly gentile Christians who had not seen Jesus before his death.

The early believers were quick to grasp the significance of resurrection, and proclaimed a changed relationship with God. The sin of Adam, which had resulted in death, had now been reversed, and Christ was hailed as the new Adam, bringing not death into the world but life. The age-old cycle of cause and effect, that is sin and death, which started at the fall had now been broken. Those incorporated mystically into union with Christ through baptism were now seen to have the certain hope of an eternal life like his. His death and resurrection at one point in time were said to have an enduring effect for all mankind. Christians were seen to be living in the new age of the spirit, and were a "new creation," as a result of Jesus' breaking the power of death. Morality and ethics could be put on a new footing—no longer were these the *sine qua non* of being saved. Instead, having been declared to be justified by grace, moral behavior is seen by Paul and others as the logical pattern of Christian life. One no longer sinned in a body that could die; sin was now seen as an act against a body destined for eternity. Thus Christ's resurrection is seen in the New Testament as a paradigm for the future destiny of his people. He is but the first-fruits of those raised from the dead.

Such is a brief summary of some New Testament teaching of resurrection. In it, attention is taken away from the purely historical element in the proclamation. Once Jesus' abiding presence was spoken of in terms of resurrection, with all that this meant about breaking out of death's grasp, then the new and revolutionary New Testament theology gave a universalism and timelessness to Christ's person and message. Resurrection belief, implying a death in which all men share, obviously had a new meaning of such value that Paul could say to the Corinthians that, if the resurrection were not true, and if Christ had not been raised, then his teaching was in vain, and the Corinthians' faith too was in vain, and that of all men Christians were most to be pitied for their false hope. For Paul and the writers of the New Testament the resurrection of Jesus was obviously a reality. Our conclusion, though, is that the resurrection of Jesus was an event only in the minds and lives of Jesus' followers. It cannot be described as an historic event. The Easter story is a faith legend, not an objective eyewitness report; but it is a myth that the Christian church through the centuries has found to be a continuing inspiration.

Albert Schweitzer

Epilogue: Results of the Jesus-Quest

ALBERT SCHWEITZER (1875-1965) was born in Upper Alsace and educated at the Münster Realschule and the University of Strasbourg, where he took his Ph.D. and licentiate in theology (1899-1900). After serving briefly as a pastor, Schweitzer became a private lecturer at Strasbourg (1902-1912). A renowned musicologist, he served as chief organist of the Societe J. S. Bach in Paris and of the Orfeo Catala in Barcelona from 1905 to 1911.

In 1913 Schweitzer received the degree of doctor of medicine from the Universities of Paris and Berlin and turned his attention to missionary work. His many important publications in the field of early Christian history include A Sketch of the Life of Jesus (1901), The Quest of the Historical Jesus (1910), Paul and His Interpreters (1912), The Mystery of the Kingdom of God (1914), and The Mysticism of Paul the Apostle (1931). He was awarded honorary degrees by many universities in Europe and America and received the Nobel Peace Prize in 1954.

There is nothing more negative than the result of the critical study of the life of Jesus.

The Jesus of Nazareth who came forward publicly as the Messiah, who preached the ethic of the kingdom of God, who founded the kingdom of Heaven upon earth, and died to give his work its final consecration, never had any existence. He is a figure designed by rationalism, endowed with life by liberalism, and clothed by modern theology in an historical garb.

This image has not been destroyed from without; it has fallen to pieces, cleft

From The Quest of the Historical Jesus by Albert Schweitzer (New York: Macmillan Publishing Co., 1968), p. 39. Copyright © 1968 by Macmillan Publishing Co. Reprinted by permission.

and disintegrated by the concrete historical problems which came to the surface one after another, and in spite of all the artifice, art, artificiality, and violence which was applied to them, refused to be planed down to fit the design on which the Jesus of the theology of the last hundred and thirty years had been constructed, and were no sooner covered over than they appeared again in a new form. The thoroughgoing skeptical and the thoroughgoing eschatological schools have only completed the work of destruction by linking the problems into a system and so making an end of the *Divide et impera* of modern theology, which undertook to solve each of them separately, that is, in a less difficult form. Henceforth it is no longer permissible to take one problem out of the series and dispose of it by itself, since the weight of the whole hangs upon each.

Whatever the ultimate solution may be, the historical Jesus of whom the criticism of the future, taking as its starting-point the problems which have been recognized and admitted, will draw the portrait, can never render modern theology the services which it claimed from its own half-historical, half-modern, Jesus. He will be a Jesus, who was Messiah, and lived as such, either on the ground of a literary fiction of the earliest Evangelist, or on the ground of a purely eschatological messianic conception.

In either case, he will not be a Jesus Christ to whom the religion of the present can ascribe, according to its long-cherished custom, its own thoughts and ideas, as it did with the Jesus of its own making. Nor will he be a figure which can be made by a popular historical treatment so sympathetic and universally intelligible to the multitude. The historical Jesus will be to our time a stranger and an enigma. . . .

The mistake was to suppose that Jesus could come to mean more to our time by entering into it as a man like ourselves. That is not possible. First because such a Jesus never existed. Secondly because, although historical knowledge can no doubt introduce greater clearness into an existing spiritual life, it cannot call spiritual life into existence. History can destroy the present; it can reconcile the present with the past—can even to a certain extent transport the present into the past—but to contribute to the making of the present is not given unto it. . . .